Harnessing Technology for Knowledge Transfer in Accountancy, Auditing, and Finance

Samuel Kwok
Xi'an Jiaotong-Liverpool University, China

Mohamed Omran
Xi'an Jiaotong-Liverpool University, China

Poshan Yu
Xi'an Jiaotong-Liverpool University, China & European Business University of Luxembourg, Luxembourg

IGI Global
PUBLISHER of TIMELY KNOWLEDGE

A volume in the Advances in Finance, Accounting, and Economics (AFAE) Book Series

Published in the United States of America by
IGI Global
Business Science Reference (an imprint of IGI Global)
701 E. Chocolate Avenue
Hershey PA, USA 17033
Tel: 717-533-8845
Fax: 717-533-8661
E-mail: cust@igi-global.com
Web site: http://www.igi-global.com

Library of Congress Cataloging-in-Publication Data

Names: Kwok, Samuel, DATE- editor. | Omran, Mohamed Aboelhamd, DATE- editor. | Yu, Poshan, editor.
Title: Harnessing technology for knowledge transfer in accountancy, auditing, and finance / edited by Samuel Kwok, Mohamed Omran, Poshan Yu.

Description: Hershey, PA : Business Science Reference, [2024] | Includes bibliographical references and index. | Summary: "This edited book explores ways in which technology, specifically augmented reality (AR) and artificial intelligence (AI), can be leveraged to enrich experiential learning and support continuous professional growth in the fields of accounting, auditing, and finance"-- Provided by publisher.
Identifiers: LCCN 2023055066 (print) | LCCN 2023055067 (ebook) | ISBN 9798369313312 (hardcover) | ISBN 9798369313329 (ebook)
Subjects: LCSH: Accounting--Study and teaching. | Auditing--Study and teaching. | Finance--Study and teaching. | Computer-assisted instruction. | Knowledge management--Technological innovations.
Classification: LCC HF5630 .H37 2024 (print) | LCC HF5630 (ebook) | DDC 657.071--dc23/eng/20231206
LC record available at https://lccn.loc.gov/2023055066
LC ebook record available at https://lccn.loc.gov/2023055067

This book is published in the IGI Global book series Advances in Finance, Accounting, and Economics (AFAE) (ISSN: 2327-5677; eISSN: 2327-5685)

British Cataloguing in Publication Data
A Cataloguing in Publication record for this book is available from the British Library.

Advances in Finance, Accounting, and Economics (AFAE) Book Series

Ahmed Driouchi
Al Akhawayn University, Morocco

ISSN:2327-5677
EISSN:2327-5685

Mission

In our changing economic and business environment, it is important to consider the financial changes occurring internationally as well as within individual organizations and business environments. Understanding these changes as well as the factors that influence them is crucial in preparing for our financial future and ensuring economic sustainability and growth.

The **Advances in Finance, Accounting, and Economics (AFAE)** book series aims to publish comprehensive and informative titles in all areas of economics and economic theory, finance, and accounting to assist in advancing the available knowledge and providing for further research development in these dynamic fields.

Coverage

- Finance and Accounting in SMEs
- Economics of Natural and Environmental Resources
- Health Economics
- Managerial Accounting
- E-Accounting
- Macroeconomics
- Economics of Agriculture and Biotechnology
- Accounting Standards
- Development Economics
- International Economics

IGI Global is currently accepting manuscripts for publication within this series. To submit a proposal for a volume in this series, please contact our Acquisition Editors at Acquisitions@igi-global.com or visit: http://www.igi-global.com/publish/.

The Advances in Finance, Accounting, and Economics (AFAE) Book Series (ISSN 2327-5677) is published by IGI Global, 701 E. Chocolate Avenue, Hershey, PA 17033-1240, USA, www.igi-global.com. This series is composed of titles available for purchase individually; each title is edited to be contextually exclusive from any other title within the series. For pricing and ordering information please visit http://www.igi-global.com/book-series/advances-finance-accounting-economics/73685. Postmaster: Send all address changes to above address.

Titles in this Series

For a list of additional titles in this series, please visit:
www.igi-global.com/book-series/advances-finance-accounting-economics/73685

Cases on Economic Crisis Impact on Multinational Corporations
Kyla Latrice Tennin (College of Doctoral Studies, University of Phoenix, USA) and Samrat Ray (International Institute of Management Studies (IIMS), ndia)
Business Science Reference • © 2024 • 225pp • H/C (ISBN: 9798369315446) • US $275.00

Harnessing Blockchain-Digital Twin Fusion for Sustainable Investments
Syed Hasan Jafar (Woxsen University, India) Raul Villamarin Rodriguez (Woxsen University, India) Hemachandran Kannan (Woxsen University, India) Shakeb Akhtar (Woxsen University, India) and Philipp Plugmann (SRH Hochschule für Gesundheit Gera, Gemany)
Business Science Reference • © 2024 • 310pp • H/C (ISBN: 9798369318782) • US $290.00

The Role of Financial Inclusion for Reaching Sustainable Development Goals
João Jungo (University of Aveiro, Portugal) Mara Madaleno (GOVCOPP, University of Aveiro, Portugal) Anabela Botelho (GOVCOPP, University of Aveiro, Portugal) and Eyup Dogan (Abdullah Gul University, Turkey)
Business Science Reference • © 2024 • 326pp • H/C (ISBN: 9798369305225) • US $275.00

Artificial Intelligence and Machine Learning-Powered Smart Finance
Sanjay Taneja (Graphic Era University (Deemed), India) Amandeep Singh (Chitkara Business School, Chitkara University, India) and Pawan Kumar (Chandigarh University, India)
Business Science Reference • © 2024 • 347pp • H/C (ISBN: 9798369332641) • US $295.00

Governance and Policy Transformations in Central Banking
Farhan Ahmed (NED University of Engineering and Technology, Pakistan) and Raza Ali Khan (NED University of Engineering and Technology, Pakistan)
Business Science Reference • © 2024 • 317pp • H/C (ISBN: 9798369308356) • US $275.00

Exploring Global FinTech Advancement and Applications
Hamed Taherdoost (University Canada West, Canada) Nam Le (University Canada West, Canada) Mitra Madanchian (University Canada West, Canada) and Yousef Farhaoui (Faculty of Sciences and Techniques, Moulay Ismail University of Meknes, Morocco)
Business Science Reference • © 2024 • 391pp • H/C (ISBN: 9798369315613) • US $290.00

IGI Global
PUBLISHER of TIMELY KNOWLEDGE

701 East Chocolate Avenue, Hershey, PA 17033, USA
Tel: 717-533-8845 x100 • Fax: 717-533-8661
E-Mail: cust@igi-global.com • www.igi-global.com

Editorial Advisory Board

Apart from expressing our gratitude to our international advisory board experts, the editors would also like to extend their thanks to The Academy of Future Education of Xi'an Jiaotong-Liverpool University and CPA Australia for their support.

Table of Contents

Detailed Table of Contents

The emergence of artificial intelligence (AI) has opened new challenges to traditional audit practices within the e-commerce industry. This chapter investigates the current state of audit professionals, who leverage audit data analysis technology to analyze client big data systems. It explores the future of audit methods by introducing intervention by the latest Do-Calculus concepts and proposing a potential connection between BDA and ADA\. The authors employ qualitative analysis, combining in-depth interviews and content analysis, to explore how external auditors use skepticism to make necessary professional judgments. The authors' analysis reveals that auditors view AI technology as a tool and still rely on a combination of manual and computer-based audit methods to ensure the quality of their professional judgments and maintain the status quo. However, the challenge remains as audit practitioners must continually improve their AI capabilities in the new AI era.

Blockchain-based technology has been recognized as a potential tool to transform corporate governance. This chapter first discusses the persisting challenges of agency costs, inefficiencies, and the need for improved transparency. It then examines the emergence of blockchain as a potential solution, offering a novel, decentralized approach to corporate governance. The analysis covers the technology's application to share registers, trading, voting, and accounting practices, emphasizing the duality of its promise for increased transparency and emergent privacy concerns. Controversial aspects, such as the threat to existing shareholder activism and the governance of blockchain itself, are critically examined. Solutions like hybrid blockchain models and regulatory nodes are proposed to address these issues. The chapter concludes with a forward-looking perspective on decentralized autonomous organizations (DAOs) as an innovative alternative to traditional corporate structures, signifying a new paradigm in corporate governance.

In the current societal landscape, consumers are increasingly concerned about the environment and are wary of greenwashing tactics when making purchasing decisions. This leads to a rise in the advertising of sustainable products. However, many of these claims about being environmentally friendly are exaggerated. So, it is necessary to develop an effective and understandable scoring framework to detect the corporate greenwashing behaviour to help monitor and push the entity reduce their greenwashing behaviour. Yet there are only several articles trying to use AI-based models to assess the corporate greenwashing and most of their database is not assessable and more importantly the criteria of the AI models to assess greenwashing is not clear enough. To move the field forward, this chapter develops a series of criteria based on the AI model formula which was come up with former scholar to help assess the greenwashing. A literature review and case study method based on Tesla have been used to demo the feasibility of proposed scoring framework.

This report analyzes the impacts of insisting on a product development strategy on XPeng's profitability from 2019 to 2022 Q2. Based on the model established by McNally, Akdeniz, and Calantone, regression analyses are used to evaluate different implementation factors' impacts on profitability. In addition, this report will combine XPeng's technological innovation points to analyze the impacts of the above factors on its profitability. Therefore, this chapter gives examples of how organizations may explore how to implement a product development strategy to enhance its profitability with advanced technology.

Creating authentic learning environments that mimic real-life workplace situations encountered by accounting professionals raises several challenges for educators. This study aims to respond to those challenges by proposing a learning prototype that enlightens the benefits of the classroom-as-organization model instructional model supported by a learning management system combined with a 360° and Virtual reality immersive learning platform. The learning prototype integrates virtual reality digital content at three levels of instructional design to fully replicate a business organization's real-life context. This chapter provides an overview of the course structure and components along with guidelines for instructional design. The prototype represents an attractive alternative to business simulations and 3-D virtual worlds to create technology-enabled immersive learning experiences. Further developments would be necessary to provide instructional design methodologies that can assist educators in creating successful immersive learning experiences for management accounting education.

The chapter examines how block chain technology can revolutionize pharmaceutical supply chain management. Through real-time tracking and traceability, the authenticity of medications can be ensured, thereby combating the persistent issue of counterfeit drugs and enhancing patient safety. Additionally, the clinical trial process stands to benefit from block chain and transparent and secure nature. Smart contracts can streamline patient recruitment, informed consent, and trial result reporting, promoting trust and accountability in the clinical trial ecosystem. Despite the potential benefits, the adoption of DeFi and block chain in healthcare presents several challenges, including regulatory compliance, scalability, and integration with existing healthcare systems. This chapter discusses the current state of block chain integration in healthcare and identifies future research directions to overcome these hurdles.

Many banks today are faced with the challenges how to appropriately store, process, use, and transfer data with the close integration of enterprise-level strategies and management. A key definition as lean theory is introduced to explain how it can lead and guide the companies to effectively conduct their digital knowledge transfer from multiple dimensions. This chapter first presents the overall background with the emphasis on different phases of data usage. Second, the main challenges on digital knowledge transfer for organizations are specified, which demonstrates the importance of using lean theory to manage data. Third, the key disciplines on lean theory and how they can be alleviated to transfer data are introduced. Finally, in order to present clear understandings, Bank F is used as a case to demonstrate how it has used lean theory to conduct effective and comprehensive digital knowledge transfer.

The banking sector plays a vital role in economic growth, offering financial services and determining interest rates, influencing borrowing and investment decisions. Traditional uniform rates based on risk assessments and market conditions may not suit today's diverse economic landscape. Leveraging big data and machine learning, the idea of personalized interest rates is explored. The proposed work examines the effectiveness of two machine learning based classification algorithms logistic regression and K-Nearest Neighbours (KNN) for predicting personalized interest rates in the banking sector. The study collects and explores a dataset from Lending Club by conducting thorough exploratory data analysis (EDA). Despite getting low accuracies, this research is pioneering in the field of interest rate prediction and provides a foundation for further research in this area. The EDA conducted during the study contributes valuable insights into the dataset's structure, enabling better understanding and identification of potential challenges and improvements for future models.

This chapter explores the effects of technological advancements on corporate social responsibility (CSR) disclosure. It examines how the evolving use of new technology is reshaping the demand for CSR disclosure from diverse stakeholders and the interconnected dynamics between them. As technology continues to evolve, understanding its far-reaching impact on CSR disclosure is critical for businesses and society as a whole. The evolution of Internet technologies at all stages, from the pre-Internet era to Web 2.0, dramatically affects the way firms interact with stakeholders. This chapter will critically examine the transformative impact of technology in CSR disclosure, as well as how these technologies in turn shape stakeholder engagement. This chapter also provides suggestions for addressing corresponding challenges in the social media era.

When it comes to maintaining their financial stability, healthcare organisations confront particular difficulties. Hospitals are constantly under pressure to maximise their financial operations due to the growing expense of healthcare, shifting reimbursement structures, and the requirement to deliver high-quality patient care. In this quickly changing environment, traditional hospital accounting techniques might not be sufficient anymore. This chapter examines how artificial intelligence (AI) can revolutionise hospital accounting and provide a way to improve financial stability. AI-driven hospital accounting uses automation, data analytics, and sophisticated machine learning algorithms to increase accuracy, expedite financial procedures, and facilitate well-informed decision-making.

Foreword

In the current era, disruptive technologies and scientific breakthroughs have been reshaping the way a business works. Business leaders and industry practitioners must embrace these emerging technologies to obtain a competitive advantage and to enhance operational efficiencies. Meanwhile, governments, regulators, policy makers and societies must handle the growing challenges and regulatory issues that emerging technologies have brought to the business world, and also prepare for future technologies.

In the same vein, emerging technologies are being increasingly applied in the areas of accountancy, auditing and finance, altering the status quo in a significant manner. As a researcher specializing in accounting and finance, I have seen a huge demand for a deeper understanding in technological advancements and applications in these areas. This has given rise to an urgent need to facilitate technology diffusion and knowledge flow between different disciplines. Importantly, there has been a call for researchers and industry partitioners to share their insights and best practices regarding technological applications in the areas of accounting and finance. In response to the call, the book "Harnessing Technology for Knowledge Transfer in Accountancy, Auditing, and Finance" makes a significant contribution to advancing the knowledge of technological applications within the fields of accounting and finance.

The book introduces the recent applications of a few important emerging technologies, such as blockchain technology, big data analytics, machine learning or AI-based models predictive analytics, data management tools and more, investigating their effectiveness in developing solutions for firms across various sectors, such as auditing sector, banking sector, health sector and new energy vehicle sector. The book links technological adoption with enhanced corporate governance, effective risk management, improved operating performance and CSR practices. In addition, it also discusses some policy issues and the implementation of new technology, i.e., virtual reality, in business education.

In conclusion, the book provides a collection of interesting chapters introducing the latest technological developments and applications within the accounting and financial professions. These case studies and policy reviews are especially valuable, not only for accounting and financial professionals, policy makers, but also for business students, researchers and educators in higher education institutions, who are willing to learn and to explore practical insights and experiences of accounting and finance technologies.

TECHNOLOGICAL ADVANCES AND TRANSFORMATION IN ACCOUNTING AND AUDITING PRACTICES AND FINANCE FUNCTIONS

The accountancy practice has evolved significantly since 1496 when the Italian mathematician and Franciscan Friar, Luca Pacioli, developed an accounting system of double-entry bookkeeping for recording mercantile transactions in Venice (Pacioli, 1523; Geijsbeek, 1914). Pacioli's innovation not only survived the Venetian Era but remains the foundation of the current system of debits and credits in journals and ledgers in accounting (Baskerville, 2012).

Today, technology has transformed accounting and auditing practices, and finance functions in many significant ways – from automation of routing tasks, digitization of finance functions, optimization of accounting workflows to real-time financial reporting and auditing (Diolas, 2019; Heller, 2022, 2023). This technological transformation has occurred in three areas: practices, processes, and methods (Hoffman, 2017), and driven by artificial intelligence, machine learning technologies – model-based learning algorithms – block chain and big data technologies.

The advances in technological innovations offer practitioners opportunities to acquire new skills and leverage those to improve efficiency and productivity. The need to acquire, harness and leverage technologies to improve accounting and auditing practices, and finance functions has not been adequately examined, contextualized or meaningfully addressed in accounting and auditing publications. This book, *Harnessing Technology for Knowledge Transfer in Accountancy, Auditing, and Finance*, fills this gap.

The book is epoch-marking in many ways. It is topical, detailed, and timely covering technologies that have implications for, and applications in accounting and auditing practices, finance functions – from blockchain technology, digitalization of audit and finance functions, machine learning, to artificial intelligence, and big data technologies. Every chapter in this book speaks to stakeholders in accountancy, auditing, finance, and educators especially those who might not be familiar, or engaging with the concept of immersive learning as applied to the teaching of accounting.

This a must-have book for accountants, auditors, financial analysts, practitioner, academics and researchers, students, and regulatory authorities. The accountancy practice of the past was all about the people; in future, it will be all about people and technology. I cannot recommend this book enough.

Peng Cheng
Xi'an Jiaotong-Liverpool University, China

James Ogunleye
Academy of Innovation and Management, London, UK & KIE/DHT Big Data Analytics Lab, London, UK

REFERENCES

Baskerville, P. (2012). The history and definition of 'Debits and Credits' in accounting. *Scoop.it! Basic Accounting Concepts.* https://www.basicaccounting concepts. education/the-history-and-definition-of-debits-and-credits-in-accounting/#:~: text=' Debits% 20and%20credits'%20is%20a, this%20system% 20in%20a%20book

Diolas, A. (2019). *Technology is transforming the accountancy profession, and has the potential to revolutionise audit/ Audit & Technology.*

Geijsbeek, J. B. (1914). *Ancient Double-Entry Bookkeeping*. Geijsbeek. https://ia802207.us.archive.org/23/items/ancientdoubleent00geijuoft/ ancientdoubleent00geijuoft.pdf

Heller, I. (2022). How Technology Is Transforming Accounting. *Forbes*. https://www.forbes.com/sites/forbestechcouncil/2022/11/30/how-technology-is-transforming-accounting/

Heller, I. (2023). How Real-Time Auditing Can Launch Us Into The 21st Century. *Forbes*. https://www.forbes.com/sites/forbestechcouncil/2023/02/23/how-real-time-auditing-can-launch-us-into-the-21st-century/

Hoffman, C. (2017). *Accounting and Auditing in the Digital Age*. https://xbrlsite.azurewebsites.net/2017/library/accountingandauditinginthedigitalage.pdf

Pacioli, L. (1523). *Summa de Arithmetica, Geometria, Proportioni et Proportionalita*. Paganino Paganini. https://digitalcollections.usfca.edu/digital/ collection/p264101coll7/id/4090/

Preface

In today's rapidly changing world, the role of technology in accountancy, auditing, and finance has become increasingly crucial. As society embraces technological advancements, professionals in these industries must understand and leverage technological tools to enhance their knowledge, increase efficiency, and improve decision-making processes. This edited book, *Harnessing Technology for Knowledge Transfer in Accountancy, Auditing, and Finance*, aims to shed light on the various aspects of technology application in these fields and provide valuable insights to professionals and researchers alike.

The relevance and significance of this book lie in its ability to address several key areas where technology plays a significant role. The chapters in the book cover a wide range of topics, reflecting the diverse and evolving landscape of the industry. It explores issues such as audit digitalization, blockchain technology, big data utilization, artificial intelligence, immersive learning, decentralized finance, and more. By examining these topics, the book positions itself at the forefront of the ongoing technological revolution within the accountancy, auditing, and finance sectors.

This book's target audience includes professionals in accountancy, auditing, and finance, including accountants, auditors, financial analysts, policymakers, and researchers. It is also relevant to educators and students seeking comprehensive insights into the impact of technology on these industries. By examining real-world case studies, policy reviews, and experimental prototypes, this book offers practical guidance, theoretical frameworks, and innovative approaches that can be implemented by practitioners and researchers alike.

Each chapter submission contributes significantly to the overall importance of this book, highlighting different facets of technology in the accountancy, auditing, and finance domains. Here is a brief description of each of the chapters:

1. "Audit Digitalization, Do-Calculus and Professional Judgment: A Practical Evidence from China" examines the practical implementation of audit digitalization, focusing on integrating do-calculus and professional judgment.
2. "Blockchain-based Technology in Corporate Governance: A Transformative Approach" explores the transformative potential of blockchain technology in enhancing corporate governance practices.
3. "Utilizing AI-Based Model to Detect Greenwashing Behavior in Corporations – A Case Study of Tesla" presents a case study of Tesla to showcase how AI-based models can effectively detect greenwashing behaviour in corporations.
4. "How to Utilize Technology to Enhance Profitability: A Study of the NPD Strategy of XPeng" focuses on the utilization of technology to enhance profitability, using the NPD strategy of XPeng as a case study.

5. "Immersive Learning in Management Accounting Education: A Prototype of Classroom-as-Organization Supported by Learning Management System and Virtual Reality" introduces a prototype that supports immersive learning in management accounting education, integrating a classroom-as-organization model, learning management system, and virtual reality.
6. "Decentralized Finance (DeFi) and Blockchain Technology in Healthcare: A Promising Confluence for Enhanced Security, Data Interoperability, and Patient" explores the promising convergence of decentralized finance and blockchain technology, highlighting enhanced security, data interoperability, and patient empowerment in healthcare.
7. "Digital knowledge transfer for banks: from a lean data management perspective" presents a lean data management perspective to examine digital knowledge transfer practices in the banking industry.
8. "Examining the Effectiveness of Machine Learning Models for Interest Rate Prediction" investigates the effectiveness of machine learning models for interest rate prediction, offering valuable insights for financial analysts and researchers.
9. "The Evolution of CSR Information Disclosure from Web 1.0 to Web 2.0" traces the evolution of CSR information disclosure, highlighting the transition from Web 1.0 to Web 2.0 and its impact on corporate social responsibility practices.
10. "AI-Driven Hospital Accounting: A Path to Financial Health" explores the application of AI-driven hospital accounting practices to improve financial health within healthcare organizations.

This collection of chapters showcases the potential impact of technology in revolutionizing the accountancy, auditing, and finance sectors. This book aims to empower professionals and researchers to embrace technology and harness its transformative potential by presenting practical evidence, case studies, policy reviews, and experimental prototypes. It contributes to the subject by offering a comprehensive overview of technology applications in these fields and providing valuable insights that can shape future practices and policies. This book aims to equip its readers with the knowledge and skills necessary to navigate the ever-evolving landscape of technology-driven accountancy, auditing, and finance by bridging the gap between theory and practice.

Samuel Kwok
Xi'an Jiaotong-Liverpool University, China

Mohamed Omran
Xi'an Jiaotong-Liverpool University, China

Poshan Yu
Xi'an Jiaotong-Liverpool University, China & European Business University of Luxembourg, Luxembourg

Chapter 1
Audit Digitalization, Do-Calculus, and Professional Judgment:
A Practical Evidence From China

Samuel Kwok
https://orcid.org/0000-0001-7320-5400
Xian Jiaotong-Liverpool University, China

Mohamed Omran
https://orcid.org/0000-0003-4968-4848
Xian Jiaotong-Liverpool University, China

Poshan Yu
https://orcid.org/0000-0003-1069-3675
Soochow University, China

ABSTRACT

The emergence of artificial intelligence (AI) has opened new challenges to traditional audit practices within the e-commerce industry. This chapter investigates the current state of audit professionals, who leverage audit data analysis technology to analyze client big data systems. It explores the future of audit methods by introducing intervention by the latest Do-Calculus concepts and proposing a potential connection between BDA and ADA\. The authors employ qualitative analysis, combining in-depth interviews and content analysis, to explore how external auditors use skepticism to make necessary professional judgments. The authors' analysis reveals that auditors view AI technology as a tool and still rely on a combination of manual and computer-based audit methods to ensure the quality of their professional judgments and maintain the status quo. However, the challenge remains as audit practitioners must continually improve their AI capabilities in the new AI era.

DOI: 10.4018/979-8-3693-1331-2.ch001

1. INTRODUCTION

As an example, let's consider a scene that auditors often come across:

An auditor was examining a hotel client's financial records. During the audit, the hotel president expressed satisfaction with the hotel's business performance, despite the unfavorable economic environment. The president attributed the success to the years of dedication and hard work put in by the management team in raising the hotel's brand awareness to a new level. The hotel president was particularly pleased with the hotel's loyal clients, whose patronage had brought in unexpected revenue. It was evident that the hotel's commitment to quality service had earned them a reputation that was paying off even in trying times.

When conducting a substantive audit test, for example, for the hotel's revenue, the auditor needs to ensure that the information provided by the management is accurate and reliable. However, it is equally important for the auditor to adopt a suspicious mindset (Brydon, 2019) throughout the audit process. This will help the auditor obtain sufficient and appropriate audit evidence that is reliable and relevant. A suspicious mindset is crucial for determining the adequacy and reliability of audit testing. This aspect can become a problematic area in many professional judgments, especially if the management's fraudulent representation is backed by fabricated business digital data stored in the client's database. In such situations, the intelligence level of the audit data analytics becomes a significant concern.

Over the past few years, there has been a remarkable rise in the application of digital tools in the fields of business and auditing due to the continuous innovation of technology (Nair and Gupta, 2021; Lehner et al., 2022). As digital auditing work involves analyzing vast amounts of data and making professional judgments based on the analysis results, the use of audit methods and tools in auditing tasks has become gradually more significant.

In the current big data environment, there are three primary paths for digital audit professional judgment (see Figure 1). The first path, i.e., path (i), shows the assistance provided by Big Data Analytics (BDA) to Audit Data Analytics (ADA), which affects Audit Professional Judgment (APJ) (ACCA, 2019). This implies that BDA can help auditors in making informed decisions by providing them with valuable insights and perspectives. The second possible path, i.e., path (ii), demonstrates that BDA directly influences APJ (Belissent, 2017). In this scenario, auditors use BDA to analyze vast amounts of data and make judgments based on the analysis results. In other words, the analysis results directly influence the auditor's judgment. The final path, i.e., path (iii), shows that machine learning may play a role in APJ.

According to Mitchell (1997, p. 2), machine learning is "A computer program is said to learn from experience E concerning some class of tasks T and performance measure P, if its performance at tasks in T, as measured by P, improves with experience E". Therefore, machine learning refers to the ability of computer systems to learn from data, identify patterns, and make decisions without human intervention. If machine learning is integrated into the auditing process, it has the potential to enhance the accuracy and efficiency of APJ.

Figure 1. Professional judgment path for digital auditing
(Mitchell, 1997)

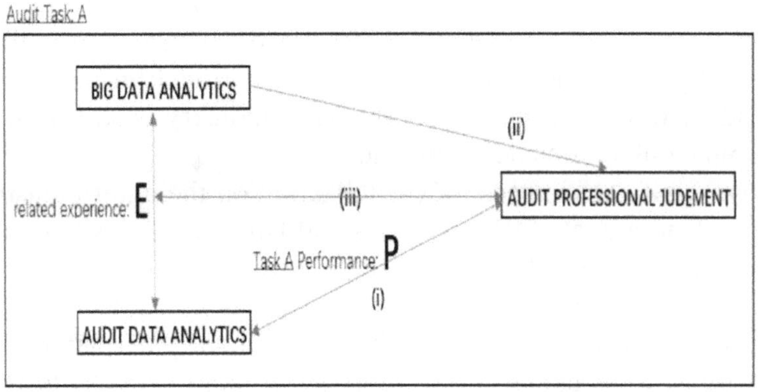

As technology continues to advance, the world of digital auditing is ever-changing, presenting digital audit professionals with new opportunities to exercise their expertise. Hence, it is essential to remain up-to-date on the latest technological developments to improve the quality and efficiency of audits.

To conduct more intelligent ADA, no matter which path we take, we must start from the current situation and understand what digital auditing means for audit professionals, as well as how to develop this relationship between people and technology to create value for all relevant stakeholders

The current study examines the impact of digital auditing on the professional judgment of auditors. To achieve this goal, we interviewed IT audit managers from the Big Four accounting firms. We also employed text analysis and a three-level coding method to investigate the connection between BDA, ADA, and APJ. The results revealed that digital auditing tools greatly assist in detecting data anomalies and enhancing the accuracy of professional judgments. In Section 5, we reveal that Auditors view AI technology as a tool and still rely on a combination of manual and computer-based audit methods to ensure the quality of their professional judgments and maintain the status quo. However, the challenge remains as audit practitioners must continually improve their knowledge and skills to reform their audit methods to meet the highest level of audit judgment required by stakeholders.

The remainder of this chapter is structured as follows: Section 2 provides a review of related literature. Section 3 presents the research objectives and applied methodology. Section 4 shows the results and findings of the current study. Section 5 discusses the results and introduces challenges and illustrations. Particularly in Section 5.2, we have presented an illustration showcasing how Path Analysis and Do-Calculus can be used to enhance the intelligence of audit machines. This approach has the potential to revolutionize the field of auditing and improve the accuracy and efficiency of the auditing process. The final section is to conclude.

2. LITERATURE REVIEW

The digitalization of the economy has a significant impact on audit firms, presenting both opportunities and challenges (Appelbaum et al., 2017; Tiberius and Hirth, 2019). This process involves the use of digital technologies to transform traditional business processes. While it has been widely adopted in other industries, the audit industry is still in the process of fully embracing and capitalizing on this development.

One of the most significant impacts of digitalization on the audit industry is the progress made in BDA (Appelbaum et al., 2017; Tiberius and Hirth, 2019). Many scholars have highlighted the relationship between BDA and audit quality. Cao et al. (2015) stated that BDA can enhance the efficiency and effectiveness of financial statement audits and improve the quality of auditors' judgments (Brown-Liburd et al., 2015) by identifying patterns and anomalies in data that may not be easily detectable through traditional auditing methods. Furthermore, it can help auditors analyze large data volumes in a shorter time, improving the efficiency of the audit process (Tiberius and Hirth, 2019).

The use of AI has the potential to significantly affect the quality of auditing work. AI can automate various repetitive tasks within the audit process, such as data entry and data analysis, freeing up auditors' time to focus on more complex tasks that require human judgment and expertise. Moreover, the use of AI can improve the accuracy and consistency of audit processes (Earley, 2015) by reducing the risk of human error (Kokina and Davenport, 2017).

Digital technologies are viewed as the most likely to revolutionize the audit process and the services offered. Audit firms are increasingly employing highly qualified data analysts and Information Technology (IT) specialists to take advantage of this trend. According to Raschke et al. (2018), digital technologies, specifically machine learning and AI, have the potential to bring significant changes to the audit process and the services offered as the use of these technologies can enhance the accuracy and efficiency of auditing procedures (Kokina and Davenport, 2017), reduce the risk of errors and fraud, and provide new opportunities for data analysis and insights. Consequently, the adoption of machine learning and AI in the auditing industry is expected to increase productivity and improve outcomes.

However, the use of BDA tools is not yet widespread in the auditing world, it is gradually adopted. While some audit firms have already embraced the use of BDA, others are still evaluating its potential benefits and challenges. Adopting BDA requires significant investment in technology and training, and many firms are still grappling with the challenges of integrating it into their existing audit processes. Over time, the audit process has progressed from sampling data to conducting a comprehensive examination of all data about a particular type of business transaction. Despite the availability of BDA tools for a while now, their use in auditing has not yet become widespread. In a recent study, De Santis and D'Onza (2021) scrutinized the elements that impact the utilization of BDA in the audit process to enhance audit excellence.

Blockchain technology also could revolutionize the auditing industry by enhancing the accuracy and reliability of financial reporting (Quattrone, 2016; Van der Stede, 2016; Dai and Vasarhelyi, 2017; Ferri et al., 2020). As a distributed ledger technology, blockchain can validate transaction reporting and ultimately eliminate the need for a monitoring phase during an audit because blockchain provides an immutable record of all transactions. However, further investigation is necessary to fully evaluate the advantages and obstacles of utilizing blockchain technology in auditing (Dai and Vasarhelyi, 2017).

Manita et al. (2020) suggest that while the adoption of digitalization in audit firms will lead to the emergence of new audit services and improve the quality of the audit process, no major disruptions are expected shortly. However, advanced technologies such as BDA and AI hold the potential to significantly transform core processes. Further research is necessary to understand the impact of these technologies on existing quality differences in the audit firm market. This knowledge is essential in helping audit firms leverage digital technologies to sustain their competitive advantage and enhance service quality.

3. RESEARCH OBJECTIVES AND METHODOLOGY

This study aims to gain a comprehensive understanding of the audit industry in China; therefore, we conducted in-depth semi-structured interviews with seven experienced audit practitioners from the Big Four accounting firms, namely KPMG, Ernst & Young, Deloitte, and Price Waterhouse. They have audit jobs all over China. The participants were managers, partners, and IT consulting managers, who were able to provide valuable insights into the industry from different perspectives. The interviews were designed to elicit information on various aspects of the audit industry, such as current practices, challenges faced, and potential areas for improvement. Hence, our study provides an in-depth analysis of the audit industry from the perspective of experienced practitioners. The current study has three objectives: First, a comprehensive understanding of the current state of audit digitalization and its application in the context of ADA. Second, exploring and examining the potential ways in which ADA can be effectively harnessed in audit interventions, using causal models as a guide. Third, it suggests a theoretical framework for an intelligent and efficient ADA, that can lead to more effective audit processes.

We present a thorough analysis of a set of scripts, utilizing text analysis and a three-level encoding method. The research methodology is grounded in qualitative research and employs a grounded theory approach to explore the relationship between BDA, ADA, and APJ. The study aims to provide a comprehensive understanding of how these elements interact with each other during the auditing process. The research methodology utilized in this study avoids theoretical sampling, ensuring that the results obtained are solely based on the collected data, making them more accurate and reliable. The analysis demonstrates that the effectiveness of big data analysis is closely tied to the quality of audit data analysis and the soundness of APJ. Furthermore, the study emphasizes the importance of the interplay between these three elements in the auditing process. The methodology highlights the need for auditors to adopt a more holistic approach, which is the theoretical framework ultimately highlighted, considering the interplay between these elements to ensure the effectiveness of the auditing process.

4. RESULTS AND FINDINGS

Our results show that the impact of digital auditing on APJ is mainly achieved through on-site data analysis using digital auditing tools, helping auditors more accurately screen out abnormal data, and ultimately make professional judgments by auditors.

During the "encoding" process, Figures 2 and 3 show the frequency and the proportion of the 23 found keywords.

The axial encoding and analysis memorandum is the result of axial encoding processing conducted by researchers (see Figure 4). In the reflective encoding process, researchers rely on keywords discovered during the analysis of memory activities as the first author is a chartered accountant at the Institute of Chartered Accountants in England and Wales (ICAEW) and an experienced professional auditor. Therefore, his reflective practice on interview scripts is combined with his practitioner background.

Figure 2. Frequency distribution of keywords

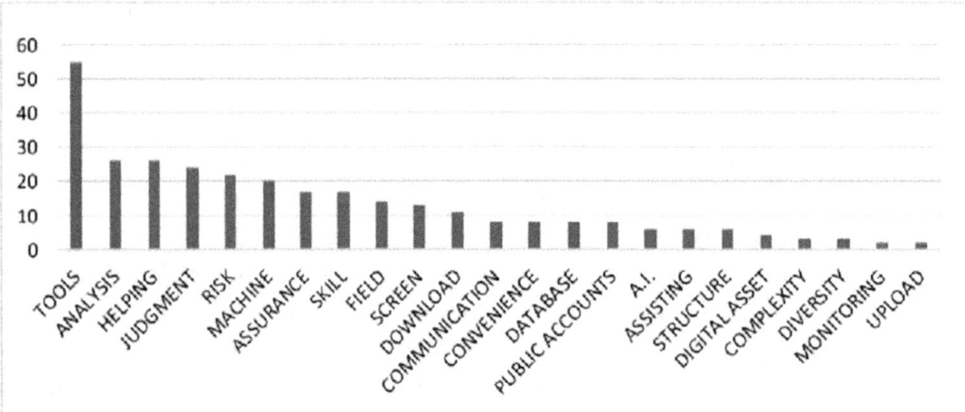

Figure 3. Keywords distribution by proportion

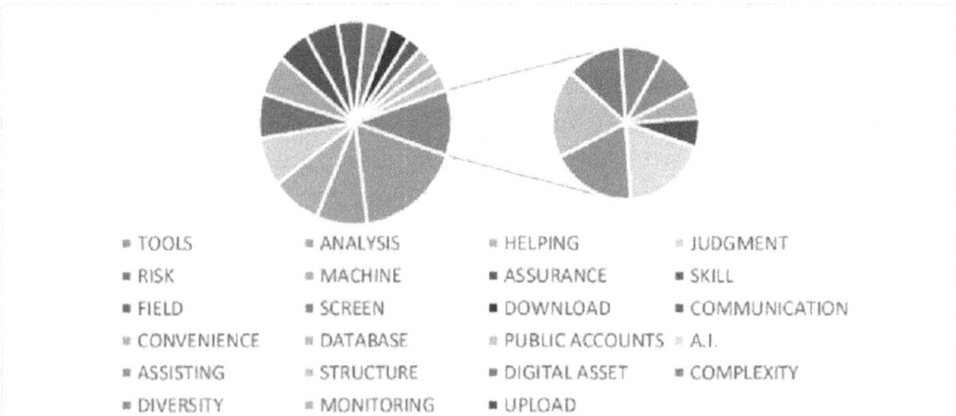

Figure 4. Spindle coding results

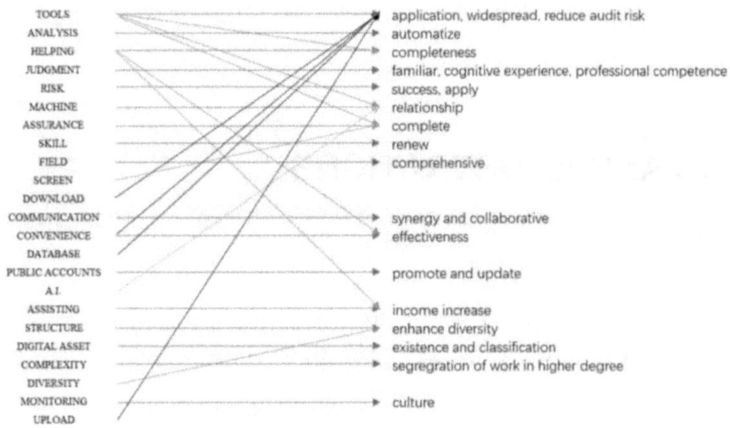

Table 1. Themes of digital auditing

Theme 1	Digitalization of the audit process means the application of new IT tools. 30% involve the application of general tools in audit tasks.
Theme 2	The application of tools is for convenience, the automation and effectiveness of the auditing (data analysis and analysis) process, rather than professional judgment.
Theme 3	The more familiar the auditor is with it, the better their perceived value ('ease of use and 'usefulness' are related to better professional judgment ').
Theme 4	The audit quality improves with the increase in diversity. The background and structure of diversified audit team members.
Theme 5	The definition of the Intelligence Level of Intelligent Audit Tool/Machine rests on the: (I.T./A.I.) – Human Relationship at the task level.
Theme 6	In most audit tasks, the degree of specialization in audit work is relatively high. The higher the multi-skilled and complexity of the digital audit environments, the higher the requirement for human resources.
Theme 7	The latest IT knowledge and skills are essential talents for audit professionals.
Theme 8	Compliance risk management is a key issue for international audit companies to successfully implement digital audit strategies in China.
Theme 9	The compliance monitoring and regulatory system catalyzes a firm's data protection culture.
Theme 10	Basic IT audit procedures and CAAT practices can still be applied to ensure the integrity of commercial operations and record systems used for financial audits.
Theme 11	Ensuring the existence and classification of digital assets through digital asset control testing is an important aspect of audit work.
Theme 12	If digital audit tools are used, they should be considered useful aids/assistance for immediate on-site investigation and completion of the purpose.
Theme 13	The client must perform additional work, for example – uploading the client's data to the ADA system, so communication is crucial for auditors and their clients when using digital auditing methods.
Theme 14	Promote the latest concept of digital audit concepts through social media accounts as public education campaigns.
Theme 15	Digital audit tools are very useful in assisting the Big Four to do cross-selling of their various professional service other than auditing.
Theme 16	The audit risk model will continue to be promoted as the authentic approach of statutory audit, thus digital audit tools are applied to reduce risks, and traditional audit review procedures will continue to play a vital role.

Our study has resulted in the following 16 themes that reflect the essence of what is currently referred to as "digital auditing" in the workplace of audit professionals. These highlights demonstrate the impact of audit technology as a tool in the clients' business big data environment. Table 1 below summarizes these themes.

5. DISCUSSION AND ILLUSTRATIONS

5.1 Discussion

After analyzing the data, it can be inferred that the top auditors in China still rely heavily on traditional concepts when it comes to utilizing audit data analysis. While big data presents some challenges, it has also created new opportunities for the auditing industry. In the face of ethical and technological challenges posed by big data, auditors have taken the lead in ensuring audit quality is not compromised. Their manual control approach is similar to traditional audit practices, with a focus on maximizing benefits while minimizing harm. Consequently, it may be assumed that the four major accounting firms representing the auditing industry may not prioritize the development of more advanced auditing data analysis techniques. The relationship between ADA and BDA is a critical aspect of expanding audit intelligence. Auditors conduct various analytical procedures to gather evidence and perform an in-depth examination of financial statements. Analyzing the data correctly helps auditors to detect fraud, errors, and other financial irregularities.

ADA is a process that uses analytics techniques to examine large volumes of data to identify patterns, trends, and anomalies. BDA, on the other hand, involves analyzing vast amounts of data from various sources to derive insights and make informed decisions. Although these two methods of analysis differ, they complement one another and can be used together to provide a more comprehensive and accurate picture of the financial situation. For example, during analytical audit procedures, auditors must conduct non-intrusive processing of source data. Based on analytical memos written during the coding process, the authors summarize each theme as follows.

5.1.1 The Application of Digital Tools in Audit Work

According to the Big Four major IT audit managers, "digital audit" refers to the use of software tools to extract, load, and transform data from client systems into auditors' data warehouses. This process streamlines audit testing programs and allows auditors to use digital tools as an aid. Digital audit tools are particularly useful for financial and internet enterprises with large business scales and data volumes. However, until now, it is important to note that digital auditing cannot replace the professional judgment of auditors in any audit procedure.

5.1.2 The Impact of Digital Audit on Audit Work

The impact of digital auditing is significant, especially when dealing with sizable amounts of data. It enhances the efficiency of audit work by automating routine tasks and enabling auditors to concentrate on more complex issues. For example, on-site work can involve utilizing digital tools to audit sales contracts. The system identifies critical data, such as transaction time, quantity, amount, and parties involved, and generates a report. Additionally, digital auditing can assist auditors in identifying risk points and forming reports, allowing them to make professional judgments more precisely and effectively.

5.1.3 Auditors Use Digital Tools

Faced with the popularization of digital auditing, accounting firms have established professional information technology departments to develop important auditing software for digital auditing. Digital auditing also requires auditors to understand digital tools, and for newly developed software, the firm should provide training on software usage. In daily office work, the firm provides programming and other training, encouraging employees to develop audit software (mini algorithms) on their own and share them on a common electronic platform to improve work efficiency. Based on this IT environment, auditors in the accounting firm are familiar with digital audit software and believe that the software is an open, authentic, and easy-to-use tool, and its reports on big data are trustworthy, authentic, and effective.

5.1.4 Auditor Structure and Audit Quality

In the environment of digital auditing, compared to traditional financial auditing, digital auditing requires personnel in the audit team to have a richer professional background. In addition to financial auditors, there should also be personnel suitable for the client industry such as architecture, chemistry, and medicine. At the same time, different functional departments should join the audit business team, such as the IT department, data analysis department, and anti-fraud audit department. Any digital audit requires a better audit team, which not only verifies the authenticity and fairness of finance but also includes aspects such as corporate strategy within the scope of audit work. Therefore, the application of digital audit does not reduce the costs for auditors and clients. The diversity of audit team members means that the audit division of labour is more detailed, the audited data is more comprehensive, and the audit quality is better.

5.1.5 The Intelligence of Digital Audit Tools

While digital audit tools have come a long way, they are not yet advanced enough to replace the judgement of human auditors. Instead, they serve as helpful assistants that aid in decision-making. Although they have not achieved the level of autonomous learning and judgement of artificial intelligence, they can identify areas of risk that may have gone unnoticed in traditional financial audits. For example, when dealing with large amounts of data, minor differences in human estimation can make it challenging to detect risks. However, machines can accurately calculate and compare data from previous years and industry averages to identify anomalies. The results of the machine's execution are reported and reviewed by auditors, who ultimately hold the final responsibility in the current digital audit environment.

5.1.6 Digital Audit Refines Audit Work

To better navigate the complex world of e-commerce, companies have assembled teams of experts from a variety of fields to oversee the various procedures involved in audit projects. By conducting digital audits, we're able to ensure that audit work is incredibly precise. Thus, the audit team is made up of financial auditors, IT specialists, anti-fraud experts, and data analysts, each with their unique responsibilities. For example, the anti-fraud team focuses primarily on analyzing operational indicators. If clients plan to go public, auditors must verify the accuracy of their operational data. To handle these complex situations, auditors need diverse teams of professionals with a wide range of skills and a strong ability to work together in a digital audit environment. This will allow auditors to provide the most detailed and comprehensive audits possible.

5.1.7 Information Technology Learning

As technology advances, IT knowledge and skills are becoming more essential for those entering the field of auditing. Audit firms often provide internal technical training programs to equip employees with the necessary expertise. Additionally, staying up-to-date with new IT technologies is crucial for professional auditors to remain competitive. Combining human expertise with machine capabilities can significantly enhance work efficiency, creating a powerful collaborative effect. Encouraging continuous learning through technical training programs fosters a culture of growth within the company, enabling employees to effectively serve clients with diverse business models.

5.1.8 Compliance and Risk Management of Applying Digital Audit

The proper handling of compliance risks is of utmost importance in the realm of digital auditing. The audit software and databases employed in this field must be situated within China's borders and adhere to the regulations stipulated by the Chinese government. This involves satisfying the requirements outlined in a variety of laws, including the National Security Law, the Data Security Law, the Personal Privacy Protection Law, and the Cybersecurity Law. To create IT systems that effectively manage evolving risks, companies can partner with tech powerhouses such as Google and Microsoft to take advantage of cutting-edge technology and develop comprehensive ADA solutions.

5.1.9 Embedding Data Security Protection Culture into Work Behavior

When conducting digital audits, accounting firms amass extensive client data. To safeguard this information, the firm must have protocols and processes in place that monitor and shield the data. All auditors must receive adequate training on data protection compliance, and the internal system of the accounting firm should regularly prompt employees to delete information or update passwords. If employees fail to adhere to the established data security procedures within the specified timeframe, they should be held accountable for their actions. This approach fosters a culture of data security within the accounting firm, promoting best practices for data protection and ensuring the ongoing safety of client's data.

5.1.10 Development of Audit Tools and Integration Into Client Systems

The accounting firm has a diverse clientele with varying business models. For companies that rely on speedy technological advancements such as the internet and e-commerce, the accounting firm must stay up-to-date with the industry's top high-tech enterprises. It is imperative to have a thorough understanding of the client's latest system flow and identify potential risks. Apart from traditional financial audits, IT system audits are also conducted to evaluate the authenticity and effectiveness of the client's IT system management environment. This includes evaluating the separation of team responsibilities, daily backups, disaster recovery drills, and more. If any issues are detected, the client is required to rectify them. Auditors continue to apply basic IT audit procedures and CAAT practices to guarantee the financial audit business operations and recording systems' integrity.

5.1.12 Digital Asset Identification

In the realm of digital auditing, control testing is paramount to verify the categorization and presence of both traditional and digital assets. While the audit of fixed assets, intangible assets, and inventory is well established, the rise of digital auditing has made it imperative to identify and audit the digital assets and information assets of clients, such as audio and video, text, and client data security. These assets are not readily discernible on financial statements, necessitating the regular implementation of penetration testing to evaluate and rate the completeness and effectiveness of the enterprise's control over them. This helps to gauge the audit risks that could impact the company.

5.1.13 Digital Auditing Requires the Integrity of Data Transfer

Ensuring the completeness of big data obtained from client systems is essential. To guarantee the authenticity and effectiveness of this data, the IT team at the front desk must thoroughly check their internal controls related to information technology. This includes verifying data transmission, underlying data logic, logs, client data modification records, password change records, and more. Throughout the data acquisition process, auditors conduct on-site supervision to detect any attempts to delete or modify data. In cases where data formats are inconsistent, the audit's information technology department should perform data cleaning for system-incompatible data. This entails unifying the client data format, importing it into the audit system for data analysis, and creating a comprehensive report.

5.1.14 Communicate With Clients on the Application of Digital Audit Tools

The field of audit is a service-based industry that caters to the unique needs of its clients. To conduct digital auditing, auditors must download a significant amount of data from the client's system. For this reason, auditors must communicate with the senior and middle management of the client to obtain authorization for the transmission of data. During these communications, auditors must clearly outline the purpose of the audit testing, the proprietary audit software use and the objectives to be achieved, and assess the client's willingness to digitize to determine whether digital auditing is appropriate.

5.1.15 Promote Digital Auditing

The auditors intend to leverage social media to promote its latest digital audit tools and raise awareness about the benefits of digital auditing. It is worth noting that not all of these tools will be utilized during on-site audits. Only the most cutting-edge and proficient digital audit tools will be utilized during on-site work, while less advanced or less capable tools will be employed solely as pilot projects. Additionally, auditors aim to communicate with a broader audience, including stakeholders beyond their clients, using social media.

5.1.16 Cross-Selling of Digital Services

Auditors' digital audit tool is constantly evolving with frequent updates and iterations. To demonstrate their successful digital audit cases and consulting services, auditors hold business-sharing meetings with potential clients. This provides them with a comprehensive understanding of a firm's capabilities. Clients tend to prefer collaborating with audit firms that possess good digital audit capabilities, as they ultimately seek a satisfactory and reasonable audit report. Once clients comprehend the benefits of digital operations, they consult auditors for digital transformation services. Auditors' digital services also facilitate cross-selling of other non-audit professional services.

5.1.17 Reducing Audit Risk Through the Application of Digital Audit

Automated systems offer a significant advantage in terms of consistency, as it is not susceptible to human error or bias. The system is capable of achieving remarkable levels of precision and safety within its designated parameters. However, its ability to learn autonomously and rooms provided for human judgment would be limited. As a result, machines cannot entirely replace auditors but provide valuable assistance in human work. As digital auditing tools continue to evolve, machines may be able to make professional judgments, provided they can adhere to high ethical standards and possess self-learning capabilities continuously.

5.2 An illustration: HUAZHU HOTEL GROUP

"On September 21, 2020, a day before the NASDAQ-listed company from China: Huazhu Hotel Group dual-listed its shares in the Hong Kong Stock Exchange, an investigative report from BONITAC Research was published. The report disclosed that the income of the Group had been overstated by HK$2 billion. The amount was misrepresented by the equal amount of fixed assets in its balance sheet which is not in existence. This means that the company had falsely represented its financial position by inflating its assets. The report also highlighted that the company had failed to disclose its related party transactions, which could potentially lead to a conflict

of interest. The report has had a significant impact on the company's reputation and its share price, which plummeted by more than 10% in a single day. This incident highlights the need for greater transparency and accountability in financial reporting and audit reporting, particularly for companies that are publicly listed." Source: Sina Finance, (2020). Huazhu Group, the second largest hotel in China, received an emergency response from short selling on the eve of its listing.https://finance.sina.com.cn/stock/hkstock/ggscyd/2020-09-22/doc-iivhuipp5842766.shtml

Huazhu Hotel Group is number two in the industry in China ranked by yearly annual revenue. The public would like to know why its income, profit and assets are significantly inflated. And, how did these account balances pass the auditor's checking? Why its auditor, Ernst & Young, which is equipped with digital audit capabilities cannot spot irregularities and fraudulent accounting entries?

This illustration aims to highlight the fallacious of arriving PAJ by following path (ii) (see Figure 1) and showcases how path (iii) (Figure 1) is possible.

When creating a Substantive Analytical Review (SAR) audit program for a hotel's yearly sales revenue, usually auditors need to establish a causal model before conducting an analysis. Firstly, the auditor needs to identify factors that affect sales revenue (R), such as occupancy rates (O), room rates (P), discount percentage (D) and the number of rooms (N) sold, i.e., *p (R, O, P, D, N, …n)*, et cetera.

5.2.1 Audit Data Analysis

During the audit process, the auditor demonstrated a comprehensive understanding of variable O by consulting with hotel management personnel. This consultation helped to clarify the definition and situation of variable O. Additionally, by examining the room price menu, it was possible to determine the rent price per night, i.e., P, with confidence. Then, the auditor could personally verify the number of rooms in the hotel, which was necessary to calculate the hotel's annual sales revenue when using the constructed equation later on. The process of determining the number of variables and their relationship was based on communication and inquiry between the auditor and client management personnel. For example, a basic SAR model is constructed with the underlining cause-and-effect chain (see Figure 5):

$$R = O\% \times N \times \$P \times 365$$

Where: R = Annual sales revenue; O = Annual average occupancy rate; N = Number of rooms; and P = Rent per night.

Figure 5. Cause-effect chain of the SAR model

Verification of policy documents is needed and it is a two-way feedback process in which the auditor reflects on the information provided by the client. For example, both O% and, therefore, $P is adjusted variables if the information of seasonal factor (S%) and discount percentage of room rate are supplied by clients and available from other sources. Also, if two categories of tenants (i.e., 'a' & 'b'), are identified during the document review process by the auditor, then the causal model may be further substantiated as follows:

$$R = Ra + Rb$$

$$Ra = (Oa\% \mid Sa\%) \times Na \times (Pa \mid Da\%) \times 365; Rb = (Ob\% \mid Sb\%) \times Nb \times (Pb \mid Db\%) \times 365$$

Where: R = Total Revenue
Ra = Annual sales revenue from client group a
Rb = Annual sales revenue of client group b
Oa% = Adjusted (by Sa) annual average occupancy rate
Ob% = Adjusted (by Sb) annual average occupancy rate
Sa = Seasonal occupancy change rate of client group a
Sb = Seasonal occupancy change rate of client group b
Na = Number of guest rooms in client group a
Nb = Number of guest rooms in client group b
Pa = Rent per night for client group a
Pb = Rent per night for client group b
Da% = Rental discount rate for client group a
Db% = Rental discount rate for client group b

This SAR process helps the auditor to determine the rationality and effectiveness of the model and the fairness of the R that is being presented in the client's financial statements.

5.2.2 Big Data Analysis

The client's database holds detailed information on variables O, N, and S, which was essential in determining the accuracy of the audit. Also, the database contains sales-related data such as check-in and check-out time, guests' gender and ID number, date of birth, occupation, nationality, membership number, other consumption information, and room rates. Auditors can then use big data analysis techniques to view the association of data from various sources to identify trends, patterns and potential associations. However, it is important to note that relying solely on big data analysis may be insufficient to determine the completeness and accuracy of annual sales amounts from random correlation analysis. Even with the availability of large amounts of data, it is not possible to accurately define each variable individually. Relying solely on big data analysis cannot effectively determine the exact number and relationship of related variables. Particularly when a fraud case is triggered by the top management.

5.2.3 Connection Between BDA and ADA

It's worth emphasizing that statistical models for BDA, while useful in many situations, may not always be applicable in audit analysis. Unique and complex situations, in particular, may require alternative approaches. For example, the hotel SAR model may need to be updated to account for different tenant clusters and seasonal changes in occupancy rates. In the context of the hotel's SAR casual model mentioned earlier, it's worth noting that the operator between "O" and "N" is multiplication, not addition. This is a key detail for anyone seeking to understand the model fully. Overall, it's important to be aware of the limitations of statistical models which itself is lacking an estimand for any cause-and-effect analysis to run.

In today's business environment, uncertainty and increased competitiveness often lead to changes in both the definition and number of variables, thus increasing their complexity in audit practice. This means that auditors face difficulties in obtaining facts from the data itself. Instead, they need to construct causal models based on data in the mirror world to clarify the facts. This leads to a crucial discussion about the essence of audit data analysis, particularly on obtaining intelligence from big data analysis. Based on Peral (1988), auditors can acquire intelligence from three categories, i.e., association, intervention, and counterfactuals. The level to which the intelligence belongs can be found in the analysis results. It is worth noting that BDA is at the very beginning of Peral's intelligence ladder, which is the association *'seeing'* layer. If auditors examine the data themselves to establish associations among different variables. They can move to the intervention layer, where they obtain intelligence output from their own ADA results. This is the core of ADA as it enables auditors to create their data and obtain out-of-the-box-in-depth insights into the data, which they can use in their APJ.

Auditing is a complex process that involves constructing causal models to answer "why" questions, as opposed to just "what" questions. To do this, auditors need to use their common sense, experience, and professional knowledge to define variables, consider quantities, select variables, and determine relationships. This approach is different from general regression statistical analysis, which relies on random connections of big data. For example, the auditor can set a conditional probability representation P (do R I D) to obtain a more accurate and comprehensive view, i.e., if D why R, to understand the dynamic of sales revenue on top of the sheer SAR formula by performing the *'do-operation'* themselves.

A way auditors can intervene in big data is by using machine learning algorithms. These algorithms can analyze large volumes of data to identify patterns and anomalies that humans might miss. This can help auditors to identify potential risks and take proactive steps to mitigate them. Another way auditors can intervene in big data is by using Do-Calculus concepts to better carry out predictive analytics. This technique involves analyzing historical data to make predictions about future events. For example, auditors can use the causal model built-in predictive analytics, and let the machine identify potential fraud risks that later human staff can take steps to prevent them from occurring.

Both ADA and BDA are essential tools for auditors. By conducting non-intrusive processing of source data during analytical audit procedures, auditors can use these techniques to detect fraud, errors, and other financial irregularities. By connecting these two areas, auditors can obtain a more comprehensive and accurate picture of the financial situation once a causal model is constructed such as the SAR causal model mentioned.

The difference between these two data analytics represents the difference between Level 1 and Level 2 intelligence (Pearl, 2019), respectively. To make auditing intelligent, auditors need to intervene in big data to achieve a constructed causal data correlation. This involves using various techniques to analyze data and extract meaningful insights from it. Overall, intervening in big data is essential for making auditing more intelligent. By using advanced techniques like predictive analytics and machine learning, auditors can gain deeper insights into their data and make more informed decisions.

Auditors are a group of professionals who ask the critical question "Why". They are not divine beings, but rather individuals who use their professional training, life experience, and common sense to examine and interpret financial data. In the case of the hotel empirical SAR analysis, the variable Sa is the seasonal occupancy change rate of client group 'a', both an existing and conjectured change rate that can be determined through big data analysis. However, auditors cannot rely solely on this calculated rate which is reached by the information of occupancy and price discounts from client's management. Auditors must apply their suspicious minds to determine what they believe is reasonable. Auditors' hypotheses are explicit representations of reason and can be widely accepted and helpful in explaining and supporting audit opinions. Therefore, it is essential to encourage auditors to conduct retrospective reasoning, which is often referred to as the reason for deterministic inquiry to analyze differences. This allows auditors to examine the data retrospectively to determine the reasons behind any discrepancies or changes in the data.

For example, during questioning, the hotel management disclosed that a student tour group was hosted during the traditional off-season in November, which increased the seasonal occupancy rate and total sales for the entire year. Similarly, in the abovementioned SAR formula, auditors can speculate on the rental discount rates of Da% and Db% for client group 'a' and 'b' by relying on their causal model for tracing. As for substantiative audit testing, the client's database may not have the adjusted O%, (Oa% | Sa%), and (Pa | Da%) data stored but only have information on the sales invoices. During this process, auditors continuously revise their causal model based on newly discovered evidence available inside and outside of the client's premises, which provides reasonable explanations for audit items. Auditors obtain new, relevant and useful information until the sufficiency of the evidence is met.

Both the conjectured rate and its relationship with other data do not exist in the client's database and the calculation from big data; therefore, it is an intervention. The reliance on common sense, prior knowledge, and external data does not exist in the big data of hotel clients. This highlights the importance of auditors' expertise in analyzing data, which goes beyond the use of automated tools and the client's existing data. Auditors' ability to use their professional judgment and experience is critical in ensuring that financial statements are free from material misstatements and provide a true and fair view of the entity's financial position. It is evident that to establish causal relationships, intervention is necessary.

To better understand this, let's consider the case of a hotel located in a scenic area that primarily caters to middle-class clients. As one would expect, the fees charged are not cheap. However, despite the global economy being worse this year than the previous year, the hotel's sales revenue has increased by 23% compared to the previous year.

Now, if an auditor were to directly examine the sales revenue, invoices, and sales amounts from tenants' checkout records and found no discrepancies, could they conclude that the completeness and cut-off of the sales amount mentioned in the financial report is factual and unbiased? Not necessarily. The auditor would need to examine other factors that could impact the sales revenue, such as the quality of the services provided, client demand, and marketing efforts. Furthermore, if the CEO in the annual report has attributed the increase in sales to an increase in the number of middle-income tenants, and that the discount sales are also lower than the previous year, the auditors should examine non-financial qualitative data outside of the financial statements to verify the authenticity and impartiality of the sales amounts mentioned in the financial statements. This could include client feedback, marketing strategies, and other factors that could impact sales revenue.

In summary, while direct examination of financial records is crucial to establish factual information, auditors must also consider non-financial qualitative data to ensure that the financial statements are unbiased, authentic and reasonable.

Based on the explanation above, it is evident that without incorporating the causal model in the ADA, the auditor cannot answer critical questions. Auditors can use BDA to attain the first layer of intelligence to complete the reconciliation process of sales documents, which generates a report outlining all unmatched sales. However, this process does not give the auditor sufficient knowledge to evaluate the CEO's explanation. Therefore, it becomes impossible to provide a professional opinion on the fairness and reasonableness of the sales amount. For instance, the actual situation could be the opposite of what the CEO claimed. Suppose the hotel's significant increase in sales is due to discounts on sales, attracting low-income guests throughout the year. In that case, it is undoubtedly an effective move in the short term, but it could harm the hotel's original client base's loyalty and sustainability. By using a causal model, the auditor can discover the actual reasons, such as Da% and Db% conjectures with supporting evidence, and refuse to provide professional opinions to the sales team until the CEO modifies their misleading explanation or provides a reasonable explanation with new evidence.

The amount of the audited accounting subject is a dependent variable under a conditional probability, namely: **P (R | (D), O, S, N, P)**. Thus, it is simply not just an amount with supporting documents that an accounting assertion has to have for its complex nature of existence. Auditors can able to analyze the underlying data by designing a targeted causal model with a *do-operator*, i.e., **P (R | do (D), O, S, N, P),** with a path diagram properly drawn. For example, the sales amount path diagram for hotel clients could be as follows (see Figures 6 and 7).

Figure 6. Auditor's causality diagram

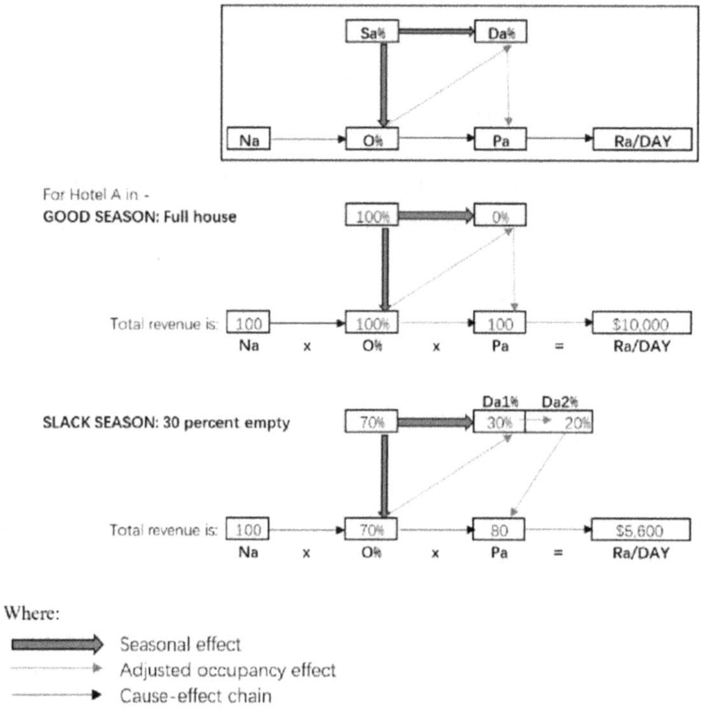

Where:

Figure 7. CEO's causality diagram

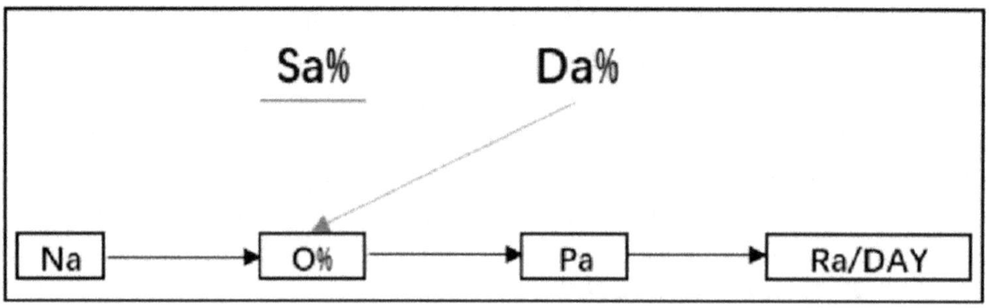

Where: **<u>Sa%</u>** means intervention made to bar the effect to the underneath variables.

The actual situation (see Figure 6) is that occupancy rates are influenced by seasonal factors, i.e., Sa%, which also affect the level of discounts given to tenants. The Da% in this case is a collider, and O% is a confounder. Then, the adjusted discount rate affected the pricing Pa. Therefore, the average annual occupancy rate is adjusted by seasonal factors so as the discount rate (adjusted from Da1% to Da2%). From the path diagrams, hotel rent cannot be the result of the unadjusted occupancy rate and unadjusted discount rate. Comparing Figures 6 and 7, it can be seen that the CEO view the discount rate, i.e., Da%, as the cause of the occupancy rate, i.e., O%. He claimed that the discount rate affects occupancy rates rather than the opposite. And, he denied the seasonal effect.

Proposing a causal model is a modelling step, and we must consider assumptions about how the world operates, what causes and what outcomes. Once we have a causal diagram, we can simulate the effectiveness of intervention by intervening in the causal network. From the above path analysis, auditors can attempt to manipulate the existence and absence of factors and the direction of the path to construct and understand the causal problem they construct, for example, assuming that seasonal factors do not exist and discount factors exist alone, the occupancy rate is the average annual occupancy rate (Figure 7). It shows how the CEO intervenes in the cause and effect of the real picture thus constructing a misrepresentation intentionally. By reconstructing the paths to obtain better audit evidence, auditors can understand better the cause and effect gradually, to be able to answer the 'why' question critically.

5.3 Challenges

As mentioned above, we presented an overview of the present digital auditing landscape, highlighting sixteen important themes. To illustrate, we explore the integration of BDA with ADA, which is frequently viewed as a seamless extension of client BDA, rather than a supplementary function. Though accounting firms might create specialized software tools to scrutinize their clients' voluminous data, it is not guaranteed that audit intelligence will advance to the second level of intelligence. Currently, the auditor's computer system conducts a fundamental analysis of the downloaded massive data, which is later incorporated into an electronic manuscript for further consideration during a manual audit. To a very large extent, his effort remained the hardship of level one intelligence.

It can be quite disheartening to observe the persistence of this issue. However, we may gain some insight by referring to Mitchell's definition of artificial intelligence (1997) again as depicted in Figure 1. According to his explanation, a program's proficiency in task performance (P) increases as it acquires more relevant experience (E) as the above path analysis explained. This can be accomplished by building a synthetic dataset from the abovementioned ADA framework for better-trained machine learning, which utilizes a causal learning approach that integrates two levels of intelligence. The resulting 'estimation formula' panel presents the outcomes derived from imparity expressions, incorporating various do-calculus principles for intelligent ADA.

The fields of causal learning and deep learning can work together harmoniously. Causal learning can be viewed as a promising avenue for deep learning that places a strong emphasis on causal reasoning. Rather than competing, these two areas of study can enhance one another. However, to successfully connect the non-intervention distribution with the intervention distribution, auditors must make additional assumptions about the causal structure of how the data is generated. Having a clear understanding of the causal relationships between variables is key to making accurate predictions about changes in the distribution due to interventions. Unfortunately, this crucial causal information isn't always obvious in the joint distribution, so auditors must employ more sophisticated techniques as shown above to form synthetic datasets for later unsupervised machine learning purposes, to train machines to learn in a meaningful way.

In the case of the Hotel's SAR model, the author utilizes a SAR model of the world (see Figure 5) alongside the observable joint distribution from the Big Data server. The illustration involves accepting the explanation from the hotel's CEO regarding the revenue increase and having no knowledge about the intervention (Figure 7) created by the CEO. Then, the auditor's causal model (Figure 6) plus his or her SAR formula as an ADA framework is a better SAR framework in providing more detailed and accurate information than a simple joint distribution of the dataset from sheer BDA. They not only acknowledge that seasonality affects the hotel's occupancy rate, but also recognize that seasonality causes the discount rate to be adjusted by both the seasonal effect and the adjusted occupancy effect ultimately impacting the room rate per night. The arrows in the Figures indicate the direction of the assumed causal relationship. The reverse of the arrow in Figure 6 (Auditor's Causality Diagram) suggests that there is no true causal effect between variables as the CEO claimed in Figure 7 depicted.

As a result, we can generate additional data for the models that these data are not available from the client's database. These are the digital assets automatically created in the machine learning process by applying the ever-improving causal model. Moreover, in constructing the path diagrams, many causality diagrams are merged into one, and the path diagrams are compatible with the same joint distribution from BDA. Therefore, generally speaking, it is impossible to make conclusive choices between different causal explanations by only looking at observed data.

5.4 How Do I Know if My Causal Model Is Right or Wrong?

Causal diagrams are important tools in understanding the relationship between variables and events in a system. However, it is important to acknowledge that we can never fully verify the accuracy and completeness of a causal diagram based solely on observed data. The validity and completeness of causal diagrams can be tested through experience, although it is important to note that certain aspects of causal models can be tested empirically. Causal diagrams imply the independence of certain conditions or the dependency relationship between variable sets. These dependencies or independencies can be empirically tested, and if they do not exist in the data, it indicates that the causal model is incorrect.

Auditors can use this method for causal discovery by attempting to infer (partial) causal models from empirical data. While causal diagrams provide a way to understand the relationship between variables in a system, it is worth noting that a complete causal model is a form of prior knowledge that auditors must consider and the imagination of the cause they made with the observed effect in their analysis to obtain answers to causal problems without actual intervention. It is not possible to use data alone for reasoning, and causal diagrams are a necessary tool for causal reasoning. Unlike prior knowledge in Bayesian analysis (used to improve data efficiency), a complete causal model is a necessary tool for auditors. With a few exceptions, randomized controlled experiments are the only alternative when causal diagrams are not available. However, these experiments are seldom feasible to use in audit practice.

6. SUMMARY AND CONCLUSION

Auditors can often answer complex questions that require controlled experiments and clear interventions by utilizing the ability to reason causally. This study has only scratched the surface of the second level of the causal ladder, with the third level - Counterfactuals - being an area that scholars should dive deeper into. Thus, we hope that our study will contribute to the development of this matter. While modeless reinforcement learning can eliminate the need to answer causal questions, in most cases, causal reasoning is the most principled approach for auditors to solve problems. Causal reasoning and do-calculus provide valuable insights into an audit problem and help auditors determine what needs to be estimated from the data based on the captured assumptions in the causal diagram. However, even with these powerful tools, deep learning is still necessary to accurately estimate the data. The authors strongly believe that the field of deep learning applied to causal reasoning has yet to be fully explored.

As we continue to make strides in AI, particularly in the realm of deep learning, it is important to consider how this will impact the relationship between humans and machines in the auditing industry. At present, this relationship can be characterized as a "boss-subordinate dynamic," with the auditor assuming the role of the boss and the machine serving as the subordinate, i.e., described as *'Tool'* in Theme 1, 2, 5, 12, and 15 of Table 1 (as demonstrated in Figure 8).

However, as AI technology progresses, we can expect to see a shift in this dynamic, as machines become increasingly sophisticated and capable of carrying out more complex tasks. This may result in a more collaborative and mutually beneficial relationship, as a partner, between auditors and AI-powered systems, with both parties working together to achieve a common goal. In today's business world, information technology plays a vital role in the auditing process. From assessing asset impairment to conducting year-end inventory counts, auditors rely on the use of advanced technology to conduct a wide range of audit tests. Thanks to the increased adoption of unsupervised AI learning and the growing sophistication of big data analysis, auditors can now perform more refined and sophisticated analysis of audit data than ever before.

Figure 8. Audit intelligence curve

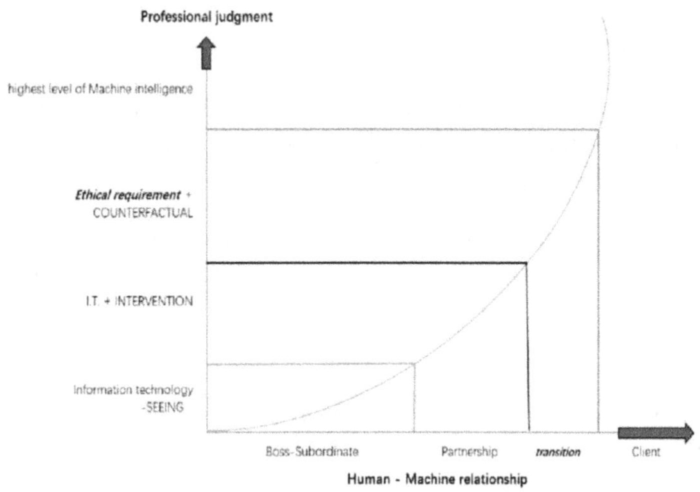

As technology continues to advance, it's natural to anticipate that the analysis of audit data will evolve in step with technological advancements. The intelligence curve, as depicted in Figure 8, is a thought-provoking representation of the potential future partnership between humans and technology. The field of audit intelligence is advancing at a rapid pace, and it has the potential to transform the traditional paradigm of auditing. By analyzing client information using big data, auditors can gain comprehensive intelligence that helps them create effective audit plans and detailed analysis recommendations. This type of analysis goes beyond mere data collection, providing auditors with a wealth of information that can help them make strategic decisions and identify potential areas of risk. For example, well-constructed metadata can be available for ADA use.

Technology is changing the way audits are conducted. Auditors need to adapt to the latest technology to conduct more efficient and effective audits. However, AI technology creates an ethical dilemma for auditors. They need to combat automation bias and meet diverse stakeholder requirements. To succeed, auditors must improve their reasoning skills with AI to provide better quality assurance for their clients. Smaller audit firms may find it challenging to leverage the benefits of AI. Nevertheless, working with AI has the potential to revolutionize the audit industry and establish a new professional-to-business relationship that benefits all stakeholders.

REFERENCES

ACCA. (2019). *Audit and Technology*. The Association of Chartered Certified Accountants.

Agnew, H. (2016). Technology transforms Big 4 hiring practices. *Financial Times*. https://www.ft.com/content/d5670764-15d2-11e6- b197-a4af20d5575e.

Alles, M. G. (2015). Drivers of the use and facilitators and obstacles of the evolution of big data by the audit profession. *Accounting Horizons*, *29*(2), 439–449. doi:10.2308/acch-51067

Appelbaum, D. A., Kogan, A., & Vasarhelyi, M. A. (2017). Big data and analytics in the modern audit engagement: Research needs. *Auditing*, *36*(4), 1–27. doi:10.2308/ajpt-51684

Belissent, J. (2021). Chief data officers: invest in your data sharing programs now. *Forrester*. https://www.forrester.com/report/chiefdata-officers-invest-in-your-data-sharing-programsnow/RES164496

Brown-Liburd, H., Issa, H., & Lombardi, D. (2015). Behavioral implications of big data's impact on audit judgment and decision making and future research directions. *Accounting Horizons*, *29*(2), 451–468. doi:10.2308/acch-51023

Brydon, D. (2019). *Assess, assure and inform: improving audit quality and effectiveness*. Assets. https://assets.publishing.service.gov.uk/government/uploads/system/uploads/attac hment_data/file/852960/brydon-review-final-report.pdf

Cao, M., Chychyla, R., & Stewart, T. (2015). Big data analytics in financial statement audits. *Accounting Horizons*, *29*(2), 423–429. doi:10.2308/acch-51068

Chandler, R. A. (2017). Questions of ethics and etiquette in the Society of Accountants in Edinburgh, 1853–1951. *Accounting History*, *22*(2), 179–192. doi:10.1177/1032373216675912

Dai, J., & Vasarhelyi, M. A. (2017). Toward blockchain-based accounting and assurance. *Journal of Information Systems*, *31*(3), 5–21. doi:10.2308/isys-51804

De Santis, F., & D'Onza, G. (2021). Big data and data analytics in auditing: In search of legitimacy. *Meditari Accountancy Research*, *29*(5), 1088–1112. doi:10.1108/MEDAR-03-2020-0838

Deloitte. (2022a). *Simplifyingrisktechnologyfordeeperinsightsandlowercostriskandregulatorydata andtechnologyinsights.* Deloitte. https://www2.deloitte.com/content/dam/Deloitte/au/Documents/risk/deloitte-au-simplifying-risktechnology-25052022.pdf

Deloitte. (2022b). *TechTrends*. Deloitte. https://www2.deloitte.com/au/en/pages/technology/articles/tech-trends.html

Earley, C. E. (2015). Data analytics in auditing: Opportunities and challenges. *Business Horizons*, *58*(5), 493–500. doi:10.1016/j.bushor.2015.05.002

Ferri, L., Spanò, R., Ginesti, G., & Theodosopoulos, G. (2020). Ascertaining auditors' intentions to use blockchain technology: Evidence from the big 4 accountancy firms in Italy. *Meditari Accountancy Research*, *29*(5), 1063–1087. doi:10.1108/MEDAR-03-2020-0829

IAASB. (2020). *Technology Frequently Asked Questions, November 2020.* IFAC. https://www.ifac.org/ system/files/publications/files/IAASB-TechnologyFAQ-Automated-Tools-Techniques.pdf

IESBA. (2021). *Handbook of the international code of ethics for professional accountants.* IESBA. https://www.ethicsboard.org/publications/2021- handbook-international-code-ethics-professional accountants.

Kend, M., & Nguyen, L. A. (2020). Big data analytics and other emerging technologies: The impact on the Australian audit and assurance profession. *Australian Accounting Review*, *30*(4), 269–282. doi:10.1111/auar.12305

Kend, M., & Nguyen, L. A. (2022). The emergence of audit data analytics in existing audit spaces: Findings from three technologically advanced audit and assurance service markets. *Qualitative Research in Accounting & Management*, *19*(5), 540–563. doi:10.1108/QRAM-01-2021-0005

Kokina, J., & Davenport, T. H. (2017). The emergence of artificial intelligence: How automation is changing auditing. *Journal of Emerging Technologies in Accounting*, *14*(1), 115–122. doi:10.2308/jeta-51730

Lehner, M., Ittonen, K., Silvola, H., & Strom, E. (2022). Artificial intelligence based intelligence-based decision-making in accounting and auditing, ethical challenges and normative thinking. *Accounting, Auditing & Accountability Journal*, *35*(9), 109–135. doi:10.1108/AAAJ-09-2020-4934

Littley, J. (2012). *Leveraging data analytics and continuous auditing processes for improved audit planning, effectiveness, and efficiency.* (KPMG White Paper).

Manita, R., Elommal, N., Baudier, P., & Hikkerova, L. (2020). The digital transformation of external audit and its impact on corporate governance. *Technological Forecasting and Social Change*, *150*, 119751. doi:10.1016/j.techfore.2019.119751

Mitchell, T. M. (1997). *Machine Learning*. McGraw-Hill.

Nair, K., & Gupta, R. (2021). Application of AI technology in modern digital marketing environment. *World Journal of Entrepreneurship, Management and Sustainable Development*, *7*(3), 318–328. doi:10.1108/WJEMSD-08-2020-0099

Pearl, J. (1988). *Probabilistic reasoning in intelligent systems: networks of plausible inference*. Morgan Kaufmann Publishers.

Pearl, J. (2019). *The Book of Why*. Penguin.

Quattrone, P. (2016). Management accounting goes digital: Will the move make it wiser? *Management Accounting Research*, *31*, 118–122. doi:10.1016/j.mar.2016.01.003

Raisch, S., & Krakowski, S. (2021). Artificial intelligence and management: The automation–augmentation paradox. *Academy of Management Review*, *46*(1), 192–210. doi:10.5465/amr.2018.0072

Richins, G., Stapleton, A., Stratopoulos, T., & Wong, C. (2017). Big data analytics: Opportunity or threat for the accounting profession? *Journal of Information Systems*, *31*(3), 63–79. doi:10.2308/isys-51805

Sina Finance. (2020). 中国第二大酒店华住集团上市前夜遭做空 华住紧急回应. Sina Finance. https://finance.sina.com.cn/stock/hkstock/ggscyd/2020-09-22/doc-iivhuipp5842766.shtml

Tiberius, V., & Hirth, S. (2019). Impacts of digitization on auditing: A Delphi study for Germany. *Journal of International Accounting, Auditing & Taxation*, *37*, 100288. doi:10.1016/j.intaccaudtax.2019.100288

Van der Stede, W. A. (2016). Management accounting in context: Industry, regulation and informatics. *Management Accounting Research*, *31*, 100–102. doi:10.1016/j.mar.2016.02.005

Widuri, R., & Gautama, Y. (2020). Computer-Assisted Audit Techniques (CAATs) for financial fraud detection: a qualitative approach. *2020 International Conference on Information Management and Technology (ICIMTech)*. KPMG. www.kpmg.com/US/en/IssuesAndInsights/ArticlesPublications/Documents/data-analytics-continuous-auditing.pdf

Yoon, K., Lucas, H., & Zhang, L. (2015). Big data as complementary audit evidence. *Accounting Horizons*, *29*(2), 431–438. doi:10.2308/acch-51076

KEY TERMS AND DEFINITIONS

Audit Data Analytics (ADA): Algorithm designed for audit software to implement audit testing procedures. ADA is used to discover and analyze patterns, identify anomalies, and obtain other useful information from data populations relevant to the audit.

Audit Professional Judgment (APJ): A behaviour that requires auditors to make decisions, analyses, or evaluations based on their knowledge, skills, training, or experience as auditors, by relevant standards, laws, regulations, or principles of applicable financial reporting frameworks.

Big Data Analytics (BDA): Big data analysis is the process of collecting, examining, and analyzing large amounts of data to discover market trends, insights, and patterns, thereby helping companies make better business decisions. These pieces of information can be quickly and effectively obtained, enabling companies to flexibly develop plans to maintain a competitive advantage.

Counterfactuals: A belief that a cause may have an impact, and its impact must be different from what would have happened without it. If it were not for it, its impact - at least partially, usually entirely - would also disappear.

Digital Audit: Digital audit refers to a comprehensive audit method that utilizes computer and information technology to inspect, analyze, and evaluate the financial accounting and internal control of enterprises. Digital auditing uses data analysis tools and techniques to collect, process, and analyze a large amount of data, automate various tasks in the auditing process, and improve auditing efficiency and accuracy.

Digitalization: Information about commercial activities is immediately digitally transformed by information technology and stored in a digital data store for further reading.

I.T. Tools: The applications and services that help people do their work more efficiently. A common tool in IT, for example, is cloud storage. Many companies run the risk of losing data in the event of power shortages, hardware problems or even unexpected software crashes.

Intervention: An intentional involvement in processes or systems designed to influence events and/or consequences. This term can refer to a single activity but typically refers to a group of activities organized within a project, plan, or tool.

Substantive Analytical Review (SAR): The analysis program includes evaluating financial information by analyzing the reasonable relationship between financial and non-financial data. They also include conducting necessary investigations into identified fluctuations or relationships that are inconsistent with other relevant information or differ significantly from expected values (ISA 520). A basic premise of applying analytical programs is that, in the absence of opposite conditions, it is reasonable to expect the existence and continuation of seemingly reasonable relationships between data.

Suspicious mindset: The initial lack of trust where auditors believe financial statements involve criminal or dishonest activities until they are convinced or reassured.

Chapter 2
Blockchain-Based Technology in Corporate Governance: A Transformative Approach

Jiaman Xu
University College Dublin, Ireland

ABSTRACT

Blockchain-based technology has been recognized as a potential tool to transform corporate governance. This chapter first discusses the persisting challenges of agency costs, inefficiencies, and the need for improved transparency. It then examines the emergence of blockchain as a potential solution, offering a novel, decentralized approach to corporate governance. The analysis covers the technology's application to share registers, trading, voting, and accounting practices, emphasizing the duality of its promise for increased transparency and emergent privacy concerns. Controversial aspects, such as the threat to existing shareholder activism and the governance of blockchain itself, are critically examined. Solutions like hybrid blockchain models and regulatory nodes are proposed to address these issues. The chapter concludes with a forward-looking perspective on decentralized autonomous organizations (DAOs) as an innovative alternative to traditional corporate structures, signifying a new paradigm in corporate governance.

1. INTRODUCTION

In an era where the digital revolution is redefining human interaction, the corporate world is experiencing a foundational shift. This transformation extends beyond mere technological advancements, challenging the long-established principles of corporate governance. Central to this change is blockchain technology, increasingly associated with notions of decentralization, transparency, and enhanced security. This chapter explores blockchain's role in redefining corporate governance, examining the challenges it seeks to address, and the innovative solutions it offers.

DOI: 10.4018/979-8-3693-1331-2.ch002

Historically, corporations have functioned as pillars of economic activity, streamlining complex transactions and operations globally. Their creation aimed to reduce transaction costs and improve market efficiency, concepts pioneered by Ronald Coase. However, these entities have continually grappled with the tension between shareholders and managers, characterized by conflicting interests and the resultant agency costs (Jensen and Meckling, 1976). This dynamic underscores the critical role of corporate governance mechanisms. They regulate information flow, power distribution, and align stakeholder interests, yet are often hindered by inefficiencies and information asymmetries.

In response, regulatory bodies have evolved, introducing reforms to strengthen governance through disclosure, shareholder empowerment, and executive accountability (La Porta et al., 2000). Despite these efforts, the persistence of agency problems indicates a need for more robust solutions (Bebchuk and Weisbach, 2010). Here, blockchain technology emerges as a beacon of hope, offering to mitigate these deep-rooted challenges. With its advent in the late 2000s, blockchain has not only been a technological breakthrough but also a catalyst for a more equitable and transparent economic system (Nakamoto, 2008; Tapscott and Tapscott, 2016).

Blockchain's potential lies in its distributed ledger system and consensus mechanisms, which collectively offer a new paradigm of transparency. However, this technology is not without its complexities and controversies. This chapter critically examines these challenges, particularly how blockchain's integration into corporate governance redefines roles, reshapes interactions, and alters the landscape of corporate oversight. From stock ownership recording to shareholder voting mechanics, and from transparent accounting practices to the implementation of smart contracts, blockchain presents a novel perspective on corporate governance (Yermack, 2017).

Nonetheless, innovation often confronts established paradigms, and blockchain is no exception. The technology's transparency, while advantageous, raises privacy concerns among market participants. Similarly, its decentralized governance prompts questions about authority and regulatory intervention in a system designed for autonomy (Buterin, 2015; Catalini and Gans, 2016).

Looking ahead, the chapter posits that the full potential of blockchain in corporate governance may be realized in alternative structures like Decentralized Autonomous Organizations (DAOs). These entities, governed by consensus and code rather than hierarchical edicts, signify a fundamental rethinking of corporate governance aligned with blockchain's ethos.

In summary, this chapter provides a comprehensive examination of blockchain's role in traditional corporate governance. It contextualizes the historical background, outlines current challenges, and anticipates future innovations. The aim is to furnish a holistic understanding of blockchain's transformative potential in reshaping the corporate governance landscape.

The chapter proceeds as follows. Section 2 discusses relevant literature on traditional corporate governance and provides a brief overview of the blockchain-based technology. Section 3 underscores the potential applications of blockchain on corporate governance and the controversies arising from the applications. Sections 4 and 5 summarize solutions and future development. Section 6 concludes.

2. BACKGROUND

2.1 Corporate Governance

Corporations were originally formed with the primary aim of reducing the transaction costs that arise from the inherent inefficiencies of market transactions. The existence of firms, as theorized by Ronald Coase, is predicated on the notion that organizing economic activity within corporate boundaries can be more efficient than transacting in the open market due to the costs associated with market transactions (Coase, 1937). This internalization of transactions is designed to mitigate the need for extensive market-based bargaining and legal enforcement, thereby streamlining economic activities.

Corporate governance serves as the framework within which corporations are directed and controlled. At the heart of corporate governance lies the principal-agent relationship, where the principals (shareholders) delegate authority to the agents (managers) to manage the enterprise on their behalf. This delegation, however, introduces the possibility of agency costs, which arise when the interests of the managers diverge from those of the shareholders (Jensen and Meckling, 1976; Fama and Jensen,1983a,b). A strand of literature posits that the market price of a company's shares should reflect the anticipated agency costs, suggesting that shareholders need not be overly concerned about these costs (Jensen and Meckling, 1976). Nevertheless, due to information asymmetries and the problem of adverse selection, it is often not possible for these costs to be fully anticipated and thus reflected in the share price.

Therefore, the overarching goal of effective governance mechanisms is to align the incentives of the principal and the agent in such a way as to minimize the costs that arise when managers prioritize their own interests over those of the shareholders. In pursuit of this alignment, shareholder value maximization has emerged as the dominant paradigm in corporate governance (Smith and Ronnergard, 2016). This approach posits that by focusing on maximizing shareholder value, the interests of managers will naturally align with those of the shareholders, thereby reducing agency costs (Fox and Lorsch, 2012).

The infrastructure of traditional corporate governance is built around shareholders, boards of directors, and, in some jurisdictions, committees that provide oversight and strategic direction. However, the agency problem persists, leading to various corporate scandals and financial crises over the years (Kirkpatrick, 2009). In response, governments have implemented a series of regulatory changes aimed at strengthening corporate governance. These changes include enhanced disclosure requirements, reforms to encourage shareholder activism, changes to proxy voting procedures, and revisions to executive compensation structures (La Porta et al., 2000; Hermalin and Weisbach, 2007). Despite these efforts, the persistence of agency problems suggests that the existing governance mechanisms are insufficient. As noted by scholars, "despite decades of governance experiments and extensive rule revisions, the existing scope of agency problems suggest that the core underlying agency problems cannot fully be resolved within the existing theoretical and legal infrastructure" (Bebchuk and Weisbach, 2010). This observation underscores the need for innovative approaches to corporate governance that can address the limitations of the current systems.

In this context, blockchain technology emerges as a potentially transformative solution. By enabling more direct and transparent interactions between shareholders and managers, blockchain has the potential to reduce or even eliminate some forms of intermediation, thereby addressing the core agency problems that have long plagued corporate governance.

2.2 Blockchain-Based Technology

Central to blockchain's innovation is its function as a distributed ledger system within a peer-to-peer network. Its defining feature is immutability; once data is recorded on the blockchain, altering it becomes exceedingly difficult. This permanence is key to establishing trust in the data's accuracy, eliminating the need for a central verifying authority (Nakamoto, 2008).

Contrasting with traditional financial systems where central authorities or intermediaries are necessary to validate transactions, blockchain operates on a decentralized model. Transactions are verified by a network of participants, each maintaining a copy of the ledger. This verification is achieved through consensus mechanisms, ensuring all parties agree on the transaction's validity (Yermack, 2017). The replication of the ledger across multiple nodes enhances both transparency and security; any discrepancies are quickly identified and addressed by the network (Catalini and Gans, 2016).

Blockchain employs various consensus mechanisms, such as Proof of Work (PoW) and Proof of Stake (PoS). While PoW is known for its use in cryptocurrencies like Bitcoin, PoS offers a more energy-efficient alternative, allocating verification power based on token ownership (King and Nadal, 2012; Saleh, 2021).

Another integral aspect of blockchain is smart contracts (Szabo, 1997). These self-executing contracts, with terms embedded in code, activate automatically under pre-defined conditions, eliminating the need for intermediaries. This feature is poised to automate complex corporate processes, thus minimizing disputes and potential litigation.

The distinction between public and private blockchains is also significant. Public blockchains are open, allowing unrestricted participation, while private blockchains limit access to specific users. Each offers distinct advantages in terms of transparency, security, and control, adaptable to various governance needs (Buterin, 2015).

Since its inception, blockchain technology has been recognized as a revolutionary force with the potential to disrupt the business world (e.g. Biais et al., 2023). Recent academic research has extensively explored the multifaceted implications of blockchain technology in the finance. Cong and He (2019) offer a theoretical framework for understanding decentralized consensus in blockchain applications, particularly in trade finance, highlighting the trade-off between enhanced market competition and the risk of collusion, especially in permissioned blockchains. Cao et al. (2020) and Cao, Cong and Yang (2023) delve into the practical applications of blockchain in streamlining auditing processes and financial reporting. They emphasize how blockchain automation can revolutionize auditing efficiency, altering traditional audit pricing models and reducing fraud. Chod and Lyandres (2023) investigate the strategic advantages of pricing products in crypto tokens, revealing how blockchain can influence market dynamics and competitive advantages. Chiu and Koeppl (2019) assess the application of blockchain in securities settlement, highlighting its potential for faster, more flexible transactions, while also considering the necessary trade-offs for sustainable blockchain finance. Finally, Ferreira, Li and Nikolowa (2022) address the governance aspect of blockchain, scrutinizing how the proof-of-work system impacts the industrial ecosystem and market structures, pointing to the risks of dominance by large firms. Collectively, these studies underscore the transformative potential of blockchain in finance, while also cautioning about its complexities and the need for careful management of its economic and competitive impacts.

Specific to corporate governance, blockchain facilitates a shift towards decentralization and transparency. As emphasized by Cong and He (2019), a carefully designed protocol on blockchains may reduce individual's incentives to manipulate and misreport, allowing more efficient information aggregation and thus enhance contracting, potentially addressing the incomplete contract problems in corporate governance. Practically, it promises more efficient management of stock ownership records, asset transfers, and corporate actions, potentially reducing costs associated with financial intermediaries and enhancing the accuracy of shareholder records (Catalini and Gans, 2016; Chiu and Koeppl, 2019). Furthermore, the immutable and transparent nature of blockchain has significant implications for financial reporting and compliance. By maintaining financial records on a blockchain, companies can decrease the likelihood of financial misreporting, thereby enhancing the credibility of their disclosures. This could also reduce the reliance on extensive auditing services, as the blockchain provides a verifiable and tamper-proof record of transactions (Tapscott and Tapscott, 2016; Cao et al., 2020; Cao, Cong and Yang, 2023).

In conclusion, blockchain technology is at the vanguard of transforming corporate governance. Its distributed ledger, consensus mechanisms, and the implementation of smart contracts constitute a framework for managing corporate affairs that is more transparent, efficient, and independent of traditional intermediaries. As blockchain continues to evolve, its potential to reshape the corporate landscape remains an area of keen interest and ongoing study in both professional and academic studies. The next section discusses specific application of blockchain technology in corporate governance, as well as controversies around the application.

3. THE APPLICATION OF BLOCKCHAIN TECHNOLOGY IN CORPORATE

While blockchain presents novel approaches to corporate governance, it simultaneously ushers in a suite of controversial issues. This transformative technology has begun to provide alternatives to traditional corporate governance, leveraging code, peer-to-peer connections, and collaborative efforts. The core of blockchain's appeal in governance lies in its capacity to minimize the role of intermediaries, thereby potentially reducing oversight costs and reshaping the principal-agent cost structure. Yet, this significant shift also brings forth a series of debates and controversies (Tapscott and Tapscott, 2016; Yermack, 2017; van der Elst and Lafarre, 2024).

3.1 Visibility of Transactions and Traders

The integration of blockchain technology into the share register is poised to redefine corporate governance by enhancing transparency. Blockchain's ledger system enables a tamper-proof and real-time record of stock ownership, which could address problems related to inaccurate and untimely records. Blockchain is transparent about the transactions in the chain, but the traders are primarily anonymous because assets on blockchains are usually stored in unidentifiable "digital wallets" that are marked by complex, serial number-like codes. For example, early Bitcoin users sought this anonymity for illicit activities like drug purchases and money laundering. However, the ability to identify users on a blockchain is debatable. On the Bitcoin blockchain, for instance, preserving anonymity has occasionally been challenging. It is relatively straightforward to link digital wallets to specific stock traders by looking for unique transaction patterns in the raw data, such as the allocation of a certain number of restricted shares to a manager on a given date.

This transparency allows for a clear identification of ownership stakes, which is instrumental in mitigating rent-seeking behaviours and reducing opportunities for regulatory arbitrage. Share owners (e.g., managers) might try to remain untraceable by using various digital wallets for different transactions or splitting their transactions across multiple wallets. To counter these tactics, regulators could mandate corporate insiders to disclose their digital wallet IDs or public keys, subject to legal penalties. Therefore, with accompanying regulations, the transparency afforded by blockchain could revolutionize managerial ownership visibility, making practices such as the backdating of stock compensation more difficult and thus potentially impacting executive behaviour.

Along the same vein, the implications for insider trading are equally profound. Blockchain could curtail managers' ability to capitalize on inside information, as a transparent ledger would make any opportunistic trades immediately visible to the market. However, Baiman and Verrecchia (1996) and Roulstone (2003), rooted in the theories of Manne (1966), argue that insider trading, whether legal or illegal, may represent an effective system that in fact aligns managers' and shareholders' interests. Consequently, firms might have to pay managers more to offset the loss of the profits that they could have gained from insider trading.

Moreover, real-time insider trading, if observed by outsiders on the chain, could be potentially valuable as managers' transactions likely signal private information about the firm. However, the transparency would also expose managers to greater scrutiny by directors and shareholders and therefore may cause them to trade less often out of concerns of sending negative signals to the markets. Hence, the managers may have diminished incentives to create valuable information that they might be able to exploit via insider trading, potentially reducing their alignment with shareholders.

3.2 Stock Liquidity, Voting and Shareholder Activism

The promise of blockchain extends to the trading floors, where shareholders could benefit from lower trading costs. The agility of blockchain technology facilitates visible, real-time observation of share transfers, potentially culminating in instantaneous settlement (Chiu and Koeppl, 2019). This efficiency obviates the need for the multiple intermediaries currently embedded within the system, who extract value in the form of commissions and bid-ask spreads. A strand of literature has shown that corporate governance benefits from improved stock liquidity as shareholders, especially institutional investors and blockholders, to sell their shares more easily and hence can discipline managers by the threat of exit (Cheung, Chung and Fung, 2015; Brogaard, Dan and Ying, 2017).

However, the introduction of blockchain in this domain is not without its controversies. One such debate centres on whether the improved liquidity and transparency provided by blockchain actually foster better corporate governance. The argument hinges on the 'exit versus voice' dichotomy, with some scholars contending that an easy exit, facilitated by liquidity, weakens shareholders' incentives to engage with management ('voice'). This disengagement could ultimately undermine corporate governance (Hirschman, 1972; Broccardo, Hart and Zingales, 2022).

Therefore, a more promising pathway is the incursion of blockchain into the domain of shareholder voting. Current custody chains complicate the relationship between issuers and shareholders, often resulting in a convoluted and opaque process where votes may not be accurately counted or attributed. Blockchain technology, with its decentralized and transparent ledger, could dismantle these complexities, facilitating a more direct line of communication and interaction between companies and their investors, potentially reshaping shareholder activism and engagement. For instance, by streamlining the voting process, blockchain could vastly simplify the exercise of voting rights, ensuring that shareholders' voices are more directly and efficiently heard. The immutable nature of blockchain records ensures the integrity of the voting process, potentially leading to an uptick in shareholder participation and a more democratic approach to corporate decision-making.

A notable application of blockchain in shareholder voting is the collaboration between Broadridge and the Tokyo Stock Exchange, as well as Banco Santander's foray into blockchain-based proxy voting. In Europe, the Shareholder Rights Directive (SRD) II has suggested a more streamlined and transparent process, which blockchain could significantly enhance. These initiatives signal a growing interest in leveraging blockchain to foster shareholder engagement, though it is clear that the technology's role in reshaping corporate governance is still in its infancy.

Furthermore, blockchain opens possibilities for rethinking the distribution of decision-making power within corporations. It could, for instance, enable a broader range of stakeholders, including employees and customers, to participate in corporate governance processes traditionally reserved for shareholders. An example can be seen in the Dutch pension fund system, where beneficiaries are involved in decisions about sustainability policies—a reflection of a growing demand for ethical and sustainable investment strategies.

However, this technological advancement does not come without its controversies. The increased transparency afforded by blockchain could, paradoxically, lead to reduced shareholder activism. Activists and corporate raiders often rely on the ability to build substantial share positions away from the public eye, taking advantage of confidentiality to avoid premature price movements (Bebchuk et al., 2020). Blockchain's transparency might discourage such strategies, potentially discourage the ardour of activists who play a vital role in monitoring management.

Another aspect of the controversy is the debate over the necessity of blockchain in shareholder voting. While blockchain promises enhanced transparency and integrity in the voting process, there are arguments to be made for centralized digital systems which could provide similar benefits without the radical overhaul required for blockchain implementation. The question remains whether the advantages of blockchain are sufficient to outweigh the costs and risks associated with its adoption.

In sum, blockchain's potential to enhance voting and shareholder activism is considerable, promising a more engaged and efficient form of corporate governance. Yet, it also raises significant debates around the need for anonymity in activist strategies and the broader implications of transparency in market behaviours.

3.3 Accounting and Earnings Management

Earnings management and accounting fraud are key issues that corporate governance attempts to prevent (Beasley et al., 2000; Cornett, Marcus and Tehranian, 2008). A more transparent accounting system, enabled by blockchain technology, may effectively reduce the probability of earnings management and fraud. Moreover, the immutable nature of blockchain records means that once financial transactions are recorded, they cannot be altered retroactively. The efficiency gains from blockchain could also reduce the need for traditional auditing services. Auditors, who are tasked with verifying the accuracy of financial records, could see their roles become less about validation and more about strategic consultation. For example, Cao et al. (2020) propose a designed Auditing Blockchain which can automate the reporting and auditing process. While this shift could save companies the high costs associated with auditing services, it could also lead to a restructuring of the accounting profession, with auditors needing to adapt to a landscape where the ledger is self-validating.

However, the integration of blockchain technology into accounting practices presents a trade-off between the significant benefits of improved transparency and the potential costs associated with the disclosure of proprietary information. Moreover, while blockchain promises to streamline accounting processes, the initial setup and ongoing maintenance of a blockchain system could be resource-intensive. The question remains whether these upfront and operational costs could be justified by the long-term savings in auditing and financial reporting.

Therefore, while blockchain in accounting offers the potential for a more transparent and efficient reporting system, one that could foster greater trust among shareholders and reduce the manipulation of financial data, this comes with the caveat that companies must carefully manage the disclosure of their financial information to protect their proprietary interests. The cost-benefit analysis of adopting blockchain in accounting will ultimately depend on a company's specific circumstances, including the competitive landscape it operates within and the value it places on the integrity and transparency of its financial records.

3.4 Smart Contract

Smart contracts, a key application of blockchain technology, warrant their own discussion beyond the previously mentioned applications. These innovative contracts represent a significant advancement in executing and enforcing terms within the blockchain framework. As self-executing agreements with the contract terms embedded directly into code, smart contracts have the potential to drastically reduce transaction and agency costs. They achieve this by automating processes that traditionally needed considerable manual supervision, marking a revolutionary shift in how contractual obligations are managed and fulfilled.

The adoption of smart contracts in corporate governance could lead to a new era of efficiency. Options embedded in derivative securities, the instant transfer of collateral upon default, and the automatic payment of employee compensation contingent upon reaching performance milestones are just a few examples of the wide array of applications. By automating these processes, smart contracts can diminish the likelihood of opportunistic behaviour, thereby reducing a considerable portion of the agency costs that plague traditional contracts.

From the perspective of corporate governance, the transparent and deterministic nature of smart contracts could serve as a recommitment mechanism for firms, signalling a refusal to engage in future opportunistic behaviour. This could enhance trust among stakeholders and potentially lower a firm's cost of capital by reducing the perceived risks associated with lending to or investing in the firm.

However, smart contracts are not without their costs and operational concerns. One significant challenge lies in their inflexibility; once a smart contract is deployed on the blockchain, altering it can be complex and sometimes impossible. This rigidity could pose problems in the dynamic business environment where contractual adjustments and negotiations are commonplace.

Moreover, the development and implementation of smart contracts require a high degree of technical expertise, and the nascent nature of the technology means that legal and regulatory frameworks are still adapting. The potential for coding errors or the exploitation of unforeseen vulnerabilities in smart contract design could lead to financial losses and legal disputes, offsetting the efficiencies these contracts are meant to introduce.

Despite these challenges, smart contracts hold immense promise for streamlining corporate governance mechanisms, provided that firms can navigate the trade-offs between the benefits of automation and the operational risks involved. As the technology matures and more safeguards are put in place, smart contracts could become a cornerstone of a new, more efficient, and transparent approach to corporate governance.

3.5 Discussion on Controversies

While the trade-offs in the adoption of blockchain technology in corporate governance are discussed separately in previous sections, this section underscores the trade-offs and provides further in-depth discussions.

At the core of the tension is the trade-offs of transparency and privacy in the context of corporate governance. While blockchain's inherent transparency regarding transactions is a significant advantage in preventing managerial strategic behaviours, it simultaneously poses a challenge for active investors who guard their strategies against potential copycats. The visibility of transactions on a blockchain means that once an investor takes a position, their strategy can be observed and potentially replicated, diluting the uniqueness and potential profitability of their approach. Active investors, such as activist shareholders or hedge funds, often rely on the element of surprise and confidentiality when building significant positions in a company. The immediate and transparent recording of transactions on a blockchain could expose their strategies to the market prematurely, allowing others to ride on their research and investment acumen, and potentially impacting the efficacy of their trades.

Concerning identity, blockchain offers a pseudonymous environment rather than anonymity. While traders' identities are not immediately transparent, over time, patterns in transaction data can potentially reveal the actors behind the trades. Sophisticated analysis of transaction times, sizes, and frequencies can unmask the identities of traders, including corporate insiders and large institutional investors. This could lead to a modern form of market surveillance, where investors' strategies and positions become decipherable to competitors and regulators. The capability to infer identities from trading patterns raises the stakes for corporate insiders, who must navigate the public nature of blockchain transactions against regulatory requirements for disclosure and the strategic desire for discretion. Companies must weigh these considerations carefully, as they may deter valuable insiders from engaging in company stock transactions, thereby impacting compensation structures and incentive alignment.

In addition, the integration of blockchain technology into accounting practices presents a trade-off between the significant benefits of improved transparency and the potential costs associated with the disclosure of proprietary information. The radical transparency that blockchain brings to accounting could also mean that sensitive financial information becomes accessible to unintended audiences, including competitors. This transparency might inadvertently disclose strategic information that could compromise a company's competitive advantage. The proprietary costs incurred could outweigh the benefits if sensitive data were to be exploited by competitors, leading to a potential reshuffling of market positions.

In essence, while blockchain technology promotes an unprecedented level of transaction transparency that can be beneficial for corporate governance, it also introduces privacy concerns that could influence investor behaviour and corporate strategies. The balance between the benefits of transparency and the protection of proprietary investment strategies is delicate and requires careful consideration by companies and regulatory bodies alike. As blockchain continues to evolve, addressing these privacy concerns and the potential for identity inference will be critical in maintaining a fair and competitive market landscape.

Finally, the governance of blockchain technology itself is a subject that sits at the heart of many debates regarding its application in corporate governance. The decentralized nature of blockchain is one of its core attractions, offering a system that is ostensibly free from the control of any single authority. However, this decentralization raises critical questions about who, or what, is responsible for the governance of the blockchain. Blockchain governance is essentially about who has the power to make changes to the protocol and under what circumstances. If blockchain attains a central role in corporate record-keeping, the authority to update its code becomes a crucial governance issue. Updates may be necessary for various reasons, from fixing security vulnerabilities to optimizing the system's efficiency or responding to changes in regulatory requirements.

The challenge is that the very features that make blockchain secure and trustworthy—its distributed nature and the consensus mechanisms for validating transactions—also introduce vulnerabilities. For example, the lack of centralized control could potentially leave a blockchain open to sabotage or manipulation by bad actors, especially if they gain control over a significant portion of the network. On the other side of the spectrum is the concept of a permissioned blockchain, where governance is more centralised, and changes can only be made by certain authorized participants. While this may enhance security and provide a clear governance structure, it also diverges from the open and permissionless nature of public blockchains, potentially reducing some of their most appealing attributes, such as resistance to censorship and reduced reliance on trust.

This governance dilemma leads to the trade-off between the decentralized ethos of blockchain and the practical need for a governance framework that can support a robust and secure infrastructure for corporate governance. Blockchain's promise of reducing the need for trust through technological means is tempered by the reality that the system itself must be trusted and, therefore, effectively governed. In navigating this trade-off, one must consider the spectrum of possibilities that blockchain governance models present, from fully decentralized public blockchains to hybrid models that incorporate elements of centralization. The implications for corporate governance are profound, as the chosen model will significantly impact how corporate records are maintained, how transparent they are, and how easily they can adapt to changing circumstances.

In conclusion, the governance of blockchain technology is a complex issue with far-reaching implications for its use in corporate governance. The centralization versus decentralization debate is not merely theoretical but has practical consequences for the security, efficiency, and adaptability of blockchain systems. As the technology continues to develop, the governance models adopted will need to balance these considerations, ensuring that blockchain can fulfil its promise as a transformative tool for corporate governance while maintaining the security and integrity of the system.

4. SOLUTIONS AND RECOMMENDATIONS

The challenges and controversies surrounding blockchain in corporate governance are substantial, but they are not insurmountable. Solutions are emerging that seek to leverage the strengths of blockchain technology while mitigating its weaknesses.

4.1 Proxy Systems and Stock Ownership Transfer

Blockchain-based technology could revolutionize proxy voting systems, making them more secure, efficient, and transparent. By recording votes on a blockchain, companies can ensure that shareholder voices are accurately represented and that results are indisputable. Similarly, blockchain can streamline the transfer of stock ownership. By automating the process through smart contracts, blockchain has the potential to make these transactions nearly instantaneous and free from the errors and fraud that can plague traditional methods.

4.2 Hybrid Blockchain Models

In response to privacy concerns and the debate over decentralization, a hybrid blockchain model offers a compelling solution. This model combines the best features of both private and public blockchains, offering the transparency and security of a public blockchain while still providing the control and privacy of a private blockchain. This approach could allow companies to keep certain sensitive transactions private while still benefiting from the public blockchain's integrity for other aspects of corporate governance.

4.3 Regulatory Nodes and Side Chains

A futuristic but increasingly viable solution is the integration of regulatory authorities directly into the blockchain network. Imagine a public blockchain where, alongside regular nodes, there are nodes or even entire side chains operated by regulatory bodies. These nodes would not have special privileges in terms of access to information but would be equipped with smart contracts that are programmed to enforce regulatory compliance automatically. If a transaction were found to be non-compliant, the smart contract could trigger an intervention by the authorities. This would maintain the decentralized nature of the blockchain while also embedding regulatory oversight within the system itself.

4.4 Smart Contracts for Compliance and Oversight

Smart contracts could be further developed to provide live, transparent oversight. These contracts would be public and auditable by anyone, yet only the regulatory authorities would have the power to execute certain functions, such as freezing assets or reversing transactions in the event of non-compliance or fraudulent activity. This approach could provide a balance between the autonomy of the blockchain and the need for regulatory control.

In conclusion, the way forward in resolving the issues and controversies surrounding blockchain in corporate governance lies in innovative solutions that combine technology with smart regulatory design. Hybrid blockchains and smart contracts offer the flexibility and adaptability needed to navigate the complex landscape of corporate governance. By incorporating these solutions, blockchain can move from a novel technology with potential pitfalls to a robust platform for transparent, efficient, and secure corporate governance.

5. FUTURE RESEARCH DIRECTIONS

In the quest for more robust governance mechanisms, it is crucial to acknowledge that blockchain's application within traditional corporate structures has its limitations. The core properties of blockchain technology—decentralization, transparency, and automation—may only be fully realized in alternative organizational forms that depart from hierarchical models.

5.1 The Rise of Decentralized Autonomous Organizations (DAOs)

Decentralized Autonomous Organizations (DAOs) represent a radical rethinking of corporate structures, harnessing blockchain technology to operate with a level of autonomy not possible in traditional organizations. A DAO is governed by rules encoded as computer programs—smart contracts—that are transparent, controlled by the organization members, and not influenced by a central government. DAOs are not burdened by the top-down hierarchy; instead, they operate on a flat structure where decisions are made by consensus or majority vote among its members.

The governance solutions offered by DAOs can address many of the issues inherent in traditional corporate governance by creating a system where the alignment of interests between shareholders and managers is built into the code. The rules of the organization and its operational procedures are embedded in the smart contracts, making the organization self-governing and largely self-enforcing.

5.2 DAO Infrastructure and Governance

The infrastructure of a DAO is designed to facilitate direct participation and control by its members, potentially leading to more efficient and responsive decision-making processes. However, the governance of DAOs is still an evolving field, with its own set of challenges and controversies, such as how to effectively manage collective decision-making and handle disputes within a purely digital framework.

In conclusion, as blockchain continues to mature, the development of alternative governance structures like DAOs may provide the most fitting application of the technology. These structures promise a more direct and engaged form of governance that could resolve many of the issues present in traditional corporate forms. However, DAOs themselves are in their infancy and will require further development and real-world testing to fulfill their potential as the next evolution in corporate governance. The journey ahead is one of exploration and innovation, with the ultimate goal of aligning governance mechanisms with the values and capabilities of blockchain technology.

6. CONCLUSION

This chapter has traversed the intricate landscape of corporate governance, examining its historical evolution, the transformation of regulatory frameworks, and the advent of blockchain technology. In doing so, it has illuminated the multifaceted impact of blockchain on aspects of corporate governance such as share registration, trading, voting, and shareholder activism. While blockchain heralds enhanced transparency and the potential for increased efficiency through mechanisms like smart contracts, it also brings forth challenges, notably in privacy concerns and the adaptability of its rigid structures.

Blockchain emerges not as a cure-all but as a potent tool that, when applied judiciously, holds the potential to revolutionize corporate governance. Its ability to directly connect shareholders and managers offers a novel approach to mitigating agency problems, embodying a significant leap in governance practices. However, this advancement necessitates a careful balancing act: harmonizing innovation with traditional practices, transparency with privacy needs, and the decentralization inherent in blockchain with necessary centralized oversight.

The proposed solutions, such as hybrid blockchain models and the incorporation of regulatory nodes, represent pragmatic steps towards leveraging blockchain's strengths while addressing its limitations. These are initial forays into a more integrated application of blockchain in the governance landscape, marking the beginning of an ongoing process of refinement.

Looking ahead, the rise of Decentralized Autonomous Organizations (DAOs) marks a shift towards more radically transparent and egalitarian governance structures. However, DAOs, like the broader application of blockchain in governance, are still in their developmental stages, brimming with potential but also facing substantial uncertainties that necessitate empirical exploration and validation.

In summary, blockchain technology, as it currently stands, is not a final solution to the complexities of corporate governance. Rather, it is a driver of innovation, a herald of transformative change. Its true potential will unfold through a continuous cycle of development, regulatory adaptation, and the evolution of governance models suited to the digital era's dynamism.

As we conclude, it is evident that the story of blockchain in corporate governance is still being crafted. The ongoing dialogue between its possibilities and challenges is shaping its trajectory, driven by the collaborative efforts of technologists, business leaders, regulators, and scholars. The promise of blockchain remains strong, its possibilities extensive, and its role in reshaping corporate governance is just beginning. This journey calls for our focused engagement, innovative thinking, and a commitment to guiding the technology towards equitable, efficient, and beneficial outcomes for the broader corporate sphere.

REFERENCES

Baiman, S., & Verrecchia, R. E. (1996). The relation among capital markets, financial disclosure, production efficiency, and insider trading. *Journal of Accounting Research*, *34*(1), 1–22. doi:10.2307/2491329

Beasley, M. S., Carcello, J. V., Hermanson, D. R., & Lapides, P. D. (2000). Fraudulent financial reporting: Consideration of industry traits and corporate governance mechanisms. *Accounting Horizons*, *14*(4), 441–454. doi:10.2308/acch.2000.14.4.441

Bebchuk, L. A., Brav, A., Jiang, W., & Keusch, T. (2020). Dancing with activists. *Journal of Financial Economics*, *137*(1), 1–41. doi:10.1016/j.jfineco.2020.01.001

Bebchuk, L. A., & Weisbach, M. S. (2010). The state of corporate governance research. *Review of Financial Studies*, *23*(3), 939–961. doi:10.1093/rfs/hhp121

Biais, B., Capponi, A., Cong, L. W., Gaur, V., & Giesecke, K. (2023). Advances in blockchain and crypto economics. *Management Science*, *69*(11), 6417–6426. doi:10.1287/mnsc.2023.intro.v69.n11

Broccardo, E., Hart, O., & Zingales, L. (2022). Exit versus voice. *Journal of Political Economy*, *130*(12), 3101–3145. doi:10.1086/720516

Brogaard, J., Li, D., & Xia, Y. (2017). Stock liquidity and default risk. *Journal of Financial Economics*, *124*(3), 486–502. doi:10.1016/j.jfineco.2017.03.003

Buterin, V. (2016). *On Public and Private Blockchain*. Ethereum. https://blog.ethereum.org/2015/08/07/on-public-and-private-blockchains

Cao, S., Cong, L. W., Han, M., Hou, Q., & Yang, B. (2020). Blockchain architecture for auditing automation and trust building in public markets. *Computer*, *53*(7), 20–28. doi:10.1109/MC.2020.2989789

Cao, S., Cong, L. W., & Yang, B. (2019). *Financial reporting and blockchains: Audit pricing, misstatements, and regulation. Misstatements, and Regulation*. (Working Paper).

Catalini, C., & Gans, J. S. (2020). Some simple economics of the blockchain. *Communications of the ACM*, *63*(7), 80–90. doi:10.1145/3359552

Cheung, W. M., Chung, R., & Fung, S. (2015). The effects of stock liquidity on firm value and corporate governance: Endogeneity and the REIT experiment. *Journal of Corporate Finance*, *35*, 211–231. doi:10.1016/j.jcorpfin.2015.09.001

Chiu, J., & Koeppl, T. V. (2019). Blockchain-based settlement for asset trading. *Review of Financial Studies*, *32*(5), 1716–1753. doi:10.1093/rfs/hhy122

Chod, J., & Lyandres, E. (2023). Product market competition with crypto tokens and smart contracts. *Journal of Financial Economics*, *149*(1), 73–91. doi:10.1016/j.jfineco.2023.04.011

Coase, R. H. (1937). The Nature of the Firm. *Economica*, *4*(16), 386–405. doi:10.1111/j.1468-0335.1937.tb00002.x

Cong, L. W., & He, Z. (2019). Blockchain disruption and smart contracts. *Review of Financial Studies*, *32*(5), 1754–1797. doi:10.1093/rfs/hhz007

Cornett, M. M., Marcus, A. J., & Tehranian, H. (2008). Corporate governance and pay-for-performance: The impact of earnings management. *Journal of Financial Economics*, *87*(2), 357–373. doi:10.1016/j.jfineco.2007.03.003

Fama, E. F., & Jensen, M. C. (1983a). Separation of ownership and control. *The Journal of Law & Economics*, *26*(2), 301–325. doi:10.1086/467037

Fama, E. F., & Jensen, M. C. (1983b). Agency problems and residuals claims. *The Journal of Law & Economics*, *26*(2), 327–349. doi:10.1086/467038

Ferreira, D., Li, J., & Nikolowa, R. (2023). Corporate capture of blockchain governance. *Review of Financial Studies*, *36*(4), 1364–1407. doi:10.1093/rfs/hhac051

Fox, J., & Lorsch, J. W. (2012). What good are shareholders. *Harvard Business Review*, *90*(7/8), 48–57.

Fox, J., Lorsch, J. W., & What, G. A. S. (2012). What are good shareholders? *Harvard Business Review*. https://hbr.org/2012/07/what-good-are-shareholders

Hermalin, B., & Weisbach, M. S. (2007). *Transparency and corporate governance*.

Hirschman, A. O. (1972). *Exit, voice, and loyalty: Responses to decline in firms, organizations, and states*. Harvard university press.

Jensen, M. C., & Meckling, W. H. (1976). Theory of the firm: Managerial behavior, agency costs and ownership structure. *Journal of Financial Economics*, *3*(4), 305–360. doi:10.1016/0304-405X(76)90026-X

King, S., & Nadal, S. (2012). Ppcoin: Peer-to-peer crypto-currency with proof-of-stake. *Self-Published Paper*.

Kirkpatrick, G. (2009). The corporate governance lessons from the financial crisis. *OECD Journal: Financial Market Trends*, *2009*(1), 61–87. doi:10.1787/fmt-v2009-art3-en

La Porta, R., Lopez-de-Silanes, F., Shleifer, A., & Vishny, R. (2000). Investor protection and corporate governance. *Journal of Financial Economics*, *58*(1-2), 3–27. doi:10.1016/S0304-405X(00)00065-9

Manne, H. G. (1966). Insider Trading and the Administrative Process. *The George Washington Law Review*, *35*, 473.

Nakamoto, S. (2008). *Bitcoin: A Peer-to-Peer Electronic Cash System.*

Rappaport, A. (1986). *Creating Shareholder Value: The New Standard for Business Performance*. Free Press.

Roulstone, D. T. (2003). The relation between insider-trading restrictions and executive compensation. *Journal of Accounting Research*, *41*(3), 525–551. doi:10.1111/1475-679X.00115

Saleh, F. (2021). Blockchain without waste: Proof-of-stake. *Review of Financial Studies*, *34*(3), 1156–1190. doi:10.1093/rfs/hhaa075

Smith, N. C., & Rönnegard, D. (2016). Shareholder primacy, corporate social responsibility, and the role of business schools. *Journal of Business Ethics*, *134*(3), 463–478. doi:10.1007/s10551-014-2427-x

Szabo, N. (1997). *The Idea of Smart Contracts.*

Tapscott, D., & Tapscott, A. (2016). *Blockchain Revolution: How the Technology Behind Bitcoin is Changing Money, Business, and The World.* Penguin.

van der Elst, C., & Lafarre, A. (2024). The Viability of Blockchain in Corporate Governance. In *Board-Shareholder Dialogue: Best Practices, Legal Constraints and Policy Options*. Cambridge University Press.

KEY TERMS AND DEFINITIONS

Blockchain-Based Technology: A system of digital record-keeping where data is stored in a chain of blocks, each containing a cryptographic hash of the previous block, transaction data, and a timestamp. This technology is characterized by its decentralized nature, transparency, security, and resistance to data modification.

Corporate Governance: The system of rules, practices, and processes by which a company is directed and controlled. It involves balancing the interests of a company's stakeholders, such as shareholders, management, customers, suppliers, financiers, government, and the community, to ensure accountability and fairness.

Decentralized Autonomous Organizations (DAOs): Organizations run by code rather than people, where decisions are made through consensus of its members, typically using blockchain technology. DAOs operate without centralized control, and their rules and financial transactions are recorded on a blockchain.

Earnings Management: The practice of using accounting techniques to produce financial reports that present an overly positive view of a company's business activities and financial position. While not necessarily illegal, earnings management involves the strategic manipulation of financial data to align with certain targets or expectations, often to make the company's performance appear better to investors, analysts, and other stakeholders. This practice can potentially mislead stakeholders about the true financial health of the company and may border on fraudulent financial reporting in extreme cases.

Shareholder Activism: The actions taken by shareholders of a corporation to influence the company's behavior, including changes in its financial or operational strategies, governance practices, or social responsibility policies. This activism can take various forms, including proxy battles, litigation, or public campaigns.

Smart Contract: A self-executing contract with the terms of the agreement directly written into lines of code, typically on a blockchain. Smart contracts automatically enforce and execute the terms of an agreement when predetermined conditions are met, reducing the need for intermediaries and increasing efficiency and security.

Stock Liquidity: The measure of how easily shares of a company can be bought or sold in the market without affecting the stock's price. High liquidity indicates a vibrant market with large volumes of trading, allowing for quick and easy transactions.

Chapter 3
Utilizing AI-Based Models to Detect Greenwashing Behavior in Corporations:
A Case Study of Tesla

Jiaqi Wang
Xi'an Jiaotong-Liverpool University, China

ABSTRACT

In the current societal landscape, consumers are increasingly concerned about the environment and are wary of greenwashing tactics when making purchasing decisions. This leads to a rise in the advertising of sustainable products. However, many of these claims about being environmentally friendly are exaggerated. So, it is necessary to develop an effective and understandable scoring framework to detect the corporate greenwashing behaviour to help monitor and push the entity reduce their greenwashing behaviour. Yet there are only several articles trying to use AI-based models to assess the corporate greenwashing and most of their database is not assessable and more importantly the criteria of the AI models to assess greenwashing is not clear enough. To move the field forward, this chapter develops a series of criteria based on the AI model formula which was come up with former scholar to help assess the greenwashing. A literature review and case study method based on Tesla have been used to demo the feasibility of proposed scoring framework.

1. INTRODUCTION

Greenwashing is a deceptive marketing strategy where a company or organization exaggerates or fabricates its environmental efforts or benefits to appear more eco-friendly than it truly is. From an accounting perspective, greenwashing falls within the domain of environmental accounting and can be seen, to some extent, as a consequence of the inadequate disclosure of

DOI: 10.4018/979-8-3693-1331-2.ch003

information in sustainability reporting. Consequently, the continuous evolution and refinement of sustainability reporting could significantly increase the difficulty for corporations to engage in greenwashing, thereby reducing its Greenwashing behavior. Greenwashing also have large impact on consumers' decision making and the assessment of environmental performance. More than half-consumers would buy more environment friendly product in recent years (Accenture,2019), so the greenwashing behavior could bring negative impact on consumer's trust and the speed we achieve the Sustainable Development Goals (SDG). Despite the increasing use of the term "greenwashing," a significant portion of the public remains unfamiliar with its implications, making it challenging for individuals to evaluate corporate sustainability claims effectively. Natural Language Processing (NLP) offers a robust methodological framework for identifying greenwashing in corporate communications. Based on the current research of using Nature language processing based formula to detect Greenwashing behavior (Kim, J.S., Sim, J.B., Kim, Y.J., Park, M.K., Oh, S.J., Doo, I.C., 2023), a more understandable tool would be developed to help enhance public awareness of corporate practices but also serve as a valuable reference to guide consumers towards making environmentally responsible purchasing decisions. This innovative approach promises to demystify the concept of greenwashing, thus empowering consumers to hold corporations accountable for their environmental impact.

2. BACKGROUND

Tesla, Inc. is a renowned American electric vehicle and clean energy company founded by Elon Musk, JB Straubel, Martin Eberhard, Marc Tarpenning, and Ian Wright in 2003. Headquartered in Palo Alto, California, Tesla has emerged as a global leader in the automotive industry, with a primary focus on designing, manufacturing, and selling electric vehicles (EVs), energy storage systems, and renewable energy products.

However, the good company that missioned to accelerate the world's transition to sustainable energy has been accused of greenwashing by environmental organizations and ratings agencies,

- In January 2020, Tesla's Shanghai factory was investigated by the Shanghai Environmental Protection Bureau and fined 500,000 RMB (approximately $77,000) for environmental violations. The investigation found that Tesla failed to conduct the required environmental impact assessment and obtain necessary approvals during the construction phase.
- In September 2020, Tesla faced accusations from German environmental organization DUH (Deutsche Umwelthilfe) regarding deforestation at its factory construction site in Berlin. Tesla was accused of clearing around 90 acres of forest, violating German environmental regulations. Tesla pledged to compensate for the deforestation, but the incident drew attention from environmental groups and the public.
- In November 2021, the German environmental authority issued a fine of 12 million euros (approximately $14.5 million) to Tesla for violating environmental permit regulations at its Berlin factory construction site. Tesla expressed regret and pledged to address the issues, ensuring compliance with German environmental standards.

In February 2022, Tesla's U.S. factory was penalized by the U.S. Environmental Protection Agency (EPA) for exhaust control violations. In May, Tesla was delisted from the S&P 500 ESG Index for, among other things, failing to disclose a low-carbon strategy. It is could be anticipated that Tesla has a high risk of involved in Greenwashing.

So it is essential to use an useful detector to assess the Greenwashing behavior of Tesla. However, processing vast amounts of textual data from corporate communications and quantifying linguistic patterns indicative of deceptive or exaggerated environmental claims would be a large project and it could be hard to complete without the help of Nature language processing model.

Specifically, machine learning algorithms can be trained to identify patterns that are suggestive of greenwashing. They do this by analyzing the language used by companies in their environmental disclosures and cross-referencing this with quantifiable data. The algorithms look for discrepancies between what companies say about their sustainability and what their data shows. Advances in natural language processing (NLP) also enable AI to better understand the context and semantics of corporate communication, further refining its capacity to detect greenwashing activities. AI-powered tools can flag potential greenwashing and provide regulators, investors, and consumers with more accurate assessments of companies' environmental claims. NLP algorithms facilitate the rapid analysis of extensive datasets by examining text, in contrast to manual methods (Yim et al., 2016). Recent bibliometric research indicates a pressing need for further investigation into NLP ((Vinuesa et al., 2020)). To conduct bibliometric analyses, tools like VosViewer make use of NLP capabilities (Jan van Eck, Waltman,2022). Closely aligned with NLP, text mining involves the conversion of unstructured text into structured data for analysis purposes, the automatic processing of text documents using NLP tools has been explored in studies (Civitani, 2021).While the current mainstream approach is to push companies to continuously improve their ESG initiatives to reduce greenwashing behaviors by continuously improving sustainable development standards in a uniform manner, AI-based NLP could also help stakeholders detect greenwashing behaviors. Although Greenwashing detection is difficult to monitor, there is still an effective learning model adopting evaluation factors available to score the 'greenwashing'.

In this chapter, a greenwashing scoring framework based on the greenwashing sentence discrimination model (Kim, J.S., Sim, J.B., Kim, Y.J., Park, M.K., Oh, S.J., Doo, I.C., 2023), which collect data from social media and analyze through sentiment analysis and BERT model to give a formula to assess the greenwashing behavior, will be broken down into more detailed factors to evaluate the Greenwashing behavior of Tesla.

3. RESEARCH QUESTIONS

The aim of this case-study is to investigate whether Tesla have involved in Greenwashing in the recent three years using the established formula based on NLP. Additionally, to assess the effectiveness of the formula by breaking down the factors in the formula into more detailed factors. Therefore, the research questions are:

i. Has Tesla engaged in greenwashing behaviours during the past three years, from 2020 to 2022?
ii. What has been the trend in Tesla's greenwashing activities from 2020 to 2022?
iii. How can greenwashing behaviours be evaluated using a scoring framework?

4. LITERATURE REVIEW

4.1 Weak Sustainability Reporting Contribute to Greenwashing

In contemporary society, the progression of sustainability reporting remains gradual, with a fully standardized reporting framework yet to materialize, resulting in considerable variability in report quality; this inconsistency provides a fertile ground for corporate greenwashing practices.

The development of sustainability reporting has evolved over time. In the 1970s, social reports were sometimes added to traditional financial reporting. In the 1980s, the focus shifted towards environmental issues, often replacing social reporting. By the late 1990s, reporting began to consider both the social and environmental dimensions in a joint report, influenced by voluntary standard-setting by the Global Reporting Initiative (GRI) (Kolk,2010). Today, the GRI (KPMG,2011) is considered the global standard for sustainability reporting.

Despite standardization efforts, there are still significant differences in the content and quality of sustainability reports among companies in different institutional environments. This variation also reflects differences in global academic interest in the topic (Fifka,2012).

The current study on the lack of a formal framework for disclosure in sustainability reporting has become a hidden danger to greenwashing. The big four firm using their special advantage collect lots of relevant information about the status of performing in the current world. KPMG (2022) noted there are still 4% of G250 companies do not report in sustainability or ESG matters and 46% of G250 not acknowledge climate change as a risk to their business. Deloitte (2022) also states that one of the most challenge the companies face are the quality and availability of the data which may impact the data accuracy and reliability. Ernst & Young (2022) stated almost 90% respondents believe sustainability reporting is very important but there are only half of leaders put the sustainable reporting in priority. Pwc (2023) reported that the SEC proposal about sustainable reporting is still pending and there are a growing number of reporting requirements worldwide really increase the difficulty for a company to manage their sustainability reporting obligations.

4.2 Impact of Greenwashing

The consequences of greenwashing can be severe. It erodes trust in ESG products and undermines the credibility of companies that engage in such practices.

On September 18, the United States Environmental Protection Agency accused Volkswagen of installing software in some of its diesel vehicles specifically designed to pass emissions tests, allowing the vehicles to comply with "high environmental standards" during inspections. The incident involves a total of 482,000 vehicles.

On September 22, Volkswagen issued a statement saying that the number of diesel vehicles involved in the suspected emissions violation could reach 11 million, and the company has allocated 6.5 billion euros to deal with this incident. This is an example of how greenwashing can lead to reputational damage, when consumers and investors discover that a company's environmental or social responsibility claims are false or exaggerated, it erodes trust and damages the company's reputation. This loss of credibility can lead to decreased sales, loss of customers, and ultimately, negative impacts on the company's bottom line and stock market value which decrease over 30% in several weeks. (Financial Conduct Authority. FCA Proposes New Rules to Tackle Greenwashing,2022).

Figure 1. The share price VOWG from 14 Sep 2015 to 25 Sep 2015
Source: The VOLK's official website

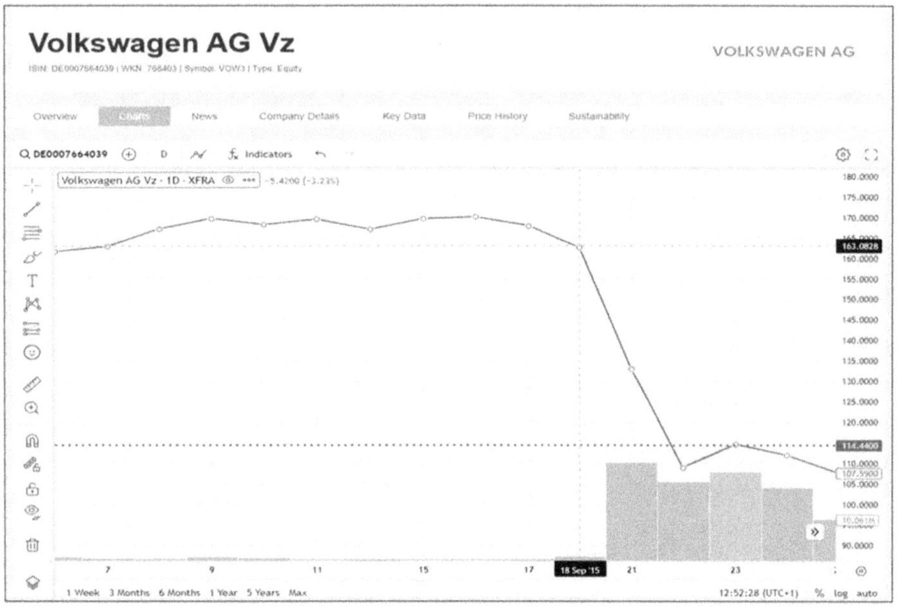

4.3 Artificial Intelligence and Machine Learning

Artificial Intelligence plays an important role in by analyzing the textual information to help detect the Greenwashing behavior through NLP model. By training AI models on vast amounts of textual data, NLP can analyze and understand the language used in sustainability reports, marketing materials, and public statements. It can identify inconsistencies, exaggerated claims, or lack of evidence that may indicate greenwashing practices. One particular subfield of AI, machine learning (ML) gained significant attention. ML utilizes algorithms to identify trend and replicate human learning and problem-solving abilities (Macpherson et al.,2021). It has emerged as a distinct area of study in academic literature, separate from general AI research ((Vinuesa et al.,2020)). The field of Natural language processing (NLP) is part of artificial intelligence and machine learning techniques and embodies a subset of artificial intelligence focusing on the interpretation and manipulation of human language by machines. This field merges the study of language with the technical expertise of computer science and has gained increasing prominence in the modern digital area.

Figure 2. Interaction 1: Sustainability reporting & Greenwashing

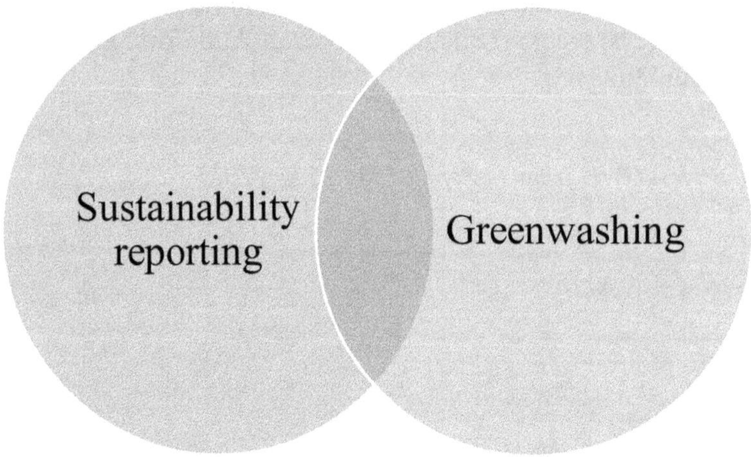

Figure 3. Interaction 2: AI &NLP & Greenwashing

5. RESEARCH METHOD

This chapter used a structured literature review to analysis the relationship between Greenwashing and sustainable reporting and Artificial intelligent. Using the case study of Tesla to show how the scoring card developed in NLP-based model could be used and analysed.

5.1 Data Collection

Data will be collected from both primary and secondary data. For the primary data, the Questionnaire will be used to collect people's overall perception about Tesla's greenwashing behavior, which comprised an important factor of the scoring framework.

Besides, the secondary data will be collected by Tesla's impact reports during 2020-2022, as it provides a updated, comprehensive, representative, and reliable assessment of the company's environmental practices and allows for the identification of long-term trends and patterns,some industry benchmark assess the footprint and water wastage, relevant news articles, interview material with Elon Musk in social media, and environment organization (like IPE and PECC)'s investigation report about Tesla's Greenwashing behavior.

This chapter is an explorative kind of research. It breakdowns the variables in the NLP-based model into more measurable factors and using the new framework to assess the greenwashing behavior of Tesla.

The initial phase of the research constituted the deployment of web scraping technology to meticulously mine the textual data contained within Tesla's Impact Reports spanning the period from 2020 to 2022. This methodical extraction was directed towards identifying the high-frequency terminology that surfaced prominently within these reports. The purpose behind isolating these recurrent words was to rigorously investigate and ascertain the salient themes and overarching priorities that Tesla has consistently highlighted in the realm of sustainable development during this three-year timeframe.

Following the collection of high-frequency words, the study proceeded to perform a detailed qualitative analysis. This entailed evaluating the context in which these words were used, understanding their connotations within the sustainability framework, and determining the frequency of their occurrence. By mapping the prevalence and distribution of these terms across the three consecutive reports, patterns indicative of Tesla's strategic focus areas and their possible evolution over time were sought out.

Figure 4. Data source logistics

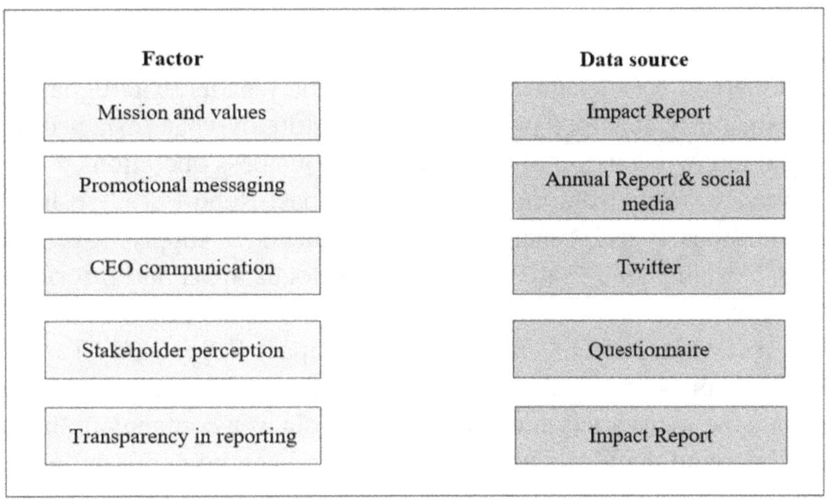

Figure 5. Data source logistics

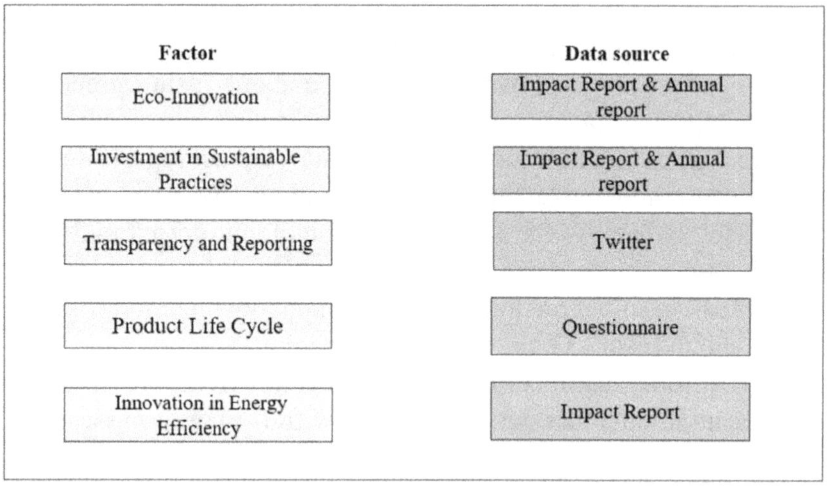

Figure 6. Data source logistics

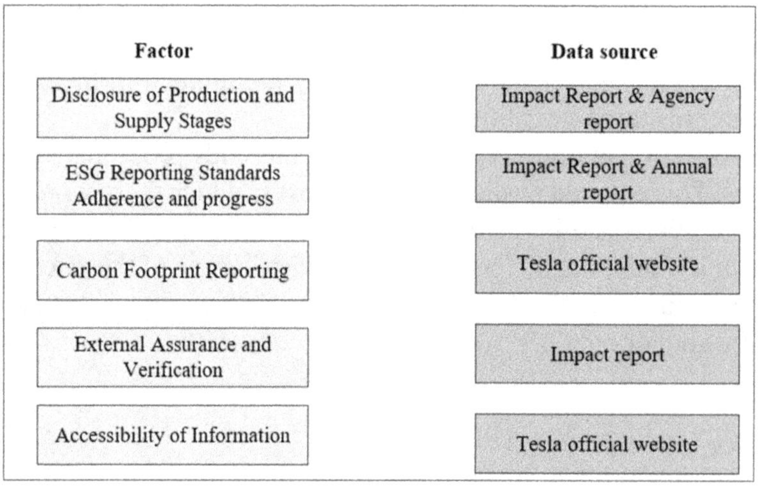

This thorough method was designed to uncover the key patterns and goals in Tesla's messaging about sustainability. It helped provide a clear picture of what Tesla wants to achieve and what it's actually doing when it comes to eco-friendly business operations.

The high-frequency words from the 2020 Tesla Impact Report are "Tesla," "model," "vehicle," "use," "emissions," "us," "energy," "manufacturing," "supply," "vehicles," "battery," "solar," "charged," "chain," and "safety" indicate the focus areas and priorities of Tesla as a company in that year.

The high-frequency words from the 2021 Tesla Impact Report are "Tesla," "emissions," "vehicle," "model", "emissions," "data," "energy," "vehicles," "supply," "vehicles," "battery," "suppliers" indicate the focus areas and priorities of Tesla as a company in that year. Compare with 2020, it can be found that Tesla pay more attention in carbon emissions management and suppliers in their supply chain.

Figure 7. High-frequency words from the 2020 Tesla Impact Report

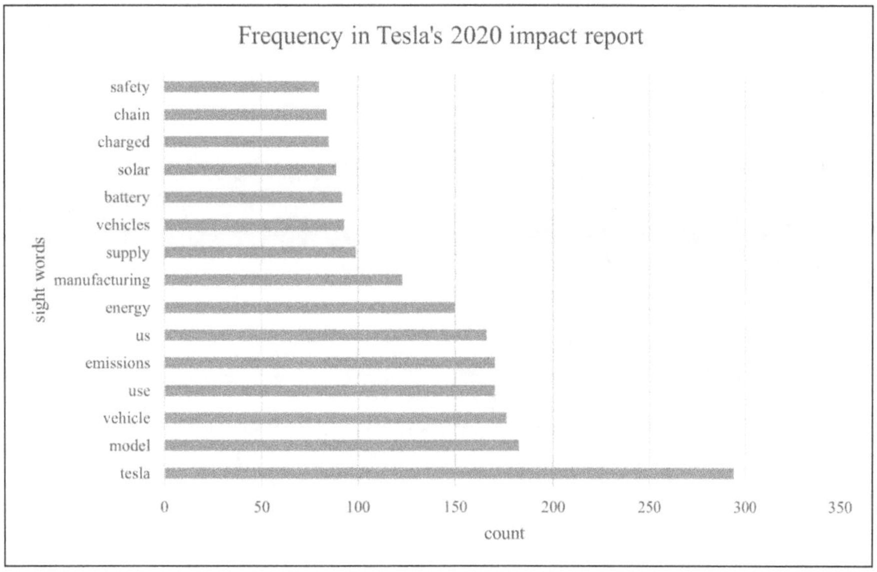

Figure 8. High-frequency words from the 2021 Tesla Impact Report

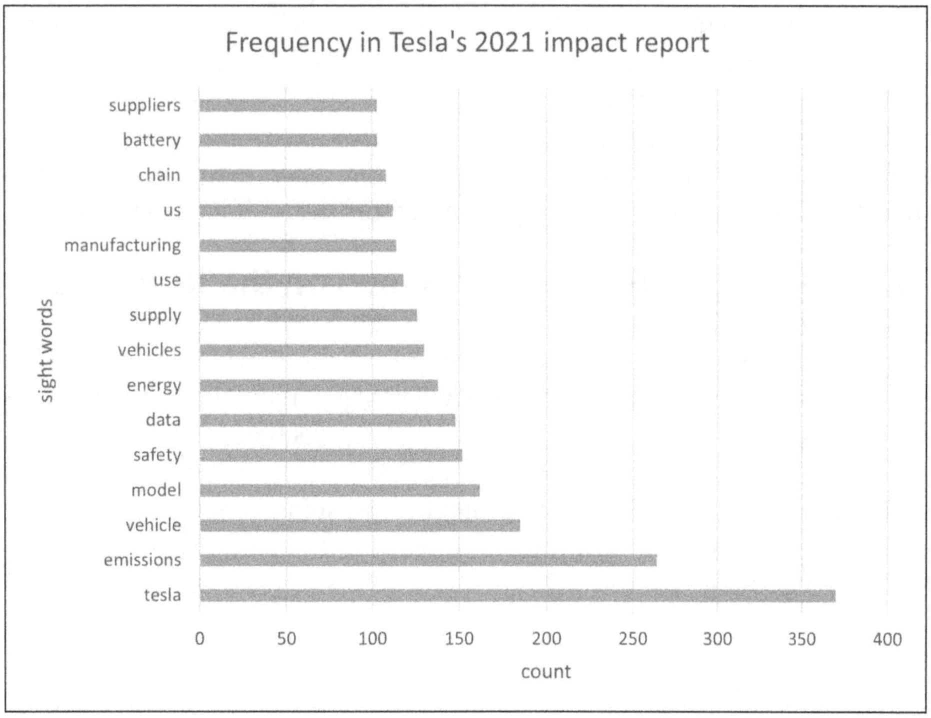

Figure 9. High-frequency words from the 2022 Tesla Impact Report

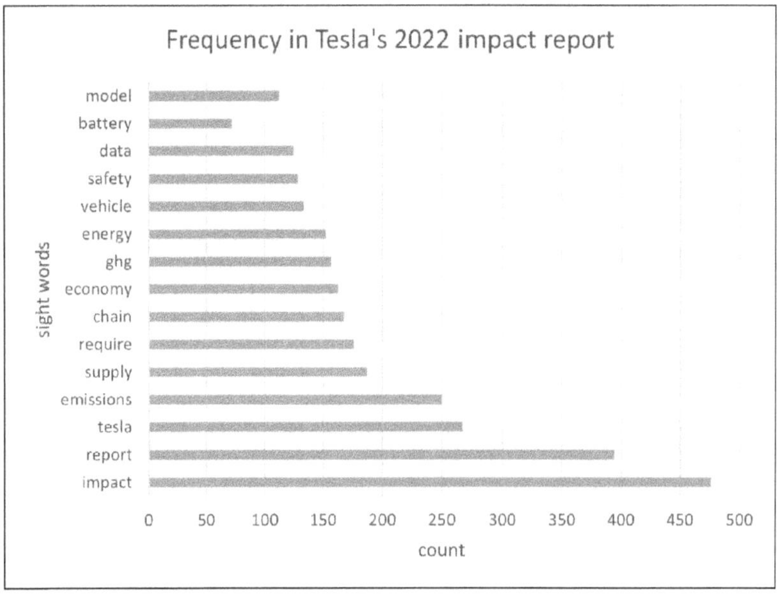

The high-frequency words from the 2022 Tesla Impact Report are "impact," "report," "tesla,", "emissions," "supply," "require," "GHG," "vehicles," "data," "vehicles," "battery," indicate the focus areas and priorities of Tesla as a company in 2022 is GHG emission, supply chain management and battery development.

So according to the most recent three year impact report, our investigation will focus on the three aspects, which is the supply chain management, emission footprint and battery development and disposal, which are shown as important factors in scoring framework.

5.2 Developed Scoring Framework Based on the NLP Model

Kim, J.S.et al.'s (2023) research come up a scoring formula of $x(y + z) * 5$ to assess the greenwashing behavior. The formula is as follows when x is directness, y is internality, and z is consistency ($0 < x, y, z <= 1$). According to their study, each number has a maximum value of 1 because all x, y, and z values range between 0 and 1. If the greenwashing score is high, it means that the entity has a high risk involved in Greenwashing behavior.

This formula collecting data by crawler python technology does provide a good tool to assess the Greenwashing behavior.

Table 1. NLP-based formula to calculate the greenwashing score

x (y + z) * 5	**X**	**Directness**	assess the direct relationship between a company and greenwashing behaviour
	Y	**Internality**	evaluates eco-friendly message behavior the entity release
	Z	**Consistency**	evaluate the transparency of information in all stages

Source: Kim, J.S.et al.'s (2023)

However, the formula exhibits a high level of generality as the directness, internality and consistency could be deep dived into more specific factors to assess the Greenwashing behavior.

For example, for the X directness which assesses the direct relationship between a company and greenwashing it could be spilt into more specific aspects to assess the relationship like Mission and values, Promotional messaging, CEO communication, Stakeholder perception and transparency in reporting.

For Y Internality, it refers to the extent to which Tesla incorporates eco-friendly practices within its internal operations and it could be assessed by Eco-Innovation, Investment in Sustainable Practices, Transparency and Reporting, Product Life Cycle and Innovation in Energy Efficiency.

For Z Consistency, it assesses the extent to which Tesla maintains coherence and transparency in its sustainability efforts over time and could be assessed by the Timeliness of disclosure, Disclosure of P&S Stages, External Disclosure, Accessibility of Information and external assurance to measure its reliability.

This could be summarized as the following figure.

Figure 10. The relationship between NLP-based model and scoring framework

Once the scoring framework is established, the primary deconstruction of the NLP model is essentially complete. However, determining the weights of various impact factors remains a challenging issue. To address this, the article conducts a questionnaire survey among ESG industry experts, employees from Apple's financial reporting department, financial institution practitioners, and individuals involved in sustainability reporting at the Big Four accounting firms, leveraging their mature industry knowledge and experience to assign weights to each factor. The more refined Greenwashing scoring system could not only help more stakeholders understand the formula, but also provide a full picture to reflect Tesla's Greenwashing behavior. The results could be shown as follow:

Table 2. Industrial experts' weighting results for the scoring system

Survey content	Option	Number of people	Percentage
1. Which of the following do you think can best evaluate the relationship between a company and greenwashing?	A. Mission and values	15	25%
	B. Promotional messaging	16	27%
	C. CEO communication	3	5%
	D. Stakeholders perception	9	15%
	E. Transparency in reporting	17	28%
2. Which of the following do you think best reflects a company's release of environmentally friendly information?	A. Eco-Innovation	18	22%
	B. Investment in Sustainable Practices	21	26%
	C. Transparency and Reporting	16	20%
	D. Product Life Cycle	10	12%
	E. Innovation in Energy Efficiency	17	21%
3. Which of the following do you think best reflects a company's efforts in information transparency?	A. Supply Chain Transparency	21	21%
	B. ESG Reporting Standards Adherence and progress	21	21%
	C. Carbon Footprint Reporting	23	23%
	D. External Assurance and Verification	19	19%
	E. Accessibility of Information	14	14%

The Greenwashing mark will normally range from 1-10 and the higher marks indicate there is lower risk of involved Greenwashing. The marks will be used to reflect the trend of the Greenwashing behavior based on the facts collected and users' judgement in respect of this issue, so the different users may give different marks even though focus on the same issue, it depends on the users' knowledge and industry experience. However, it could give individuals a full picture about a company's Greenwashing trend in recent years as their judgement will be consistent.

As the scoring framework will range from 1-10, the benchmark to assess Greenwashing mark could be divided three stages. For the Low mark range between 1.0 to 3.3 may indicate the behaviour of a company in its commitments and behaviour would be poor and have a high risk involved in Greenwashing. The higher risk may indicate better behaviour and involve less Greenwashing behaviour.

Figure 11. The benchmark to assess the greenwashing mark

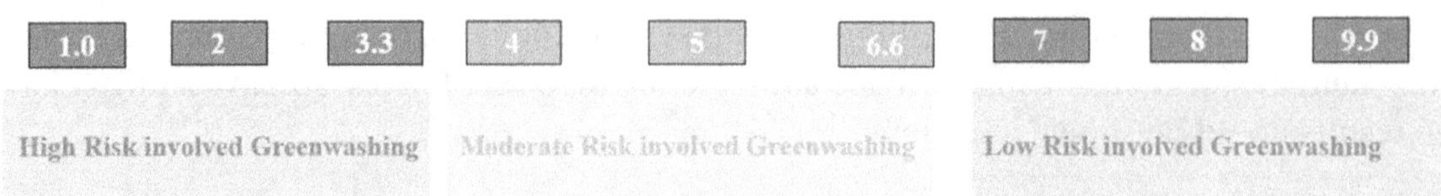

6. FINDINGS

6.1 Mission and Values (25%)

Table 2 shows that 15% of the evaluation criteria assess Tesla's potential for greenwashing by exploring the congruence between its actions and its commitment to sustainable energy over the last three years. Tesla, championing the transition to clean energy, has advanced significantly with its electric vehicles and innovations, upholding its environmental dedication.

Despite past critiques over opaque environmental and social disclosures, with its first impact report emerging in 2018, Tesla has since improved. The Transition Pathway Initiative had previously marked Tesla down for not sharing its environmental policies and performance. In a constructive turn, by 2022, Tesla began reporting on customers' emissions savings, advancing past mere sales-related mission statements. This shift indicates a stronger adherence to their environmental goals, meriting an elevated 2022 score. Consequently, Tesla's mission and values score remains high, reflecting its inherent environmental ethos.

Table 3. Tesla's mission section in the impact report from 2020 to 2022

At Tesla, we strive to be the best on every metric relevant to our mission to accelerate the world's transition to sustainable energy. In order to maximize our impact, we plan to continue increasing our production volumes and the accessibility of our products. In more concrete terms, this means that by 2030 we are aiming to sell 20 million electric vehicles per year (compared to 0.5 million in 2020) as well as to deploy 1,500 GWh of energy storage per year (compared to 3 GWh in 2020).	**2020 Tesla impact report**
We strive to be the best on every metric relevant to our mission to accelerate the world's transition to sustainable energy. To maximize our impact, we plan to continue increasing our production volumes and the accessibility of our products. In more concrete terms, this means that by 2030 we are aiming to sell 20 million electric vehicles per year (compared to 0.94 million in 2021) and deploy 1,500 GWh of energy storage per year (compared to 4 GWh in 2021).	**2021 Tesla impact report**
Our mission is to accelerate the world's transition to sustainable energy. Through our electric vehicles and zero emission energy products, we are accelerating the world's transition to sustainable energy. In 2022, our customers avoided emitting 13.4 MmT of CO2e	**2022 Tesla impact report**

Source: Tesla impact report 2020-2022

6.2 Promotional Messaging (27%)

This factor, accounting for 16% of the assessment, evaluates a company's potential for greenwashing. Tesla Inc. champions sustainable transport and energy. While Tesla's innovations in electric vehicles (EVs) and renewable energy promote a shift from fossil fuels and cut operational greenhouse gas emissions, critiques arise regarding the full environmental narrative. Tesla EVs boast zero tailpipe emissions, offering clear advantages during the usage phase compared to combustion engine vehicles. However, the complete environmental impact, covering manufacturing, battery production, and disposal must be considered. The substantial environmental costs, especially from energy-intensive and carbon-heavy battery production and the use of rare earth elements with associated ecological and human impacts, receive less prominence in Tesla's environmental messaging.

It could be clearly observed the Tesla's lifecycle emission has been expanded from manufacturing to upstream supply chain, which could better assess and evaluate the complete footprint of the EV of Tesla.

Table 4. Lifecycle emission calculation comparison

2020Tesla impact report	Furthermore, each product we make must be continuously improved at each step of its lifecycle: from manufacturing to consumer use to recycling. We must also improve every metric.
2020Tesla impact report	Furthermore, each product we make must be continuously improved at each step of its lifecycle: from manufacturing to consumer use to recycling.
2020Tesla impact report	The per-mile lifecycle emissions of our vehicles include emissions from upstream supply chain, direct emissions from manufacturing and electricity consumption an use-phase emissions when charged from a grid with a generation mix that reflects the geographic distribution of Model 3 and Model Y deliveries in the U.S., Europe and China.

Source: Tesla impact report 2020-2022

6.3 CEO Communication (5%)

CEO communication plays a pivotal role in shaping a company's public image and conveying its commitment to environmental responsibility. From the survey results, it appears that only a small number of experts (5%) believe CEO communication is the most significant factor in evaluating a company's relationship with greenwashing. Despite this low percentage, the influence of a CEO's statements should not be underestimated.

Elon Musk is known for his active presence on social media platforms, especially Twitter, where he shares updates, thoughts, and engages directly with the public. This approach has been a double-edged sword. Musk frequently discusses sustainability and the environmental benefits of Tesla's products. By promoting electric vehicles and clean energy, Musk reinforces Tesla's position as a leader in the fight against climate change. His communication helps to shape public perception of electric vehicles as not just environmentally friendly but also high-performance and desirable.

Tesla CEO Elon Musk (2022) called ESG "an outrageous scam" after S&P Dow Jones Indices removed the electric-vehicle maker from its ESG index. "Exxon is rated top ten best in world for ESG by S&P 500, while Tesla didn't make the list!" Musk said on Twitter, adding that ESG "has been weaponized by phony social justice warriors. This could reflect the Tesla's CEO's high confidence about the Tesla's environment behaviour.

6.4 Stakeholders Perception (15%)

This option emphasizes the relevance of stakeholders' views on the company's environmental claims, serving as a measure of credibility and greenwashing. A survey targeting about 500 members of the ESG Group—including Tesla customers, industry experts, and investors—

yielded 50 valid responses. The majority have a moderate view of Tesla's environmental efforts, acknowledging the need for improvement. Although perceptions are generally positive, expectations are higher given Tesla's leading position in the EV market, casting a somewhat negative shadow on the survey results.

Figure 12. Survey about the stakeholder's perception about towards Tesla
Source: Questionnaire I

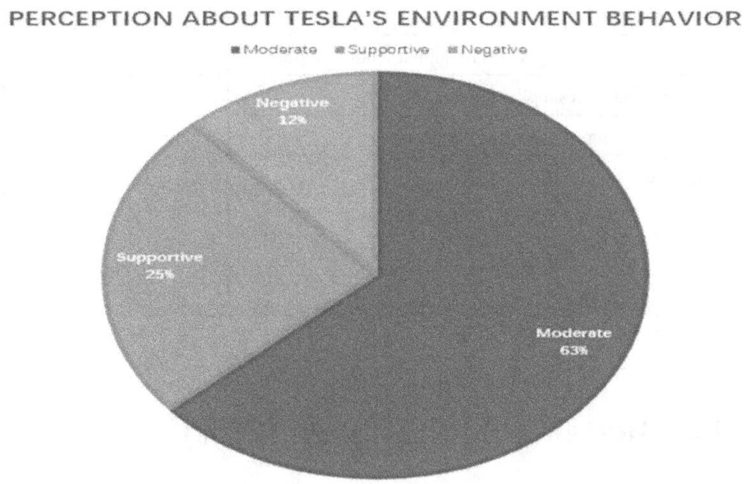

6.5 Transparency in Reporting (28%)

The highest percentage of experts consider transparency in reporting as the best way to evaluate greenwashing. Clear, detailed, and honest reports about environmental impact, sustainability goals, and progress are seen as key indicators of genuine commitment. As a listed company, Tesla published it is impact report in their website annually, however when it face the accuse of environment organizations, IPE & PECC (2021) stated the potential supply chain pollution did not closured in their impact report and until now there is no reply in respect of supply chain issue. And according to the impact report, it is until 2021 it published the formal supply chain policy and until 2022, it began the supply chain audit in their management.

6.6 Eco-Innovation (22%)

A significant portion of experts regards eco-innovation, which could include developing new, less environmentally damaging products or processes, as an important indicator of a company's release of environmentally friendly information. As Tesla impact report (2020&2021) state, the materiality of Company's Intellectual Property, Innovation, R&D has always been put higher impact to Tesla Business, which means Tesla pays higher attention in this issue.

Table 5. The supply chain status shown in Tesla impact report from 2020 to 2022

year	Topic	If have formal clear supply chain policy?	If perform supply chain audit?
Supply Chain2020 impact report	Responsible Material Sourcing	✗	✗
	Cobalt in our Supply Chain		
	Battery Materials Sourcing		
Supply Chain2021 impact report	Battery Recycling	✓	✗
	Alignment with Best Practices		
	Battery Supply Chain		
	Responsible Sourcing &Tesla Supplier Audit Program		
Supply Chain2022 impact report	Engagement with supplier directly	✓	✓
	Measurable improvement supply chain		
	Increase visibility		
	More strict supply contracts and policies		
	Audit		
	Production control		

Source: Tesla impact report 2020-2022

6.7 Investment in Sustainable Practices (26%)

This factor is preeminent, indicating that proactive investment in sustainability is a direct measure of a company's environmental dedication. Tesla has maintained a robust sustainability agenda, apparent in themes across its annual reports from 2020-2022. The strategy is dual-pronged: adopting energy-saving factory designs and renewable energy, notably solar, to cut fossil fuel use, and localizing production with streamlined supply chains to lower emissions from transport. Furthermore, technological advancements are fundamental to Tesla's approach, from developing cathode materials to producing innovative 4680 battery cells, merging energy storage improvements with financial benefits from higher efficiency. In 2021, Tesla also advanced its use of artificial intelligence to enhance factory efficiency, underlining its commitment to leveraging technology for better resource utilization. These consistent initiatives underscore Tesla's aim to minimize its environmental impact, making it a leader in integrating sustainability within its core operations and the sustainable automotive and energy sectors.

6.8 Transparency and Reporting (20%)

Transparency and regular reporting about environmental initiatives suggest a company is open about its efforts and willing to be held accountable.

6.9 Product Life Cycle (12%)

A smaller proportion of experts consider product life cycle analysis—which evaluates the environmental impact from raw material extraction to disposal—as critical for complete transpar-

Table 6. Tesla's investment in sustainable practice from 2020 to 2022

Year	Investment in Sustainable Practice
2020 Tesla impact report	Building new, better designed, more efficient vehicle factories
	Production localization
	Supply chain localization
	Covering roof space with solar panels
	Transitioning to in-house cathode material manufacturing
	Utilizing renewable energy as much as possible throughout all our operations
2021 Tesla impact report	Transitioning to in-house manufactured 4680 Tesla cells
	Building new, better designed and more efficient factories
	Covering roof space with solar panels
	Leveraging AI to make our factories more efficient
	Utilizing renewable energy as much as possible throughout all our operations
2022 Tesla impact report	Building more sustainable factories from the grounded up
	Covering roof space with solar panels
	Leveraging AI to make our energy use more efficient

Source: Tesla impact report 2020-2022

Table 7. Tesla's impact report published time from 2020 to 2022

Report	Published time
2020 Tesla impact report	August 11,2021
2021 Tesla impact report	May 6, 2022.
2022 Tesla impact report	April 25, 2023.

Source: Tesla impact report 2020-2022

ency. Tesla's recent impact reports illustrate a move towards transparency in capturing lifecycle emissions. Originally focusing on production and use-phase emissions, Tesla's 2022 report now includes the environmental costs of mining critical battery materials like lithium, cobalt, and nickel. This approach not only improves the precision of impact assessments but also aligns with industry-wide shifts towards full supply chain accountability. By integrating these initial stages, Tesla's reporting practices now better conform to the Global Reporting Initiative (GRI) Standards for sustainability reporting, showcasing a comprehensive examination of the company's environmental impact.

6.10 Innovation in Energy Efficiency (21%)

Investments and breakthroughs in energy efficiency could also signify a company's dedication to reducing its carbon footprint, and over a fifth of experts see this as a key indicator. As MSCI

Table 8. Product average lifecycle emission calculation from 2020 to 2022

Year	Product Average Lifecycle Emission Calculation
2020 Tesla impact report	Manufacturing Phase + Use-phase
2021 Tesla impact report	Manufacturing Phase + Use-phase
2022 Tesla impact report	Raw material mining + Product + Use and disposal

Source: Tesla impact report 2020-2022

(2023) states, the absolute amount of R&D input of Tesla is always increase 74% from 2020 to 2021 and 18.6% in 2022. The eco-innovation performs well in general although the growth of R&D input was slow down.

6.11 Supply Chain Transparency (21%)

Disclosure of and Supply stages means revealing detailed information about the manufactur-

Figure 13. The R&D input of Tesla from MSCI

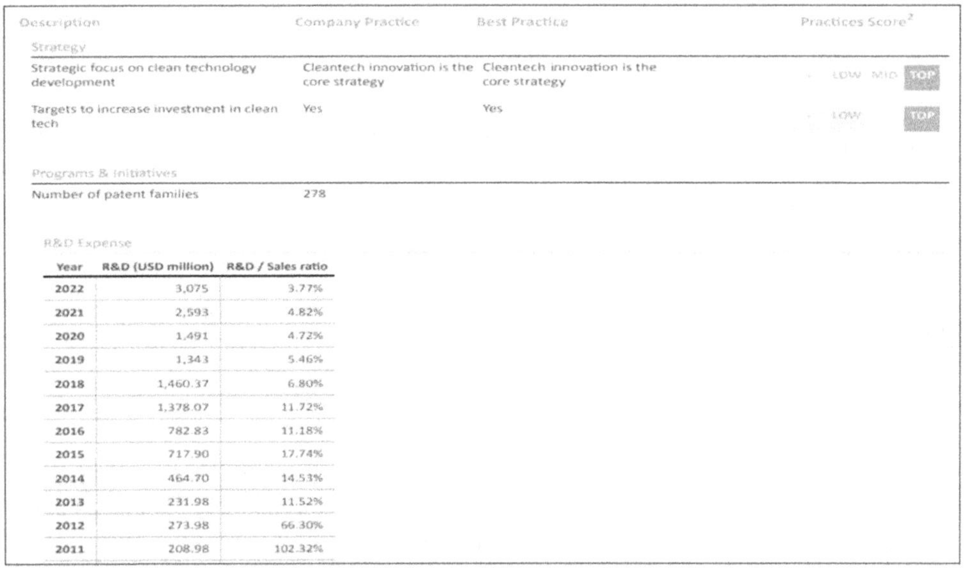

Description	Company Practice	Best Practice	Practices Score[2]
Strategy			
Strategic focus on clean technology development	Cleantech innovation is the core strategy	Cleantech innovation is the core strategy	LOW MID TOP
Targets to increase investment in clean tech	Yes	Yes	LOW TOP
Programs & Initiatives			
Number of patent families	278		

R&D Expense

Year	R&D (USD million)	R&D / Sales ratio
2022	3,075	3.77%
2021	2,593	4.82%
2020	1,491	4.72%
2019	1,343	5.46%
2018	1,460.37	6.80%
2017	1,378.07	11.72%
2016	782.83	11.18%
2015	717.90	17.74%
2014	464.70	14.53%
2013	231.98	11.52%
2012	273.98	66.30%
2011	208.98	102.32%

ing process and supply chain. Given the complexities and potential impact in these areas, clear disclosure is seen as a crucial component of transparency. Based on the IPE & PECC (2022) Report, the Tesla still do not make any response in respect of their supply chain issue may indicate there is a risk of disclosure in supply chain

6.12 ESG Reporting Standards Adherence and Progress (21%)

Currently, most of companies adhere to recognized ESG standards like the Global Reporting Initiative (GRI), the Sustainability Accounting Standards Board (SASB), and the Task Force on Climate-related Financial Disclosures (TCFD) to standardize its reporting. And according to the survey, this factor also take a large percentage of importance in scoring. When considering the ESG Reporting Standards Adherence and progress it should consider Frameworks and Guidelines, Comparability and Benchmarking, it may need great efforts to assess these factors, so this paper rely on the ESG agencies' rating score from 2020 to 2022 to evaluate the Tesla's Adherence and progress which could be shown as follow figure:

Table 9. Tesla ESG rating from 2020 to 2022 by MSCI and Sustainalytics

Year	MSCI ESG Rating	Sustainalytics (the lower, the better)
2020	A	Not available
2021	A	28.5
2022	A	25.2

Source: MSCI and Sustainalytics

6.13 Carbon Footprint Reporting (23%)

Scope 1 emissions stem from direct sources that are either owned or effectively within the control of the entity. For Tesla, such emissions rose from 185,000 metric tons of CO2 equivalent (tCO2e) in 2021 to 202,000 tCO2e in 2022—an augmentation that suggests increased activity in the company's operational footprint. This could be a reflection of Tesla's expansion in its production and operational infrastructure necessitating greater energy consumption, which is directly correlated to the emissions under Scope 1.

Scope 2 covers indirect emissions from the generation of purchased electricity, heat, or steam. Tesla's increase from 403,000 tCO2e to 408,000 tCO2e could indicate a growing reliance on energy sources that may not have been fully mitigated by the deployment of renewable energy solutions, despite Tesla's investment in such technologies.

The Scope 3 emissions, under Category 11 (Use of Sold Products), are particularly relevant for Tesla given the nature of its products—electric vehicles (EVs), whose usage phase emissions are predominantly related to EV charging. In this regard, there was a substantial hike from 1,954,000 tCO2e to 3,409,000 tCO2e from 2021 to 2022. The leap in Scope 3 emissions can be attributed to the increased adoption of Tesla's vehicles, translating to higher electricity consumption during the operation of these vehicles.

Table 10. Tesla GHG emission from 2020 to 2022

Year	Metric	Unit of Measure	Manufacturing	Sales, Service & Delivery	Other	Total
2020	Not available	-	-	-	-	-
2021	Scope 1 GHG emissions	tCO2e	124,000	31,000	30,000	185,000
	Scope 2 GHG emissions (location-based)	tCO2e	342,000	35,000	26,000	403,000
	Scope 3 I Category 11: Use of Sold Products (EV charging)	tCO2e				1,954,000
2022	Scope 1 GHG emissions	tCO2e	148,000	27,000	27,000	202,000
	Scope 2 GHG emissions (location-based)	tCO2e	305,000	74,000	29,000	408,000
	measure all Scope 3emissions categories, but focuson the largest: product use andsupply chain	tCO2e				3,409,000

Source: Tesla impact report 2020-2022

6.14 External Assurance and Verification (19%)

This refers to third-party validation of a company's sustainability claims. The fact that nearly a fifth of the experts' value this suggests that independent verification is key to credibility.In recent years, the advent of comprehensive sustainability reports has grown increasingly pivotal for corporations with significant environmental footprints. Tesla, a leader in the electric vehicle space, hasn't always included external audits in their sustainability reports, but that changed in 2021 and 2022 with PwC evaluations, particularly focusing on Tesla's greenhouse gas emissions. While only a portion of the data was verified, suggesting a gradual improvement strategy, it does raise concerns about the veracity of the unverified 81%. As Tesla moves toward full transparency, the expectation is that comprehensive external audits will become standard in the industry, driven by stakeholder expectations and regulatory standards.

Table 11. The audit status of the Tesla's impact report from 2020 to 2022

Year	GHG Emissions audit or not
2020 Tesla impact report	NO
2021 Tesla impact report	Yes, audit by Pwc
2022 Tesla impact report	Yes, audit by Pwc

Source: Tesla impact report 2020-2022

6.15 Accessibility of Information (14%)

The accessibility of information ties into how easily stakeholders can understand and obtain sustainability data. While this is the least selected option, it still represents an important aspect of transparency because the best data is of little use if stakeholders can't access or understand it. Tesla provides substantial information on its sustainability practices making it accessible online and understandable to a broad audience, there's consistent room for improvement, especially in terms of expanding the depth, breadth, and frequency of their disclosures. As stakeholder demands evolve and global expectations rise, Tesla, along with other corporations, will likely continue to refine their approach to sustainability reporting to meet these heightened standards of transparency and accountability. So in this aspect, Tesla deserve a relevant high mark like most of listed companies.

7. DISCUSSION

Owing to the asymmetry of information and the relative cost-effectiveness of 'greenwashing,' there is an increasing propensity among firms to engage in such deceptive practices within the market. For the general populace, the deployment of a scoring card-based on an NLP (Natural Language Processing) model can significantly facilitate a more profound comprehension of corporate 'greenwashing' trends, thereby mitigating informational disparities. This chapter, employing Tesla as an illustrative case, analyses the company's 'greenwashing' trends over the past three years through the lens of such a scoring mechanism. The overall trajectory of scores is ascending, suggesting a decrement in the risk of 'greenwashing' and illustrating Tesla's escalating prioritization of the Sustainable Development Goals (SDGs) pertinent to environmental conservation.

Table 12. Greenwashing card of Tesla in respect of 2020 impact report

Greenwashing scorecard		
In respect of Tesla 2020 impact report		
KEY ISSUE	**WEIGHT**	**SCORE(0-1)**
weighted-average Key issue score	**100%**	**4.27**
> X Directness	0<X<1	0.70
Mission and values	25%	0.80
Promotional messaging	15%	0.70
CEO communication	5%	0.70
Consumer perception	27%	0.60
transparency in reporting	28%	0.70
> Y Internality	0<Y<1	0.62
Eco-Innovation	22%	0.70
Investment in Sustainable Practices	26%	0.60

Table 12. Continued

Greenwashing scorecard		
In respect of Tesla 2020 impact report		
KEY ISSUE	WEIGHT	SCORE(0-1)
weighted-average Key issue score	100%	4.27
Transparency and Reporting	20%	0.60
Product Life Cycle	12%	0.60
Innovation in Energy Efficiency	21%	0.60
> Z Consistency	$0<Z<1$	0.60
Supply Chain Transparency	21%	0.60
ESG Reporting Standards Adherence and progress	21%	0.60
Carbon Footprint Reporting	23%	0.60
External Assurance and Verification	19%	0.60
Accessibility of Information	14%	0.60

Table 13. Greenwashing card of Tesla in respect of 2020 impact report

Greenwashing scorecard		
In respect of Tesla 2021 impact report		
KEY ISSUE	WEIGHT	SCORE(0-1)
weighted-average Key issue score	**100%**	**4.60**
> X Directness	$0<X<1$	0.7
Mission and values	25%	0.8
Promotional messaging	15%	0.7
CEO communication	5%	0.7
Consumer perception	27%	0.6
transparency in reporting	28%	0.7
> Y Internality	$0<Y<1$	0.68
Eco-Innovation	22%	0.75
Investment in Sustainable Practices	26%	0.7
Transparency and Reporting	20%	0.65
Product Life Cycle	12%	0.6
Innovation in Energy Efficiency	21%	0.65
> Z Consistency	$0<Z<1$	0.64
Supply Chain Transparency	21%	0.6
ESG Reporting Standards Adherence and progress	21%	0.6
Carbon Footprint Reporting	23%	0.6
External Assurance and Verification	19%	0.8
Accessibility of Information	14%	0.6

Table 14. Greenwashing card of Tesla in respect of 2020 impact report

Greenwashing scorecard		
In respect of Tesla 2022 impact report		
KEY ISSUE	**WEIGHT**	**SCORE(0-1)**
weighted-average Key issue score	**100%**	**5.00**
> X Directness	**0<X<1**	**0.7**
Mission and values	25%	0.8
Promotional messaging	15%	0.7
CEO communication	5%	0.7
Consumer perception	27%	0.6
transparency in reporting	28%	0.7
> Y Internality	0<Y<1	0.75
Eco-Innovation	22%	0.85
Investment in Sustainable Practices	26%	0.8
Transparency and Reporting	20%	0.7
Product Life Cycle	12%	0.65
Innovation in Energy Efficiency	21%	0.7
> Z Consistency	**0<Z<1**	**0.68**
Supply Chain Transparency	21%	0.65
ESG Reporting Standards Adherence and progress	21%	0.6
Carbon Footprint Reporting	23%	0.7
External Assurance and Verification	19%	0.8
Accessibility of Information	14%	0.65

8. CONCLUSION

8.1 Conclusion for Objective One

In the earlier stages, Tesla faced risks associated with greenwashing, potentially due to less stringent regulations and less mature sustainable reporting practices. The initial lower scores in directness, internality, and consistency indicate that Tesla's environmental claims were not fully substantiated by clear, direct actions and transparent reporting. Moreover, the consumer perception of the company's environmental mission and values, alongside the transparency in its corporate communication, may have been weaker. This, coupled with the infancy of sustainability norms and reporting frameworks, may have contributed to the greenwashing risk.

8.2 Conclusion of Objective Two

However, as seen in the scorecard, Tesla has demonstrated a notable year-on-year improvement in its Greenwashing Scorecard metrics. The rise in scores across all three key categories suggests that Tesla has invested in more eco-friendly innovations, maintained more transparent internal practices, and improved management of product life cycles and energy efficiencies. Increased transparency in supply chain management and greater adherence to ESG (Environmental, Social, and Governance) standards have contributed to this positive trend.

The application of a robust evaluative framework is paramount to discern the extent and nature of greenwashing. The aforementioned metrics serve as pivotal indicators:

Figure 14. The greenwashing trend of Tesla from 2020 to 2022

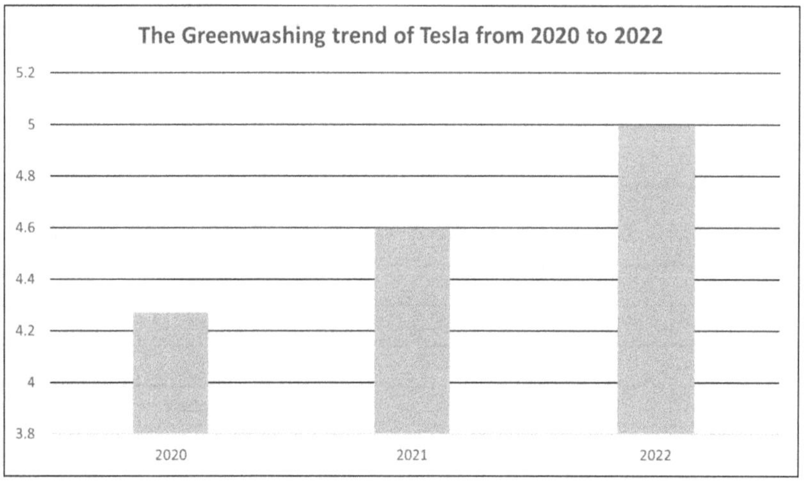

8.3 Conclusion of Objective Three

Directness encapsulates the degree to which a corporation's environmental contentions are substantiated by palpable ecological advancements. Augmentation in this metric indicates an enhanced transparency in Tesla's assertions regarding its environmental impact.

Internality measures the degree to which sustainable practices are assimilated into the company's operational ethos. A progressive score intimates the infusion of sustainability within the organizational DNA of Tesla.

Consistency pertains to the harmony between Tesla's projected environmental image and its practical initiatives. Improvements in this domain denote an integrative approach to conveying veracious information and deploying consistent sustainable practices throughout all company echelons.

Tesla's commitment to enhancing the consistency of its practices, especially by providing external assurance and verification, as well as making information more accessible, is indicative of serious efforts to reduce greenwashing risks. These improvements are likely responses to evolving regulations, as well as a more profound understanding of the expectations from consumers and investors for genuine sustainable practices.

Looking ahead, assuming continuous strengthening of regulations and sustainable reporting standards, Tesla's trajectory suggests it is likely to further diminish greenwashing concerns. By continually investing in transparent and direct sustainability efforts, and aligning their reporting with best practice standards, the company is set to lower its greenwashing risks in the coming years. This projection not only implies a better environmental impact but also reinforces Tesla's commitment to its core mission of accelerating the world's transition to sustainable energy.

9. RECOMMENDATION

To effectively combat corporate greenwashing, stakeholders—including governments, regulators, consumers, NGOs, and businesses—must collaborate. Developing comprehensive, standardized sustainability reporting frameworks is critical for transparent and accountable business practices, allowing clear differentiation between true sustainability and greenwashing. Adopting universal frameworks will ensure that companies' sustainability data is accurate, transparent, and comparable.

Furthermore, deploying advanced tools, possibly powered by AI and real-time data analytics, is key to detecting greenwashing risks, thus protecting consumer and investor interests, and maintaining the green movement's integrity.

Collectively, these initiatives can diminish greenwashing and support a sustainable and ethical global economy. Only through joint efforts and leveraging technology can we hold corporations to their environmental pledges and foster meaningful contributions to sustainable development.

10. LIMITATIONS

The framework measures Tesla's environmental claims but may struggle outside its specific industrial context. For instance, it assumes a manufacturing setting for sustainability integration, not fitting as neatly with service or digital industries that have other sustainability needs. Different sectors also face varying regulatory and market drives regarding sustainability efforts. Less regulated industries might lack sufficient data, risking misrepresentation of environmental efforts.

Furthermore, the metrics' scalability and adaptability are questionable; businesses of different sizes and operations might find the framework inflexible, risking misapplication or oversimplification and challenging the reliability of cross-industry use. Thus, while the framework sheds light on Tesla's sustainability, its effectiveness is limited by sector differences and the challenges in gathering accurate sustainability data..

10.1 Ethical Issues

The asymmetrical nature of present impact report within businesses results in limitations to the data collected for this study. Furthermore, the analytical approach incorporates elements of subjectivity. This, in turn, could potentially lead to misunderstandings among stakeholders and those utilizing the information.

REFERENCES

Accenture. (2019). *More than half of consumers would pay more for sustainable products designed to be reused or recycled, Accenture survey finds*. Accenture. https://newsroom.accenture.com/news/2019/more-than-half-of-consumers-would-pay-more-for-sustainable-products-designed-to-be-reused-or-recycled-accenture-survey-finds

Afolabi, H., Ram, R., & Rimmel, G. (2022). Harmonization of sustainability reporting regulation: Analysis of a contested arena. *Sustainability (Basel)*, *14*(9), 5517. doi:10.3390/su14095517

Bowen, S. A. (2014). The relationship between corporate social responsibility and greenwashing: An exploratory study. *Business & Society*, *53*(1), 38–72.

Buchholz, R. A., & Rosenthal, S. B. (2005). Toward a contemporary conceptual framework for stakeholder theory. *Journal of Business Ethics*, *58*(1-3), 137–148. doi:10.1007/s10551-005-1393-8

Cojoianu, T., Hoepner, A. G. F., Ifrim, G., & Lin, Y. (2020). *Greenwatch-shing: Using AI to Detect Greenwashing*. https://papers.ssrn.com/sol3/papers.cfm?abstract_id= 3627157

Deloitte. (2022). *Deloitte us survey findings on esg disclosure and preparedness*. Deloitte. https://www2.deloitte.com/content/dam/Deloitte/us/Documents/audit/us-survey-findings-on-esg-disclosure-and-preparedness.pdf

Dixon, L. (2020). Autonowashing: The greenwashing of vehicle automation. *Transportation Research Interdisciplinary Perspectives*, *5*, 100113. doi:10.1016/j.trip.2020.100113

Dong Soo, K. (2022). Recent ESG disclosure trends and greenwashing. *Future Growth Research*, *8*(1), 101–107.

EY. (2022). *C-suite insights sustainability and esg trends index*. EY. https://assets.ey.com/content/dam/ey-sites/ey-com/en_us/topics/sustainability/ey-c-suite-insights-sustainability-and-esg-trends-index.pdf

Fifka, M. (2012). The development and state of research on social and environmental reporting in global comparison. *Journal Für Betriebswirtschaft*, *62*(1), 45–84. doi:10.1007/s11301-012-0083-8

Financial Conduct Authority. (2022). *FCA Proposes New Rules to Tackle Greenwashing*. FCA. https://www.fca.org.uk/news/press-releases/fca-proposes-new-rules-tackle-greenwashing

Herzig, C., & Schaltegger, S. (2006). Corporate sustainability reporting: An overview. In S. Schaltegger, M. Bennett & R. L. Burritt (Eds.), *Sustainability Accounting and Reporting* (pp. 301-324). Springer. https://www.sec.gov/news/statement/lee-statement-esg-052522

IPE & PECC. (2021a). *Tesla & More Electric Vehicle Investigative Report I*. IPE. https://wwwoa.ipe.org.cn/Upload/202109140452005929.pdf

IPE & PECC. (2021b). *Tesla & More Electric Vehicle Investigative Report II*. IPE. https://wwwen.ipe.org.cn/reports/report_21270.html

Kim, J. S., Sim, J. B., Kim, Y. J., Park, M. K., Oh, S. J., & Doo, I. C. (2023). Establishment of NLP-Based Greenwashing Pattern Detection Service. In J. S. Park, L. T. Yang, Y. Pan, & J. H. Park (Eds.), *Advances in Computer Science and Ubiquitous Computing* (pp. 1–9). Springer. doi:10.1007/978-981-99-1252-0_32

Kolk, A. (2010). Trajectories of sustainability reporting by MNCs. *Journal of World Business, 45*(4), 367–374. doi:10.1016/j.jwb.2009.08.001

KPMG. (2011). *KPMG International Survey of Corporate Responsibility Reporting*. KPMG. https://www.in.kpmg.com/securedata/aci/files/corporateresponsibility2011.pdf

KPMG. (2022). *Big shifts, small steps, Survey of Sustainability Reporting 2022*. KPMG. https://kpmg.com/xx/en/home/insights/2022/09/survey-of-sustainability-reporting-2022.html

Laplume, A. O., Sonpar, K., & Litz, R. A. (2008). Stakeholder theory: Reviewing a theory that moves us. *Journal of Management, 34*(6), 1152–1189. doi:10.1177/0149206308324322

Li, M., Chen, L., Zhao, J., & Li, Q. (2021). Sentiment analysis of Chinese stock reviews based on BERT model. *Applied Intelligence, 51*(7), 5016–5024. doi:10.1007/s10489-020-02101-8

Limited, J. S. E. (2022). *Leading the Way for a Better Tomorrow: JSE Sustainability Disclosure Guidance*. JSE. https://www.jse.co.za/sites/default/files/media/documents/JSE%20Sustainability%20Disclosure%20Guidance%20June%202022.pdf

Lozano, R., & Huisingh, D. (2011). Inter-linking issues and dimensions in sustainability reporting. *Journal of Cleaner Production, 19*(2-3), 99–107. doi:10.1016/j.jclepro.2010.01.004

Macpherson, M., Gasperini, A., & Bosco, M. (2021). Implications for Artificial Intelligence and ESG Data. SSRN Electronic Journal. doi:10.2139/ssrn.3863599

Min, Y. L., Zheng, Q., & Zhu, Y. (2022) *MGTF 490 capstone project: identify "Greenwashing" funds using NLP in firms' prospectuses, as you sow*. Semantic Scholar. https://www.semanticscholar.org/paper/MGTF-490-Capstone-Project%3A-Identify-%E2%80%9CGreenwashing%E2%80%9D-Li-Hsu/aa59e82a5ed86ab76272925bb73ce6d298527a71

MSCI. (2023). *Tesla ESG rating report*. MSCI. https://www.alliancebernstein.com/sites/ campaign/theme/resources/pdfs/msci_tsla_esg_ratings_report.pdf

Musk, E. (2022a). *ESG is an outrageous scam! Shame on SPGlobal* [Twitter]. https://twitter.com/elonmusk/status/1526957672200908801

Musk, E. (2022b). *Exxon is rated top ten best in world for environment, social & governance (ESG) by S&P 500, while Tesla didn't make the list! ESG is a scam. It has been weaponized by phony social justice warriors* [Twitter]. https://twitter.com/elonmusk/status/1526958110023245829

Nemes, N., Scanlan, S. J., Smith, P., Smith, T., Aronczyk, M., Hill, S., Lewis, S. L., Montgomery, A. W., Tubiello, F. N., & Stabinsky, D. (2022). An integrated framework to assess greenwashing. *Sustainability (Basel), 14*(8), 4431. doi:10.3390/su14084431

Nemes, N., Scanlan, S. J., Smith, P., Smith, T., Aronczyk, M., Hill, S., Lewis, S. L., Montgomery, A. W., Tubiello, F. N., & Stabinsky, D. (2022). An integrated framework to assess greenwashing. *Sustainability (Basel)*, *14*(8), 4431. doi:10.3390/su14084431

Ning, X., Yim, D., & Khuntia, J. (2021). Online Sustainability Reporting and Firm Performance: Lessons Learned from Text Mining. *Sustainability (Basel)*, *13*(3), 1069. doi:10.3390/su13031069

Pearson, J. (2010). Turning Point. Are We Doing the Right Thing? Leadership and Prioritisation for Public Benefit. *Journal of Corporate Citizenship*, *2010*(37), 37–40. doi:10.9774/GLEAF.4700.2010.sp.00006

PwC. (2023). *Comparison of the big three sustainability frameworks*. PwC. https://viewpoint.pwc.com/dt/gx/en/pwc/in_depths/in_depths_INT/in_depths_INT/Navigating-the-ESG-landscape.html?ep=eml_15_08_2023_gx_en_ext

U.S. Securities and Exchange Commission (2022). It's Not Easy Being Green: Bringing Transparency and Accountability to Sustainable

Sensharma, S., Sinha, M., & Sharma, D. (2022). Do Indian firms engage in greenwashing? Evidence from Indian firms. *Australasian Accounting*. *Business and Finance Journal*, *16*(5), 67–88. doi:10.14453/aabfj.v16i5.06

Sheehy, B. (2014). Greenwashing in corporate environmental discourse: A discursive approach. *Journal of Business Ethics*, *123*(3), 635–649.

Swann, C., Jackman, P. C., Lawrence, A., Hawkins, R. M., Goddard, S. G., Williamson, O., Schweickle, M. J., Vella, S. A., Rosenbaum, S., & Ekkekakis, P. (2023). The (over) use of SMART goals for physical activity promotion: A narrative review and critique. *Health Psychology Review*, *17*(2), 211–226. doi:10.1080/17437199.2021.2023608 PMID:35094640

Tahir, R., Athar, M. R., & Afzal, A. (2020). The impact of greenwashing practices on green employee behaviour: Mediating role of employee value orientation and green psychological climate. *Cogent Business & Management*, *7*(1), 1781996. doi:10.1080/23311975.2020.1781996

TerraChoice. (2009). *The seven sins of greenwashing: Summary Report*. TerraChoice. https://www.e-education.psu.edu/emsc302/sites/www.e-education.psu.edu.emsc302/files/TerraChoice_2010.pdf

Tesla Inc. (2020). *Impact Report 2020*. Tesla. https://www.tesla.com/ns_videos/2020-tesla-impact-report.pdf

Tesla Inc. (2021). *Impact Report 2021*. Tesla. https://www.tesla.com/ns_videos/2021-tesla-impact-report.pdf

Tesla Inc. (2022). *Impact Report 2022*. Tesla. https://www.tesla.com/ns_videos/2022-tesla-impact-report.pdf

Tettamanzi, P., Venturini, G., & Murgolo, M. (2022). Sustainability and financial accounting: A critical review on the ESG dynamics. *Environmental Science and Pollution Research International*, *29*(11), 16758–16761. doi:10.1007/s11356-022-18596-2 PMID:35025042

U.S. Securities and Exchange Commission. (2022). *It's Not Easy Being Green: Bringing Transparency and Accountability to Sustainable Investing*. U.S. Securities and Exchange Commission. https://www.sec.gov/news/statement/lee-statement-esg-052522

Uyar, A., Karaman, A. S., & Kilic, M. (2020). Is corporate social responsibility reporting a tool of signaling or greenwashing? Evidence from the worldwide logistics sector. *Journal of Cleaner Production*, *253*, 119997. doi:10.1016/j.jclepro.2020.119997

Vinuesa, R., Azizpour, H., Leite, I., Balaam, M., Dignum, V., Domisch, S., Felländer, A., Langhans, S. D., Tegmark, M., & Fuso Nerini, F. (2020). The role of artificial intelligence in achieving the Sustainable Development Goals. *Nature Communications*, *11*(1), 233. doi:10.1038/s41467-019-14108-y PMID:31932590

Yim, W. W., Yetisgen, M., Harris, W. P., & Kwan, S. W. (2016). Natural language processing in oncology: A review. *JAMA Oncology*, *2*(6), 797–804. doi:10.1001/jamaoncol.2016.0213 PMID:27124593

KEY TERMS AND DEFINITIONS

Greenwashing: Greenwashing was defined as the Gap between an entity's claims and their actual performance.

APPENDIX A

Questionnaire One

请问你认为哪几项最能评估企业和洗绿之间的关系? Which of the following do you think can best evaluate the relationship between a company and greenwashing?

A. Mission and values - 使命与价值
B. Promotional messaging - 推广信息
C. CEO communication - 首席执行官沟通
D. Consumer perception - 消费者感知
E. Transparency in reporting - 报告透明度
请问你认为哪几项最能体现企业是在释放环境友好的信息?

Which of the following do you think best reflects a company's release of environmentally friendly information?

A. Eco-Innovation - 生态创新
B. Investment in Sustainable Practices - 可持续实践投资
C. Transparency and Reporting - 透明度与报告
D. Product Life Cycle - 产品生命周期
E. Innovation in Energy Efficiency - 能源效率创新
请问你认为哪几项最能体现企业在信息透明性上的努力?

Which of the following do you think best reflects a company's efforts in information transparency?

A. Disclosure of Production and Supply Stages - 生产及供应阶段披露
B. External Disclosure - 对外披露
C. Timeliness of Disclosure - 披露时效性
D. External Assurance and Verification - 外部审核和核实
E. Accessibility of Information - 信息可获取性

APPENDIX B

Questionnaire Two

Greenwashing is when companies deceive people by pretending to be environmentally friendly when they're actually not.

1. Have you ever heard of the company Tesla?
   - Yes
   - No
2. Were you familiar with the concept of Greenwashing before this questionnaire?
   - YES
   - No
3. To the best of your knowledge do you think Tesla is involved in Greenwashing?
   - YES
   - No
   - Unsure
4. Please briefly explain your reasons for thinking that Tesla is involved in Greenwashing.
   - Leadership in electric vehicles
   - Promotion of zero-emission vehicles
   - Renewable energy use
   - Environmental advocacy by CEO Elon Musk
5. What factors do you think may have contributed to Tesla's alleged involvement in Greenwashing (please select all that apply)
   - False advertising
   - Opaque information about production and supply chain
   - Lack of environmentally friendly practices
   - Deceptive environmental claims
6. Do you believe that Tesla is transparent in its ESG management?
   - Yes
   - No
   - Unsure
7. Please briefly describe your view on Tesla's transparency in ESG management (optional)
   - Tesla is very transparent in its ESG management by providing detailed reports and data.
   - Tesla is transparent in ESG management but there is still room for improvement.
   - Tesla lacks transparency in ESG management and does not provide sufficient information
8. Do you consider Tesla to be an environmentally friendly company?
   - Yes
   - No
   - Unsure

9. Are you willing to continue supporting Tesla despite allegations of greenwashing?
    - Yes
    - No
    - Unsure
    - Other Please specify __________
10. Do you have any comments about Greenwashing or Tesla's greenwashing behaviror

Chapter 4
How to Utilize Technology to Enhance Profitability: A Study of the NPD Strategy of XPeng

Yuhan Gao
Yanching Institute of Technology, China

Samuel Kwok
Middlesex University, China

ABSTRACT

This report analyzes the impacts of insisting on a product development strategy on XPeng's profitability from 2019 to 2022 Q2. Based on the model established by McNally, Akdeniz, and Calantone, regression analyses are used to evaluate different implementation factors' impacts on profitability. In addition, this report will combine XPeng's technological innovation points to analyze the impacts of the above factors on its profitability. Therefore, this chapter gives examples of how organizations may explore how to implement a product development strategy to enhance its profitability with advanced technology.

1. INTRODUCTION

1.1 Company Background

XPeng Inc. is a smart electric vehicle (EV) enterprise that designs, manufactures, and retails intelligent EVs including coupes and sport utility vehicles. XPeng was established in 2014, and it has been listed on the US Stock Exchange since August 2020 and listed in Hong Kong on July 7, 2021, which is the first new energy company listed in both US and Hong Kong shares in China (Mena Report, 2022). The headquarters of XPeng is in Guangzhou, and it has set six worldwide research and development (R&D) centres as main offices to achieve its global de-

DOI: 10.4018/979-8-3693-1331-2.ch004

velopment roadmap (XPeng, 2022a). XPeng's mission is to accelerate smart EV transformation with data and technology, shaping future mobility experience, and its development strategy is resolved to utilize its full-stack R&D to lead the smart EV industry (XPeng, 2021a), which means XPeng insists on the product development strategy as its growth strategy and engages in developing new technologies by itself.

XPeng emphasized its technological innovations in safety, driving experience, and other aspects in its latest ESG report, and it obtained 694 new patents in 2022 (XPeng, 2023). In addition, XPeng clearly stated that its new product development strategy is technology specific, hence it is called technology research and development strategy, and it continues to invest heavily in R&D, setting up international R&D centres and teams, which is to achieve technological leadership in the EV industry and enhance its profitability (XPeng, 2023).

Figure 1. Ten years of global electric vehicle sales
Source: 'Visualizing 10 Years of Global EV Sales by Country' (Bhutada, 2022).

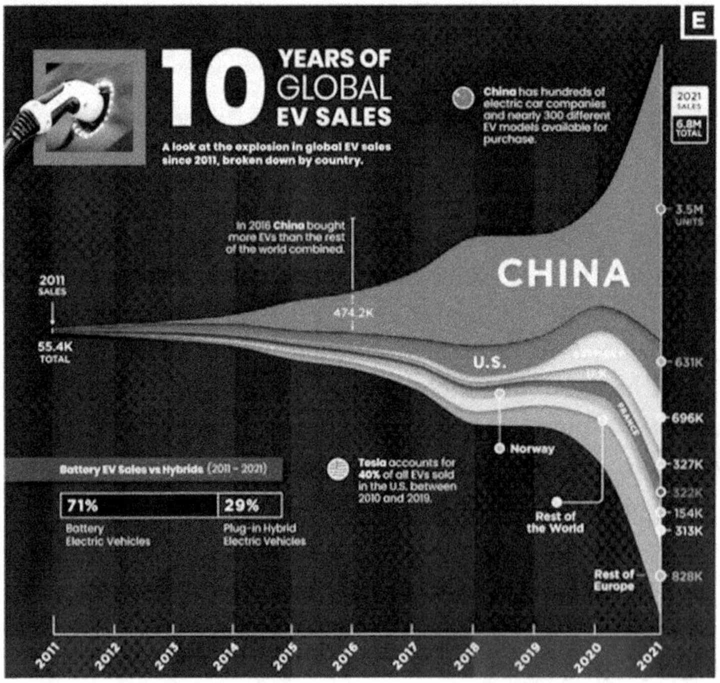

In 2020, total electric vehicle sales in China were more than one million, so the growth of several electric-vehicle manufacturers has been accelerated such as XPeng, which is a signal that the Chinese EV market has entered the growth period from the introduction period (Fox, 2022). Under this trend, XPeng has become a multibillion-dollar business after being listed on the NYSE (XPeng, 2021a). However, after the breakout year, the macro-environment of the electric vehicle industry has struggled since 2021. As the largest vehicle market in the world, Chinese automakers' operations have been disrupted due to the squeeze by Covid-related lockdowns (Flannery, 2022). The supply chain of many enterprises has experienced rupture due to the shortage of raw materials caused by epidemic prevention and control measures (Yang, 2022). However, the demand for electric vehicles is still increasing, which has caused large pressure on the manufacturers and intensified competition, so the Chinese EV sector is currently trading under a backdrop of strong sales but not-so-strong earnings (Yang, 2022). Figure 1 indicates the superior growth rate of the Chinese EV market compared with other countries.

In this situation, although there may be an optimistic future for EV manufacturers in the long run, investors still care about the profitability of entities as a reference for investment decisions (Flannery, 2022). Like other smart EV makers, XPeng's developments and operations mainly rely on external finance, so profitability is a significant figure for XPeng to obtain continuous support from their investors (XPeng, 2022a).

1.2 Motivations

The two main competitors of XPeng are NIO and Li Auto. Diagram 1 is drawn to illustrate the changes in the gross profit margin of the three companies' vehicle businesses from 2020 to 2022 Q2 based on the table in Appendix 1 (ZheShang Securities, 2022). XPeng's gross profit margin has been continuously lower than that of the other two companies.

The business model of XPeng is providing an innovative mobility experience through smart EVs, software, and services, and its primary source of revenue is vehicle sales (XPeng, 2021a). In the fourth quarter of 2021, XPeng's vehicle sales hit new records and the sales of P7 reached their peak. However, since 2022, the quarterly sales volume has declined slightly, and the monthly sales have fluctuated significantly as shown in Diagram 2. There has been no significant year-to-year increase in sales from 2022. In addition to fluctuations in sales, the gross profit margin from vehicle sales was 9.1% for the second quarter of 2022 in comparison with 11% for 2021 Q2, so there is a year-over-year decrease of 1.9% (XPeng, 2022a). Moreover, XPeng's net losses increased by around 1.26 times compared with the second quarter of 2021.

Figure 2. Gross profit margin from vehicle sales

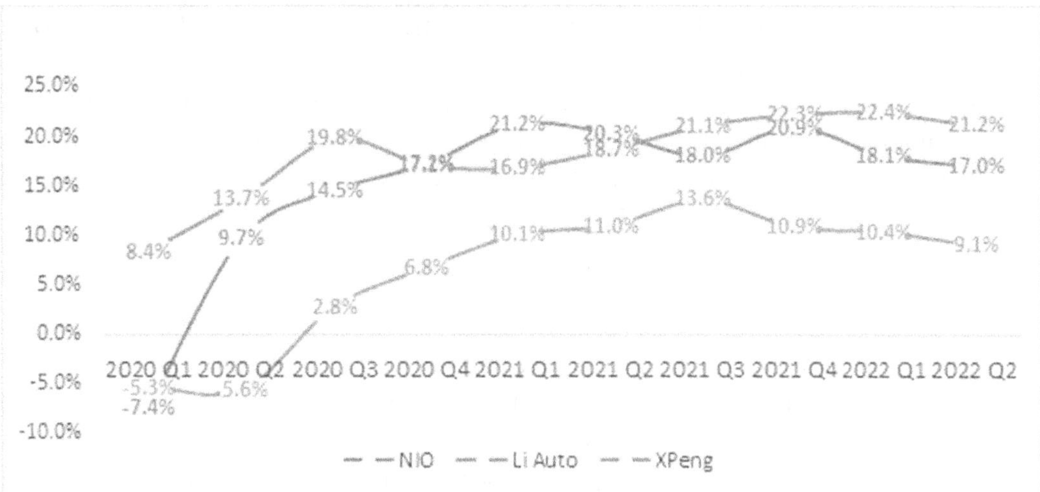

Figure 3. Sales of XPeng's different products from September 2020 to September 2022
Source: 'Automotive Industry Weekly Report' (DongHai Securities, 2022).

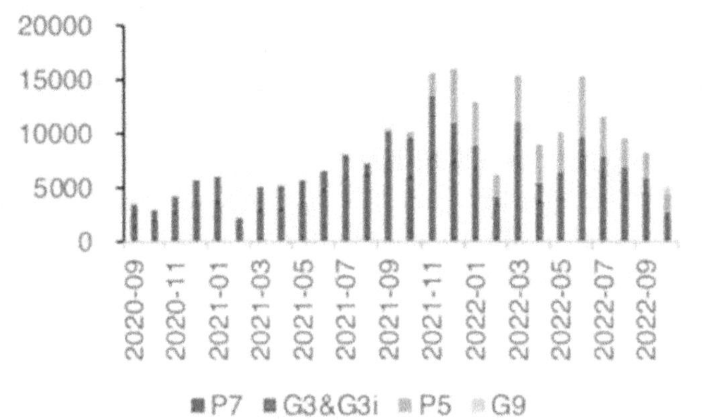

In summary, both horizontal and vertical analyses demonstrate that XPeng's profitability grew rapidly in 2020 and 2021 and has become weak since 2022. XPeng's chairman announced that XPeng will achieve better cost control through advanced manufacturing technologies, and the medium goal is to increase the overall gross profit margin of the company to more than 25% through new models (XPeng, 2021a), which indicates that XPeng insists on the product development strategy to improve its profitability. However, according to the results of Diagram 1, XPeng's previous highest gross profit margin was only 13.6%, so it is crucial to consider how to utilize technology in research and development to enhance its profitability.

1.3 Problem Statement

It can be inferred from both XPeng's strategic planning and resource input that it attaches great importance to product R&D strategy, but from Diagram 1, we can see that its gross margin has not shown a rising trend. Therefore, the research question for this case study is how the implementation of the product development strategy affects XPeng's profitability from 2019 to the second quarter of 2022. By analyzing the influencing factors, the ultimate goal of this study is to help XPeng's managers better plan their new product development (NPD) strategy and thereby enhance profitability with advanced technology. Moreover, the results of this study may also provide some reference for other companies in the intelligent vehicle industry on how to use NPD strategies to enhance profitability.

1.4 Structure

The rest of the project will be organized according to the following structure. The following chapter will be the literature review and divide the research question into three objectives. Furthermore, based on the literature, there will be three detailed parts in the following section showing the process of hypothesis development. Section four will describe the research methods for different hypotheses. Section five will present and primarily analyze the research results. The penultimate part will discuss the results found. The final section of this project will conclude and give some recommendations.

2. LITERATURE REVIEW

On account of climate and energy problems, the smart electric vehicle industry has developed rapidly, and its growth highly relies on the supporting architecture, so many companies insist on new product development strategies (Bhatti, Mohan and Raja Singh, 2021). New product development (NPD) means product improvements and modifications based on research and development (R&D) efforts and new brands introduced by the firm (Andaleeb and Hasan, 2016). It is usually the foundation for an entity's growth and profitability, and the risks of NPD are high due to many uncertainties and large investments (Yang and Xu, 2017). For an NPD project, its success and ability to enhance the profitability of an entity are affected by the research plan in the early phase, mainly depending on whether the management has considered the commercial feasibility of the future product and whether it matches the current business model of the enterprise (Florén, 2018). After establishing a suitable product definition, product design should be considered together with marketing, and their relationship plays a decisive role in the success of an NPD project (Beverland, Gemser and Karpen, 2017). The success of an NPD project can be measured by various indicators, such as rising financial performance, expanding market share, and an increasing number of patents (Sivasubramaniam, Liebowitz and Lackman, 2012). This case study will evaluate NPD's impacts on financial performance on account that realizing a superior financial performance is the current strategic objective of XPeng which has attracted extensive attention from the investors as well.

There is a complementary role in the relationship between product design and marketing, which can promote the success of the product development strategy (Millson and Wilemon, 2019). Marketing is a multi-faceted concept, and in many commercial cases, management usually takes notice of customer needs which is often the most important indicator for them to decide the R&D direction (Verhoef and Leeflang, 2009), which is due to three main reasons. Firstly, better knowledge of customers can be helpful for enterprises to identify the implicit needs of customers, and thus the newly developed products can meet more customer expectations and beef up their sales (Verhoef and Leeflang, 2009). Secondly, the design-marketing relationship may be beneficial to create product differentiation, which is useful to maintain the current market share and expand the market (Kumar, Townsend and Vorhies, 2015). Thirdly, this relationship can help brand renewal for newly developed products (Casoni, 2010). The realization of these benefits depends on how the enterprise implements the NPD strategy.

There is a combination of various implementable factors that influence a new product's outstanding performance. Management usually adjusts the development process according to the actual progress and the market's desire for products, which is reflected in the speed to market, so it is a typical factor of product development strategy affected by the market (Hemonnet, Manceau and Abecassis, 2019). For industries with rapid changes, enterprises usually choose to speed up the launch of new products to meet the changing needs of customers and adapt to the growth rate of the industry, which is to maintain their market share (Kiss and Barr, 2017). Quality and safety are one of the core advantages of products, especially for vehicle manufacturers (Ding et al., 2022). Moreover, on account of that product profitability can be reflected by financial figures, development expenditure will create both direct impacts on the profitability and indirect impacts through other mediators. Development expenses recognized in financial statements reduce profit generated during the financial period based on the accounting logic, but higher development expenditures are associated with higher quality, more innovations and even higher sales performance after launch (Swink, Talluri and Pandejpong, 2006). From a comprehensive perspective, speed to market, quality and development expenditure is necessary to be considered when implementing the NPD strategy, which can increase the new products' advantages in the competitive industry (McNally, Akdeniz and Calantone, 2011).

Based on the above literature, this case study is to evaluate XPeng's product development strategy based on its actual situation and operating results, so this research will select quantifiable implementation factors for analysis in terms of the financial and non-financial data made public by XPeng. The theoretical model applied for this research is mainly established regarding the model set by McNally, Akdeniz & Calantone (2011) and divides the research question into three objectives. Speed to market, product quality and development expenses have direct impacts on product profitability separately (Ernst, Hoyer and Rübsaamen, 2010), and the logic supporting quality issues as mediators between development expenditure and the dependent variable of profitability will be explained in the next section. Therefore, there are **three objectives** corresponding to the research question set in the last part:

i. Determine the speed that theoretically maximizes XPeng's profitability. In terms of the model established by Langerak and Hultink (2006), speed to market has larger and more complex impacts on profitability, so this research will first explore the relationship between speed to market and profitability.
ii. This research will evaluate the impacts of R&D expenditure and quality on profitability respectively based on the empirical research conducted by McNally, Akdeniz & Calantone (2011).
iii. Thirdly, the following will estimate how the effect of development expenses on profitability is mediated by quality.

The next part will develop three hypotheses corresponding to the literature and the three research objectives.

3. HYPOTHESES DEVELOPMENT

3.1 Objective One

In terms of Kiss and Barr (2017), the relationship between financial performance and new product development duration depends on the environmental turbulence level reflected in an industry's growth rate, and a shorter NPD implementation duration is suggested for turbulent and fast-growing industry environments. For specific products, speed to market which can be referred to as development cycle time or lead time is the period incurred between the initial announcement of an idea and final commercialization (George et al., 2005). Quick speed to market represents fast innovation, which can turn consumers' insights into ideas that will achieve more return on investment for the entity and investors (George et al., 2005). If a firm can launch new products as soon as possible, there will be fewer uncertainties in forecasting customer tastes and developing the products' concepts in terms of attractiveness found by customers (Kessler and Bierly, 2002), so quicker speed to market is beneficial to the product profitability.

On the other hand, faster is not always equal to higher profitability. Fast launch can make products be adjusted in time according to customer acceptance and preference to improve quality. However, Jayaram and Narasimhan (2007) verified that the speed to market is negatively related to profitability in some cases. Products that have been developed for a longer time and launched slowly will be more innovative in most instances, which will be more attractive to customers (Ali, 2000), and thus slower launch speed is associated with higher profitability, which is contrary to the research findings mentioned in the last paragraph.

These conflicts may be on account that there is an inverted U-shaped relationship between speed and profitability (Langerak and Hultink, 2005). In terms of the above empirical research results, managers need to make trade-offs in planning and managing the speed of product launches to maximize product profitability. Therefore, the first objective of this research is to search the properest speed to market for XPeng to achieve an increase in its profitability.

Chinese smart electric vehicle industry is rapidly growing, and the competition is fierce. To satisfy the needs of different customers, XPeng has been constantly expanding its product portfolio and gradually accelerating the launch of new models. Figure 2 is drawn to show the launch time of each product in XPeng's product portfolio.

Figure 4. The product portfolio of XPeng until September 2022
Source the '2021 annual report' (XPeng, 2021b).

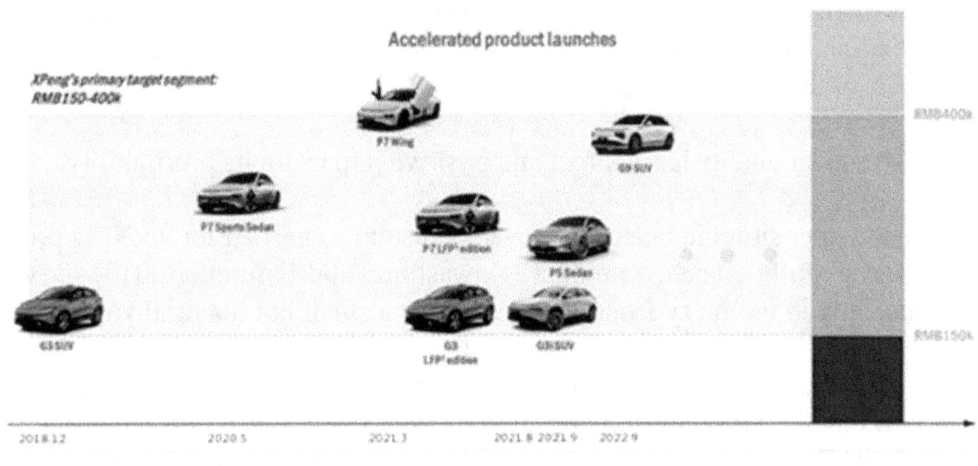

For the main products, the delivery time interval between G3 and P7 is about 18 months, and it is around 16 months between P7's launch and P5's. Until September 2022, XPeng has launched the latest G9 model, only 12 months before the last new product launch. This trend indicates that XPeng speeds up new products to market and continues upgrading its technology on original models. 2021 is the year with the largest number of new and improved models being launched, which is consistent with the upward trend of profitability shown in Diagram 2. Therefore, this report initially plans to assume that the relationship between XPeng's product launching speed and profitability conforms to the inverted U-shaped relationship, and a speed that would theoretically maximize profitability can be found.

H1: There is an inverted U-shaped relationship between speed to market and XPeng's profitability.

3.2 Objective Two

High quality of products is a competitive advantage, and from the customer's perspective, quality is influenced by comparing with the competing products (Sethi, 2000). In detail, quality reflects the advantages of the product in appearance, functions, workmanship and useful life (Aaker and Jacobson, 1994). Product quality is significant to interpreting the marketplace success of products because there are two elements affecting customer feelings: design quality, which is the extent to which the design satisfies consumers' expectations, and conformance quality, which is the production ability for design specifications (Jayaram and Narasimhan, 2007). From a long-term perspective, quality will affect the entity's future operating performance. There is a positive relationship between quality and returns on equity, and quality measures perceived by the market may even affect the stock price of a listed entity (Aaker and Jacobson, 1994), which indicates that quality is positively related to profitability in most empirical studies.

For XPeng, since the establishment of the company, XPeng has insisted on formulating a quality culture, and its efforts on product quality are increasing, which is roughly consistent with the growing trend of its profitability (XPeng, 2021a). In addition, the sales volume of XPeng's new car P5 has continued to increase from September 2021 to now, so it can be inferred that P5 meets consumers' expectations, and XPeng has the production capacity. Therefore, it can be assumed that increasing product quality can enhance profitability, which should be proved to complete part of the second research objective.

H2a: XPeng's product quality has a direct and positive impact on its profitability.

Development expenditure indicates the level of resources needed for an NPD project from an idea to a successfully launched product (Kuwashima and Fujimoto, 2013). Development expenses, especially in the fuzzy front phase, indicate a small but materially direct impact on product profitability (McNally, Akdeniz and Calantone, 2011). In terms of the results of the above empirical research, development has a significantly positive and direct impact on profitability. For XPeng, its gross profit margins from vehicle sales generally indicate an upward trend as shown in Diagram 2, and there is an almost half-fold annual increase in its development expenditure. Therefore, it can be supposed that the increasing development expenditure has contributed to profitability.

H2b: The higher development expenditure has led to the profitability increase.

3.3 Objective Three

Swink, Talluri and Pandejpong (2006) found that higher development expenses are strongly related to higher productive power with minor defects (i.e., conformance quality), as well as improved properties of products to better satisfy consumers' demands (i.e., design quality), which demonstrates that there is a positive relationship between development expenditure and quality. In consequence, combined with the general negative impact on cash flow brought by higher development expenditures, management usually needs to trade off quality and R&D expenditure when making product development strategies (Kessler and Bierly, 2002). The results of empirical research conducted by McNally, Akdeniz and Calantone (2011) demonstrate the impact of expenses on profitability is partially mediated by the quality issue as well. Additionally, quality can mediate the influence of expenses occurring in the fuzzy-front end stage on a product's profitability, but the expenses in the latter stages that may be capitalized exhibit less influence on profitability (Kessler and Bierly, 2002).

XPeng's vehicle operations highly rely on its proprietary software, such as XPILOT and Xmart OS, so its increasing R&D investments are to enhance such intelligent technology functions to reduce uncertainties brought by their inherent complexity (XPeng, 2021b). In terms of XPeng's latest quarter report, R&D expenses were 1,265 million for 2022 Q2, representing a year-over-year increase of 46.5% and an increase of 3.6% compared with that for the first quarter of 2022. Additionally, from March 2019 to September 2020, some G3 models had quality problems and were recalled, but with the increase in R&D investment, there was no serious recall of the later-developed models (XPeng, 2021a). Therefore, the increase in R&D expenditure may be able to enhance product quality, and the enhanced quality may improve profitability as discussed in the last part, which means that quality may play a regulatory role.

H3: The effect of development expenses on profitability is mediated by product quality.

In summary, the above three issues in the product development strategy have direct and indirect impacts on XPeng's profitability. The relationships and hypotheses can be described as the following model:

Figure 5. The research model

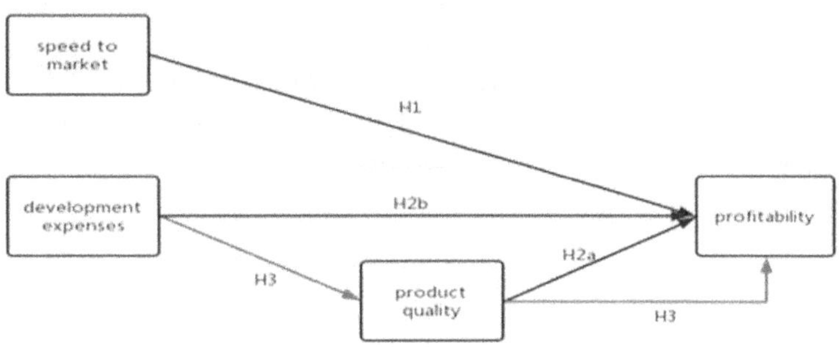

4. METHODOLOGY

This part will describe the research methodology applied to achieve the above research objectives. This project is to evaluate the impacts of different implementation factors of product development strategy on XPeng's profitability, so this type of research is mainly quantitative research based on archival data. In this case study, data is selected based on the actual performance of XPeng. On account of its limited disclosed information, quarterly data will be collected to expand the sample size as large as possible compared with yearly data. The sampling technique used is purposive sampling because certain criteria are tailored to the research objectives with a small data population. Moreover, the measurement scale for the quality issues is an interval scale, and scales for others are ratio scales, so all the analyses can use the F test to test whether the linear relationship of the regression equation is significant through the significance levels. Therefore, three hypotheses will be tested through SPSS by different methods, and samples will be collected differently corresponding to particular objectives. The following sections in this part will state the model used for each hypothesis, the measurement for different variables and different data collection ways for each variable.

To eliminate errors caused by different measurement methods, all of the sample data will be standardized by the Z-score standardization method because the measurements of each variable are different. Z-score standardization will scale the data uniformly to the range around zero, which can remove the limitation of units but will not change the sequence and overall regularity of the data (Andrade, 2021), and the formula is:

$$x'(\text{standarded observation}) = \frac{x - \grave{\imath}}{\acute{o}}$$

In consequence, all of the data included in the following figures have been Z-standardized before tests.

4.1 Research Method for H1

4.1.1 Model

This project will apply multiple regression analysis to determine the relationship between speed to market and profitability referred to in the research model established by Langerak and Hultink (2006). XPeng's profitability is the dependent variable (Y), and the speed to market is the independent variable (X). Although there is merely one independent variable, the multiple regression method will reveal the linear effect of speed to market on profitability and the quadratic effect, and there is an error term ε in this formula:

$$Y = \hat{a}_1 X + \hat{a}_2 X^2 + \mathring{a}$$

If $\hat{a}_1$ is a positive number and $\hat{a}_2$ is a negative number, the inverted U-shaped relationship has been proved. In addition, the absolute values of $\hat{a}_1$ and $\hat{a}_2$ can estimate the respective influence of speed to market and its squared term on profitability.

4.1.2 Measurements of Variables

According to Langerak and Hultink (2006), new product profitability and speed to market can be measured by two approaches. The first method is that they can be measured by the absolute amount from respondents or public information, which is to objectively measure these variables. The second approach is subject, which requires interviewees to judge the speed and profitability of the company's product R&D projects based on their cognition. This case analysis will take the first way, which is measured by the information disclosed by XPeng to maintain the objectivity of the research. Therefore, XPeng's profitability will be measured by the gross loss margin from vehicle sales which represents how much gross profit is generated as a percentage of revenue, which can demonstrate the product profitability (Ahmeti and Iseni, 2022). Furthermore, the financial goal of XPeng is to achieve a gross profit margin of more than 25%, so the measurement is consistent with XPeng's objective. The speed to market is measured by the number of months expired from the concept was announced to market launch. To measure the dependent variable and independent variable, the dependent variable will be measured by the gross profit rate of the next quarter after the product is launched.

4.1.3 Data Collection

In general, all of the data used in the report is collected quarterly by the purposive sampling method. For H1, the estimation of the inverted U-shaped relationship normally requires the profitability and speed data from numerous completed product development projects. In this case study, the research period is from 2019 to the second quarter of 2022. During this period, XPeng has not only released three major models G3, P7 and P5 but also continuously upgraded them. As shown in Figure 4, XPeng has included the upgraded products in the product portfolio. To expand the sample size, this research regards the upgraded products and the new batteries developed as units of analysis, which are six products in total that have been launched by XPeng. Therefore, due to XPeng's actual situation, the sample size for this multiple analysis is six. XPeng's quarterly gross profit margins are collected from its quarterly and annual financial reports that have been summarized in Appendix 2 and 4. Additionally, the speed to market of six products has been disclosed in XPeng's annual reports shown in Appendix 4.

4.2 RESEARCH METHOD FOR H2

4.2.1 Model

A single regression analysis approach will be utilized to evaluate the two relationships in H2 respectively. The formula for the two single regression analyses refers to McNally, Akdeniz & Calantone (2011), which are

H2a: $\text{Y}\left(\text{profitability}\right) = \text{å}_3\text{Quality} + \text{å}_2$

H2b: $\text{Y}\left(\text{profitability}\right) = \text{å}_4\text{Development expense} + \text{å}_3$

In terms of this model, å_3 and å_4 4 will separately demonstrate how and how much the quality and development expenses affect the profitability, which is to test Hypotheses 2a and 2b respectively.

4.2.2 Measurements of Variables

Profitability in this model is measured by the gross profit margins from vehicle sales as same as the measurement in the first model. The quality issue usually utilizes the defective rate or the judgment of managers and customers as the measurement standard (McNally, Akdeniz & Calantone, 2011). For this research, XPeng's annual report (2021b) has stated that there may be some defects in design or manufacturing that make them not perform as expected or that require repairs, and some certain features of smart vehicles may take longer than expected to be launched, and thus it has recognized some warranty for future possible quality problems. Additionally, XPeng has not disclosed the total amount of defects arising in the production process. Therefore, this project will use the opposite of the proportion of expenses paid during the warranty period in revenue earned in the corresponding period to represent the product quality. The warranty expense applied in this research refers to the expense spent by XPeng to repair the quality defects of the sold products within the warranty period and scope in this quarter, so it means that the higher quality will cause fewer warranty expenses. Furthermore, this project will use the proportion of the development expenditure to corresponding revenue figures disclosed in XPeng's statements of profit or loss for each period to measure the scale of XPeng's R&D investment.

4.2.3 Data Collection

As data is collected every quarter to expand the sample size, the research period starts from the first quarter of 2019 when public information can be collected to the second quarter of 2022, so the sample size for H2 and H3 is both fourteen. The data relating to profitability and development expenses are both collected from XPeng's quarterly and annual reports, which are shown in Appendix 2 and 4. The data relating to quality is recorded in the ESG reports listed in Appendix 3.

4.3 RESEARCH METHOD FOR H3

4.3.1 Model

A mediator is included in this hypothesis, so the analysis of intermediary function will be used to explore causal relationships among development expense, quality and profitability, which is developed by McNally, Akdeniz & Calantone (2011) as well. It will analyze whether quality has played an intermediary role in the relationship between R&D expenditure and profitability as the red line in Figure 5.

4.3.2 Measurements of Variables and Data Collection

Development expenditure is the independent variable, and profitability is the dependent variable, which is the same as the measurement applied for H2b. To test the intermediary role of quality, quality issues are set as a mediator variable. On account of that this model is based on the model set for Hypothesis 2, the variables involved in this model are the same as those in Hypothesis 2, which means that the variable measurements, data collection ways, period and sample size are the same as those used for H2.

Data used in the project are summarized in Table 1.

Table 1. Summary of data measurements and sources of collection

Variables		Hypothesis	Measures	Collection sources	Data type	References
Dependent	Profitability	H1, H2, H3	Gross profit margin	Quarterly FRs (Appendices 2&4)	Scale	Ahmeti and Iseni, 2022
Independent	Speed to market	H1	The number of months expired from a concept to a market launch	Quarterly FRs (Appendices 2&4)	Scale	Langerak and Hultink, 2006
	Quality	H2, H3	-Warranty/revenue	ESG reports (Appendices 3)	Interval	McNally, Akdeniz & Calantone, 2011
	Development expenditure	H2, H3	Development expenses/ revenue	Quarterly FRs (Appendices 2&4)	Scale	McNally, Akdeniz & Calantone, 2011

5. FINDINGS

In terms of the above methods, this section will show the test results and simply analyze their meanings mainly from an arithmetical perspective. Additionally, there are some limitations of the sample size, and the results of this research may be influenced by other commercial factors, which result in the research methods not meeting the statistical standards and the results may differ from the theoretical values. Therefore, this analysis is conducted at the firm level to test the relationships between speed to market, quality, development expenditure and XPeng's profitability respectively and evaluate whether the relationship between development expense and XPeng's profitability is mediated by quality issues. This research is based on XPeng's current conditions and its product development history from 2019 to the second quarter of 2022, and the different results for different tests are shown as follows.

5.1 Result of Hypothesis One

To test hypothesis 1, multiple regression analysis is utilized by SPSS to evaluate the relationship between speed to market and XPeng's profitability. There is a squared term of speed to market, which is to test the proposed relationship between speed to market and profitability. If the coefficient of the quadratic item is negative and the coefficient is positive of the linear speed to a market variable, the inverted U-shape will be approved (Langerak and Hultink, 2006). In addition, this research performs the T-test and F-test in this multiple regression analysis as well to verify the existence of the causal relationships between the independent and the dependent variable (Sun, 2000). There may be some deviations due to the limitations of the sample size. The data collected for this analysis is based on XPeng's product development process and product portfolio, so the sample size is six which is much less than 30. The limitation of sample data acquisition may lead to the problem of colinearity between sample data, which cannot be reduced by data standardization (Wichers, 1975). Therefore, this part will simply discuss the linear relationship between listing speed and profitability in terms of the results summarized in Diagram 3 and Table 2.

Before the test, Diagram 1 shows the relationship between the launch speed and profitability of different products of XPeng drawn according to the original data. The horizontal axis represents the products' launch speed in months, and the vertical axis represents quarterly profitability. It can be seen that with the acceleration of the listing speed, the relationship between them roughly conforms to the inverted U-shaped relationship. To obtain a more rigorous relationship, this research completed a regression analysis of z-standardized data by SPSS, and the results are shown in Table 2.

Figure 6. The scatter diagram based on the original data for H1

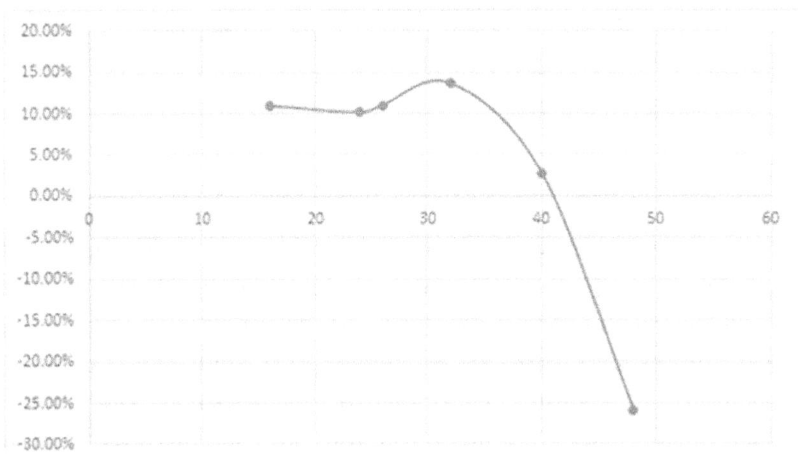

As the results are shown in Table 2, all of the sample data has been standardized by the Z-score method before implementing the linear regression. In this model, the coefficient of speed to market (X) is 2.855 which is positive for profitability, and the coefficient of the quadratic item is -3.693 which illustrates a negative impact on XPeng's profitability. The result is consistent with the inverted U-shaped relationship. In addition, the coefficient of determination (R-squared) in this model is 0.940, and the adjusted R^2 is 0.900. The R^2 may exaggerate the interpretation of independent variables to dependent variables, and the adjusted R^2 can eliminate the influence of the number of independent variables (Bar-Gera, 2017). On account of that the number of independent variables in the multiple regression can be regarded as two, this model utilizes the adjusted R^2 to reduce the inflated impact. Therefore, the value of the adjusted R^2 can prove that X can explain 90.0% change in the dependent variable, and the tested formula in the research model is

$$Y= -3.693X + 2.855X^2 + 0.000$$

These findings have successfully proved the inverted U-relationship assumed in Hypothesis 1. In addition, to make the model more meaningful, the model was F-tested, and it passed the F test. The result (F=23.470, p=0.015<0.050) indicates that at least one of the speed to market and its squared item has impacts on profitability. Furthermore, T-tests were conducted on each of them to verify their specific impact on profitability separately. As a result, the t-value of x (speed to market) is 3.016 (p=0.057>0.050), and thus considered in conjunction with the regression coefficients, speed to market has a positive but non-significant effect on profitability. On the contrary, the t-value of the quadratic item is -3.901 (p=0.030<0.050), which indicates that the squared item has a significantly negative impact on the dependent variable of profitability.

Table 2. Results of hypothesis one

Parameter Estimates (n=6)					
	Unstandardised Coefficients		**Standardised Coefficients**	**t**	**p**
	Beta	**Std. Error**	**Beta**		
Constant	0	0.129	-	0	1
S_x^2	-3.693	0.947	-3.693	-3.901	0.030*
S_speed to market (X-months)	2.855	0.947	2.855	3.016	0.057
R^2	0.94				
Adj R^2	0.9				
F	F (2,3)=23.470,p=0.015				
Dependent Variable: S_profitability					
* p<0.05 ** p<0.01					

5.2 RESULTS OF HYPOTHESIS 2A

Table 3 demonstrates the results of evaluating the linear relationship between quality issues and profitability through SPSS. As the independent variable, the coefficient of quality is 0.640, so the formula of this model after linear regression is

Y(profitability)= 0.640 × Quality + 0.000

The adjusted R-square is equal to 0.360 which means that the independent variable (quality) can explain a 36.0% change in the dependent variable (profitability). In addition, this sample data has passed the F test as well, which illustrates that quality factors must have an impact on product profitability. Additionally, the t-test yielded a p-value (0.014) that is less than 0.050. The combination of the above indicators concluded that product quality has a significant positive impact on its profitability, which is consistent with the predicted relationship in Hypothesis 2a.

Table 3. Results of hypothesis 2a

Parameter Estimates (n=14)					
	Unstandardised Coefficients		**Standardised Coefficients**	**t**	**p**
	Beta	**Std. Error**	**Beta**		
Constant	0	0.214	-	0	1
S_quality	0.64	0.222	0.64	2.884	0.014*
R^2	0.409				
Adj R^2	0.36				
F	F (1,12)=8.317,p=0.014				
Dependent Variable: S_profitability					
* p<0.05 ** p<0.01					

5.3 Results of Hypothesis 2b

The results of the regression analysis of R&D expenses and corresponding profitability are shown in Table 4. From the above figure, the linear relationship between R&D expenses and profitability based on the financial data of XPeng for fourteen quarters can be concluded as

Y(profitability)= –0.964 × R&D expenditure + 0.000

The value of the adjusted R-square is 0.924 which signifies that a 92.4% change in the dependent variable (profitability) can be explained by R&D expenditures. In addition, this sample data passed the F test, and the F-value of this sample data is 159.110. Through conducting the T-test, the p-value of 0.000 is lower than the limit of 0.010 and much less than 0.050, which proves R&D expenditures' significant impact on profitability. On account of that the coefficient is -0.964, this linear regression analysis confirms the significantly negative impact of R&D expenditure on profitability, which has rejected Hypothesis 2b.

Table 4. Results of hypothesis 2b

Parameter Estimates (n=14)					
	Unstandardised Coefficients		Standardised Coefficients	t	p
	Beta	Std. Error	Beta		
Constant	0	0.074	-	0	1
S_R&D expenditure	-0.964	0.076	-0.964	-12.614	0.000**
R^2	0.930				
Adj R^2	0.924				
F	F (1,12)=159.110,p=0.000				
Dependent Variable: S_profitability					
* p<0.05 ** p<0.01					

5.4 Results of Hypothesis Three

To assess hypothesis 3, SPSS is utilized to test the mediation role of quality factors. To evaluate the intermediary effect of quality factors, the model adds research on the linear relationship between development expenditure and quality based on the linear relationship tested by Hypothesis 2b. Finally, hypothesis 3 will be tested by analyzing the regression coefficients of R&D expenditure and quality on profitability. In general, the results are shown in Table 5 and can be summarized into the following three relations:

$$Y(\text{profitability}) = -0.964 \times \text{R\&D expenditure} + 0.000$$

$$Y(\text{quality}) = -0.450 \times \text{R\&D expenditure} + 0.000$$

$$Y(\text{profitability}) = -0.848 \times \text{RD expenditure} + 0.258 \times \text{Quality} + 0.000$$

In the above relationship, the regression coefficient -0.964 represents the total effect without intermediary variables, which has been discussed in the results for hypothesis 2b. The regression coefficient of R&D expenditure to quality is -0.450 and the p-value is 0.106 (>0.050), indicating that the negative impact of development expenditure on quality is not significant. When the quality factor is treated as an intermediary variable, its regression coefficient to profitability is 0.258, and the p-value of the t-test is 0.000 (< 0.010), which demonstrates that its positive impact is more significant. At the same time, after mediating by the quality, the coefficient of R&D expenditure to profitability is -0.848 and the p-value is 0.000 (< 0.010). In consequence, R&D expenditure still has a significantly negative impact on profitability, but after considering the quality factor, the absolute value of its correlation coefficient decreases from 0.964 to 0.848.

Table 5. Results of hypothesis three

Mediation analysis results (n=14)															
	S_profitability					S_quality					S_profitability				
	B	Std. Error	t	p	β	B	Std. Error	t	p	β	B	Std. Error	t	p	β
constant	0	0.074	0	1	-	0	0.248	0	1	-	0	0.038	0	1	-
S_R&D expenditure	-0.964**	0.076	-12.614	0.000	-0.964	-0.450	0.258	-1.746	0.106	-0.450	-0.848**	0.044	-19.276	0.000	-0.848
S_quality											0.258**	0.044	5.867	0.000	0.258
R 2	0.930					0.203					0.983				
Adj R 2	0.924					0.136					0.980				
F value	F (1,12)=159.110,p=0.000					F (1,12)=3.047,p=0.106					F (2,11)=318.355,p=0.000				
* p<0.05 ** p<0.01															

Table 6 is the summary table of the evaluation of the intermediary effect, in which the product of the regression coefficient of the independent variable (R&D expenditure) to the intermediary variable (quality) and the coefficient of the mediator to the dependent variable (profitability) is - 0.116, which represents the mediation effect. 95% BootCI means the 95% confidence interval calculated by SPSS using Bootstrap sampling. If the interval does not contain 0, the mediation effect is significant. The interval of this model is from -0.322 to -0.056, excluding 0, so the mediation effect of quality issues exists. Figure c' represents the regression coefficient of development expense to profitability when there is an intermediate variable in the model, so it indicates the direct effect on profitability.

Table 6. Results of the mediation test

Summary of Mediation Test Results								
Terms	**c**	**a**	**b**	**a*b**	**a*b (Boot SE)**	**a*b (95% BootCI)**	**c'**	**Result**
S_R&D expenditure=>S_quality=>S_profitability	-0.964**	-0.450	0.258**	-0.116	0.071	-0.322 ~ -0.056	-0.848**	Partial mediation

In this model, the p-value of c' is 0.000 which is lower than 0.010, so the direct effect is significant, and the product of a and b and c's are both negative numbers. Under this condition, if one of the regression coefficients of the independent variable to the intermediate variable and the intermediate variable to the dependent variable is not significant, and the 95% confidence interval of their product does not contain 0, the mediation variable plays a part of the mediation role (MathWorks, 2022). Therefore, after comprehensively considering the regression coefficients and confidence interval in the model, it can be concluded that quality can partially mediate the impact of R&D expenditure on profitability in this case, which has partially proved hypothesis 3 in terms of the test results.

5.5 Summary

This section has introduced the results of each research model established for each hypothesis, and the mathematical meanings of these results have been simply analyzed in this part. In summary, hypotheses 1 and 2a have been proved, and the medicated role of the quality issue mentioned in hypothesis 3 has been partially proved, and development expense has an insignificantly negative impact on quality as the above results show. Hypothesis 2b has been rejected. Figure 4 summarizes the significant relationships and the adjusted R-squares obtained from the above tests, which shows that the squared term of speed to market has the largest impact on profitability, and the R&D expense has the most significant impact. In addition to the significance, the results have indicated that in this research model, only the quality issue has a positive impact on profitability, and other factors are negative on XPeng's product profitability. Moreover, the general fitting degree reflects the error of the mathematical model. The closer the R-square is to 1, the higher the fitting degree of the model is, which demonstrates a higher coincidence between the predicted results and the actual situation (MathWorks, 2022). The results summarized in Table 5 illustrate that the R&D expenditure has the highest fitting degree, indicating that its impact on profitability is closer to the actual situation.

This section has introduced the test results and mathematical findings in the research model. To explain the above findings, the following section will discuss them and explore the reasons for the above relationships based on XPeng's business conditions, which is to combine the theoretical model with actual operations.

6. DISCUSSION AND IMPLICATION

The fifth chapter demonstrated the mathematical results of the research model. On account that this report is a case study, this part will explain the reasons for the formation of the above indicators in combination with XPeng's operations. Before discussing the impacts of each factor on profitability, it is necessary to confirm whether XPeng's product development strategy has been successful because if the strategy itself fails, the analysis of its implementation factors will be invalid. According to Florén et al. (2018), the commercialization of developed products is a sign of the success of the product development strategy. Figure 2 shows that XPeng has successfully launched a series of products, and its deliveries have won the championship of smart electric vehicles in China for four consecutive quarters from 2021 Q3 to the second quarter of

2022. Therefore, XPeng's product development strategy is successful. Based on this success, the next part will explore the respective impacts of each factor on profitability and explain the reasons for these impacts.

Figure 7. Summary of significant variables and the R-square amount

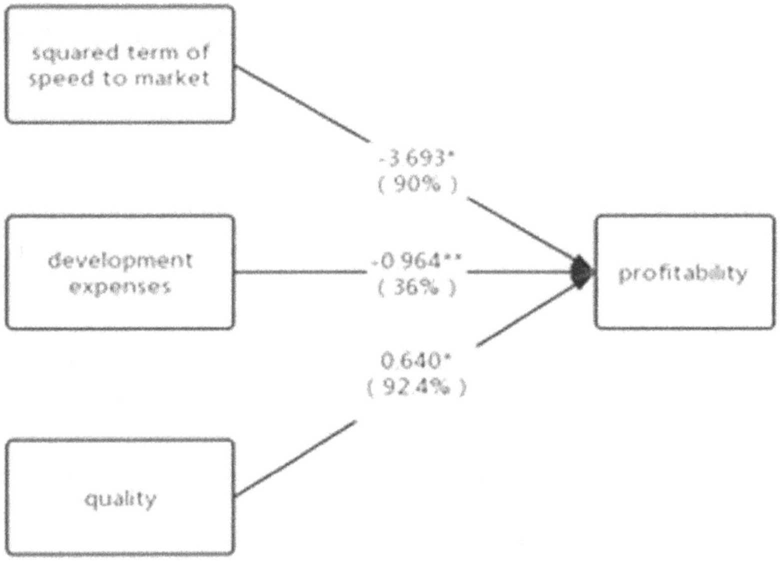

6.1 Speed to Market

The above coefficients and functional relationship have proved the inverted U-shaped relationship between speed to market and XPeng's profitability, which means that too fast or too slow to market both have negative impacts on the profitability of the product. From the release of G3 to P7wing, acceleration of the launch of new products has steadily improved XPeng's profitability. With the accelerated release speed, new products have been published constantly in 2021, but XPeng's profitability started to decline slightly rather than continue to increase. The following two aspects can explain this trend. The first one is related to the attractiveness of products, and the second one is related to technical risks.

Firstly, the acceleration of the speed to market has a positive impact on profitability because products can be adjusted in time based on customer needs to enhance product attractiveness to meet different customers' needs, which promotes adding more innovative points during the product planning and designing stages to attract future customers (Kessler and Bierly, 2002). These features will make the product more popular in the future and enhance its profitability. For XPeng, it spent about 48 months launching the G3 and 32 months launching its upgraded model G3i (XPeng, 2020). The profitability of G3i is higher than that of G3. The launch speed and profitability of P7 and P7wing prove this trend as well. Compared with the original model, the upgraded model has been listed quicker and made better financial performance. For example,

G3i has not only carried out intelligent upgrading based on the G3 but also has been designed with a more colourful appearance for the needs of different customers. The P7 Wing has not only made changes in appearance but also added the all-wheel-drive and high endurance version that consumers expect on the P7 model. This improvement has successfully attracted more young consumers. Therefore, after the launch of the P7 Wing in the fourth quarter of 2020, XPeng's vehicle delivery volume in the first quarter of 2021 increased by 130% month on month and 384% year on year (DongHai Securities, 2022). These sales performance illustrates that XPeng has achieved profitability growth by turning consumers' needs into R&D innovation points.

On the other hand, over-fast speed may lead to fewer innovation points of new products and may be unable to meet customer expectations, leading to a decline in profitability. For instance, although P5 was listed on the market faster than G3i, some consumers complained that P5 had poorer practicality, which led to a decline in deliveries and profitability after its launch (Yang, 2022). As for the newly released G9, its data is not included in the test of the above model because of its late launch. From its launch speed and current sales performance, it is only 12 months away from the release of P5, which is the model most rapidly launched by XPeng. However, on the complaint platform, some consumers pointed out that the G9 is not as superior as advertised, such as its poor UI and small space (Insideevs, 2022). These disappointments with G9 from consumers have led to the delivery of 623 and 1546 G9 vehicles in October and November respectively, which hurts profitability, mainly reflected in the increase of net loss to 2.38 billion (XPeng, 2022c). Therefore, the inverted U-shaped relationship between speed to market and profitability partly depends on whether the quicker speed to market can adjust the innovation points in time according to customers' preferences.

Secondly, according to the research conducted by Akram Afzal (2017), technological rapidity risk and financial risk are the two main risks that will affect the success of an entity's NPD program, and enterprises in the growth stage are more vulnerable to these risks than larger enterprises in the mature stage. For XPeng, the occurrence of technological risk means that a quicker speed to market may reduce the risk of technology obsolescence. The competition in the smart electric vehicle market is becoming fierce, and many traditional vehicle enterprises have transformed into this emerging market recently (Flannery, 2022). On account of the rapid updating speed of new products and high scientific and technological risks in the market, a quicker launching speed means faster innovation. For example, the launch of XPeng G3i is closely followed by the release of Tesla's Model Y which is one of its main competitors, and G3i has been one of the most profitable products for XPeng with a 13.6% gross profit margin. Therefore, speeding up the launch may avoid the unsalable risk caused by outdated technology that has been updated by competitors. However, the premise of this positive effect is that speeding up is not achieved through the sacrifice of innovation points, otherwise, a negative effect on profitability will be caused by the useless launch.

6.2 Quality

Both the literature and test results in this research model have proved that quality issue has a significantly positive impact on profitability. In the process of product research and development of XPeng, the quality factor has always been thought highly of by management. XPeng has gradually established a handling mechanism to deal with any quality problems (XPeng, 2021a).

Firstly, XPeng collects and identifies quality problems through various channels, such as hotline complaints, maintenance records, and return ratios. After finding the deficiencies, those will be analyzed according to the "Three Reality Principle" which requires proper countermeasures in terms of the real situation, practical scene, and actual objects. Finally, the quality problems are solved through some internal mechanisms of the company, including daily meetings for quality issues, weekly meetings with directors and meetings chaired by the president. With the improvement of the quality management mechanism, from 2019 to the second quarter of 2022, the proportion of the warranty expenses that are used to compensate for the problems caused by poor quality to the revenue illustrates a general downward trend, which implies that the quality of products has been promoted continuously. At the same time, the profitability starts to increase gradually with the decrease of the warranty expenditure, and the overall trend is shown in Diagram 4.

Figure 8. Curves of profitability and the proportion of warranty to revenue

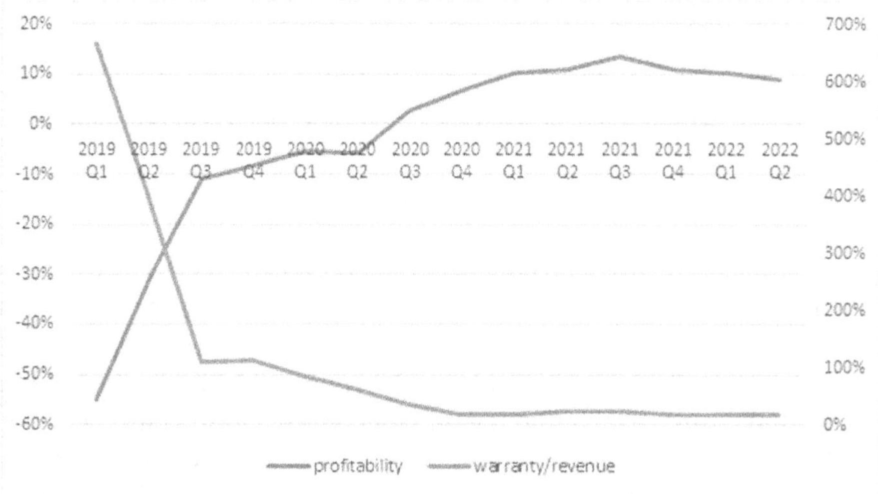

In addition, the G3 model has ranked top in quality among the compact smart electric vehicles in the study of 2021 China New-Energy Vehicle Quality, which has reflected consumers' approbation of XPeng's vehicle quality (Moloughney, 2021). It can be speculated that XPeng's profitability has risen sharply since the first quarter of 2019 because of the launch of G3. Moreover, XPeng's quality management has also been extended to the corresponding improvement of service quality, proposing the concept of a "3 km Energy Replacement Life Circle", thereby reducing the charging time of owners (XPeng, 2023). Therefore, although the findings for the H2a have concluded quality can merely explain a 36.0% change in profitability, continuous improvement of product quality and strengthening of quality control mechanisms during the research and development process can effectively improve product profitability.

6.3 Development Expenses

6.3.1 Direct Impact

The impact of development expenditure on profitability is comprehensive, so this part will discuss the findings in the research for H2b to evaluate the direct impact on profitability. The result from the test of H2b's relationship indicates that XPeng's R&D expenditure has a significant negative impact on its profitability, which has rejected Hypothesis 2b for the following reasons. The research conducted by Zhao (2019) found that in the manufacturing industry, larger R&D investment would weaken the profitability of enterprises, and after further research being conducted, the results demonstrate that there is a critical point for R&D expenditure. When the development expenditure is lower than the critical point, R&D investment will enhance enterprise profitability; When the critical point is exceeded, higher expenditure will make a negative impact on the profit of the enterprise. Additionally, Zhao (2019) concluded two main reasons for this result. The first reason is that the investment in R&D is excessive. The costs invested in research and development can help to enhance the competitiveness of enterprises and establish a superior image of them, thus easily causing excessive R&D investment, especially for the high-tech industry. Secondly, it is because the transformation efficiency of R&D investment is low. The R&D investment costs have been recognized as expenses, which cannot be converted into assets that can bring benefits to the enterprise in time, so the low conversion efficiency has led to a negative impact on profitability.

For XPeng, the R&D expenditure in the first quarter of 2019 was about 6.66 times of the revenue, but by the fourth quarter of 2020, the proportion of XPeng's R&D investment had reduced to 19% of its revenue. After that, although the proportion has increased, it is merely a small fluctuation. In consequence, initial R&D investment may be excessive. In the early stage of R&D, XPeng's R&D directions were diversified. With the launch of some achievements, XPeng began to focus on the main concerns of consumers based on consumer feedback, such as battery endurance, intelligent control systems, and auxiliary driving functions (XPeng, 2021a). Additionally, XPeng conducted blind expansion. Some of its R&D expenditure has been used for research on hovercars and robots, but its income mainly comes from the vehicle business, which is one of the reasons for its abnormal R&D expenditure. Therefore, the negative impact of development expenditure on profitability may be due to the excessive initial investment and low efficiency. With the optimization of the R&D process and the concentration of the direction, the profitability has been improved.

6.3.2 Indirect Impact

The findings in H3 illustrate the indirect impact of development expense on profitability. The mediation role has been partially proved for Hypothesis 3, which indicates that part of the impact of R&D expenditure on profitability is to affect quality first, and then quality affects profitability. The positive impact of quality on profitability has been confirmed above, and the results in Table 5 need to be thought highly of about the negative impact of R&D expenditure on quality. Although the impact is not significant, previous empirical studies show that R&D expenditure has a positive effect on quality. According to the tested data of XPeng, while the proportion of R&D investment decreases, product quality improves. Combined with the results discussed in section 6.3.1, this relationship may be formed due to the lack of attention to quality factors in the initial stage of XPeng's product development. In reality, some vehicles of the first G3 model were recalled due to quality problems, which is consistent with this view. In addition, the ESG report mentioned that XPeng has put product quality and safety first in the current R&D process since the recall (XPeng, 2021a). Therefore, the unusual finding is caused by XPeng's operations. XPeng's product development strategy has gradually become systematic and targeted from the initial stage of excessive investment and scope, which is the reason why profitability has gradually increased as the proportion of R&D investment has decreased. In this process, the positive impact of quality medicates some negative impacts of R&D expenditures on profitability.

This section has explained the findings combined with the actual situations of XPeng. In summary, the impacts of insisting on a product development strategy on XPeng's profitability from 2019 to the second quarter of 2022 can be discussed from three aspects, which are the speed to market, quality and development expenditure. These findings are mainly in line with previous studies except for the relationship between development expense and profitability. As a case study, although there are some limitations of the study scope and sample size, the findings about each implement factor's impact on profitability are still valuable to improve XPeng's product development strategy.

7. LIMITATIONS

7.1 Literature Limitations

The determinants of profitability are various and complex, which include both internal and external issues. For example, according to Tan and Floros (2014), market competitiveness related to an industry's characteristics is an essential external issue, which is a critically dominant factor of an entity's profitability. Moreover, a firm's profitability may be influenced by its risk management level, size, and financing capacity (Seo, 2016). Therefore, the first limitation is that this research merely focuses on product development strategy's impacts on profitability.

In addition, the model used in this research is based on that developed by McNally, Akdeniz and Calantone (2011), which further analyzed the relationship between cross-functional integration and profitability. However, it is difficult to interview XPeng's management and collect the key informant perceptions to quantify this dimension, so the model was truncated. Therefore, the other inherent defect of this research is that XPeng's profitability may be affected by other management factors which have not been evaluated in this case study.

7.2 Methodology Limitations

XPeng has been listed since 2020, so there were no financial records before 2019. Additionally, the product range of XPeng is limited as well. Those reasons result in the limitations of the study scope and sample size, so the research methods may not meet the statistical standards and the results may differ from the theoretical values.

8. CONCLUSION AND RECOMMENDATION

This study is a case study, and its primary objective is to analyze how the implementation of the product development strategy affects XPeng's profitability from 2019 to the second quarter of 2022. Based on the research model established by McNally, Akdeniz and Calantone (2011), this research utilizes separate regression models and mediation analysis models to investigate how the speed to market, quality, and development expenses affect XPeng's profitability. In terms of the findings, the three implementation factors in the product development strategy have significant impacts on XPeng's profitability. Only the quality issue has a positive impact on profitability continuously. The other two factors' impacts are comprehensive. The detailed conclusions and recommendations are as follows.

Firstly, the inverted U-shaped relationship between speed to market and profitability has been proved based on XPeng's product portfolio. Therefore, to maximize product profitability, speed to market should not be too quick or too slow, and the above coefficients and functional relationship have demonstrated that XPeng is theoretically able to find a proper research speed to maximize its profitability. XPeng believes that accelerating the products' launch speed can make its product portfolio expand in the short term to satisfy the needs of customers of different levels (XPeng, n.d.), which may be absolute. As shown in Figure 3, G3i took about 32 months from the concept release to the final launch, and its gross profit margin after the launch was the highest of all products. Therefore, for XPeng, around 30 months may be the suitable speed that can maximize profitability. If the speed is too slow, it may not keep up with the speed of industry changes due to technological risks, and if it is too fast, it cannot meet consumers' expectations for example, consumers are more interested in seeing performance improvements than appearance.

Secondly, the emphasis on quality issues during the product R&D process has been proven to have a positive impact on its profitability. Quality is one of the key points that customers attach importance to, especially for the vehicle manufacturing industry, which should be taken seriously in the research and development process (Ding et al., 2022). Quality and safety are one of the core advantages of products, so XPeng is recommended to focus on the navigating ability, quality of workmanship, and comprehensive improvement of intelligence to increase its competitive advantages and avoid the recurrence of recall.

Thirdly, the negative effect of R&D expenditure on profitability has been proved based on XPeng's quarterly data. This result is consistent with the findings by Curtis, Mcvay and Toynbee (2020), which indicate that the largest increase in R&D expenditures is related to the greatest average decline in R&D profitability, which supports the assumption of diminishing marginal returns to R&D expenditures. In consequence, management should pay attention to the efficiency of R&D investments and make rational research decisions, so R&D expenditure is not the more the better. It is recommended that XPeng should seek and approach the critical point of R&D investment according to the characteristics of the company and the industry, to improve the transformation efficiency of R&D investment. In addition, to avoid blind expansion, XPeng should reduce the expenditure on research and development of hover cars and robots, focus on the research of the automobile business, and avoid being disconnected from the core vehicle business.

In conclusion, the product development strategy has an impact on XPeng's profitability. To enhance profitability, XPeng's managers need to pay attention to the above three factors. The NPD strategy is mainly aimed at improving the performance and appearance of vehicles, so new energy-intelligent vehicle companies such as XPeng should focus their main energy on their main products, and research and development should focus on product quality, appropriately improving the speed of new product launches. Other factors that will affect XPeng's profitability, however, due to the limitations of this case study, this report only discusses the above issues which are valuable to help XPeng explore how to implement the product development strategy to enhance its profitability.

REFERENCES

Aaker, D. A., & Jacobson, R. (1994). The Financial Information Content of Perceived Quality. *Journal of Marketing Research (JMR)*, *31*(2), pp. 191–201. https://eds-s-ebscohost-com.ez.xjtlu.edu.cn/eds/detail/detail?vid=0&sid=b8d20eb7-83c8-4c90-83f8-70f2a37f3053%40redis&bdata=JnNpdGU9ZWRzLWxpdmUmc2NvcGU9c2l0ZQ%3d%3d#AN=9411112939&db=bsu.

Ahmeti, Y., & Iseni, E. (2022). Factors Affecting Profitability of Insurance Companies. *Academicus,* (25), pp. 122–142. [Online]. https://eds-s-ebscohost-com.ez.xjtlu.edu.cn/eds/detail/detail?vid=0&sid=00dd95f5-c2a7-417f-bbb4-2760d329b36a%40redis&bdata=JnNpdGU9ZWRzLWxpdmUmc2NvcGU9c2l0ZQ%3d%3d#db=hlh&AN=154767036

Akram Afzal, M. (2017). Risks in new product development (NPD) projects. ebsCohost. https://search-ebscohost-com.ez.xjtlu.edu.cn/login.aspx?direct=true&db=edsble&AN=edsble.738624&site=eds-live&scope=site

Ali, A. (2000). The Impact of Innovativeness and Development Time on New Product Performance for Small Firms. *Marketing Letters*, *11*(2), 151–163. https://search-ebscohost-com.ez.xjtlu.edu.cn/login.aspx?direct=true&db=edsjsr&AN=edsjsr.40216567&site=eds-live&scope=site

Andaleeb, S. S., & Hasan, K. (2016) *Strategic Marketing Management in Asia : Case Studies and Lessons Across Industries.* [Place of publication not identified]: Emerald Group Publishing Limited. [Online]. https://search-ebscohost-com.ez.xjtlu.edu.cn/login.aspx?direct=true&db=edsebk&AN=1423724&site=eds-live&scope=site

Andrade, C. (2021). Z Scores, Standard Scores, and Composite Test Scores Explained. *Indian Journal of Psychological Medicine*, *43*(6), 555–557. https://eds-s-ebscohost-com.ez.xjtlu.edu.cn/eds/detail/detail?vid=0&sid=58922e84-ed8e-4cb8-9d9d-c2e19877d938%40redis&bdata=JnNpdGU9ZWRzLWxpdmUmc2NvcGU9c2l0ZQ%3d%3d#AN=153685949&db=asn

Bar-Gera, H. (2017). The Target Parameter of Adjusted R-Squared in Fixed-Design Experiments. *American Statistician*, *71*(2), 112–119. https://eds-p-ebscohost-com.ez.xjtlu.edu.cn/eds/detail/detail?vid=0&sid=d23f04d3-7f78-46a0-b9d0-bfe8b0f789a5%40redis&bdata=JnNpdGU9ZWRzLWxpdmUmc2NvcGU9c2l0ZQ%3d%3d#db=asn&AN=123952667

Beverland, M. B., Gemser, G., & Karpen, I. O. (2017). Design, consumption and marketing: outcomes, process, philosophy and future directions. *Journal of Marketing Management*, 33(3/4), pp. 159–172. https://eds-s-ebscohost-com.ez.xjtlu.edu.cn/eds/detail/detail?vid=0&sid=3f3dedd8-5c7d-4dd9-9885-c5bd60ab08e9%40redis&bdata=JnNpdGU9ZWRzLWxpdmUmc2NvcGU9c2l0ZQ%3d%3d#AN=121630773&db=bsu (Accessed: 21 November 2022).

Bhatti, G., Mohan, H., & Raja Singh, R. (2021). Towards the future of smart electric vehicles: Digital twin technology. *Renewable and Sustainable Energy Reviews, 141*. https://eds-s-ebscohost-com.ez.xjtlu.edu.cn/eds/detail/detail?vid=0&sid=fd935fcc-49df-4462-b790-1e03b402e74a%40redis&bdata=JnNpdGU9ZWRzLWxpdmUmc2NvcGU9c2l0ZQ%3d%3d#AN=S1364032121000964&db=edselp

Bhutada, G. (2022). *Visualizing 10 Years of Global EV Sales by Country* [Online]. Visual Capitolist. https://www.visualcapitalist.com/visualizing-10-years-of-global-ev-sales-by-country/

Casoni, G. (2010). Design and creativity in open innovation processes: The case of Italian industrial districts. *Strategic Design Research Journal*, *3*(2), 33–40. https://eds-s-ebscohost-com.ez.xjtlu.edu.cn/eds/detail/detail?vid=0&sid=62795653-a518-46da-a314-4fd50176908a%40redis&bdata=JnNpdGU9ZWRzLWxpdmUmc2NvcGU9c2l0ZQ%3d%3d#AN=60870568&db=asn

Cooper, R. G., Edgett, S. J., & Kleinschmidt, E. J. (2004). Benchmarking Best Npd Practices-Ii', *Research Technology Management, 47*(3), pp. 50–59. https://search-ebscohost-com.ez.xjtlu.edu.cn/login.aspx?direct=true&db=edsjsr&AN=edsjsr.43238109&site=eds-live&scope=site

Ding, H. (2022). *Vehicle Driving Risk Prediction Model by Reverse Artificial Intelligence Neural Network*. Computational Intelligence & Neuroscience. https://eds-p-ebscohost-com.ez.xjtlu.edu.cn/eds/detail/detail?vid=0&sid=cf20a4ef-0ea7-4827-b638-900d1c5f2f19%40redis&bdata=JnNpdGU9ZWRzLWxpdmUmc2NvcGU9c2l0ZQ%3d%3d#AN=159695525&db=asn doi:10.1155/2022/3100509

DongHai Securities. (2022). *Automotive Industry Weekly Report*. DongHai Securities. http://www.iwencai.com/unifiedwap/infodetail?uid=1b11ba4603306623&w=小鹏销量&querytype=report

Ernst, H., Hoyer, W. D., & Rübsaamen, C. (2010). Sales, Marketing, and Research-and-Development Cooperation Across New Product Development Stages: Implications for Success', *Journal of Marketing*, *74*(5), 80–92. https://search-ebscohost-com.ez.xjtlu.edu.cn/login.aspx?direct=true&db=edsjsr&AN=edsjsr.41228575&site=eds-live&scope=site

Flannery, R. (2022). China EV Maker XPeng Loss More Than Doubles Amid Covid Woes. *Forbes*. https://search-ebscohost-com.ez.xjtlu.edu.cn/login.aspx?direct=true&db=bsu&AN=157033656&site=eds-live&scope=site

Florén, H. (2018). Critical success factors in early new product development: a review and a conceptual model. *International Entrepreneurship and Management Journal*, *14*(2), 411–427. https://eds-s-ebscohost-com.ez.xjtlu.edu.cn/eds/detail/detail?vid=0&sid=29e5f1f5-2243-4556-b322-7dfeb350965d%40redis&bdata=JnNpdGU9ZWRzLWxpdmUmc2NvcGU9c2l0ZQ%3d%3d#AN=edssjs.F01DC038&db=edssjs

Fox, R. (2022). XPeng Stock Shows Strong Q2 Delivery Numbers; Is It A Buy Now? Here's What Charts, Analysis Show. *Investors Business Daily*. https://search-ebscohost-com.ez.xjtlu.edu.cn/login.aspx?direct=true&db=bwh&AN=159350087&site=eds-live&scope=site

George, M. (2005) *Fast Innovation: Achieving Superior Differentiation, Speed to Market, and Increased Profitability*. McGraw-Hill Education. https://eds-s-ebscohost-com.ez.xjtlu.edu.cn/eds/detail/detail?vid=0&sid=59cb4dbc-5523-480d-bdc5-5fb0e798b719%40redis&bdata=JnNpdGU9ZWRzLWxpdmUmc2NvcGU9c2l0ZQ%3d%3d#AN=edsely.0071457895&db=edsely (Accessed: 4 October 2022).

Hemonnet, G. A., Manceau, D., & Abecassis, M. C. (2019). Drivers and Pathways of NPD Success in the Marketing–External Design Relationship. *Journal of Product Innovation Management, 36*(2), 196–223. https://eds-p-ebscohost-com.ez.xjtlu.edu.cn/eds/pdfviewer/pdfviewer?vid=1&sid=ea2bb025-ba8d-4eba-812c-534f7d1dba62%40redis

Insideevs. (2022). 'XPeng Electric Car Sales Decreased By Almost 63% In November 2022. Inside EVS. https://insideevs.com/news/624618/xpeng-electric-car-sales-november2022/

Jayaram, J., & Narasimhan, R. (2007). The Influence of New Product Development Competitive Capabilities on Project Performance. *IEEE Transactions on Engineering Management, Engineering Management, IEEE Transactions on, IEEE Trans. Eng. Manage, 54*(2), 241–256. https://eds-p-ebscohost-com.ez.xjtlu.edu.cn/eds/detail/detail?vid=0&sid=cfdf6fb5-162f-4cae-a39f-c31c10920c1f%40redis&bdata=JnNpdGU9ZWRzLWxpdmUmc2NvcGU9c2l0ZQ%3d%3d#AN=edseee.4160162&db=edseee

KaiYuan Securities. (2022). *XPeng total deliveries until September 2022*. IWENCAI. http://www.iwencai.com/unifiedwap/inforesult?w=%E5%B0%8F%E9%B9%8F&querytype=report&tab=2

Kessler, E. H., & Bierly, P. E., III. (2002). Is faster better? An empirical test of the implications of innovation speed. *IEEE Transactions on Engineering Management, Engineering Management, IEEE Transactions on, IEEE Trans. Eng. Manage, 49*(1), 2–12. https://eds-p-ebscohost-com.ez.xjtlu.edu.cn/eds/detail/detail?vid=0&sid=a42b9fe2-a446-45e7-8cda-fa16525054c1%40redis&bdata=JnNpdGU9ZWRzLWxpdmUmc2NvcGU9c2l0ZQ%3d%3d#AN=edseee.985742&db=edseee

Kiss, A. N., & Barr, P. S. (2017). New Product Development Strategy Implementation Duration and New Venture Performance. *Journal of Management, 43*(4), 1185–1210. https://eds-p-ebscohost-com.ez.xjtlu.edu.cn/eds/detail/detail?vid=0&sid=750872be-f362-44c6-a5c4-02a88cdccbdb%40redis&bdata=JnNpdGU9ZWRzLWxpdmUmc2NvcGU9c2l0ZQ%3d%3d#AN=121615690&db=bsu

Kumar, M., Townsend, J. D., & Vorhies, D. W. (2015). Enhancing Consumers' Affection for a Brand Using Product Design. *Journal of Product Innovation Management, 32*(5), 716–730. https://eds-p-ebscohost-com.ez.xjtlu.edu.cn/eds/detail/detail?vid=0&sid=6d3ea559-8df6-4500-9968-a7e770a918c1%40redis&bdata=JnNpdGU9ZWRzLWxpdmUmc2NvcGU9c2l0ZQ%3d%3d#AN=108541949&db=bsu

Kuwashima, K., & Fujimoto, T. (2013). Performance Measurement in Product Development Research: A Literature Review. *Annals of Business Administrative Science*, *12*(4), 213–223. https://eds-s-ebscohost-com.ez.xjtlu.edu.cn/eds/detail/detail?vid=0&sid=35581885-aa72-4407-ae9a-77b232e4df7a%40redis&bdata=JnNpdGU9ZWRzLWxpdmUmc2NvcGU9c2l0ZQ%3d%3d#AN=119369235&db=bsu (Accessed: 21 November 2022).

Langerak, F., & Hultink, E. J. (2005). The impact of new product development acceleration approaches on speed and profitability: lessons for pioneers and fast followers. *IEEE Transactions on Engineering Management, Engineering Management, IEEE Transactions on, IEEE Trans. Eng. Manage.* IEEE. https://eds-p-ebscohost-com.ez.xjtlu.edu.cn/eds/detail/detail?vid=0&sid=fe052f67-ee0d-4fac-81f7-c5d5d1bfc36a%40redis&bdata=JnNpdGU9ZWRzLWxpdmUmc2NvcGU9c2l0ZQ%3d%3d#AN=edseee.1388696&db=edseee

Langerak, F., & Hultink, E. J. (2006). The Impact of Product Innovativeness on the Link between Development Speed and New Product Profitability. *Journal of Product Innovation Management, 23*(3), 203–214. https://eds-s-ebscohost-com.ez.xjtlu.edu.cn/eds/detail/detail?vid=0&sid=e4a18c29-bdcb-4c00-bf29-eb3c8878a64a%40redis&bdata=JnNpdGU9ZWRzLWxpdmUmc2NvcGU9c2l0ZQ%3d%3d#AN=20535319&db=bsu

MathWorks. (2022) *BootCI*. Mathworks. https://de.mathworks.com/help/stats/bootci.html

McNally, R. C., Akdeniz, M. B., & Calantone, R. J. (2011). New Product Development Processes and New Product Profitability: Exploring the Mediating Role of Speed to Market and Product Quality. *Journal of Product Innovation Management*, (s1), 63–77. https://eds-s-ebscohost-com.ez.xjtlu.edu.cn/eds/detail/detail?vid=0&sid=0349b761-5727-41bb-9841-cea04d0046cd%40redis&bdata=JnNpdGU9ZWRzLWxpdmUmc2NvcGU9c2l0ZQ%3d%3d#AN=66592359&db=bsu

Curtis, A., McVay, S., & Toynbee, S. (2020). The changing implications of research and development expenditures for future profitability [Preprint]. *Review of Accounting Studies*, *25*(2), 405–437. doi:10.1007/s11142-019-09528-6

Mena Report. (2022). EB CoHost. https://search-ebscohost-com.ez.xjtlu.edu.cn/login.aspx?direct=true&db=edsgea&AN=edsgcl.693449837&site=eds-live&scope=site (Accessed: 17 October 2022).

Millson, M. R., & Wilemon, D. (2019). The Npd Speed-Market Success Relationship: A Meta-Analysis', *International Journal of Innovation Management*, *23*(6), N.PAG. https://eds-s-ebscohost-com.ez.xjtlu.edu.cn/eds/detail/detail?vid=0&sid=c5118752-88cf-467b-9168-d98359264dc6%40redis&bdata=JnNpdGU9ZWRzLWxpdmUmc2NvcGU9c2l0ZQ%3d%3d#AN=137684240&db=edb

Moloughney, T. (2021). XPeng G3 Earns Top Quality Ranking By J.D. Power In Latest Study. Inside EVS. https://insideevs.com/news/524097/xpeng-g3-jd-power-quality/

Seo, J. Y. (2016). What Factors Influence Profitability in the Korean Credit Card Business?. *International Journal of Business & Society*, *17*(1), 19–27. https://search-ebscohost-com.ez.xjtlu.edu.cn/login.aspx?direct=true&db=bsu&AN=116157302&site=eds-live&scope=site (Accessed: 8 October 2022).

Sethi, R. (2000). New Product Quality and Product Development Teams. *Journal of Marketing*, *64*(2), 1–14. https://eds-s-ebscohost-com.ez.xjtlu.edu.cn/eds/detail/detail?vid=0&sid=46478820-e48d-43e9-b952-0f1ed41b8dba%40redis&bdata=JnNpdGU9ZWRzLWxpdmUmc2NvcGU9c2l0ZQ%3d%3d#AN=3043546&db=bsu

Sivasubramaniam, N., Liebowitz, S. J., & Lackman, C. L. (2012). Determinants of New Product Development Team Performance: A Meta-analytic Review. *Journal of Product Innovation Management*, *29*(5), 803–820. https://eds-p-ebscohost-com.ez.xjtlu.edu.cn/eds/detail/detail?vid=0&sid=0973782c-e37f-47fc-a0b6-c0d1609cf14e%40redis&bdata=JnNpdGU9ZWRzLWxpdmUmc2NvcGU9c2l0ZQ%3d%3d#AN=78301272&db=bsu

Sun, D. (2000). Selection of the Linear Regression Model According to the Parameter Estimation. *JOURNAL OF NATURAL SCIENCES*, *5*(4), 400–405. https://search-ebscohost-com.ez.xjtlu.edu.cn/login.aspx?direct=true&db=edscoj&AN=edscoj.whdxxb.e200004005&site=eds-live&scope=site.

Swink, M., Talluri, S., & Pandejpong, T. (2006). Faster, better, cheaper: A study of NPD project efficiency and performance tradeoffs. *Journal of Operations Management*, *24*(5), 542–562. https://eds-p-ebscohost-com.ez.xjtlu.edu.cn/eds/detail/detail?vid=0&sid=7409c5bb-9ebd-4d23-845b-e103f0cec522%40redis&bdata=JnNpdGU9ZWRzLWxpdmUmc2NvcGU9c2l0ZQ%3d%3d#AN=S0272696305001488&db=edselp

Tan, Y., & Floros, C. (2014). Risk, Profitability, and Competition: Evidence from the Chinese Banking Industry. *Journal of Developing Areas*, *48*(3), 303–319. https://eds-s-ebscohost-com.ez.xjtlu.edu.cn/eds/detail/detail?vid=0&sid=b5a78bbc-27f3-4183-b7ae-c92a21a751ca%40redis&bdata=JnNpdGU9ZWRzLWxpdmUmc2NvcGU9c2l0ZQ%3d%3d#AN=97125404&db=bsu (Accessed: 6 October 2022).

Verhoef, P. C., & Leeflang, P. S. (2009). Understanding the Marketing Department's Influence Within the Firm', *Journal of Marketing*, *73*(2), 14–37. https://eds-s-ebscohost-com.ez.xjtlu.edu.cn/eds/detail/detail?vid=0&sid=e93cac68-4161-4f9c-a461-06f8f5a61d2f%40redis&bdata=JnNpdGU9ZWRzLWxpdmUmc2NvcGU9c2l0ZQ%3d%3d#AN=36441948&db=bsu

Wichers, C. R. (1975). The Detection of Multicollinearity: A Comment. *The Review of Economics and Statistics*, *57*(3), 366–368. https://search-ebscohost-com.ez.xjtlu.edu.cn/login.aspx?direct=true&db=edsjsr&AN=edsjsr.10.2307.1923926&site=eds-live&scope=site

XPeng. (2020) *2020 Annual Report* [Online]. XPeng. https://ir.xiaopeng.com/static-files/c75210a2-1b8d-4a52-8a41-8190e000822c

XPeng. (2021a) *2021 Environmental, Social and Governance Report* [Online]. XPeng. https://ir.xiaopeng.com/system/files-encrypted/nasdaq_kms/assets/2022/05/25/21-12-58/2021-ESG-220524-vS-EN.pdf (Accessed: 1 October 2022).

XPeng. (2021b) *2021 Annual Report* [Online]. XPeng. https://ir.xiaopeng.com/static-files/8707a7a3-2645-45a7-9cb4-02364ce5cf57 (Accessed: 4 October 2022).

XPeng. (2022a) *XPENG CORPORATE STORY* [Online]. XPeng. https://heyxpeng.com/brand?prentId=5 (Accessed: 1 October 2022).

XPeng. (2022b) *XPeng Reports Second Quarter 2022 Unaudited Financial Results* [Online]. XPang. https://ir.xiaopeng.com/static-files/fd52d251-717e-49b6-b39e-f5bb5c66b44c

XPeng. (2022c) *XPeng Reports Third Quarter 2022 Unaudited Financial Results* [Online]. XPeng. https://ir.xiaopeng.com/static-files/d18ce2b8-2d45-4b7d-961b-b74e0b7766f7

XPeng. (2023) *2022 Environmental, Social and Governance Report* [Online]. XPeng. https://ir.xiaopeng.com/system/files-encrypted/nasdaq_kms/assets/2023/04/12/5-18-25/小鹏汽车2022年ESG报告-英文版.pdf

XPeng. (n.d.) *About XPeng*. XPeng. https://ir.xiaopeng.com/?mobile=1

Yang, C. (2022). China's Popular EV Companies Enter Crucial Earnings Season. *Bloomberg*. https://search-ebscohost-com.ez.xjtlu.edu.cn/login.aspx?direct=true&db=bsu&AN=158489758&site=eds-live&scope=site

Yang, Y., & Xu, D. (2017). A methodology for assessing the effect of portfolio management on NPD performance based on Bayesian network scenarios. *Expert Systems*, *34*(2). https://eds-p-ebscohost-com.ez.xjtlu.edu.cn/eds/detail/detail?vid=0&sid=535cc033-c759-4831-a8e1-81a49f94d36e%40redis&bdata=JnNpdGU9ZWRzLWxpdmUmc2NvcGU9c2l0ZQ%3d%3d#AN=122404448&db=bsu

Zhao, H. X. (2019) *R&D investment and enterprise profitability*. R&D. https://www.fx361.com/page/2019/0910/10034472.shtml

ZheShang Securities. (2022). *Weekly report for the automotive industry*. ZheSheng. http://www.iwencai.com/unifiedwap/inforesult?w=%E5%B0%8F%E9%B9%8F%20%E7%90%86%E6%83%B3%20%E8%94%9A%E6%9D%A5%20%E6%AF%9B%E5%88%A9&querytype=report&tab=2

APPENDIX

Industry Comparison Data

财务数据		20Q1	20Q2	20Q3	20Q4	21Q1	21Q2	21Q3	21Q4	22Q1	22Q2
汽车业务营收	特斯拉（亿美元）	51.3	51.8	76.1	93.1	90.0	102.1	120.6	159.7	168.6	146.0
	YOY	37.8%	-3.7%	42.2%	46.3%	75.4%	97.1%	58.4%	71.4%	87.3%	43.1%
	蔚来（亿元）	12.6	34.9	42.7	61.7	74.1	79.1	86.4	92.2	92.4	/
	YOY	-18.2%	146.5%	146.1%	130.0%	489.8%	127.0%	102.4%	49.3%	24.8%	/
	理想（亿元）	8.4	19.2	24.6	40.6	34.6	49.0	73.9	103.8	93.1	84.8
	YOY					311.8%	155.5%	199.7%	155.7%	168.7%	73.0%
	小鹏（亿元）	3.7	5.4	18.9	27.4	28.1	35.8	54.6	81.9	70.0	69.4
	YOY			373.7%	375.8%	655.2%	562.4%	189.0%	199.3%	149.0%	93.6%
汽车业务毛利率	特斯拉	25.5%	25.4%	27.7%	24.1%	26.5%	28.4%	30.5%	30.6%	32.9%	27.9%
	蔚来	-7.4%	9.7%	14.5%	17.2%	21.2%	20.3%	18.0%	20.9%	18.1%	/
	理想	8.4%	13.7%	19.8%	17.1%	16.9%	18.7%	21.1%	22.3%	22.4%	21.2%
	小鹏	-5.3%	-5.6%	2.8%	6.8%	10.1%	11.0%	13.6%	10.9%	10.4%	9.1%
净利润	特斯拉（亿美元）	0.2	1.0	3.3	2.7	4.4	11.4	16.2	23.2	33.2	22.6
	蔚来（亿元）	-17.2	-12.1	-11.9	-14.9	-48.7	-6.6	-28.6	-21.8	-18.3	/
	理想（亿元）	-2.3	-3.5	-3.2	1.1	-3.6	-2.4	-0.2	3.0	-0.1	-6.2
	小鹏（亿元）	-9.4	-11.4	-20.3	-7.9	-7.9	-11.9	-15.9	-12.9	-17.0	-27.0
R&D margin	特斯拉	5.4%	4.6%	4.2%	4.9%	6.4%	4.8%	4.4%	4.2%	4.6%	3.9%
	蔚来	40.3%	14.7%	13.1%	12.5%	8.6%	10.5%	12.2%	18.5%	17.8%	/
	理想	22.3%	10.3%	13.3%	9.0%	14.4%	13.0%	11.4%	11.6%	14.4%	17.5%
	小鹏	75.4%	54.1%	31.9%	16.1%	18.1%	23.0%	22.1%	17.0%	16.4%	17.0%
SG&A margin	特斯拉	10.5%	11.0%	10.1%	9.0%	10.2%	8.1%	7.2%	8.4%	5.3%	5.7%
	蔚来	61.8%	25.2%	20.8%	18.2%	15.0%	17.7%	18.6%	23.8%	20.3%	/
	理想	13.2%	12.0%	13.6%	10.4%	14.3%	16.6%	13.1%	10.6%	12.6%	15.2%
	小鹏	78.1%	80.8%	60.5%	32.2%	24.4%	27.4%	26.9%	23.6%	22.0%	22.4%
交付量		20Q1	20Q2	20Q3	20Q4	21Q1	21Q2	21Q3	21Q4	22Q1	22Q2
特斯拉	ModelS/X	12230	10614	15275	18966	2030	1895	9289	11766	14724	16162
	Model3/Y	76266	80277	124318	161701	182847	199409	232102	296884	295324	238533
蔚来	ES8	195	2263	3530	4873	4516	4433	5418	5683	4341	3681
	ES6	3643	8068	8660	7574	8088	9935	11271	12180	13620	9914
	EC6			16	4906	7456	7528	7750	7171	7644	4715
	ET7									163	6749
理想	理想one	2896	6604	8660	14464	12579	17575	25116	35221	31716	28687
小鹏	P7		325	6210	8527	7974	11522	19731	21342	19427	15983
	G3i	2271	2903	2368	4437	5366	5876	5691	12788	4648	5591
	P5							244	7621	10486	12848
单车数据		20Q1	20Q2	20Q3	20Q4	21Q1	21Q2	21Q3	21Q4	22Q1	22Q2
单车收入	特斯拉（万美元/车）	5.1	4.9	5.0	4.8	4.4	4.7	4.7	4.9	5.0	5.4
	蔚来（万元/车）	32.7	33.7	35.0	35.6	36.9	36.1	35.3	36.8	35.9	/
	理想（万元/车）	29.0	29.1	28.5	28.1	27.5	27.9	29.4	29.5	29.3	29.6
	小鹏（万元/车）	16.4	16.8	22.0	21.1	21.1	20.6	21.3	19.6	20.3	20.2
单车毛利	特斯拉（万美元/车）	0.9	0.8	1.1	0.9	0.9	1.2	1.3	1.4	1.5	1.4
	蔚来（万元/车）	-2.4	3.3	5.1	6.1	7.8	7.3	6.4	7.7	6.5	/
	理想（万元/车）	2.5	4.0	5.6	4.8	4.6	5.2	6.2	6.6	6.6	6.3
	小鹏（万元/车）	-0.9	-0.9	0.6	1.4	2.1	2.3	2.9	2.1	2.1	1.8
单车R&D	特斯拉（万美元/车）	0.4	0.3	0.3	0.3	0.4	0.3	0.3	0.2	0.3	0.3
	蔚来（万元/车）	14.4	5.3	4.8	4.8	3.4	4.0	4.9	7.3	6.8	/
	理想（万元/车）	6.6	3.1	3.9	2.6	4.1	3.7	3.5	3.5	4.3	5.3
	小鹏（万元/车）	13.7	9.9	7.4	3.5	4.0	5.0	4.9	3.5	3.5	3.7
单车SG&A	特斯拉（万美元/车）	0.7	0.7	0.6	0.5	0.6	0.5	0.4	0.5	0.3	0.4
	蔚来（万元/车）	22.1	9.1	7.7	7.0	6.0	6.8	7.5	9.4	7.8	/
	理想（万元/车）	3.9	3.6	4.0	3.0	4.1	4.8	4.1	3.2	3.8	4.6
	小鹏（万元/车）	14.2	14.8	14.0	7.1	5.4	5.9	6.0	4.8	4.7	4.8
单车净利润	特斯拉（万美元/车）	0.0	0.1	0.2	0.1	0.2	0.6	0.7	0.8	1.1	0.9
	蔚来（万元/车）	-44.9	-11.7	-9.7	-8.6	-24.3	-3.0	-11.7	-8.7	-7.1	/
	理想（万元/车）	-8.1	-5.2	-3.7	0.7	-2.9	-1.3	-0.1	0.8	-0.03	-2.15
	小鹏（万元/车）	-41.2	-35.4	-23.6	-6.1	-5.9	-6.9	-6.2	-3.1	-4.9	-7.8

备注：单车收入和单车毛利采用汽车业务相关指标计算；特斯拉单车收入和单车毛利采用汽车销售业务（不含积分、租赁）相关指标计算

来源：各公司公告、浙商证券研究所

1. Quarterly financial reports. 2019 Q3 and 2020 Q3: https://ir.xiaopeng.com/static-files/fc1ce69c-0fd8-4918-a8f4-a3dc0e3cc446 . 2019 Q4 and 2020 Q4: https://ir.xiaopeng.com/static-files/e8ee5915-0007-4706-983d-e3d49917036e . 2021 Q1: https://ir.xiaopeng.com/static-files/aa459178-2519-4c3a-9659-bfb766ffa474 . 2021 Q2: https://ir.xiaopeng.com/static-files/8b791d14-f9a5-4ff2-b5aa-668583684829 . 2021 Q3: https://ir.xiaopeng.com/static-files/f58be5e4-6366-42a3-991a-440e20058fc3 . 2021 Q4: https://ir.xiaopeng.com/static-files/abeadcc0-0a0b-48bb-bd52-1b846c878f53 . 2022 Q1: https://ir.xiaopeng.com/static-files/73765847-a430-492f-9b79-7d04acc26f85 . 2022 Q2: https://ir.xiaopeng.com/static-files/fd52d251-717e-49b6-b39e-f5bb5c66b44c

2. ESG reports. 2021: https://ir.xiaopeng.com/system/files-encrypted/nasdaq_kms/assets/2022/05/25/21-12-58/2021-ESG-220524-vS-EN.pdf. 2020: https://ir.xiaopeng.com/system/files-encrypted/nasdaq_kms/assets/2022/05/02/3-54-02/XPeng-Inc.-2020-Environmental-Social-and-Governance-Report_EN.pdf
3. Annual reports. 2021: https://ir.xiaopeng.com/static-files/8707a7a3-2645-45a7-9cb4-02364ce5cf57 (2). 2020: https://ir.xiaopeng.com/static-files/c75210a2-1b8d-4a52-8a41-8190e000822c (1) . 2019: https://www.doc88.com/p-49816042298019.html

Chapter 5
Immersive Learning in Management Accounting Education:
A Prototype of Classroom-as-Organization Supported by Learning Management System and Virtual Reality

Jean-Yves Le Corre
Xian-Jiaotong Liverpool University, China

Shaozhe Xu
University of Liverpool, UK

ABSTRACT

Creating authentic learning environments that mimic real-life workplace situations encountered by accounting professionals raises several challenges for educators. This study aims to respond to those challenges by proposing a learning prototype that enlightens the benefits of the classroom-as-organization model instructional model supported by a learning management system combined with a 360° and Virtual reality immersive learning platform. The learning prototype integrates virtual reality digital content at three levels of instructional design to fully replicate a business organization's real-life context. This chapter provides an overview of the course structure and components along with guidelines for instructional design. The prototype represents an attractive alternative to business simulations and 3-D virtual worlds to create technology-enabled immersive learning experiences. Further developments would be necessary to provide instructional design methodologies that can assist educators in creating successful immersive learning experiences for management accounting education.

DOI: 10.4018/979-8-3693-1331-2.ch005

INTRODUCTION

Today's VUCA (Volatile, Uncertain, Complex, Ambiguous) environment calls for a new set of professional skills in management accounting. Social and cognitive skills are increasingly essential to a management accountant's skillset. Data analytics technologies make the production of standard reports easily automated, resulting in the value-adding role of management accountants increasingly relying on their ability to create new data insights by combining different forms of data, which is not purely a technical process but also a cognitive and social process (CGMA, 2016). Experts in management accounting education have advocated for more extensive applications of constructivist learning strategies in management accounting education to adapt to this new context. Constructivism-based learning strategies can provide essential methodological and conceptual elements in developing, understanding, and guiding the application of management accounting techniques in the contemporary VUCA context. Jakobsen et al. (2019) claimed that constructivist learning theory might not have received appropriate attention as a means for innovative teaching strategies in the field of management accounting education as compared with other disciplines and advocated for constructivism as a foundation for educating advanced students in management accounting. They argued that this would help foster more research-based teaching practices to prepare accounting students to act as business partners in business organisations. Jayasinghe (2020) conducted a study to evaluate the feasibility of implementing radical constructivism for teaching management accountant students and concluded that this could provide learners with innovative, constructive learning structures and cultures.

From the early stages of developing constructivist learning strategies, experts have claimed that using advanced digital technologies might contribute new opportunities to design and implement constructivist learning experiences. The recent progress in Information Technology and software development allows the creation of Virtual Constructivist Learning Environments (VCLEs), bringing new features and potentialities to online learning. Dabbagh et al. (2018) argued that immersive learning tools can significantly support affordances and significance in designing meaningful learning experiences. Immersive learning design can greatly benefit from developments in new applications like Learning Management Systems (LMS) and Virtual Reality (VR) for designing and implementing innovative constructivist-based learning strategies, representing the multiple affordances needed in learning to varying degrees. Integrating Virtual Reality (VR) digital content into one existing course supported by an LMS may represent an attractive alternative to instructional strategies using 2-D or 3-D virtual worlds or business simulation packages.

However, several conditions are necessary to successfully integrate virtual Reality (VR) digital content into one existing course supported by an LMS. Firstly, the overall pedagogical approach and instructional strategy should be underpinned by constructivist learning. Secondly, educators must combine the resources from VR immersive learning technology solutions with LMS-embedded tools as effectively and efficiently as possible. Thirdly, it is very likely that a progressive approach where the immersive learning experience can be developed, tested, and refined through iterative steps and multiple reviews of the learning experience must be adopted. Instructional designers and educators need to follow a number of steps, like creating scenarios and scripts of speaking, using a special camera to shoot 3-D images and 360 interactive videos, rethinking those scenarios, and creating, redesigning, restructuring, or deleting learning activities.

BACKGROUND

This chapter features a learning prototype called *MPP business simulation* developed from preparing and successively delivering one course entitled 'Business Strategy & Data Analytics' at a Sino-foreign Higher Education institution in China from 2018 until 2022. The course was delivered online, in the classroom, and in a blended format. The course emphasises the development of behavioral and cognitive skills, which are highly in demand in the management accounting profession nowadays. Participants are immersed in the company's virtual environment as if they were acting like consultants and are assigned the responsibility of proposing a strategic plan and dashboard of performance indicators for the company. A business case scenario was created featuring a fictitious company *called Mengxiang Plastics Products*, which operates in the plastics manufacturing sector. The case scenario recreates the workplace environment of this fictitious company.

MPP business simulation follows the CaO instructional model, which lays the foundations for the structure and components of the immersive learning experience while integrating various contexts where learners encounter typical workplace scenarios of creating a dashboard of performance measures. In addition, *MPP business simulation* simulates various interactions with fictitious roles to support active and collaborative learning behaviors. Thomas et al. (2020) recommended that a structure be defined for CaO instructional design, including collaborative team-based or group-based learning activities, designing the learning process through authentic, inquiry-based activities for learners to access content, share ideas, and revisit their thinking. Students, teachers, and the community engage in collaborative activities to solve the driving question, mirroring the complex social situation of expert problem-solving. While engaged in the inquiry process, students are scaffolded, which helps them participate in activities usually beyond their ability (potentially with learning technologies). Students are expected to not only collect resources, organize work, and manage long-term activities but also collaborate, design, revise, and share their ideas and experiences with authentic audiences and supportive peer groups in the classroom in the organisation's context.

CaO provides a valuable framework for designing immersive learning experiences that replicate real-life contexts and situations encountered by management accountants in business organizations. According to Thomas et al. (2020), CaO is a learning approach capable of creating genuine organizational issues for learners and immersing them into the position of a corporate member who must deal with organizational problems. In the CaO instructional model, learners must face and solve an issue faced by the organisation and prepare for a solution. According to Thomas et al. (2020), the purpose of CaO is 'not to simulate an organization, but rather to create genuine organizational issues for students, to put them in the position of an organizational member who must deal with such problems as: how does work get allocated; how does one work with others who bring different expertise to tasks; how does one influence and motivate subordinates, peers, and superiors; how does one cope with ambiguity in solving difficult tasks which do not have any correct single answer; how can disagreements among coworkers be resolved; and how will decisions be made' *(p. 4)*

EMBRACING DIGITAL LEARNING TECHNOLOGIES

Numerous studies have highlighted the benefits of Information Technology and Communication Tools (ICTs) for constructivist learning. Al-Huneidi et al. (2011) argued that combining constructivism and conversation theories in blended learning environments can enhance learning performance. Ahmad and Schreurs (2012) proposed a model of constructivist learning in a blended environment where ICTs can be used to increase the level of communication and interaction between students. Singh (2019) argued that interaction and collaboration between learners should be supported by information and communication technologies (ICTs) to be more effective. Tóth & Bessenyei (2008) argued that Moodle, a widely used LMS in Higher Education, can advantageously embrace a social-constructivist approach and efficiently support problem-solving and knowledge construction. Some other studies have investigated the role of online discussion forums in creating favourable conditions for learners to resolve socio-cognitive conflicts (Rivera et al., 2023).

Regarding immersive learning technologies, Alves (2017) evidenced that using a virtual learning environment positively affects students' performance in the context of constructivist learning. Dabbagh et al. (2018) categorised digital learning tools in their affordances and significance to the design of immersive learning experiences. To varying degrees, those external tools represent the multiple affordances needed in immersive learning experiences. For example, for collaboration and communication tools, those affordances may include multiple modes of communication, multiple modes in terms of timing, formal and informal channels of communication, or shared access to collaborative artefacts.

The advancement of combining VR immersive technologies and LMSs brings greater potential and opportunities while learners switch from place to place, mimicking a continuous tour experience in real life. Using an application programming interface, X-API, to create immersive learning experiences that combine the resources of an LMS and Virtual Reality platform opens the door to other possibilities by allowing illimited data storage and using advanced features such as voice recognition. For example, X-API is an option to exchange data between various systems, applications, and websites, where a client entity (a course, app, simulation, etc.), also called an Activity Provider, generates X-API statements and a Learning Record Store (LRS) endpoint receives statements and stores them in a database.

It is commonly recognised that, in the field of management accounting education, immersive learning is still in its infancy, being mostly confined to games-based learning practices (Silva, 2021). Indeed, several questions must be addressed to ensure the benefits of combining resources from both LMS and Virtual Reality (VR) technology solutions to create immersive learning experiences. How effective is the process to integrate existing learning activities? Which new types of learning activities supported by VR immersive technology solutions should be considered? How efficient is designing, customizing, and integrating VR digital content (full-size 3D models, interactive 360° images, and 360° photos) into the learning experience?

INSTRUCTIONAL DESIGN

Existing literature suggests that one reason for the limited implementation of immersive virtual environment applications is a lack of recommendations for their practical design (Tycho, 2021). The instructional design of *MPP business simulation* was investigated in several case studies conducted from 2018-2022 using a learning prototype, which led to formulating recommendations and guidelines for instructional goals for successfully designing and implementing VCLEs in an LMS (Moodle) to support cognitive learning, situated learning, or collaborative learning in the learning experience. Those studies contributed to improving instructional design through action research, investigating a causality model to predict learners' behavioral intentions, exploring psychological determinants as research constructs of learners' behaviors towards socio-cognitive conflicts, as well as developing a methodology roadmap for designing and implementing immersive learning experiences using Virtual Real-life-based Organizational Contexts (VROCs). Those case studies used explanatory sequential mixed-method research, including scenario-based experiments (quasi-experimental design) to investigate the behavioral intentions of learners. *MPP business simulation* gradually improved through continuous improvements while embracing new technological developments in digital learning technologies. In its final development phase, *MPP business simulation* was supported by a VR immersive technology platform commercialised by a software company that allows to get started in immersive learning quickly.

Table 1. summarizes the structure of the *MPP business simulation* learning prototype in its final development phase. Activities in the LMS (Moodle) are either synchronous or asynchronous. All activities in the VR immersive learning platform are supposed to be real-time synchronous, with several activities available on an asynchronous basis in the LMS if learners like to retake them. External digital learning tools could be taken from the LMS or VR immersive platforms. Several functions, like peer assessment, forum discussions, or knowledge-sharing databases, are embedded in the LMS and can serve to coordinate sequential learning activities or multitasking in the VR platform. Combining asynchronous and synchronous learning activities or dividing problems into sub-problems where learners perform only one task at a time helps create immersive learning environments for learners. LMSs also provide several types of Information and Communication tools (ICT). Virtual meeting rooms are useful to support interactions between students and groups of students or external participants. LMSs also provide peer-review assessment tools where documents can be more easily processed, monitored, and recorded in a Learning Management System, for example, *Workshop* in Moodle. External Digital Tools, besides those provided by LMS and VR platforms, might also be necessary to design immersive learning environments.

MPP business simulation is supported by a virtual reality immersive platform (Uptale) where the digital environments are generated. 3-D images and videos are imported and integrated to create an immersive learning experience and virtual(work) space by adding features to the space such as an information text plane, 2-D images/videos, voice guide, navigation arrows as well as other interactive buttons. Those features are essential to provide an understandable organizational context and background demonstration for students. The immersive learning platform also supports the complete virtual simulation of a learning space, which requires dynamic navigation, messages, and actions that can be triggered by clicking or timeouts. A door-type switching button can be added to the virtual space to inform and guide learners to switch from place to place, mimicking a continuous tour experience in real life. Fictitious roles like the CEO of MPP company are reproduced in interactive videos where the CEO, for example, can introduce the different phases and lead students from the first perspective into the next place. The switching buttons to enter different online breakout rooms in *Big Blue Button* can be inserted into the virtual space for synchronous communications, including project team meetings, department meetings, and group discussions. The integration of VR digital content and the LMS is facilitated by weblinks or QR codes that can be inserted into the course page in the LMS to showcase immersive, real-time interactive and comprehensive experiences.

In summary, instructional design goals can be categorised at three levels of instructional design (learning environment, learning process, and performance tasks)

1. Learning environment, defined as the combination of locations and various forms of interactions to create contexts and cultures where learners are immersed.
2. Learning process, defined as a series of structured and coordinated learning and assessment (formative and summative) activities in situated scenarios.
3. Performance tasks, defined as tasks that require students to perform to demonstrate their understanding, competency, and knowledge.

Table 1. MPP business simulation: Instructional goals

	LMS	**VR Immersive Learning Platform**	**Digital learning tools**
Learning Environment	Case scenario External information (market, stakeholders) Roles (internal/external) Peer-reviews for preparation	Virtual space Social context Social presence	Library resources Internet resources
Learning Process	Summative assessments Formative assessments Access to external data and information Teacher's presence Virtual meeting rooms	Scenario-based situations Magic tags Triggering events Pre-recorded lectures Time management Cognitive presence	Knowledge representation tools Collaborative Learning Tools Online questionnaires
Performance Tasks	Discussion Forums Questionnaires	Self-reflection questionnaires	Slides Presentations Data Analytics Dashboard

LEARNING PROTOTYPE

Table 1. provides an overview of the structure and main components of the '*MPP business simulation*' learning prototype supported by a Learning Management System (Moodle) and a VR immersive learning technology solution (Uptale) to support innovative solutions for management accounting education.

Learning Environment

Overview

MPP business simulation learning experience comprises three main phases: a preparation phase, a phase of familiarisation with the digital learning environment (*MPP Factory visits*), and a more extensive phase where learners complete their project (*Strategy Away Week*). During the completion of *MPP Factory visits*, learners familiarise themselves with the working environments of the company and start interacting with others or with fictitious roles such as the CEO office or fictitious members of the departments of the MPP company. During the completion of *Strategy Away Week*, groups of learners (*MPP Project Teams*) undertake the primary three phases to prepare a business case in the form of an authentic assessment. *Strategy Away Week features* the environment of a fictitious university where learners prepare for the three main components of their business case as indicated below:

1. Project Teams prepare a keynote speech to communicate their strategy and vision for the company and convince the senior management team; the keynote speech should be recorded and submitted as a video file.
2. Project Teams propose performance indicators to implement and monitor the strategy from different categories of performance indicators in alignment with principles of strategic management accounting.
3. Project Teams produce a simple version of their performance dashboard using data analytics software to showcase the dashboard (*Analytics dashboard*) as a digital artefact.

Authentic Learning Environment

Figure 1. below describes the project phases in the authentic learning environment for learners. *MPP business simulation* learning prototype recreates the organisational context of a business organization where learners construct performance measures by interacting with each other, communicating values with others, understanding facts, reflecting on possibilities, and making decisions on their values and desires. It promotes collaborative learning and deepens teammates' rapport, underscoring its significance in fostering a dynamic and autonomous learning environment. Project teams must submit and present their business case to a fictitious Board of Directors. The business case can be divided into three phases described above and represents the three summative assessment components in the MPP business simulation. Immersive situations are created through virtual open spaces where learners enter different web conference meeting rooms (*Big Blue Button*), which can be accessed directly via the VR immersive platform while configuring within the LMS (*Moodle*).

Figure 1. MPP business simulation: Project phases

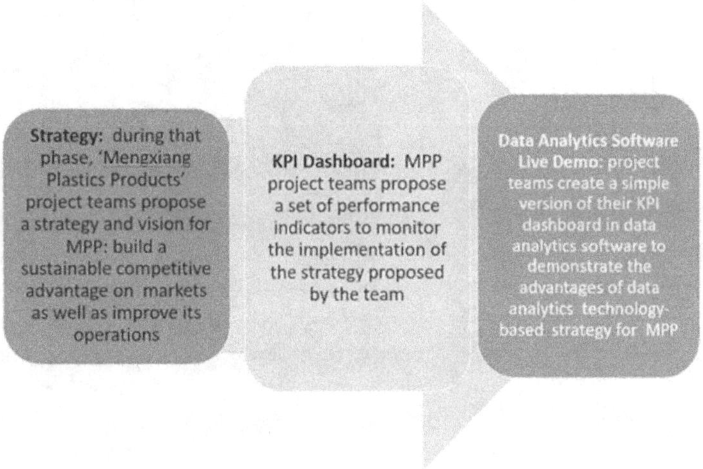

Learner Interaction Methods

During the completion of *MPP Factory visits*, familiarisation with the learning environment is facilitated by quiz questionnaires, where choosing correct answers becomes a prerequisite for proceeding to the following scenarios: for example, being required to pass the quiz in a limited time in a particular circumstance such as selecting the correct number of production lines of the factory when visiting the Production Department of the company, or prioritising a ranking for the four types of competitive advantages for plastic bags when visiting the Research & Development Department. In this way, learners' comprehension level regarding course materials, data files, and organizational infrastructures is evaluated and instructed simultaneously. In addition to quizzes, students can also interact with the learning environment, for example, selecting items from an extrusion machine in the factory site to learn about its usage or picking up a phone call from the marketing manager of the fictitious company. Figure 2. below provides an example of a scenario where learners are enquired about their knowledge of the workplace environment of the company.

In addition, materials are provided in one section of the course page in the LMS (*Library Resource*) about generic topics that participants might decide to use if necessary to revise or upgrade their basic knowledge of theories, concepts, methods, and techniques they will need to apply in the preparation of their business case for the company.

Figure 2. MPP factory visit: Virtual tour

Learning Activities

Learning activities represent authentic activities taking place in the organizational environment of the fictitious organization, like meeting with the accounting department to collect data or gathering data from external sources. *MPP business simulation* features several learning activities for social collaboration and negotiation. Online discussions, collaborative project work, and presentations are essential. For example, learners can enter the mentor room to get supporting advice and the conference hall to attend seminars from business experts. This simulates an authentic seminar classroom, as illustrated in Fig.3 below.

Figure 3. Lectures and expert seminars

Synchronous and Asynchronous Activities

As the learning environment needs to be informal and complex to reflect real-life organizational contexts, it is wise to think about learning activities as a 'mix' of relatively unstructured activities, allowing learners to navigate between them, for example, by mixing real-time synchronous with asynchronous activities that can be performed at any time. Creating a more informal learning environment may also facilitate scaffolding and opportunities for triggering events.

- Synchronous (real-time) activities involve the simultaneous engagement of students and company staff, physically or digitally, coalescing in the same time and space. On the first day of *Strategy Away Week*, students must participate in project team meetings in virtual rooms, facilitating team bonding, data gathering, and mutual knowledge exchange. The VR immersive learning platform can generate entrances in virtual spaces to online breakout rooms to achieve synchronous communications. Learners can discuss their plan for a business solution they would like to propose to the company's management. On the second day of *Strategy Away Week*, students start attending meetings with members of the company departments to develop and share knowledge about the company's operations. This facilitates interactions, enhances efficiency, and enriches the learning experience.
- Asynchronous learning activities aim to increase student engagement as these learning activities are perceived as more voluntary and impressive to the students, which tends to achieve better learning results. Those activities are integrated clearly and comprehensively through the LMS and coordinated with other learning activities completed in the virtual environment via the VR immersive learning platform. As a pivotal component of learning activities, asynchronous activities guarantee flexibility, letting students get access at their own pace and work through multiple iterations as they wish. For example, students can replay the lectures and seminars attended during the *Strategy Away Week* asynchronously. Also, interactions with the CEO and CFO offices cannot be supported on a real-time basis in the VR immersive learning platform but made possible by using asynchronous discussion forums in the LMS. This also includes online forum discussions where students are invited to engage and receive advice from mentors. Figure 4. below provides an example of the scene allowing learners to enter the virtual rooms.

Social Context-Based Activities

In immersive learning, the lack of "real" interpersonal connections makes students feel isolated and disengaged (Patel, 2021). Building a social context is also essential to bring learners a happy and helpful experience in the immersive learning environment. Students must be immersed in that social context to ensure an authentic learning environment. The social context should be supported by collaborative learning activities where learners work in groups and interact with each other and with external participants. Those learning activities should allow learners to negotiate, confront opinions, and make decisions to solve complex problems. The social context might also involve co-curricular activities like community work, practicums, internships, and fieldwork studies potentially organized with industry partners. Third-party organisations may engage in various learning activities with learners, including review panels for feedback or mentoring, using email communication or discussion forums. Figure 6. gives an example of interactive videos to support the social context created for learners.

The real-time synchronous activities involve the simultaneous engagement of learners and company fictitious staff members, physically or digitally, coalescing simultaneously and in space. The VR immersive learning platform can generate entrances in virtual spaces to online breakout rooms to achieve synchronous communications. For example, *Social Room is* a virtual space where all participants can join online gatherings while completing the learning experience. Mentors may also participate in events in the Social Room.

Figure 4. Department meeting virtual space

Figure 5. Interactive 360 video

Storytelling

On the first day of *Strategy Away Week*, students participate in project team meetings in virtual rooms, facilitating team bonding, data gathering, and mutual knowledge exchange. Students discuss the business solution, including a proposal for a strategic plan and a dashboard of performance indicators. After the foreshadowing of the discussion and meeting learning activities, project teams are invited to submit their preferences for which department they would like to meet for group discussions. Project teams should submit the *MPP Meeting Request for Discussion* form via the *CEO forum discussions*. During those group discussions, each project team meets with one or two departments of the company for around 15 minutes. The objective of those group discussions is for each project team to receive feedback and seek collaboration from the departments to prepare their business case, discuss and negotiate uncertainties, and make agreements on resolving areas of uncertainties in the project team's business case proposal. For example, suppose the project team decides some market data forecast on the targeted market segment is unavailable. In that case, the project team should explain its assumptions and seek feedback from the department or identify actions to help reduce the uncertainty of assumptions made by the project team.

On the second day of *Strategy Away Week*, students attend the department meetings to complete several tasks to support project teams collaboratively. Each department meeting will have detailed instructions and guidelines given to participants. The department's role is to support project teams in collecting and disseminating information in their respective fields of competencies. *MPP Knowledge Platform* provided in the LMS is a collaborative space where all the company's departments can share general information about the internal and external environment in the plastics manufacturing industry (for example, current trends and competition landscape, key competencies, technologies....). In each phase of the *MPP business simulation*, departments will be invited to share content on the Intranet Page with all project teams. In doing this, departments do not have to respond to specific requests from project teams but should provide them with new insights to explore possibilities for their business case.

Feedback Mechanisms

It is necessary to distinguish between formative and summative types of assessment, where summative assessments are evaluations of what someone has learned throughout a course. In contrast, formative assessments evaluate someone's learning progress in a classroom. Alves et al. (2019) argued that authentic assessment needs to contain assessment tasks that authentic assessment promotes self-regulation of learning, i.e., resolving problems through concrete experience, collaborative discourse, and reflection. Designing for learning using VROCs requires authentic assessment forms to evaluate whether students can successfully transfer knowledge and skills gained in the classroom to various contexts, scenarios, and situations. Authentic assessments in the organisational environment should focus on learning, perception, and problem-solving and embed social elements as an essential part of the assessments. Assessment must become an integrated, ongoing, seamless part of the learning environment and provide important feedback to both teachers and students. It should be complex and require authentic consent or prior knowledge and integrating knowledge from multiple areas (Wachira et al., 2015).

Including feedback sessions as a learning activity is indispensable as they provide participants with deeper insights into their progress and opportunities to seek advice and clarification. During feedback sessions, participants can discuss and plan progress in building their business case. They interact with fictitious roles like CEO *Office Assistants* to ask for advice on difficulties they may face, enquire for feedback, and receive explanations on how to conduct learning activities. Feedback mechanisms are supported by several fictitious roles, as explained below:

1. Departments have a role in reviewing the data requests submitted by project teams to discuss and communicate their response to the request.
2. *MPP CEO Office* has a role in supporting project teams to monitor their progress in preparing their business case. Project teams interact with the CEO's Office through asynchronous forum discussions supported by the LMS.
3. *MPP CFO Office* has a role to assist project teams in their need for information and data necessary for their business case. Project teams interact with the CEO Office through asynchronous forum discussions supported by the LMS.

Forum discussion allows learners to engage and discuss online to get answers to their questions or corresponding feedback. Interactions with fictitious roles like *MPP CEO Office* or *MPP CFO Office* cannot be supported in real-time in the VR platform via avatars but are made possible by using discussion forums in the LMS on an asynchronous basis. Those activities aim to facilitate feedback and advice to project teams along the different preparation steps of their business case. Correspondingly, the objective of feedback sessions is to facilitate the process of data requests in *MPP business simulation.* Figure 6 gives an example of an interaction that can initiate reflection and seek feedback behaviors from the learners.

Figure 6. MPP business simulation: Virtual tour

Performance Tasks

Expert Seminars

Expert seminars introduce essential theories, concepts, methods, and techniques that participants may decide to apply (or 'think over') in preparing their business case for the company. Expert Seminars will address essential issues in contemporary strategic management, management innovation, and digitalisation.

Direct Instruction

Cheng (2014) argued that learning activities involving interactions should be analysed using instructional scripts that contain theoretical and empirical underpinnings of cognitive learning theories. Internal and external scripts are essential, considering that simply assigning group tasks may not be sufficient and that clear guidance and scaffolding techniques need to be provided to learners (Weinberger et al., 2005). Those scripts can be used to specify and sequence learning tasks, specify, and sequence learners' interactions to facilitate collaborative learning and knowledge construction (Weinberger et al., 2005). Socio-cognitive conflicts are beneficial for learning to the extent that conflict is regulated. Instructional designers may rely on instructional models at the activity level to design performance tasks to create conditions in immersive situations to ensure that learning outcomes are met, e.g., that confronting diverging ideas results in positive outcomes.

In *MPP business simulation*, instructional scripts at the performance tasks level are necessary for students to learn from one another in groups and for communication to be productive. They provide detailed instructions to learners when participating in meetings or interactive sessions to ensure clarity in the performance tasks. Figure 7. gives an example of an interaction that can trigger direct instruction.

Figure 7. Interaction with specific objectives

SITUATED COGNITION

Scholars in situated cognition have examined the effects of situated learning on knowledge acquisition and evidenced that learning in situated environments makes knowledge transfer more efficient and facilitates the acquisition of transferable knowledge in real-life contexts. The core assumption of situated cognition is that learning inherently ties to the social and cultural contexts in which it occurs. A critical assumption of situated cognition theory is that learning cannot be abstracted from the situations in which it is learned and merely be transferred or applied. Zheng (2010) compared learning performance between situated and traditional learning and found a positive correlation between situated learning and learner performance.

Immersive tools are widely recognised for offering the potential for fully immersive environments that can enhance learners' cognitive development. In the field of management accounting education, immersion in a reality-based environment, engagement with complex and ambiguous situations and information, and interaction with space can significantly enhance situated cognition. Townley et al. (2003) argued that performance measurement should embed twin dimensions of rationalization in the pursuit of reason in human affairs, that is, the process of bringing to light the justifications by which actions and policies are pursued and rationalization for dominance of a means–end instrumental rationality. Similarly, several other experts in managerial control theory argued that any Managerial Control System (MCS) is dominated by rationalities that can be collectively described as either 'instrumental rationality' or 'communicative rationality' (Broadbent & Laughlin, 2009). The construction of MCSs `should embed socially constructed but inherently connected opposite dimensions as part of the same rationalization process. The interplay between two dimensions of rationalisation is important to the organizational dynamics of individuals' responses to MCS design as a continuous process for organizational change (Townley et al, 2003).

In *MPP business simulation*, learners prepare for a dashboard of performance indicators by encountering a series of situated scenarios supported by the VR immersive learning platform to enhance learners' cognitive development. Cognitive learning in *MPP business simulation* is related to learners' behavioral intentions in response to socio-cognitive conflicts encountered when learners interact in groups during knowledge construction. Participants are invited to answer questionnaires on their behavioral intentions before interacting in meetings with other participants and reflecting on their behavioral learning styles. They are also invited to receive feedback and guidance from mentors to assist and give advice on preparing for meetings. This aims to help significantly enhance learners' cognition in knowledge construction of performance measures as explained above.

Situated cognition represents another challenge for instructional designers and educators because it requires balancing what is known and what is currently being experienced (the incoming information and new knowledge) along the learning process of 'cognitive regulation'. Darnon (2019) argued that socio-cognitive conflicts benefit learning because conflict is regulated through specific mechanisms to ensure that the conditions under which confronting diverging ideas results in positive cognitive and relational outcomes are met. Conflict regulation is defined as the meaning people attribute to conflict when facing another's idea that contradicts their own, which determines the conditions under which confronting diverging ideas results in positive cognitive and relational outcomes (Darnon, 2019). Truhlar (2018) investigated the factors that influence students' engagement in synchronous online discussions and found that assigning roles increases the proportion of critical student–student interactions. Existing literature on socio-cognitive conflicts suggests that learners demonstrate various types of behavioral intentions in response to socio-cognitive conflicts when learners interact in groups to construct organizational performance measures (Cheng, 2014).

RESEARCH AVENUES

The *MPP business simulation* learning prototype advances the field of instructional design by helping to formulate strategies, methodologies, and tools vital for the success of both immersive educational environments based on CaO instructional model. Several scholars like Tycho (2021) acknowledged a dearth of practical guidelines for learning design in immersive environments: '*MPP business simulation*' learning prototype attempts to bridge this gap. The pedagogical approach employs a multi-faceted viewpoint encompassing the learning environment, processes, tasks, socio-cognitive, technological aspects, and learning design. Our insights augment existing literature, particularly emphasising educational models tailored to managerial accounting. However, a more nuanced instructional design framework for creating and deploying immersive learning experiences using VROCs still requires further exploration. We encourage educators passionate about practice-based educational research in this realm to take up this mantle. More effort would be necessary to advance the development of instructional strategies and methodologies that ensure the efficacy of immersive learning environments, particularly for learning and teaching in managerial control and management accounting.

CONCLUSION

Instructional designers and educators in management accounting and controlling may find it difficult to find practical methodologies or frameworks for designing and implementing successful immersive learning experiences. This chapter contributes to instructional strategies and methodologies for designing and implementing successful immersive learning environments for managerial control and management accounting education in response to the need for clear instructional design goals and suitable instructional design frameworks or guidelines. It will provide useful guidelines to address several critical dimensions of instructional design frameworks for managerial accounting and controlling education. This will ensure educators are well prepared to design and implement successful learning experiences most effectively and efficiently. *MPP business simulation* learning prototype is a valuable tool for creating a successful immersive learning experience supported by an LMS combined with a VR immersive learning technology solution.

ACKNOWLEDGMENT

The authors would like to acknowledge the contribution of the Uptale Inc. company, which kindly offered the researchers the use of the Uptale immersive learning platform for the purpose of this study.

REFERENCES

Al-Huneidi, A. M., & Schreurs, J. (2011). Constructivism Based Blended Learning in Higher Education. [iJET]. *International Journal of Emerging Technologies in Learning*.

Alves, P., Miranda, L., & Morais, C. (2017). The Influence of Virtual Learning Environments in Students' Performance, *Universal. The Journal of Educational Research*, *5*(3), 517–527.

Broadbent, J., & Laughlin, R. (2009). Performance Management Systems: A conceptual model. *Management Accounting Research*, *20*(4), 283–295. doi:10.1016/j.mar.2009.07.004

Butera, F., Sommet, N., & Darnon, C. (2019). Sociocognitive Conflict Regulation: How to Make Sense of Diverging Ideas. *Current Directions in Psychological Science*, *28*(2), 145–151. doi:10.1177/0963721418813986

CGMA. (2016). *Business Analytics and Decision Making? The human dimension*. CGMA. www.cgma.org/resources/reports/business-analytics-and-decision-making.html

Cheng, S. C. (2014). *Effects of Socio-Cognitive Conflicts on Group Cognition and Group Performance*. [Unpublished doctoral dissertation, Harvard Graduate School of Education].

Dabbagh, N., Marra, R. M., & Howland, J. L. (2018). *Meaningful Online Learning: Integrating Strategies, Activities, and Learning Technologies for Effective Designs* (1st ed.). Routledge. doi:10.4324/9781315528458

Jakobsen, M., Mitchell, F., Nørreklit, H., & Trenca, M. (2019). Educating Management Accountants as Business Partners. *Qualitative Research in Accounting & Management*, *16*(4), 517–541. doi:10.1108/QRAM-10-2017-0099

Jayasinghe, K. (2021). Constructing constructivism in management accounting education: Reflections from a teaching cycle with innovative learning elements. *Qualitative Research in Accounting & Management*, *18*(2), 282–309. doi:10.1108/QRAM-05-2020-0067

Patel, N. S. (2021). Establishing Social Presence for an Engaging Online Teaching and Learning Experience. *International Journal of TESOL Studies*, *3*(1), 162–178.

Rivera, D. A., Frenay, M., & Swaen, V. (2023). The Learning Design of MOOC Discussion Forums: An Analysis of Forum Instructions and Their Role in Supporting the Social Construction of Knowledge. *Technology, Knowledge, and Learning*.

Silva, R., Rodrigues, R., & Leal, C. (2021). Games-based learning in accounting education – which dimensions are the most relevant? *Accounting Education, 30*(2), 159–187. doi:10.1080/09639284.2021.1891107

Singh, V., & Thurman, A. (2019). How Many Ways Can We Define Online Learning? A Systematic Literature Review of Definitions of Online Learning (1988–2018). *American Journal of Distance Education, 33*(4), 289–306. doi:10.1080/08923647.2019.1663082

Thomas, D. R., Chappell, S. F., & Bright, D. S. (2020). *Classroom as Organization.* Edward Elgar Publishing. doi:10.4337/9781788979856

Townley, B., Cooper, D. J., & Oakes, L. (2003). Performance Measures and the Rationalization of Organizations. *Organization Studies, 24*(7), 1045–1071. doi:10.1177/01708406030247003

Truhlar, A. M., Williams, K. M., & Walter, M. T. (2018). Case study: Student engagement with course content and peers in synchronous online discussions. *Online Learning : the Official Journal of the Online Learning Consortium, 22*(4), 289–312.

Tycho, T., De Back, A., Tinga, M., & Louwerse, M. (2021). Learning in immersed collaborative virtual environments: Design and implementation. *Interactive Learning Environments, 31*(1), 1–19.

Wachira, M. (2018). Constructionism in Accounting Research: An Investigative Tool for Corporate Social Disclosure Practices'. *European Journal of Business and Management, 10*, 10.

Weinberger, A., Ertl, B., Fischer, F., & Mandl, H. (2005). Epistemic and social scripts in computer-supported collaborative learning. *Instructional Science, 33*(1), 1–30. doi:10.1007/s11251-004-2322-4

Zheng, R. (2010). Effects of situated learning on students' knowledge acquisition: An individual differences perspective. *Journal of Educational Computing Research, 43*(4), 467–487. doi:10.2190/EC.43.4.c

Tóth, Z., Bessenyei, I. (2008). *Moodle and social constructivism.* NETIS textbook

KEY TERMS AND DEFINITIONS

CaO: Classroom-as-Organization - This instructional model treats the classroom as an organization, enhancing real-world relevance and applicability.

LMS: Learning Management System - A software application for the administration, documentation, tracking, reporting, automation, and delivery of educational courses, training programs, or learning and development programs.

VCLE: Virtual Constructivist Learning Environment - A learning environment that is based on constructivist pedagogy and is virtual or digital.

VR: Virtual Reality, a computer created environment.

VROC: Virtual (real-life based) organizational contexts – A learning environment that mimics the real business environment.

Chapter 6
Decentralized Finance (DeFi) and Blockchain Technology in Healthcare:
A Promising Confluence for Enhanced Security, Data Interoperability, and Patient

Jaspreet Kaur
Chandigarh University, India

ABSTRACT

The chapter examines how block chain technology can revolutionize pharmaceutical supply chain management. Through real-time tracking and traceability, the authenticity of medications can be ensured, thereby combating the persistent issue of counterfeit drugs and enhancing patient safety. Additionally, the clinical trial process stands to benefit from block chain and transparent and secure nature. Smart contracts can streamline patient recruitment, informed consent, and trial result reporting, promoting trust and accountability in the clinical trial ecosystem. Despite the potential benefits, the adoption of DeFi and block chain in healthcare presents several challenges, including regulatory compliance, scalability, and integration with existing healthcare systems. This chapter discusses the current state of block chain integration in healthcare and identifies future research directions to overcome these hurdles.

1. INTRODUCTION

Decentralized Finance (DeFi) and block chain technology are two groundbreaking innovations that have the potential to revolutionize traditional financial systems and various industries, including healthcare. Each concept brings distinct advantages and challenges to the table. This chapter aims to explore the convergence of DeFi and block chain technology in the healthcare sector, focusing on the potential benefits of enhanced security, data interoperability, and patient-

DOI: 10.4018/979-8-3693-1331-2.ch006

centric solutions [Gramlich, 2023; Zhou, 2023; Wronka, 2023]. DeFi refers to a decentralized ecosystem of financial applications and services built on block chain technology, predominantly Ethereum [Auer, 2023; Pineiro-Chousa, 2023; Kitzler, 2023; Wieandt & Heppding, 2023; Far, 2023]. It leverages smart contracts to create trust less, automated, and peer-to-peer financial transactions without the need for intermediaries like banks or brokers. Key elements of DeFi include lending and borrowing platforms, decentralized exchanges (DEXs), stablecoins, yield farming, and liquidity provision [Ozili, 2023].

Figure 1. Advantages of DeFi
Source: Ozili (2023)

Accessibility
DeFi platforms are accessible to anyone with an internet connection, enabling broader financial inclusion.

Global Reach
DeFi operates without borders, making it possible for individuals worldwide to participate in financial activities.

Transparency
All transactions and activities on DeFi platforms are recorded on a public block chain, ensuring transparency and auditability.

Elimination of Intermediaries
DeFi eliminates the need for intermediaries, reducing fees, enhancing efficiency, and minimizing counterparty risk.

Figure 2. Challenges of DeFi
Source: Kitzler (2023)

Security Vulnerabilities:
Smart contract vulnerabilities can lead to hacking incidents and financial losses.

Regulatory Uncertainty:
The decentralized nature of DeFi challenges traditional regulatory frameworks, leading to legal ambiguities.

Scalability:
Congestion on block chain networks can lead to slow transaction speeds and high fees during peak usage.

User Experience:
The complex nature of DeFi platforms can be intimidating for newcomers, hindering mass adoption.

Figure 3. Advantages of block chain technology
Source: Wieandt & Heppding (2023).

Investment Requirements for the AI Era Market Opportunity	Competitive Advantage	Operational Efficiency	Team Experience
Data Monetization	Proven Traction	Innovation in Technology	Scalability

Figure 4. Challenges of block chain technology
Source: Far et al. (2023)

Scalability	Data Privacy	Energy Consumption	Regulatory Compliance
• Some block chains struggle with scalability issues, leading to slower transaction processing.	• Striking a balance between data transparency and privacy, especially in sensitive sectors like healthcare, is challenging.	• Proof of Work block chains can have high energy requirements, leading to environmental concerns.	• Integrating block chain solutions with existing regulatory frameworks can be complex.

The healthcare sector stands to benefit significantly from the convergence of DeFi and block chain technology. Block chain's security features can protect patient data from breaches, ensure interoperability among diverse healthcare systems, and empower patients with control over their medical information. DeFi principles can be leveraged for patient financing, insurance, and innovative funding mechanisms for medical research [Kaur, 2023; Han et al., 2023]. Addressing the long-standing issues facing the industry is the driving force behind investigating the convergence of DeFi and block chain technologies in healthcare. These issues include patients' restricted control over their health data, data security breaches, and a lack of interoperability amongst healthcare systems. The healthcare industry may transition to a more patient-centric, safe, and connected environment by fusing the security and transparency of block chain with the accessibility and effectiveness of DeFi [Han et al., 2023; Jensen, 2021; Werner, 2022; Zetzsche et al.,2020]. Block chain technology has a wide range of applications in healthcare, offering significant potential to enhance data security, interoperability, and patient-centred care [Wenhua et al., 2023]. Figure 5 depicts text-based representation of how block chain technology can be applied in healthcare and can make a transformative impact:

Figure 5. Application of block chain technology in healthcare
Source: Meisami et al. (2023)

```
Identify Use Case
|
Determine Data Sharing Needs
|
Choose Blockchain Type:
|---- Public, Private, Consortium
|
Design Blockchain Network
|---- Nodes, Consensus Mechanism
|
Develop Smart Contracts
|---- Define Rules, Logic
|
Implement Blockchain in Healthcare
|---- Data Storage and Transactions
|
Data Security & Privacy
|---- Encryption, Decentralization
|
Improve Interoperability
|---- Health Information Exchange
|
Enhance Clinical Trials
|---- Data Integrity, Transparency
|
Strengthen Supply Chain
|---- Authenticity Verification
|
Secure Telemedicine
|---- Encrypted Data Exchange
|
Facilitate Insurance
|---- Claims Processing, Fraud Prevention
|
Monitor and Update
|---- Continuous Improvement
```

Block chain technology has the potential to completely change how electronic health records are handled. Authorised parties can securely keep and access patient data, including medical history, medications, test results, and treatment plans. With the help of smart contracts and cryptographic keys, patients may manage consent and restrict access to their records, protecting the privacy of their data. This strategy improves data security and gives individuals the ability to actively manage their health data [Wu et al., 2023; Zhang et al., 2023].

The use of blockchain to trace and verify the provenance, calibre, and distribution of medicines, medical equipment, and supplies. This increases the overall security and effectiveness of the healthcare supply chain, ensures the validity of medical equipment, and aids in preventing the entry of fake medications onto the market. A safe and uncheckable platform for storing telemedicine and remote patient monitoring data can be provided via block chains. In order to facilitate remote consultations, diagnoses, and therapy modifications while protecting patient privacy, patients can securely communicate real-time health data with healthcare professionals [Meisami et al., 2023]. By providing a transparent and auditable record of patient interactions with insurers, block chains help expedite the health insurance process. Smart contracts can automate the processing of claims, lowering administrative costs, cutting down on fraud, and increasing the accuracy of claim reimbursement [Fayard et al., 2012; Wenhua et al., 2023].

Block chain's inherent features, including immutability and cryptographic security, play a vital role in safeguarding sensitive patient data and preventing unauthorized access in healthcare settings as depicted in figure 6. These features combine to create a robust and secure environment for storing and managing patient information [Shrestha et al.,2020]. Immutability refers to the inability to alter or delete data once it's recorded on the block chain. This characteristic is fundamental for maintaining the integrity of patient data and preventing unauthorized modifications. When patient data is added to the block chain, it becomes a permanent part of the ledger, and any subsequent changes are recorded as new transactions. This prevents unauthorized tampering with health records and maintains a transparent and verifiable history of data modifications. Block chain employs cryptographic techniques to enhance the security of patient data in several ways as depicted in figure 6 and 7:

Figure 6. Cryptographic security in healthcare
Source: Wang (2021)

Data Encryption	Access Control	Digital Signatures
• A block chain can be used to hold encrypted patient data. With encryption, you can make sure that even if someone gets access to your data without your permission, they won't be able to decipher it without the right decryption keys.	• Access to patient data can be restricted using cryptographic keys. The data can only be decrypted and accessed by people who have the proper cryptographic keys. This restricts access to authorised staff and makes it harder for unauthorised users to access critical data.	• Digital signatures, which are cryptographic tools that guarantee data integrity and offer confirmation of the sender's identity, can be used to sign transactions on the block chain. By doing this, unauthorised individuals are prevented from acting as legitimate users and from making unauthorised changes.

Data is dispersed over a network of nodes rather than being stored in a single, centralised location because block chain operates in a decentralised fashion. Because of this decentralisation, there is a lower chance of a single point of failure and it is harder for bad actors to undermine the entire system. Multiple organisations, including hospitals, clinics, and patients, work together to ensure the data's integrity in a decentralised healthcare block chain. Block chain networks employ consensus procedures to verify and concur on the ledger's current state. Network participants must agree that the transaction is genuine before data is added to the block chain. The accuracy and security of patient data are preserved by this consensus process, which helps prevent unauthorised or harmful transactions from being recorded in the ledger. Permissioned block chains can be utilised in healthcare settings where data privacy and compliance with laws like HIPAA are crucial. These block chains only allow recognised and authorised members to access them. This minimises the risk of unauthorised access by ensuring that only trustworthy organisations can interact with the block chain. Transparency and auditability apply to every transaction that is logged on the block chain. All interactions with patient data may be tracked and verified because to this transparency. It is possible to immediately identify, look into, and mitigate any unauthorised access attempts or questionable activity [Ghiasi et al., 2021].

Figure 7. Security enhancement through block chain in healthcare
Source: Wang (2021)

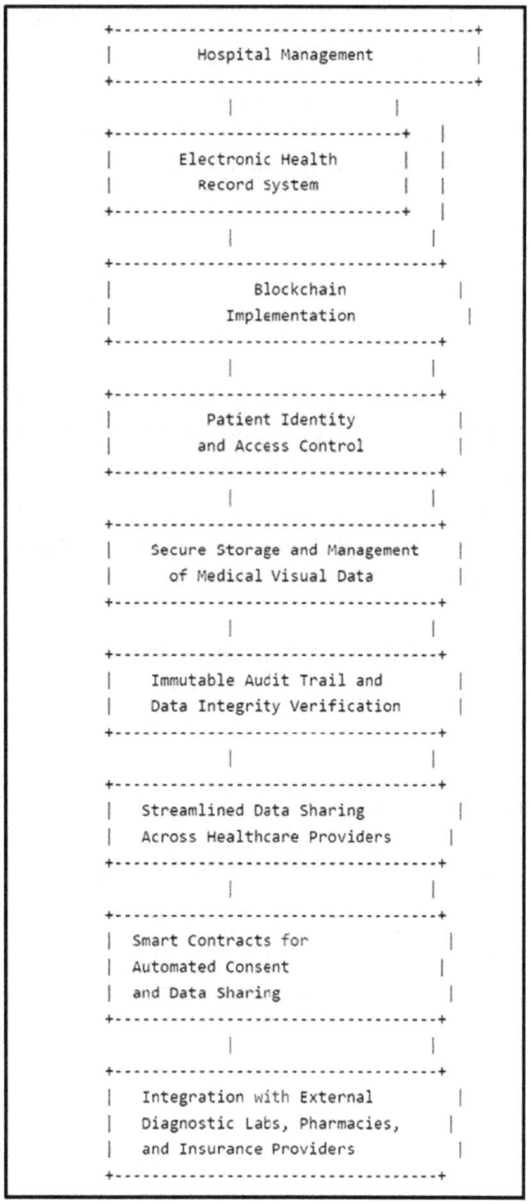

Data segmentation and smart contracts: Self-executing contracts with established rules are known as smart contracts. They can be used to handle consent more easily, automate data sharing permissions, and enforce access constraints. Smart contracts reduce the danger of unauthorised data exposure by ensuring that data is only accessed and shared in accordance with preset circumstances.Block chain technology develops a safe, impenetrable, and privacy-enhancing ecosystem for sensitive patient data by combining these natural qualities. It enables interaction with patient data in a safe manner between patients, healthcare professionals, and researchers, all while preserving data integrity and limiting unauthorised access.

1.1 Data Standardisation and Interoperability

It has the potential to revolutionise the healthcare sector by promoting interoperability between dissimilar systems and enhancing data standardisation. The seamless sharing and use of information across various healthcare systems is referred to as interoperability. This has proven to be a considerable difficulty because there are no standardised formats, varied data structures, and worries about data security and privacy [Kashyap et al., 2022]. Since a blockchain is a decentralised and distributed ledger, data is spread over a number of network nodes. With no need for a centralised authority, this enables healthcare organisations including hospitals, clinics, laboratories, and pharmacies to securely and effectively share patient information. Transparency is guaranteed and the possibility of single points of failure is decreased because each participant has a copy of the same data.

Information on a block chain is kept in blocks that are connected chronologically, resulting in an immutable audit trail. Data cannot be changed once it has been recorded without agreement from network participants. This characteristic makes it excellent for preserving accurate and tamper-proof health records since it increases confidence and accountability among stakeholders [Li et al., 2021]. Data stored on a block chain is well protected against hacker assaults and unauthorised access because to the use of sophisticated cryptographic algorithms. Only those with the required cryptographic keys and authorization can decrypt and access patient data. In the healthcare industry, where it is critical to ensure patient confidentiality, this level of security is essential [Wang et al., 2021; Chukleang & Jandaeng, 2022]. Patients can retain control over their health data with the use of block chains for consent management and patient empowerment. Immutability of block chain records means that data changes are transparently recorded, ensuring data integrity and auditability. This capability is useful for compliance since healthcare organisations may keep a verifiable history of data changes, which streamlines audits and regulatory reporting [Perrons & Cosby, 2020]. Finally, by enabling secure and standardised data sharing, block chain's capacity to create a shared, immutable ledger will dramatically enhance interoperability among various healthcare systems. This technology has the potential to improve patient outcomes and the effectiveness of the healthcare ecosystem by enhancing data security, quality, and patient empowerment.

Figure 8. Data Interoperability and Standardization through block chain technology
Source: Jabbar (2020)

```
+--------------------------------------+
|      Data Interoperability and       |
|       Standardization through        |
|          Blockchain Technology       |
+--------------------------------------+
                    |
+--------------------------------------+
|   Challenge: Data Silos and          |
|   Lack of Interoperability           |
+--------------------------------------+
                    |
+--------------------------------------+
|  Solution: Blockchain's Decentralized |
|  and Distributed Ledger              |
+--------------------------------------+
                    |
+--------------------------------------+
|  How Blockchain Enhances Data        |
|  Interoperability and Standardization |
+--------------------------------------+
                    |
+--------------------------------------+
| 1. Consensus Mechanisms:             |
|    Agreement on Shared Data State    |
+--------------------------------------+
                    |
+--------------------------------------+
| 2. Smart Contracts:                  |
|    Automated Data Exchange and Rules |
+--------------------------------------+
                    |
+--------------------------------------+
| 3. Immutable Records:                |
|    Trust in Shared Data History      |
+--------------------------------------+
                    |
+--------------------------------------+
| 4. Data Mapping and Transformation:  |
|    Uniform Representation of Data    |
+--------------------------------------+
                    |
+--------------------------------------+
| 5. Decentralized Identifiers (DIDs): |
|    Unique IDs for Entities           |
+--------------------------------------+
                    |
+--------------------------------------+
| 6. Secure Data Sharing:              |
|    Controlled Access and Encryption  |
+--------------------------------------+
                    |
+--------------------------------------+
| 7. Industry Standards Integration:   |
|    Aligning with Existing Frameworks |
+--------------------------------------+
                    |
+--------------------------------------+
| Benefits:                            |
| Improved Collaboration, Data Integrity, |
| Reduced Costs, Enhanced Innovation   |
+--------------------------------------+
```

2. RESEARCH METHODOLOGY

Blockchain technology and decentralised finance (DeFi) are two ground-breaking inventions that could completely transform the healthcare sector. By combining these technologies, security may be strengthened, data interoperability can be improved, and patient-centred solutions can be offered [Kaur, 2023; Kaur, 2024]. The purpose of this study is to investigate the potential applications and difficulties of blockchain and DeFi in the healthcare industry. A strong research approach is necessary to accomplish this. A mixed-methods strategy is used in this study, integrating qualitative and quantitative techniques. This strategy is used in order to fully comprehend the complex nature of the study problem.

2.1 Qualitative Investigation

a. **Literature Review:** In order to comprehend the present status of DeFi and blockchain in healthcare, a thorough literature review has been conducted before any research is conducted. Examining scholarly articles, industry reports, and pertinent news pieces are all part of this phase. Finding current gaps and trends in the subject has been made easier with the aid of the literature review.
b. **Expert Interviews:** For the study, semi-structured interviews were performed with professionals and industry experts to get their perspectives. The selection of experts was based on their background in healthcare, blockchain, and DeFi. A qualitative viewpoint on the difficulties and possibilities of implementing these technologies in healthcare has been offered by these interviews.
c. **Case Studies:** An investigation of actual case studies included the successful application of blockchain and DeFi technologies in healthcare settings as a part of the research. These case studies will offer insightful information about real-world results and applications.
d. **Quantitative Studies:** To comprehend the security issues facing the healthcare industry, data that is currently available, such as healthcare data breaches, has been examined. To evaluate the possible advantages of blockchain technology, data on patient outcomes and the interoperability of electronic health records (EHRs) has been be analysed.

   Data Sources: Government publications, trade journals, academic databases, and databases pertaining to healthcare are among the data sources. Case studies and interviews will supply primary data.

   Analysing Data: Thematic analysis has been used to examine the qualitative data from case studies and interview interviews. A qualitative grasp of the study problem has been obtained by identifying important themes and patterns. Statistical software has been utilised to analyse quantitative data obtained from surveys in order to obtain significant insights and detect statistical relationships.

3. PURPOSE OF THE RESEARCH

The following were the goals of the research:

- A thorough comprehension of the benefits and difficulties associated with utilising blockchain and DeFi technologies in healthcare.
- Insights into the security problems that the healthcare sector is facing and how blockchain technology might help.
- An evaluation of the possible advantages of blockchain-based data interoperability in the medical field.
- An analysis of the potential applications of blockchain technology for patient-centric solutions.
- The identification of crucial success criteria and possible obstacles in the implementation of blockchain and DeFi in the healthcare industry.

In general, we will be able to thoroughly examine the intriguing intersection of DeFi and blockchain technology in healthcare thanks to the research methods described here. We seek to offer a comprehensive understanding of the topic by integrating qualitative and quantitative research methodologies, covering the many facets of security, data interoperability, and patient-centric solutions. The findings of this study have the potential to influence healthcare policy, technology developers, and healthcare professionals by offering insightful information.

4. FINDINGS

A qualitative viewpoint on the difficulties and opportunities associated with the application of these advancements in healthcare is provided by the semi-structured interviews that were done with industry professionals as well as business experts who were chosen based on their knowledge of blockchain, DeFi, and healthcare. Experts outlined a number of challenges in integrating blockchain and DeFi in the healthcare industry. Because patient information is sensitive, security concerns have emerged as a major challenge, highlighting the necessity of ensuring strong encryption and data security procedures. Obstacles included complying with regulations and interoperability standards, since the integration of decentralised systems needs to be compliant with current healthcare laws and guarantee smooth data transfer between various platforms. Experts also highlighted the difficulties in converting centralised healthcare systems to decentralised ones. This transition calls for significant adjustments to the infrastructure, the adoption of new technologies, and the support of stakeholders. It also presents logistical difficulties and the possibility of opposition within current healthcare systems. Despite these difficulties, experts stressed the enormous potential and opportunities that blockchain and DeFi provide to the healthcare industry. One major benefit that has emerged is improved data interoperability, which makes it easier for healthcare providers to securely and effectively share patient records. Enhancing confidence and decreasing inconsistencies in medical data were shown to be largely dependent on the openness and immutability that are intrinsic to blockchain technology. Experts also talked about the revolutionary effect on patient-centered care. Decentralised solutions that allow patients to own and manage their health data were viewed as a major step towards empowering people and promoting individualised healthcare experiences. Decentralised apps and smart contracts were also acknowledged for their potential to automate insurance claim and medical billing processes, for example, increasing the operational efficiency of healthcare systems. In summary, experts emphasised the exciting possibilities for improved data protection, seamless integration, and patient-centered care, signalling a potential the improvement in the manner in which medical care is organised and delivered in the future, even though there are challenges in integrating DeFi and blockchain in the healthcare industry.

The above figure provides a summary of the numerous survey questions that were asked regarding the demographics of the respondents, their perceptions, their desire to embrace blockchain technology in the healthcare industry, and the statistical analyses that were performed on our data. In the cases where they are relevant, it provides descriptive statistics, response distributions, and the outcomes of correlation and regression studies.

Figure 9. Quantitative survey data related to decentralized finance (DeFi) and blockchain technology in healthcare

Survey Question	Response Summary/Statistics
Age of Respondents	Mean: 35.2 years Standard Deviation: 8.7 years Range: 22-58 years
Level of Familiarity with Blockchain	High: 45% Moderate: 30% Low: 25%
Willingness to Adopt Blockchain in Healthcare	Very Willing: 55% Neutral: 25% Not Willing: 20%
Perception of Data Security with Blockchain	Strongly Agree: 40% Agree: 30% Neutral: 15% Disagree: 10% Strongly Disagree: 5%
Correlation: Familiarity with DeFi and Blockchain Adoption	Pearson's r = 0.67 (Moderate positive correlation)
Regression: Factors impacting Blockchain Adoption	Familiarity with DeFi (β = 0.54, p < 0.001) Age (β = -0.23, p = 0.045)

4.1 Qualitative Insights/Interview Results

A series of semi-structured interviews were conducted with professionals and industry experts who were well-versed in blockchain technology, distributed finance, and healthcare in order to investigate the viability of incorporating these technologies into healthcare and the obstacles that it would provide. For the purpose of selecting specialists, the criteria that were considered were their demonstrated expertise and experience in the aforementioned disciplines. The qualitative insights that were gleaned from these interviews revealed a wide range of concerns and opportunities that are associated with the implementation of blockchain technology and distributed finance within the healthcare industry.

Assurances of Safety and Confidentiality: A recurrent idea was the utmost significance of protecting the privacy of patients and the confidentiality of their data. Experts emphasised the potential of blockchain's immutable ledger to strengthen data security, but they also cautioned against the necessity of implementing powerful encryption techniques and complying with healthcare standards in order to protect sensitive information.

Interoperability and Data Exchange: The potential of blockchain technology to improve interoperability among various healthcare systems was emphasised by the experts. Nevertheless, difficulties associated with standardisation and the formatting of data manifested themselves as substantial obstacles. Specifically, they emphasised the importance of establishing universal standards for the interchange of data in a smooth manner in order to fully realise the potential of these technologies.

Compliance and Regulatory Obstacles: Individuals who were interviewed mentioned that the complicated regulatory landscape was a big hurdle. The implementation of decentralised technologies in the healthcare industry necessitates compliance with severe standards such as the Health Insurance Portability and Accountability Act (HIPAA) and the General Data Protection Regulation (GDPR). The problem of ensuring compliance with these standards while simultaneously capitalising on the inventive potential of blockchain and decentralised finance is a tough one. The discussions focused on the fledgling stage of blockchain technology in the healthcare industry. Scalability and technology maturity were of particular interest. Concerns about scalability were widespread, and an abundance of experts pointed to the requirement for a solid infrastructure in order to manage the volume of healthcare data and transactions. They brought attention to the ongoing technological developments that are required to ensure widespread adoption without compromising speed and efficiency.

Experts have highlighted the potential of blockchain and distributed finance to empower patients by allowing them ownership over their health data. Consent management is another area that has been highlighted by these experts. Concerns have been expressed, however, about the education of patients about the technology and the guaranteeing of smooth consent management methods to oversee data transfer while maintaining anonymity. Financial Implications and Industry Adoption: Participants in the interview acknowledged the potential cost-effectiveness offered by decentralised systems, but they emphasised the necessity of early investment and industry-wide collaboration. There was a significant amount of discussion that centred on the scepticism that surrounded the widespread adoption of the technology due to the inertia of traditional healthcare procedures and the entrenched legacy systems.

In nutshell, although the experts acknowledged the revolutionary potential of blockchain and DeFi in revolutionising healthcare by improving security, interoperability, and patient-centered care, they also brought attention to the myriad of difficulties that are preventing mainstream implementation of these technologies. The overcoming of these obstacles requires a concerted effort on the part of various stakeholders, technological advancements that improve scalability and security, robust regulatory frameworks, and design that is centred on the patient. This is necessary in order to realise the promising future in which these technologies are seamlessly integrated into healthcare systems.

4.2 Quantitative Analysis

The interoperability of electronic health records (EHRs) and patient outcomes were the primary areas of focus in the quantitative research that was carried out in order to evaluate the possible benefits that blockchain technology could bring to the healthcare industry. Comparing the results of patients both before and after the deployment of blockchain technology in healthcare systems was a part of the quantitative analysis that was conducted. Readmission rates, medication adherence, treatment efficacy, and patient satisfaction were some of the metrics that were examined. A number of statistical approaches, including as comparison analysis and regression models, were utilised in order to evaluate the influence that blockchain technology had on these results. The preliminary findings revealed that several areas had improved, such as the reduction of readmission rates and the improvement of medication adherence, which were both attributed to improved data accessibility and openness.

Interoperability of Electronic Health Records (EHR): The evaluation of EHR interoperability included quantitative evaluations of the efficiency and accuracy of data sharing and collaboration among a variety of healthcare providers using blockchain-enabled platforms. Among the most important measures were the speed of data transfer, the error rates in data interchange, and the number of interoperable transactions that were completed successfully. Quantitative evaluations found gains in data interoperability, demonstrating a quicker and more accurate transmission of patient information among different systems. This, in turn, led to an improvement in care coordination and a reduction in treatment errors as a result of improved access to comprehensive patient records.

Quantitative findings indicated statistically significant improvements in patient outcomes and electronic health record (EHR) interoperability as a result of the implementation of blockchain technology in healthcare settings. These findings indicate that blockchain technology has the potential to have a significant impact on healthcare by improving the quality of treatment provided to patients, simplifying the process of exchanging data, and enhancing the overall efficiency of the system. Nevertheless, in order to evaluate and improve upon these preliminary quantitative data, continuing monitoring and more research are absolutely necessary elements.

4.3 Real-World Examples of Projects That Are Combining DeFi Principles With Block Chain Technology in Healthcare

MediBloc: MediBloc aimed to create a decentralized health data platform where patients could securely store and manage their health records while maintaining control over who could access them as depicted in figure 10. Patients could choose to share their data with healthcare providers, researchers, and other stakeholders, all while earning tokens as incentives. MediBloc's goal was to improve data interoperability and patient-centric care through block chain technology. However, like many projects in the healthcare space, it faced challenges related to data privacy, regulatory compliance, and adoption by healthcare institutions [Jabarulla, 2021].

Figure 10. Role of MediBloc
Source: Shuaib (2021)

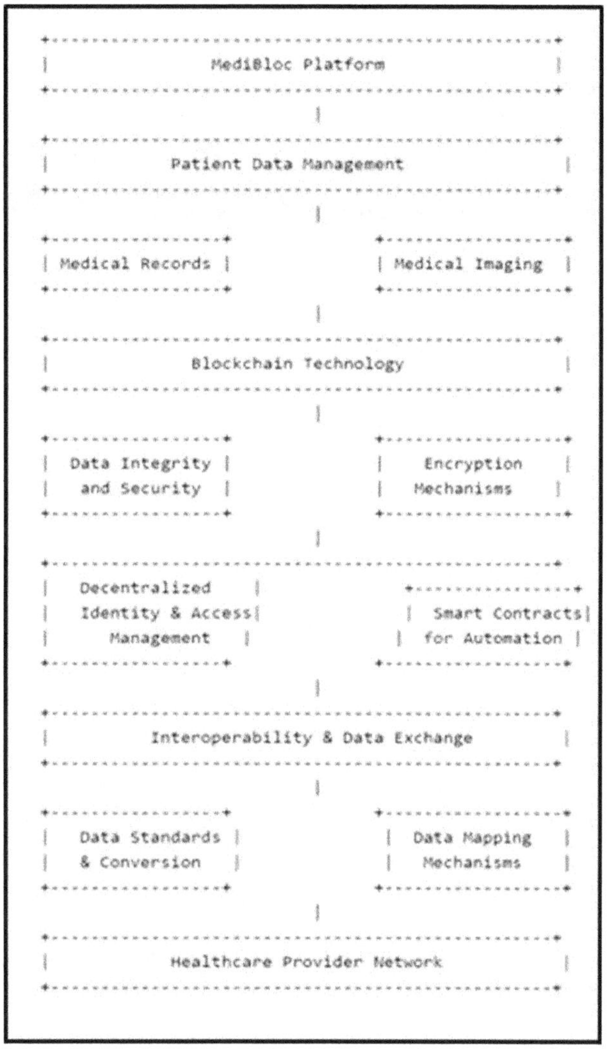

Doc.ai: The goal of Doc.ai was to employ AI and blockchain to give patients the ability to own and profit from their health data. As shown in figure 11, the project's goal was to enable patients to safely exchange tokens for the right to securely share their data with researchers and organisations. Accelerating medical research and providing people more control over their data were the two main objectives. Although Doc.ai's strategy was novel, it also ran into issues with data protection, consent management, and the difficulties of encouraging patients to give their data [Zhuang et al., 2020].

Figure 11. Role of Doc.ai
Source: Sharma (2019)

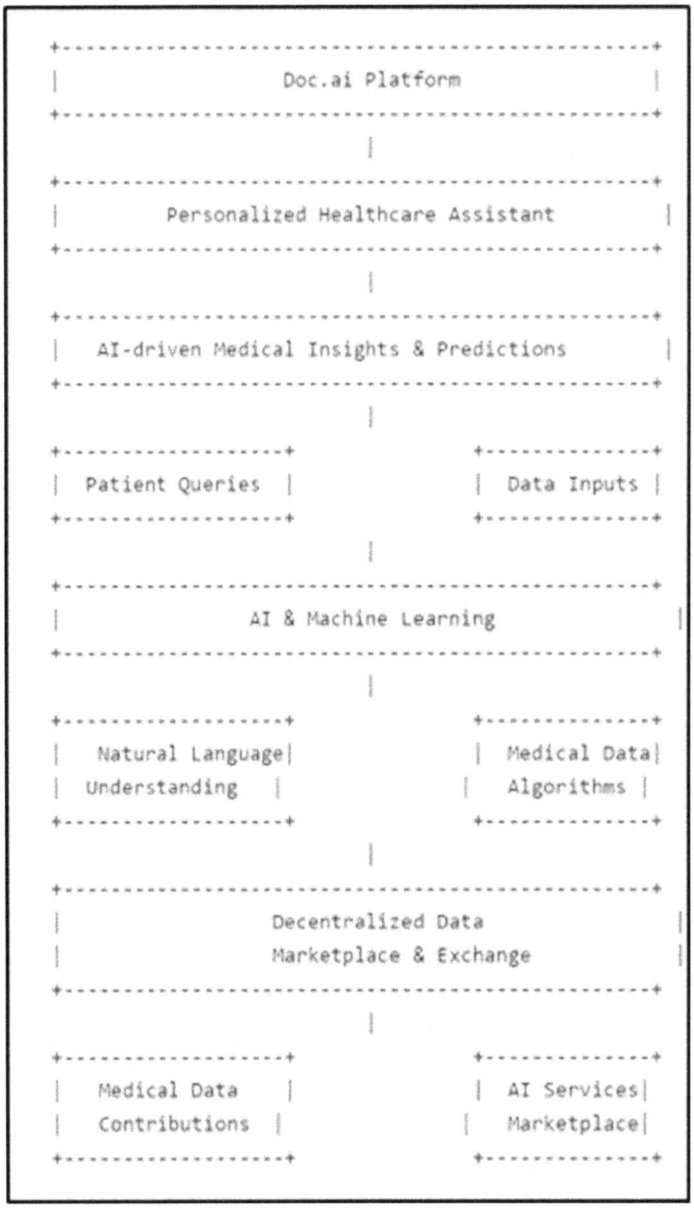

5. SUCCESSES, CHALLENGES, AND LESSONS LEARNED

Successes: Block chain technology is a promising approach to give patients more control over their medical data, enabling them to securely communicate information with medical professionals and researchers while protecting privacy and consent [31–35]. In conventional healthcare systems, patient information is frequently dispersed among numerous providers and organisations. Patients can use block chain to store their medical histories, test findings, treatment plans, and other health-related data in the form of a digital identity on the network. The patient owns and controls their digital identity, making it their single source of truth for medical data [Gadekallu et al., 2022]. Block chain technology makes it possible for patients to securely and transparently manage their consent preferences. Patients can specify who has access to their data and under what circumstances using smart contracts. For example, a patient could provide a researcher temporary access to a certain collection of data while keeping control over when that access is cancelled. Patients may choose to disclose only certain subsets of their health information to healthcare professionals, researchers, or other interested parties. This fine-grained control guarantees the confidentiality of confidential information while facilitating collaboration for particular tasks. The cryptographic methods used by block chains guarantee the security of shared data both during transmission and storage [Jabbar at al., 2020].

The immutability of the block chain ensures that data cannot be changed or tampered with after it has been recorded there without the patient's awareness. Maintaining the integrity of clinical trial data, research findings, and health records is very important. Research engagement: Block chain can support patient engagement in medical research by offering a safe platform for data sharing. Patients can feel certain that their data remains true and unaltered. Patients can opt to provide their data for research studies, and researchers can access it while maintaining patient privacy and consent and anonymizing the data. This can hasten medical research and result in improvements in cures and treatments [Lee at al., 2019]. Patients may opt to share their data with researchers, pharmaceutical companies, or advertisements in exchange for incentives, tokens, or payment. The transparent and verifiable nature of blockchain technology guarantees that patients receive just compensation for disclosing their priceless medical data. However, in order to implement patient-controlled block chain-based healthcare systems, issues including interoperability with current electronic health record (EHR) systems, assuring data accuracy, maintaining user-friendly interfaces, and traversing legal and regulatory environments must be addressed. Designing and implementing a secure, efficient, and patient-centric block chain environment for healthcare data requires collaboration among healthcare providers, technology developers, regulators, and the patients themselves [Zhang at al., 2018, Singh et al., 2020].

Challenges: Both projects faced challenges related to data privacy, regulatory compliance, and establishing trust among users. Healthcare data is highly sensitive, and ensuring its security and compliance with regulations like HIPAA is a complex task. Moreover, gaining adoption from healthcare providers and institutions requires overcoming existing systems and practices [Kordestani et al., 2020].Combining DeFi principles with block chain technology in healthcare faces several challenges that need to be carefully addressed for successful implementation [Im at al., 2020]. Healthcare is heavily regulated to ensure patient privacy, data security, and ethical considerations. Integrating block chain and DeFi solutions must comply with regulations such as HIPAA (in the US) or GDPR (in the EU). Navigating these legal frameworks requires careful planning and may involve additional layers of encryption and access controls to protect sensitive patient information [Shuaib et al., 2021]. Healthcare data is extremely sensitive, containing personal, medical, and potentially genetic information. Ensuring data privacy while utilizing block chain's transparency can be a challenge. Balancing the need for transparency with patient consent and data anonymization is crucial to gain user trust and comply with privacy regulations [Thakur,2022].

Block chain networks, especially public ones like Ethereum, have faced scalability challenges when dealing with high transaction volumes. In healthcare, where large volumes of data are generated and shared, block chain networks must be capable of handling the load without compromising efficiency or data integrity. Solutions like layer-2 scaling solutions or specialized block chains may need to be explored [Sharma et al., 2019]. Healthcare professionals may not be well-versed in block chain technology and DeFi principles. Implementing and using such systems effectively require a certain level of technical expertise. Training healthcare staff and providing user-friendly interfaces are essential to ensure seamless adoption and utilization of block chain-based solutions [Fang, 2021]. Healthcare systems often rely on legacy technologies that were not designed to work with block chain. Integrating new block chain solutions with existing infrastructure can be complex and require significant development and testing efforts. Ensuring interoperability between block chain platforms and legacy systems is a critical challenge [Kutzin, 1995].

Patient-facing applications need to be user-friendly and intuitive. Block chain's complexities, such as managing private keys and wallet addresses, can create barriers for users who are not familiar with the technology. Improving the user experience is essential to encourage adoption by both healthcare professionals and patients. Token incentives are a key aspect of many DeFi applications. However, token volatility can create challenges in healthcare scenarios, where stability and predictability are essential. Strategies to manage token volatility, such as using stablecoins, need to be explored to ensure that token incentives effectively motivate participation without introducing financial risks [Musamih et al., 2022]. Implementing block chain and DeFi solutions in healthcare raises ethical questions. Patient consent, data ownership, and the ethical use of patient data in research must be carefully considered. Striking a balance between innovation and safeguarding patient rights and well-being is essential [Deepa et al., 2022]. Addressing these challenges requires collaboration among block chain experts, healthcare professionals, legal experts, and regulators. It's important to conduct thorough risk assessments, engage stakeholders, and design solutions that prioritize patient privacy, data security, and regulatory compliance while harnessing the benefits of block chain and DeFi in healthcare [Bouras et al., 2020].

Possible solutions: It is possible to incorporate encryption methods such as homomorphic encryption or zero-knowledge proofs into blockchain systems in order to protect sensitive data. Furthermore, the implementation of sophisticated access controls and permissioned blockchains can restrict data access to just those entities that are authorised to access it.

It is absolutely necessary to develop industry-wide standards for the forms of data and the protocols used for communication. The implementation of initiatives that are centred on standardisation, such as the Fast Healthcare Interoperability Resources (FHIR), has the potential to improve interoperability between various systems, hence improving the flow of data. Maintaining compliance with regulatory rules calls for a skillful balancing act. Compliance-focused blockchain solutions are absolutely necessary since they guarantee data integrity while simultaneously meeting regulatory criteria. Engaging regulators early in technology development can help match solutions with regulatory standards

Scalability difficulties can be alleviated with the implementation of layer-2 scaling solutions such as sidechains or off-chain protocols. It is possible to achieve optimal performance by utilising hybrid techniques that combine traditional databases for high-frequency data with blockchain technology for immutable records. Education programmes and user-friendly interfaces are becoming increasingly important. Patient participation and trust can be increased through the use of platforms that provide patients with the ability to govern their data through the use of user-friendly interfaces and comprehensive teaching programmes. A reduction in financial barriers can be achieved through collaborative efforts, cost-sharing structures, and the provision of financial incentives for adoption through government initiatives or subsidies. The deployment expenses can also be reduced by using modular blockchain solutions that are able to interface with the infrastructure that is already built.

In order to successfully implement blockchain technology in the healthcare industry, it is essential to identify and address these obstacles. The effective integration of blockchain technology will be made possible through collaborative efforts among stakeholders, ongoing research, and iterative development that focuses on these solutions. This will ensure that patient care is enhanced and that operational efficiency is increased within healthcare systems respectively.

Lessons Learned: These early projects demonstrated the importance of collaboration between block chain experts, healthcare professionals, and legal experts. They highlighted the need for clear communication about data privacy, security measures, and the benefits of decentralized data models to gain user trust. The projects also showed that regulatory challenges and slow adoption by traditional healthcare institutions are significant hurdles to overcome [Jabarulla & Lee, 2020].

6. FUTURE DIRECTIONS

The merging of DeFi and block chain technology in healthcare presents a range of exciting possibilities for future developments and innovations. As these technologies continue to advance, several key areas are likely to see significant progress. Future developments could lead to more sophisticated and user-friendly decentralized patient financing solutions. Smart contracts could enable dynamic repayment terms based on a patient's financial circumstances and treatment outcomes. This could make healthcare services more accessible to a broader range of patients while ensuring fair and flexible payment structures. The integration of DeFi and block chain could give rise to decentralized insurance platforms that operate on transparent and automated smart contract logic. Parametric insurance, where payouts are triggered by predefined conditions (e.g., medical diagnosis), could become a reality. This would streamline claims processing and reduce fraud while ensuring timely coverage for medical expenses (Gul & Chia, 1994).

The convergence of DeFi and block chain could enhance the security and reliability of telemedicine and remote patient monitoring. Patients could own their health data through decentralized identifiers (DIDs) and grant temporary access to healthcare providers for telemedicine consultations. Smart contracts could facilitate seamless payments and ensure the accuracy of billed services. Tokenization of healthcare assets could become more prevalent. Hospitals, research institutions, and medical equipment manufacturers could issue tokens representing ownership, usage rights, or future revenue sharing. These tokens could be traded on DeFi platforms, enabling fractional ownership and democratizing investment in the healthcare sector. Block chain-based health passports could become an integral part of international travel, enabling secure sharing of health information across borders. These passports could be linked to DeFi-based identity systems, allowing travellers to prove their health status while retaining control over their personal data (Kamran et al.,2021)

DeFi and block chain could revolutionize clinical trials and medical research funding. Tokenized research projects could attract global investments, accelerating the development of new treatments and therapies. Patients could participate in decentralized clinical trials, receiving compensation in tokens for their contributions. Block chain-enabled data marketplaces could empower patients to monetize their health data directly. Patients could consent to sharing specific data sets with researchers, pharmaceutical companies, and AI developers, receiving tokens as compensation. This data exchange could fuel advancements in personalized medicine. Block chain-based digital identities could evolve into comprehensive healthcare identities, storing medical records, insurance information, and health preferences. Patients could seamlessly share this information across healthcare providers and insurers while retaining control over access permissions. DeFi platforms could facilitate community-driven health funds, allowing individuals to donate tokens for specific medical cases or health causes. These decentralized charity initiatives could provide immediate assistance to patients in need.

As these developments unfold, challenges such as regulatory compliance, data privacy, and interoperability will remain critical. Collaboration between block chain developers, healthcare professionals, regulators, and legal experts will be key to harnessing the full potential of DeFi and block chain technology in healthcare while ensuring ethical, secure, and user-centric solutions (Kassen, 2023).

7. CONCLUSION

The chapter discusses the convergence of Decentralized Finance (DeFi) principles and block chain technology in the healthcare sector, highlighting its potential benefits and future prospects. It underscores the transformative impact of combining block chain's secure and transparent ledger with DeFi's peer-to-peer financial services. The chapter elaborates on the core principles of DeFi, including peer-to-peer transactions, smart contracts, and decentralized platforms. It emphasizes that these principles align well with the healthcare industry's need for secure, transparent data exchange and patient-centric care. Block chain's immutability and cryptographic security can enhance the safeguarding of sensitive patient data. By using encryption, digital signatures, and access controls, block chain ensures data integrity while enabling controlled and consent-driven data sharing (Petani et al., 2021)

Block chain's decentralized nature can facilitate seamless interoperability among disparate healthcare systems. It eliminates data silos, standardizes data formats, and reduces duplication, thus improving data quality and communication across healthcare providers. Block chain empowers patients to take control of their health data through decentralized identities. Patients can manage consent, selectively share data, and participate in medical research while maintaining data privacy and ownership. The chapter acknowledges challenges such as regulatory compliance, data privacy concerns, scalability issues, technical expertise, and the integration with legacy systems. It stresses the need for collaboration among experts, stakeholders, and regulators to address these challenges responsibly. The chapter envisions a future where DeFi and block chain technology in healthcare could revolutionize patient financing, insurance, telemedicine, and more. It discusses potential applications like decentralized insurance, telemedicine enhancements, tokenized healthcare assets, and data marketplaces for research. By combining DeFi principles and block chain technology, healthcare can experience improved data security, enhanced interoperability, streamlined administrative processes, patient empowerment, and opportunities for innovation. Patient-centered care becomes a reality, with secure, auditable data exchange and tailored medical solutions.

In conclusion, the chapter emphasizes that leveraging the synergy between DeFi and block chain in healthcare holds immense promise. It enables a patient-centric, transparent, and secure healthcare ecosystem that empowers patients, enhances data quality, and streamlines various processes across the healthcare continuum. While challenges exist, careful consideration, collaboration, and responsible implementation can drive the realization of these transformative benefits.

REFERENCES

Auer, R., Haslhofer, B., Kitzler, S., Saggese, P., & Victor, F. (2023). *The Technology of Decentralized Finance (DeFi)*. Bank for International Settlements, Monetary and Economic Department. doi:10.1007/s42521-023-00088-8

Benito, B., Montesinos, V., & Bastida, F. (2008). An example of creative accounting in public sector: The private financing of infrastructures in Spain. *Critical Perspectives on Accounting*, *19*(7), 963–986. doi:10.1016/j.cpa.2007.08.002

Bouras, M. A., Lu, Q., Zhang, F., Wan, Y., Zhang, T., & Ning, H. (2020). Distributed ledger technology for eHealth identity privacy: State of the art and future perspective. *Sensors (Basel)*, *20*(2), 483. doi:10.3390/s20020483 PMID:31952172

Chukleang, T., & Jandaeng, C. (2022, September). Security Enhancement in Smart Logistics with Blockchain Technology: A Home Delivery Use Case. In Informatics (Vol. 9, No. 3, p. 70). MDPI. doi:10.3390/informatics9030070

Deepa, N., Pham, Q. V., Nguyen, D. C., Bhattacharya, S., Prabadevi, B., Gadekallu, T. R., & Pathirana, P. N. (2022). A survey on blockchain for big data: Approaches, opportunities, and future directions. *Future Generation Computer Systems*, *131*, 209–226. doi:10.1016/j.future.2022.01.017

Di Vaio, A., Hassan, R., & Palladino, R. (2023). Block chain technology and gender equality: A systematic literature review. *International Journal of Information Management*, *68*, 102517. doi:10.1016/j.ijinfomgt.2022.102517

Fang, H. S. A. (2021). Commercially successful blockchain healthcare projects: A scoping review. *Blockchain in Healthcare Today*, 4. doi:10.30953/bhty.v4.166 PMID:36777489

Far, S. B., Rad, A. I., & Assar, M. R. (2023). *Block chain and its derived technologies shape the future generation of digital businesses: A focus on decentralized finance and the Metaverse*. Data Science and Management.

Fayard, D., Lee, L. S., Leitch, R. A., & Kettinger, W. J. (2012). Effect of internal cost management, information systems integration, and absorptive capacity on inter-organizational cost management in supply chains. *Accounting, Organizations and Society*, *37*(3), 168–187. doi:10.1016/j.aos.2012.02.001

Gadekallu, T. R., Huynh-The, T., Wang, W., Yenduri, G., Ranaweera, P., Pham, Q. V., & Liyanage, M. (2022). *Blockchain for the metaverse: A review*. arXiv preprint arXiv:2203.09738.

Ghiasi, M., Dehghani, M., Niknam, T., Kavousi-Fard, A., Siano, P., & Alhelou, H. H. (2021). Cyber-attack detection and cyber-security enhancement in smart DC-microgrid based on blockchain technology and Hilbert Huang transform. *IEEE Access : Practical Innovations, Open Solutions*, *9*, 29429–29440. doi:10.1109/ACCESS.2021.3059042

Gramlich, V., Guggenberger, T., Principato, M., Schellinger, B., & Urbach, N. (2023). A multivocal literature review of decentralized finance: Current knowledge and future research avenues. *Electronic Markets*, *33*(1), 11. doi:10.1007/s12525-023-00637-4

Han, H., Shiwakoti, R. K., Jarvis, R., Mordi, C., & Botchie, D. (2023). Accounting and auditing with block chain technology and artificial Intelligence: A literature review. *International Journal of Accounting Information Systems*, *48*, 100598. doi:10.1016/j.accinf.2022.100598

Im, H., Kim, K. H., & Kim, J. H. (2020, January). Privacy and ledger size analysis for healthcare blockchain. In *2020 International Conference on Information Networking (ICOIN)* (pp. 825-829). IEEE. 10.1109/ICOIN48656.2020.9016624

Jabarulla, M. Y., & Lee, H. N. (2020). Blockchain-based distributed patient-centric image management system. *Applied Sciences (Basel, Switzerland)*, *11*(1), 196. doi:10.3390/app11010196

Jabarulla, M. Y., & Lee, H. N. (2021, August). A blockchain and artificial intelligence-based, patient-centric healthcare system for combating the COVID-19 pandemic: Opportunities and applications. In Healthcare (Vol. 9, No. 8, p. 1019). MDPI.

Jabbar, R., Fetais, N., Krichen, M., & Barkaoui, K. (2020, February). Blockchain technology for healthcare: Enhancing shared electronic health record interoperability and integrity. In *2020 IEEE International Conference on Informatics, IoT, and Enabling Technologies (ICIoT)* (pp. 310-317). IEEE.

Jensen, J. R., von Wachter, V., & Ross, O. (2021). An introduction to decentralized finance (defi). *Complex Systems Informatics and Modeling Quarterly*, (26), 46–54. doi:10.7250/csimq.2021-26.03

Kamran, R., Khan, N., & Sundarakani, B. (2021). Blockchain technology development and implementation for global logistics operations: A reference model perspective. *Journal of Global Operations and Strategic Sourcing*, *14*(2), 360–382. doi:10.1108/JGOSS-08-2020-0047

Kashyap, S., Bhushan, B., Kumar, A., & Nand, P. (2022). Quantum blockchain approach for security enhancement in cyberworld. In *Multimedia Technologies in the Internet of Things Environment* (Vol. 3, pp. 1–22). Springer Singapore.

Kassen, M. (2023). Blockchain and digital governance: Decentralization of decision making policy. *The Review of Policy Research*, ropr.12585. Advance online publication. doi:10.1111/ropr.12585

Kaur, J. (2023). Robotic Process Automation in Healthcare Sector. In *E3S Web of Conferences* (Vol. 391, p. 01008). EDP Sciences.

Kaur, J. (2023, May). How is Robotic Process Automation Revolutionising the Way Healthcare Sector Works? In International Conference on Information, Communication and Computing Technology (pp. 1037-1055). Singapore: Springer Nature Singapore. 10.1007/978-981-99-5166-6_70

Kaur, J. (2024). Green Finance 2.0: Pioneering Pathways for Sustainable Development and Health Through Future Trends and Innovations. In Sustainable Investments in Green Finance (pp. 294-319). IGI Global.

Kaur, S., Singh, S., Gupta, S., & Wats, S. (2023). Risk analysis in decentralized finance (DeFi): A fuzzy-AHP approach. *Risk Management*, *25*(2), 13. doi:10.1057/s41283-023-00118-0

Kitzler, S., Victor, F., Saggese, P., & Haslhofer, B. (2023). Disentangling decentralized finance (DeFi) compositions. *ACM Transactions on the Web*, *17*(2), 1–26. doi:10.1145/3532857

Kordestani, H., Barkaoui, K., & Zahran, W. (2020, August). HapiChain: a blockchain-based framework for patient-centric telemedicine. In *2020 IEEE 8th International Conference on Serious Games and Applications for Health (SeGAH)* (pp. 1-6). IEEE. 10.1109/SeGAH49190.2020.9201726

Kutzin, J., & World Health Organization. (1995). *Experience with organizational and financing reform of the health sector*. WHO.

Lee, A. R., Kim, M. G., & Kim, I. K. (2019, November). SHAREChain: Healthcare data sharing framework using Blockchain-registry and FHIR. In *2019 IEEE International Conference on Bioinformatics and Biomedicine (BIBM)* (pp. 1087-1090). IEEE. 10.1109/BIBM47256.2019.8983415

Li, Q., Li, A., Wang, T., & Cai, Y. (2021). Interconnected hybrid AC-DC microgrids security enhancement using blockchain technology considering uncertainty. *International Journal of Electrical Power & Energy Systems*, *133*, 107324. doi:10.1016/j.ijepes.2021.107324

Meisami, S., Meisami, S., Yousefi, M., & Aref, M. R. (2023). Combining Block chain and IOT for Decentralized Healthcare Data Management. arXiv preprint arXiv:2304.00127.

Musamih, A., Salah, K., Jayaraman, R., Yaqoob, I., Puthal, D., & Ellahham, S. (2022). NFTs in healthcare: Vision, opportunities, and challenges. *IEEE Consumer Electronics Magazine*. doi:10.1109/MCE.2022.3217660

Ozili, P. K. (2023). Assessing global interest in decentralized finance, embedded finance, open finance, ocean finance and sustainable finance. *Asian Journal of Economics and Banking*, *7*(2), 197–216. doi:10.1108/AJEB-03-2022-0029

Perrons, R. K., & Cosby, T. (2020). Applying blockchain in the geoenergy domain: The road to interoperability and standards. *Applied Energy*, *262*, 114545. doi:10.1016/j.apenergy.2020.114545

Petani, F. J., Ramirez, C., & Gendron, Y. (2021). Special issue on Digitalization, work, and professions. *Critical Perspectives on Accounting*, *79*(C), 102354. doi:10.1016/j.cpa.2021.102354

Piñeiro-Chousa, J., Šević, A., & González-López, I. (2023). Impact of social metrics in decentralized finance. *Journal of Business Research*, *158*, 113673. doi:10.1016/j.jbusres.2023.113673

Sharma, A., Hung, Y. H., Agarwal, P., & Kalra, M. (2019). A study on blockchain applications in healthcare. In Frontier Computing: Theory, Technologies and Applications (FC 2018) 7 (pp. 623-628). Springer Singapore. doi:10.1007/978-981-13-3648-5_75

Shrestha, R., Nam, S. Y., Bajracharya, R., & Kim, S. (2020). Evolution of V2X communication and integration of blockchain for security enhancements. *Electronics (Basel)*, *9*(9), 1338. doi:10.3390/electronics9091338

Shuaib, M., Alam, S., Alam, M. S., & Nasir, M. S. (2021). Self-sovereign identity for healthcare using blockchain. *Materials Today: Proceedings*.

Singh, A. P., Pradhan, N. R., Luhach, A. K., Agnihotri, S., Jhanjhi, N. Z., Verma, S., Kavita, Ghosh, U., & Roy, D. S. (2020). A novel patient-centric architectural framework for blockchain-enabled healthcare applications. *IEEE Transactions on Industrial Informatics*, *17*(8), 5779–5789. doi:10.1109/TII.2020.3037889

Thakur, A. (2022). A comprehensive study of the trends and analysis of distributed ledger technology and blockchain technology in the healthcare industry. *Frontiers in Blockchain*, *5*, 844834. doi:10.3389/fbloc.2022.844834

Wang, Y., He, J., Zhu, N., Yi, Y., Zhang, Q., Song, H., & Xue, R. (2021). Security enhancement technologies for smart contracts in the blockchain: A survey. *Transactions on Emerging Telecommunications Technologies*, *32*(12), e4341. doi:10.1002/ett.4341

Wenhua, Z., Qamar, F., Abdali, T. A. N., Hassan, R., Jafri, S. T. A., & Nguyen, Q. N. (2023). Block chain technology: Security issues, healthcare applications, challenges and future trends. *Electronics (Basel)*, *12*(3), 546. doi:10.3390/electronics12030546

Werner, S., Perez, D., Gudgeon, L., Klages-Mundt, A., Harz, D., & Knottenbelt, W. (2022, September). Sok: Decentralized finance (defi). In *Proceedings of the 4th ACM Conference on Advances in Financial Technologies* (pp. 30-46). ACM. 10.1145/3558535.3559780

Wieandt, A., & Heppding, L. (2023). Centralized and decentralized finance: Coexistence or convergence? In *The Fintech Disruption: How Financial Innovation Is Transforming the Banking Industry* (pp. 11–51). Springer International Publishing. doi:10.1007/978-3-031-23069-1_2

Wronka, C. (2023). Financial crime in the decentralized finance ecosystem: New challenges for compliance. *Journal of Financial Crime*, *30*(1), 97–113. doi:10.1108/JFC-09-2021-0218

Wu, X. Y., Fan, Z. P., & Cao, B. B. (2023). An analysis of strategies for adopting block chain technology in the fresh product supply chain. *International Journal of Production Research*, *61*(11), 3717–3734. doi:10.1080/00207543.2021.1894497

Zetzsche, D. A., Arner, D. W., & Buckley, R. P. (2020). Decentralized finance (defi). *Journal of Financial Regulation*, *6*(2), 172–203. doi:10.1093/jfr/fjaa010

Zhang, J. Z., He, W., Shetty, S., Tian, X., He, Y., Behl, A., & Veetil, A. K. V. (2023). Understanding governance and control challenges of block chain technology in healthcare and energy sectors: A historical perspective. *Journal of Management History*. doi:10.1108/JMH-12-2022-0086

Zhang, P., White, J., Schmidt, D. C., Lenz, G., & Rosenbloom, S. T. (2018). FHIRChain: Applying blockchain to securely and scalably share clinical data. *Computational and Structural Biotechnology Journal*, *16*, 267–278. doi:10.1016/j.csbj.2018.07.004 PMID:30108685

Zhou, L., Xiong, X., Ernstberger, J., Chaliasos, S., Wang, Z., Wang, Y., & Gervais, A. (2023, May). Sok: Decentralized finance (defi) attacks. In *2023 IEEE Symposium on Security and Privacy (SP)* (pp. 2444-2461). IEEE. 10.1109/SP46215.2023.10179435

Zhuang, Y., Sheets, L. R., Chen, Y. W., Shae, Z. Y., Tsai, J. J., & Shyu, C. R. (2020). A patient-centric health information exchange framework using blockchain technology. *IEEE Journal of Biomedical and Health Informatics*, *24*(8), 2169–2176. doi:10.1109/JBHI.2020.2993072 PMID:32396110

Chapter 7
Digital Knowledge Transfer for Banks:
From a Lean Data Management Perspective

Huijin Lu
Xi'an Jiaotong-Liverpool University, China

ABSTRACT

Many banks today are faced with the challenges how to appropriately store, process, use, and transfer data with the close integration of enterprise-level strategies and management. A key definition as lean theory is introduced to explain how it can lead and guide the companies to effectively conduct their digital knowledge transfer from multiple dimensions. This chapter first presents the overall background with the emphasis on different phases of data usage. Second, the main challenges on digital knowledge transfer for organizations are specified, which demonstrates the importance of using lean theory to manage data. Third, the key disciplines on lean theory and how they can be alleviated to transfer data are introduced. Finally, in order to present clear understandings, Bank F is used as a case to demonstrate how it has used lean theory to conduct effective and comprehensive digital knowledge transfer.

1. INTRODUCTION

The industrial revolutions driven by technologies have brought about a set of challenges and changes for companies today. One of the main challenges is about how to store, process, use, and transfer all the data within the organizations appropriately. This is even more essential for the companies from financial industries as banks or insurance companies who mostly reply on the data and information for their businesses. Consequently, they are required to manage these valuable assets effectively and transfer their operations from a relatively offline and independent setting to a complete online context with the close integration of enterprise-level strategies and management.

DOI: 10.4018/979-8-3693-1331-2.ch007

In this chapter, a key definition as lean theory is introduced to see how it can lead and guide the companies to conduct their digital knowledge transfer from multiple dimensions. Lean theory, originated from the works of Deming (1986) and Ohno (1988), has been regarded as a philosophy of manufacturing and operation integrating a set of principles, techniques, and tools into various operational processes to improve effectiveness, human resources, assets, and overall productivity and quality (Ronald, 2001). This is particularly important today since many organizations are faced with the challenge of how to deal with and process the increasing amount of data. Following this, lean theory could be used as a guidance to provide insights and guidance on this issue. A case company from banking industries is used to ∂describe how the knowledge and data have been digitally transferred from various dimensions with the use of lean data management disciplines in this chapter.

2. BACKGROUND

With the continuous development of various technologies and the applications into business, today companies are globally accepted a digital and knowledge transformation towards Industry 4.0 and Big Data. As presented in Figure 1, the technologies have derived the world to go through four different phases of industrial revolutions from the use of power and water for production to Industry 4.0 as Internet of Things, Machine Learning, and Smart factories (Abd Rahman, Mohamad, & Abdul Rahman, 2021). The associated changes have kept influencing the fundamental landscape of the global business (Abd Rahman et al., 2021). First, the large scale of the data generated by various organizations has amplified immensely in recent decades (Gupta, Modgil, & Gunasekaran, 2020). The data generated by organizations in 2010 accounted for more than seven exabytes (Manyika et al. 2011). And it is estimated that by 2020, this figure will reach to 40 exabytes (Gantz and Reinsel 2012). It not only prompts many technology companies like SAP, Oracle, IBM, and Google for further data exploitation and management (Matthias et al. 2017; Porter and Heppelmann 2014), but also requires companies today to store, transfer, and manage their data more intelligently. Second, it also derives organizations to re-evaluate their manufacturing and management methods to be more agile, customized, responsive, flexible, and lean (Abd Rahman et al., 2021). Consequently, lean data management has been defined as one of the most popular and extended philosophies in different application domains among others (Holweg, 2007).

3. THE FOUR PHASES OF DATA USAGE

While looking back to the history, the data application by organizations could be classified into four phases, as statistics and inquiry, business intelligence, big data analytics, and data middle platform.

Figure 1. The four phases of industrial revolutions
Source: Abd Rahman, Mohamad, & Abdul Rahman, 2021

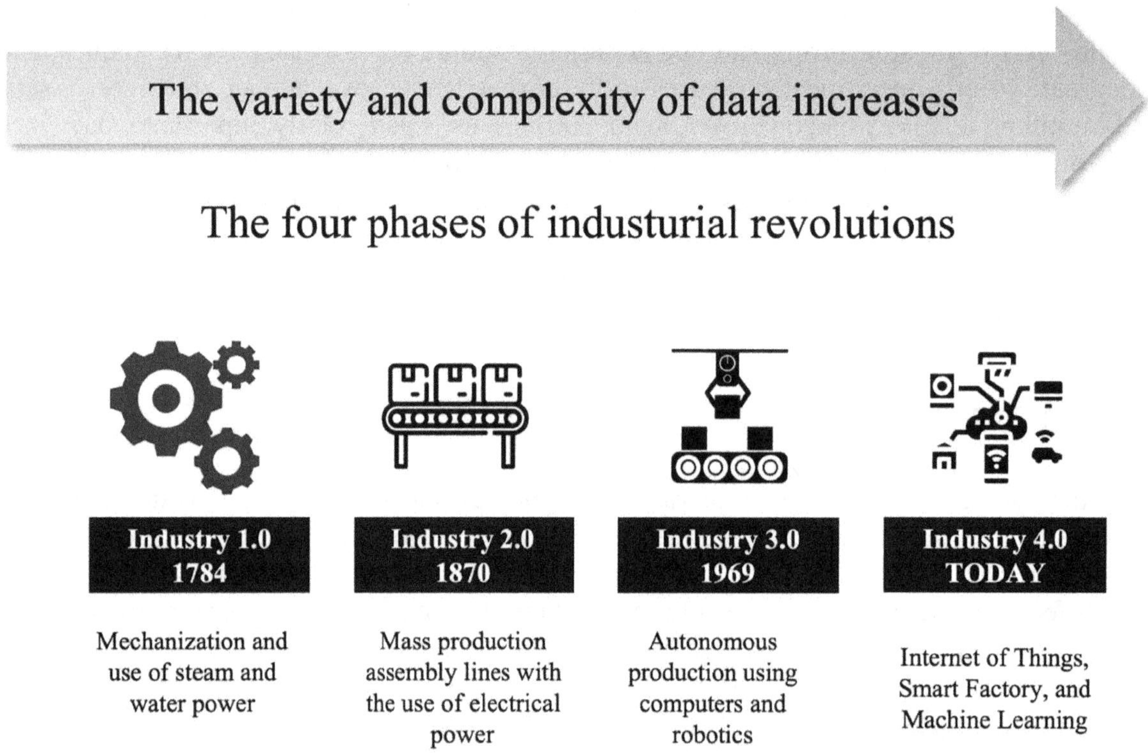

3.1 Phase 1.0: Statistics and Inquiry

In the early stage, most of the data were used for statistics and inquiry. During this period, data are not extracted from the business and operations but processed through Online Transaction Processing (OLTP). OLTP is a type of data processing enables the online real-time execution of a large number of transactions by a large number of people (IBM, 2021).The main objective of OLTP is to complete a specific business through online processes, wherein the data generated are by-products and only part of the data are stored. Researchers suggest that OLTP enables up-to-date data and the reporting of data more flexibly (Bog, Kruger, & Schaffner, 2008). It has the following characteristics:

- Systems need to process a large number of straightforward tasks, normally as adding, deleting, inquiring, or modifying the data.
- Systems need to ensure the overall integrity of data since there is a large number of clients visit the same type of data.
- Systems should support the high-speed processing tasks and the reply time should be measured in milliseconds.
- Systems need to provide quick searching and inquiring functions.

Based on above characteristics, the application of data based on OLTP has the following specifics:

- Data are regarded as the by-products of software functionalities, and only a small part of data are stored during this procedure.
- Data and applications are stored in a whole infrastructure. Data are stored based on the logics of applications, so while searching for the data, the same tables should be used through SQL.
- Only administrators or clients of the business systems are able to enquire data.

3.2 Phase 2.0: Business Intelligence

In the Phase 1.0, data searching is only applicable to specific business personnel. While more and more businesses being supported by computer software, managerial levels need to hold a comprehensive picture on the business information to make decisions. This is the Phase 2.0 Business Intelligence. Business Intelligence is a software process for data analysis and management of business information through integrating strategies and technologies used by companies (IBM, 2019). The main objective of Business Intelligence is to "improve the timeliness and quality of inputs to the decision process, hence facilitating managerial work" (Negash, 2004, p. 178).

During this phase, data were processed based on relational data and Online Analytical Processing (OLAP). OLAP is one of the systems used by Business Intelligence to generate information (Negash, 2004). OLAP is a technology good at processing a large amount of data from different dimensions (Microsoft, 2020). Different from OLTP, OLAP focuses more on the overall trends of data changes and analysis results. OLTP only needs to visit and process the same data origins, however, OLAP can gather and analyze the data sources from multiple systems.

The main objective of OLAP is to gain business insights from data and can be regarded as a general infrastructure for data mining, business intelligence, and complicated analysis and calculations (Conn, 2005). It is frequently applied in financial analytics, budgeting development, and sales forecasting etc. The key focus of most OLAPs is to provide clients with multi-dimensional data to quickly enquire, report, and analyze them.

Table 1. Difference between OLTP and OLAP

	OLTP	OLAP
Targeted clients	Business and operations staff	Managerial people and data analytics
Focus	A small amount of data for modification and inquiry	Complicated analysis based a specific theme with a large amount of data
Data sources	Single relational database	Multi-dimensional data sources
Processing time	Measured by milliseconds	Shorter than OLTP
Concurrent visit volumes	High	Low
Data comprised	Include currently processed data	Historic data from different databases
Business values	Process current businesses	Provide business analysis and insights

In the phase of Business Intelligence, the requests from organizations management on data analytics increases steadily leading to emergence of many data techniques and products. The data processing of this phase could be classified into layers presented in Figure 2 (Ong, Siew, & Wong, 2011).

- Layer 1: Systems extract the original data to this level to formulate a data mart. Data mart is a subset of data warehouse used for supporting analytical needs (Bukhbinder, Krumenaker, & Phillips, 2005). Then the data are gathered into the data warehouse to form an enterprise-level unified data mart which provides data model to businesses. In this phase, how to manage the increasing amount of data become a specific issue and organizations' information management turns into a data management method which has been paid close attention to.
- Layer 2: It is the modeling layer. Systems model the data extracted from the data warehouse to form a set of data serving various business themes and provide quick responses.
- Layer 3: The front-end data is the application level of organizational data, using the data which has been machined by OLAP in many ways, including enquiring, reporting, real-time analysis, and data mining.

Figure 2. Three layers of data processing in Business Intelligence

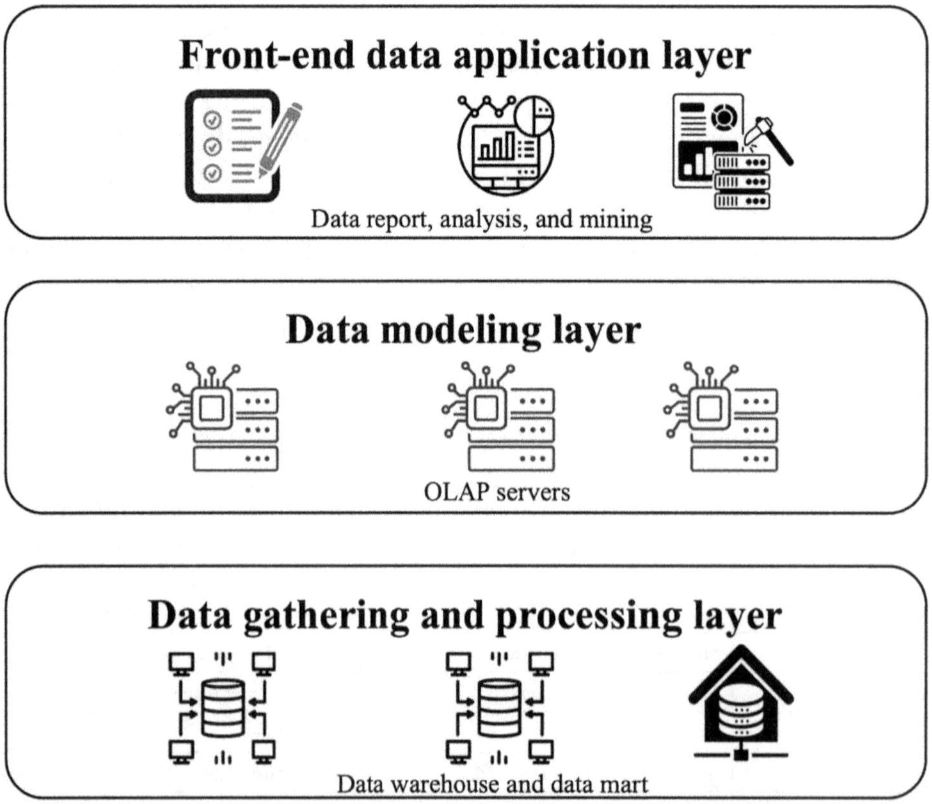

3.3 Phase 3.0: Big Data Analytics

In the Phase 2.0, many data are managed through various enterprise management systems represented by Enterprise Resource Planning system (ERP). ERP is a software that organizations use to manage their daily operations and business activities, including accounting, procurement, risk management and compliance (Oracle, 2018).

With the development of mobile development, many organizations have formulated its own e-business and membership systems and paid more attention to their client experiences. The data focus on clients' bills and the basic information could not meet organizations' analytic requests on their clients anymore. Consequently, organizations start to do the data mining from customers' behaviors and social media platforms to gain more in-depth insights on clients.

Despite the requests on data quantity and data types, organizations also have stronger value demands on their data leading to the emergence of various digital techniques such as cloud computing, big data, Internet of Things, and mobile internet techniques (Elgendy & Elragal, 2014). Consequently, a new period of big data has come. During this period, organizations rely on big data platform to process larger amount of data. Different from the previous phase, it has the following characteristics:

- The huge increase on data amount, categories, and development speed. During this phase, what organizations need is a more comprehensive, multi-dimensional, and real-time data process and analysis method, to make sure the digitalized results are consistent with the businesses and provide insights (Elgendy & Elragal, 2014).
- The data could serve all staff. In the Phase of Business Intelligence, most of the data are used to serve only managerial level, which means they are historic data instead of real-time data since they are extracted from previous business to form statistical and analytical business information. In the Phase of Big Data, the data could serve and support all functions across the organization (Russom, 2011). And the emergence of mobile internet and Internet of Things enables the connections with the front lines. Different users also have different requests on the data and digital products which requires organizations to develop the data capabilities to respond to the diversified requests quickly.
- From batch processing to real-time processing. In the previous phase, the data were processed based on OLAP, most of the work were non-real-time basis. However, in the Phase of Big Data, organizations start to have stronger demands on real-time data processing.

During this phase, data become increasingly important to organizations and the concept of data-driven organization concept is generally and widely accepted by more and more organizations.

3.4 Phase 4.0 Artificial Intelligence

In Phase 4.0, it has been transformed from Business Intelligence to Artificial Intelligence. Artificial Intelligence is an advanced technique enables developing smart machines to perform tasks and think and function as human beings (Sarker, 2022). It makes computers smart and intelligent through providing them with capabilities to think, make decisions, and learn using various techniques and programs (Sarker, 2022). In the previous phases, most of the operating decisions are made by staff and data were used as the aid decision making. In this phase, the technologies including Artificial Intelligence, Machine Learning, and Deep Learning have provided very different insights on operations compared with the traditional data analytic techniques based on statistics (Hunt, 2014). These techniques rely on algorithms and organizations entering into the times of data-driven period. Artificial Intelligence will generally become the major engine of the data-driven period, and the large amount of historic data and deal data become the valuable material for training and algorithm improvement which presents that the role of data has been changed from supporting the decision-making to directly participating into decision-making (Ertel, 2018). More specifically, organizations start to use Artificial Intelligence to conduct data modeling to develop the algorithm data to guide the business optimization.

4. MAIN CHALLENGES ON DIGITAL KNOWLEDGE TRANSFER FOR ORGANIZATIONS

To understand how the lean data management could guide organizations to transfer their data scientifically, it is important to understand the issues and difficulties they have been faced with (Tornjanski, Petrovic, & Nesic, 2020). More specifically, driven by the technology and large data scale mentioned above, today's organizations are faced with five main challenges for digital knowledge transformation including lack of data mindset, connections with businesses, high-quality data, appropriate data management platforms and tools, as well as the relevant company cultures. These challenges must be investigated and understood to drive corresponding solutions.

4.1 Challenge 1: lack of data mindsets

Data mindsets refer to the capabilities of identifying and solving problems, which determine whether employees are able to effectively analyze the data and provide corresponding solutions. It requires a high level of data sensitivity and the experiences of data processing. Employees need to be very sensitive to the data to have in-depth understandings on the business activities, explore the business laws underneath the data, and be able to develop a landscape of the data with fragmentation and lack of interconnections (Meadows et al., 2022). With the high sensitivity, people should know the ways to manage the data through segmenting, mapping, filling, or computing to transform the surface data to those with business values, opportunities, or problems (Meadows et al., 2022).

4.2 Challenge 2: lack of integrations into businesses

All the data are serving the business and should be integrated into business activities closely, which requires a valuable business scenario (Zahedi, Shahin, & Ali Babar, 2016). However, what is a valuable business scenario? This has been a challenging question for most companies today. It needs to be able to solve a specific problem and motivate relevant parties to share their data. Consequently, innovative solutions are needed to guide companies to explore the valuable business scenarios step by step.

4.3 Challenge 3: lack of high-quality data

Most companies today might be faced with the problem of lack of data. However, data are everywhere, most of them are in the mode of "deep sleep" since they lack consistencies and standards. The primary reason on this issue is the lack of an integrated structure on data application (Bond, Shipton, Jones, Butler, & Gibbs, 2007). More specifically speaking, developers focus on the business functions for data development and storage. However, most companies today are still classifying and developing their businesses based on different positions or departments, leading to the lack of overall planning. To solve the issue, companies should develop data blueprint first, and then plan the business lines.

4.4 Challenge 4: lack of data management platforms and tools (Hossain & Lassen, 2017)

Excel is still the most popular tool for many companies to manage, process and report data based on various requests. However, it leads to the management, coordination, or safety issues. It is also challenging to effectively process the large volume of data. Consequently, these organizations are faced with the dilemmas as "We do not know how to explore the values of the data in hand". Following this, they need to construct an overall data development platform to serve the business values, i.e., data center. This will be introduced in the later session.

4.5 Challenge 5: lack of company culture

As Alibaba states "We only use data to talk". Taking TikTok as another example, employees are advocated to use A/B test for problem solving wherein quantified results are derived first by data before decision making. However, most companies are still lack of data-driven culture. It acts as the foundation to explore the data value to serve business and define data as assets to generate values (Tornjanski et al., 2020). However, with the lack of company culture, the quality of data is normally neglected by the organizations. Consequently, the company culture should be regarded as the foundation for digital transformation (Tornjanski et al., 2020).

Based on the five challenges raised above, companies are required to manage the issues of data development and utilization through new solutions with the disciplines of focusing on client values, constructing autonomous data value chains, and continuous optimization. These three disciplines are the primary principles of lean theory, which has been used to guide industrial manufacture. Meanwhile, we argue that lean management is also applicable to data management and digital knowledge transfer.

6. LEAN THEORY AND LEAN DATA MANAGEMENT

6.1 Lean theory

Lean is a philosophy of manufacturing and operation integrating a set of principles, techniques, and tools into various operational processes to improve effectiveness, human resources, assets, and overall productivity and quality (Ronald, 2001). Lean theory, originated from the works of Deming (1986) and Ohno (1988), has been regarded as an essential product of the Third Industrial Revolutionary and widely adopted into the industrial production. Following this, it leads to the theory of lean manufacturing developed by Toyota Production System in the Japanese auto industry of the 1970s and 1980s (Holweg, 2007; Shah & Ward, 2007).

After World War II, the production method that dominated by American Ford Motor Company in the automobile industry was the low-variety and high-volume assembly line production method. It represented the advanced management ideas and methods which was to achieve cost reduction and productivity improvement through mass production. Compared with the American automobile industry, Japan's automobile industry was in a relatively preliminary stage during that period. Within more than ten years from its establishment to 1950s, the total output of Toyota Motor Company was not even as much as the one-day output of Ford Motor Company in the same period. Consequently, a large number of people were sent to United States for inspection.

After visiting several major automobile factories, Toyota Motor Company investigators found that there was still room for further improvement in the method of reducing costs through mass production. They believed that the strategy of large-volume and low-variety production was not applicable in Japanese market from a long-term perspective.

The founders of lean production, represented by Taiichi Ohno of Toyota Motor Corporation (Kemp, 2018), after continuous exploration, finally found a new automobile production method suitable for the Japanese market as just-in-time production, overall quality management, concurrent engineering, as well as integrated supply chain relationship management (Figure 3). Gradually, a unique lean production method of multiple varieties, small batches, high quality, and low consumption was created. The oil crisis of 1973 brought Japan's automobile industry to the world stage. Due to changes in the market environment, the weaknesses of the mass production method had become increasingly obvious, but Toyota Motor Corporation was not impacted. This was due to the implementation of lean production.

The principles of learn production method could be summarized into two sets, value creation and waste elimination (Čiarnienė & Vienažindienė, 2012). More specifically, Shah and Ward (2003) conceptualize lean production into just-in-time, total quality control, overall productive maintenance, and human resource management. Figure 4 presents the overall framework of lean production.

Focus 1: Value creation (Čiarnienė & Vienažindienė, 2012)

> Value creation has been regarded as a prominent manufacturing philosophy for customer-focused process improvements. Consequently, the key and first point for lean management is understanding and defining the values of business.

Focus 2: Waste elimination (Čiarnienė & Vienažindienė, 2012)

> Lean theory advocates for just-in-time production and eliminating wastes on human resources and equipment with limited time and space. Consequently, lean theory requires the support of just-in-time production and automation.

Figure 3. The overall framework of lean production

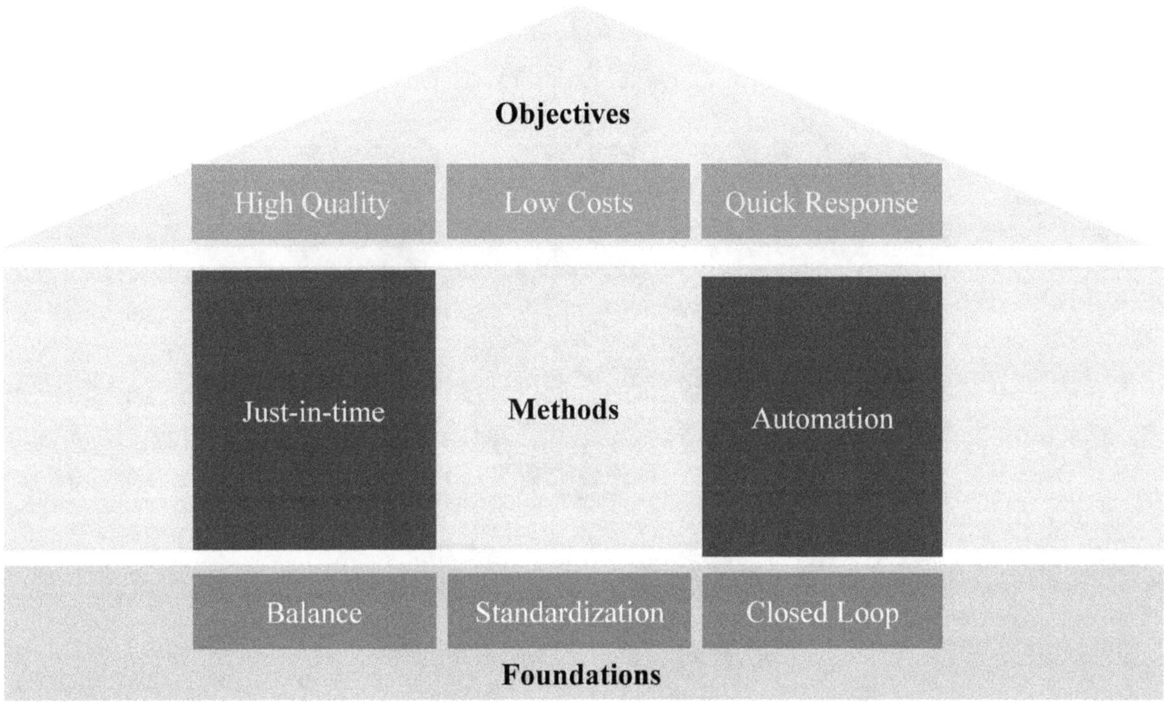

6.2 Lean Data Management

In the digital era, lean theory has been updated and widely adopted in company digitalization for data management. Following this, lean data management is the application of lean theory for transferring digital knowledge and processing data within an organization (Demirdöğen, Işık, & Arayici, 2020). Lean data management, oriented towards user value in various business scenarios, have guided companies to transfer its knowledge to a lean digitalized organization successfully. It could be regarded as a set of methodologies for digital transformation, which needs to be fully integrated into whole procedure of data development and helps organizations to achieve the following seven functions (Figure 5).

Function 1: Being visible

The first function enables relevant parties to be able to know what data they have, where the data is stored, and how the quality of the data is (Parry & Turner, 2006). The users should be authorized to access to the data they need and have a clear picture on the data categories, including the descriptions, positions, visit methods, and samples etc. Further, the data in hand should be catalogued appropriately and easy for users to search and retrieve (Parry & Turner, 2006). More importantly, to comprehensively manage the data, a data portal across the whole organization should be established and maintained to achieve the above functions.

Figure 4. The seven functions of lean data management

Function 2: Being addressable

The data should provide access to the relevant users in appropriate time and location based on appropriate methods. There are five main ways to access data.

1. Access data through documents, database, and applications.
2. Access data through data warehouse.
3. Automatically access data through Application Programming Interface (API).
4. Access, develop, search, and manage data through organizational level data directory.
5. Further modify and update data though organizational level data directory and map the relevant data based on users' requirements.

Function 3: Being trustworthy

The lean data management defines the following six objectives for data trustworthiness.

1. The data should be able to be used as the key references for decision-making.
2. The full lifecycle of data development, use, and modifications should be appropriately categorized and stored.
3. The original data of the full lifecycle should be managed appropriately to ensure that every data could be traced back to the sources.
4. The data quality assurance platforms should be developed to evaluate and improve the data quality.
5. Artificial Intelligence techniques should be applied automatically to check the key data and identify the potential issues in time.

6. The data trustworthiness and authenticity should be published regularly to invite developers and consumers for further improvement.

Function 4: Being connectable

Through formulating a unified data standard, the data could be connected and integrated (Chiarini & Kumar, 2021). Lean data management requires data connectivity to achieve the following objectives:

1. Organizations should develop standardized identifiers to make the data more easily identified, connected, searched, and referenced.
2. Quickly and easily integrate data based on data standards.
3. Using Artificial Intelligence to integrate and group data automatically and intelligently.

Function 5: Being interoperable

Being interoperable means the organizations should develop disciplines to all systems and industrial partners. And the disciplines should also include the original data needed (Chiarini & Kumar, 2021). Further, the sharing and exchange of data should also be standardized by organizations based on various levels and categories. More importantly, standards on data dissemination and acquisition should be developed to promote data integration, sharing, and interoperation (Chiarini & Kumar, 2021).

Function 6: Being understandable

The data should satisfy the following requirements to be understandable by relevant parties.

1. Clearly and comprehensively describe the original data, including names, business definitions, technique descriptions, and formats etc.
2. Easily browse the data samples. Consequently, the corresponding tools of searching data samples could be developed to let users determine whether the data provided are the ones they want through sampling.
3. Determine the data tags independently. Once users have found the data they wanted, they should be able to add data tags by themselves, which could save efforts on searching and testing the data.
4. Connect to the data use scenarios. The data should be connected to the usage scenario so that uses could better understand the data based on the contextual scenarios.
5. Be able to trace back to the original data. In the complicated scenarios, tracing back to the origins of data development and processing could help users to better understand the data.
6. Intelligent data interpretation. Through intelligent systems to manage, transform, group, or derive data, more comprehensive interpretations could be achieved.

Function 7: Being safe and controllable

Based on the lean data management theory, organizations should develop a system for data management and control, apply techniques to ensure the safety and controllability of the data (Chiarini & Kumar, 2021).

1. Refine the authority management to standardize the data access, use, and management.
2. Regularly evaluate the data categories.
3. Develop standards on data management and security check.
4. Develop prevention measures on data loss and accidental disclosure.
5. Conduct full audit on data access, use, and management.

6. Comprehensively collect, record, and monitor the procedures of data development, processing, use, sharing and dissemination and achieve automatic warnings through risk gradings and classifications.

7. CASE: DIGITAL KNOWLEDGE TRANSFORMATION JOURNEY OF BANK F BASED ON LEAN DATA MANAGEMENT APPROACH

7.1 Background information of Bank F

With more than one hundred years of history, Bank F has been recognized as one of the best retail banks in Country A and famous for its innovation and impressive customer experiences.

Bank F has started to develop its own enterprise-level data warehouse since 1980s to highlight its focus on data management. Before 2017, Bank F's digitalization started with the focus on various business lines, every business department and function had its own data management systems, which were highly dispersive and challenging to share and inquire. For instance, the credit card department did not have any information on their clients' mortgage and investment businesses.

To solve the issues, Bank F has initiated its digitalization journey since 2017 to establish a highly centralized and concentrated data management and operation team and develop an integrated data platform with a dedicated team for advanced data analytics. Generally speaking, the digital knowledge transformation journey of Bank F could be summarized as the following four aspects:

1. Achieve the organizational-level data asset management and governance.
2. Identify the future oriented business scenarios.
3. Construct an organizational-level data platform.
4. Establish data management and operation teams.

The digitalization project supported Bank F to identify a set of high value, standardized and unified data assets. And the enterprise-level data platform enabled each business department to manage its own data and develop excellent digital products in various business aspects to better understand their clients. Consequently, the management capabilities have been improved and risks have been reduced. The Chief Data Officer stated that "The data makes our company to be more agile and effective" (Newsroom, 2021).

7.2 Digital knowledge transformation journey of Bank F

7.2.1 Digital Transformation Task 1: Achieve the organizational-level data asset management and governance

Bank F has established a Chief Data Office (CDO) to lead and formulate a list of very important business documents such as data management strategies and enterprise data standards to specify the effective methods for data asset management and maintenance. These documents are consistent with the original policies on corporation, loans, information security, record management, and data protection and security to meet the supervision requirements and laws. The data governance has improved the overall operation effectiveness and client experience significantly. The following four objectives have been determined:

1. Develop organization data catalogues to enable users to clearly understand the sources of data, data products, and services.
2. Ensure the original data could be traced back on relevant systems, enabling the process of data transformation to be clearly recorded.
3. Integrate the commonly used data into unified version to make it convenient for users or regulators to inquire and acquire.
4. Establish the data communication language, platform, and tools to let different functions and departments to acquire the consistent and standardized data.

Through implementing the above data management practices, Bank F could better manage its risks, use data to solve issues, and explore opportunities of various businesses within the bank.

The data governance of Bank F includes not only the standards and procedures, but also the fundamental framework of data management techniques, and standards on the data integration and exchange. While managing the data, Bank F has also comprehensively gathered its own data assets. In 2017, Bank F analyzed the full picture of its financial data, constructed the whole lifecycle of its enterprise level data asset management, including the analysis of operational data, pricing data, and user data etc., and uniformly analyzed and designed the data sources, categories, as well as analysis methods, to make sure the overall consistency between enterprise level data management standards and top-level consistency.

This is aligned with the principles of lean data management, which advocates for enterprise data asset blueprint, i.e., constructing an overall data governance whole picture based on which to manage the data which have been generated, being generated, and to be generated in the future.

To better manage the data, Bank F also set up a position for data management and exploration. The main responsibility of this position is using and managing the data based on business objectives, explore the potential clients and customers, and make sure the practices meet the requirements of regulators. Different business lines have their own data management and exploration positions.

In summary, Bank F's data management is targeted on data application on various business lines, as well the integration of business, technologies, and the responsibilities of data management positions. It is not a pure technique work.

7.3 Digital Transformation Task 2: Identify future-oriented business scenarios and blueprint

One of the most important parts of data management for Bank F is that it not only analyzed the current status of Bank F but also designed and planned the future-oriented business scenarios and data management and application. Bank F stated that "we need to prioritize data framework designed before IT system design".

Based on the business scenarios and blueprint, Bank F has constructed the Analytic Target Operation Model focused on business analysis, through which all business departments are capable of managing data intelligently, including improving client experience, gaining insights on users and markets, managing risks and focusing on enterprise clients.

1. **Improving client experiences.**
   The data management team of Bank F analyzed more than 70 million client data to gain insights from various data and deepen understandings on client behaviors. Consequently, the client experiences have been improved dramatically.
2. Gaining insights on clients and markets.
   Through gathering clients' effective information, Bank F has been able to gain the history data to analyze the business transactions and understand various business consequences and action modes based on different client types. Following this, Bank F could be able to predict the customer behaviors and design products based on client information in hand. For instance, based on the large amount of the standardized data, Bank F has constructed Client Data Platform (CDP), through which a lot of analysis applications have been conducted, including the Chatbot for customer service, and using client service on Facebook applications such as managing cashflows, balancing outcomes and incomes, and acquiring financial management suggestions.
3. Risk management
   Risk management has been the most important task for financial companies, which can also be managed appropriately through the intelligent data. Bank F is able to implement data and intelligent technique into the risk management, including anti-money laundering, credit card frauds etc., as follows:
   a. Credit card frauds: Bank F data management team have developed an Artificial Intelligent Model to continuously monitor the fraud probabilities of credit cards. Artificial Intelligence Model is a set of programs to analyze data to find patterns and make forecasting. The model alerts while the probabilities are beyond the thresholds and take actions automatically.
   b. Bank card frauds: Bank card frauds are the most typical business scenarios for banks. The model could help banks to identify high risk events on brokerages, violations, and loan restructure.
4. Focusing on enterprise clients
   Bank F has developed a list of digital products and services based on its own data and platforms, which not only have been applied to enterprise businesses, but also changed into value-added services for enterprise clients to create values based on the following two aspects.
   a. Focusing on clients: Many companies plan for wok based on data, but Bank F has paid more attention to customer values. Bank F has identified the key clients and their journeys along with the potential issues. This has been further defined as the plans for digital knowledge transfer.
   b. Grading and classifying the plans: It is not possible for Bank F to achieve all the plans at one time. So, the plans have been graded and classified based on business strategies. Consequently, the most essential, riskiest plans are prioritized.

7.4 Digital Transformation Task 3: constructing enterprise-level advanced data management platform for Bank F

Bank F has constructed its own enterprise data platforms since 1983, including SAS, Teradata, and Oracle. For the digital knowledge transfer based on lean data management, Bank F has planned to construct a unified and fundamental data structure and used Hadoop for advanced data management platform, including the following components.

1. Advanced data management platform
   Bank F has continuously kept transferring data from traditional Teradata, Oracle, SAA independent data platforms to cloud-based or Hadoop based open data infrastructure in order to integrate and unify the enterprise data. Throughout this procedure, more than 100 independent data centers were closed to reduce costs and improve data consistency and usability. Since originally all the data of Bank F were distributed among every department, business lines, or branch, the data platform transfer was based the overall digital strategy to ensure the data were interconnected among each other and aligned with the top-level design.
2. Enterprise level data lake
   Data lake is a centralized data repository to store, management, process, and secure all structured and unstructured data at any scale (AWS, 2023a). Bank F's data consist of the following categories:
   a. Internal data: the structural data on client accounts and transaction records; unistructural data on customer service audio records, branch video records, and online business records.
   b. External data: the data on credit ratings and reports of every client, information provided by credit rating authorities or courts, or the consumption information of clients.

   Bank F has established a distributed data storage architecture based on Hadoop and data management platform to manage the enterprise level data through various techniques and unified standards.
3. Client data platform
   Bank F has focused on clients and connected every business line to construct a "horizontal client view", i.e., client data platform. Consequently, business staff could acquire the comprehensive and consistent client information, help them to develop the most accurate and real time business decisions.
4. Original data management
   To manage and define the original data, Bank F has developed a language to describe the data comprehensively and consistently and applied the data governance structure from the bottom level to ensure the overall consistency and uniqueness.
5. Data mart
   Bank F has constructed a data mart based on the data lake. Data mart is a subset of data warehouse specializing in a particular business line, department, or subject (IBM, 2023). As a result, all the data service could be developed on the data mart to provide more effective support.

6. Data Application Programming Interface (API)
   API is a mechanism enables two or more computer software or programs to communicate with each other (AWS, 2023b). Bank F has constructed its own API, and data have been provided based AIP to both internal and external departments to develop its own ecosystems. Overall, Bank F has made data to be visible and intelligent. The businesses have been more intelligent through integrating data products and service API into business systems to impact businesses on a real-time basis.
7. Machine learning
   Bank F announced to establish its own Artificial Intelligence Team in 2018 to implement machine learning and other Artificial Intelligence techniques into businesses. In February 2018, Bank F introduced the forecasting functions based on Artificial Intelligence to clients to analyze their activities and provide them suggestions and warnings, to help them manage their fortunes actively to avoid any potential loses.
8. Natural language processing
   People are more and more inclined to communicate with digital devices through natural languages instead of typing information through keyboards. Based this trend, natural language processing techniques could become the connections between our voices and control systems. In banking industries, voice verification is more straightforward, effective, and safer than passwords. It could also provide more options and convenience while clients paying the bills, transforming cash, or doing other businesses. Bank F is one of the finance companies who has applied natural language processing techniques into data management areas and constructed intelligent customer service systems based on this technique.
9. Automatic data processing
   Artificial Intelligence techniques could learn how to collect, organize, and explain data when the data appear in the same location with the same formats across time. Consequently, the time on manual and repetitive work could be saved. For instance, while banks approving the requests of opening accounts from clients, in the past, business personals need to spend a large amount of time on reviewing more than ten documents and systems. After the Artificial Intelligence techniques have been applied, business personals could focus more on clients and their requests, and the Artificial Intelligence systems could provide correct information and filter the content need to be reviewed.

Through the modern data platform, Bank F has completed the unified data gathering and storage process across the whole bank, constructed a standardized data processing chain, and developed the most important data products based on it.

7.5 Digital Transformation Task 4: Establish data management and operation teams

Bank F has set up its own Chief Data Officer since 2014 and developed its own unified data operation and management team with more than five thousand members to support every business line and function to operate and explore data, and better achieve the business objectives through data.

Figure 5. The hierarchy of data management team

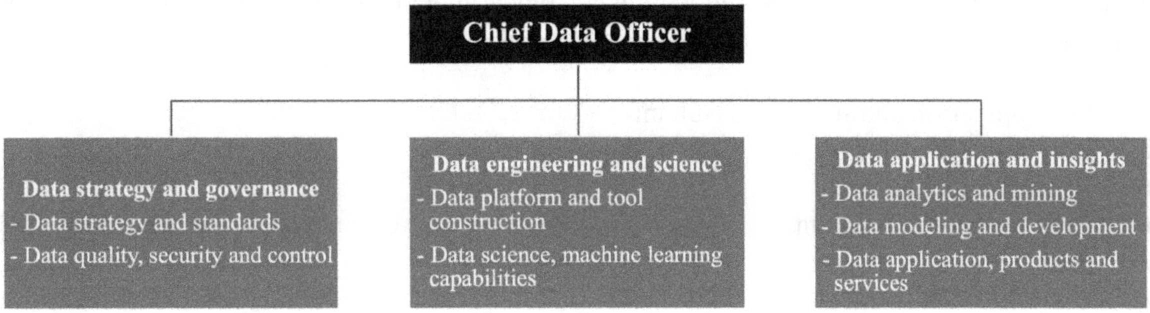

1. The key roles of Bank F data management team

The whole data management team of Bank F have been led by the Chief Data Officer with the following three lines:

a. Data strategy and governance

Data strategy and governance team are mainly responsible for developing data strategies and standardized systems, including ensuring data qualities, safeties, and controls. The team have following positions:

- Data strategy consultant
- Data governance expert
- Data gathering consultant
- Data privacy officer

b. Data engineering and science

Data engineering and science team are mainly responsible for constructing data platforms and tools and providing capabilities of data science and machine learning for organizations. The team have following positions:

- Machine learning or Artificial Intelligence engineer
- Data scientist
- Big data center engineer or data platform engineer
- Data processing personnel
- Data testing engineer

c. Data application and insights

Data application and insight team are mainly responsible for working with business teams for data analysis and exploration, data modeling and development, and data operation, application, products and services. The team have following positions:

- Data operation and insight consultant
- Data modeling consultant
- Host data management
- Data analysis consultant
- Data analysis consultant
- Data risk management team
- Data product manager

2. Organizational structures and corporation patterns of Bank F's data management team

Bank F's data strategies clearly state that the most important task to become a data-driven company is to define the data as a new element for business operations and everybody needs to have the data capabilities. To better drive data to be implemented into businesses, Bank F has set up a data team with more than five thousand people and categorized the team into every functionality which consist of two types to form a matrix and can more closely cooperate with business teams.

The first type is the centralized data management team responsible for data planning, data standards development, and the construction of general data systems, application and product services, as well as providing data capabilities and techniques to other business teams.

The second type is dedicated to a specific business line and distrusted to every business and function. The team works with the business analytics and operation personnel everyday, deal with the requests and queries from the frontlines to better understand the business and leverage data and digital techniques to solve problems.

Consequently, the team are able to diffuse data thinking, data value and data capability across the whole organization through the close collaborations with other business teams and to formulate the data organization and culture from bottom to top.

7.6 Bank F Today

Bank F never stops and has kept optimizing its digital infrastructure strategy. In 2021, Bank F announced its new digital infrastructure strategy, with the combination of a multi-cloud approach with external parties to improve its technological speed, business agility, and scalability. The head of Technology states that "our tomorrow will be digital-first and offer easier-to-use products and services, and all of that starts with the driving speed, scalability, and enhanced user experience through the next generation digital infrastructure strategy we're announcing today".

8. CONCLUSION

Digital knowledge transfer has gone through four phases of data usage, from Phase 1.0 as Statistics and Inquiry to Phase 2.0 as Business Intelligence, to Phase 3.0 as Big Data Analytics to the current period of Phase 4.0 as Artificial Intelligence. From which, it can be seen that data is transferring its role from supporting the business to making strategic decisions as human beings for companies (Ong et al., 2011). Consequently, it is important for companies today to manage and transfer their data in hand appropriately.

A very important theory as lean data management is proposed and a case as Bank F is used to see how the company followed this theory to conduct digital knowledge transfer from multiple perspectives. Bank F has been treated as the industrial benchmark of data transformation and has accepted many media publications. Based on this case, it is found that the data strategy of Bank F is the foundation of the successful digital transformation. The insights on this case could be summarized as follows:

1. Analyze the requests by focusing on customers. Among the above four tasks introduced, three of them take clients as the center. Following this, it is more important to analyze the requests through focusing on customers instead of the organization per se.
2. Business value is the key driven for data transformation. The nature of data transformation is to make data to create values for business, instead of achieving high quality data governance. So the data should be governed and leveraged through connecting with business values to achieve a sustainable data governance.
3. Data platform should be connected with business values. To construct a unified data platform to gather data assets and let frontline business personnel to acquire comprehensive client and market insights, all these should be driven by connecting with business values. Otherwise, the data will "sleep deadly" into database if the data are not applied into business scenarios.
4. The diffusion of data-driven culture should be integrated into the practices of data management teams. It is a long-term task of digital transformation, everybody should be equipped with the corresponding data capabilities to be successful finally. So the data management team should collaborate with business personnel closely to diffuse the data-driven culture across the whole organization.

To conclude, organizations should have clear and implementable data management strategies to guide the constructions of organizational data assets and the development of data element values. Lean data management strategy is to learn from the successful methods and practices of Bank F's strategic planning, being driven by business values and focusing on business scenarios, constructing the blueprints of data assets and digital techniques, which could help organizations to achieve successful digital transformation and construct lean and digital data organizations.

REFERENCES

Abd Rahman, M. S. B., Mohamad, E., & Abdul Rahman, A. A. B. (2021). Development of IoT—Enabled data analytics enhance decision support system for lean manufacturing process improvement. *Concurrent Engineering, Research and Applications*, *29*(3), 208–220. doi:10.1177/1063293X20987911

AWS. (2023a). *What is a data lake?* AWS. https://aws.amazon.com/big-data/datalakes-and-analytics/what-is-a-data-lake/

AWS. (2023b). *What is an API (Application Programming Interface)?* AWS. https://aws.amazon.com/what-is/api/#:~:text=API%20stands%20for%20Application%20Programming,other%20using%20requests%20and%20responses

Bog, A., Kruger, J., & Schaffner, J. (2008). A Composite Benchmark for Online Transaction Processing and Operational Reporting. Paper presented at the *2008 IEEE Symposium on Advanced Management of Information for Globalized Enterprises (AMIGE)*. IEEE. 10.1109/AMIGE.2008.ECP.30

Bond, C. E., Shipton, Z. K., Jones, R., Butler, R. W. H., & Gibbs, A. D. (2007). Knowledge transfer in a digital world: Field data acquisition, uncertainty, visualization, and data management. *Geosphere*, *3*(6), 568–576. doi:10.1130/GES00094.1

Bukhbinder, G., Krumenaker, M., & Phillips, A. (2005). *Insurance Industry Decision Support: Data Marts*. OLAP and Predictive Analytics.

Chiarini, A., & Kumar, M. (2021). Lean Six Sigma and Industry 4.0 integration for Operational Excellence: Evidence from Italian manufacturing companies. *Production Planning and Control*, *32*(13), 1084–1101. doi:10.1080/09537287.2020.1784485

Čiarnienė, R., & Vienažindienė, M. (2012). Lean manufacturing: theory and practice. *Economics and management, 17*(2), 726-732. doi:10.5755/j01.em.17.2.2205

Conn, S. S. (2005). OLTP and OLAP data integration: a review of feasible implementation methods and architectures for real time data analysis. Paper presented at *IEEE SoutheastCon, 2005*. IEEE.

Deming, W. E. (1986). *Out of the Crisis*. MIT Press.

Demirdöğen, G., Işık, Z., & Arayici, Y. (2020). Lean management framework for healthcare facilities integrating BIM, BEPS and big data analytics. *Sustainability (Basel)*, *12*(17), 7061. doi:10.3390/su12177061

Elgendy, N., & Elragal, A. (2014). Big Data Analytics: A Literature Review Paper. Paper presented at the *Advances in Data Mining*. Applications and Theoretical Aspects, Cham.

Ertel, W. (2018). *Introduction to artificial intelligence*. Springer.

Gupta, S., Modgil, S., & Gunasekaran, A. (2020). Big data in lean six sigma: A review and further research directions. *International Journal of Production Research, 58*(3), 947–969. doi:10.1080/00207543.2019.1598599

Holweg, M. (2007). The genealogy of lean production. *Journal of Operations Management, 25*(2), 420–437. doi:10.1016/j.jom.2006.04.001

Hossain, M., & Lassen, A. H. (2017). How do digital platforms for ideas, technologies, and knowledge transfer act as enablers for digital transformation? *Technology Innovation Management Review*, *7*(9), 55–60. doi:10.22215/timreview/1106

Hunt, E. B. (2014). *Artificial intelligence.* Academic Press.

IBM. (2019). *What is business intelligence?* IBM. https://www.ibm.com/topics/business-intelligence

IBM. (2021). *What is OLTP?* IBM. https://www.ibm.com/topics/oltp#:~:text=OLTP%2C%20or%20online%20transactional%20processing,of%20data%20in%20a%20database

IBM. (2023). *What is a data mart?* IBM. https://www.ibm.com/topics/data-mart

Kemp, A. (2018). *Taiichi Ohno: Hero of the Toyota Production System.* QAD. https://www.qad.com/blog/2018/03/taiichi-ohno-toyota-production-system

Meadows, M., Merendino, A., Dibb, S., Garcia-Perez, A., Hinton, M., Papagiannidis, S., Pappas, I., & Wang, H. (2022). Tension in the data environment: How organisations can meet the challenge. *Technological Forecasting and Social Change*, *175*, 121315. doi:10.1016/j.techfore.2021.121315

Microsoft. (2020). *Online analytical processing (OLAP).* Microsoft. https://learn.microsoft.com/en-us/azure/architecture/data-guide/relational-data/online-analytical-processing

Negash, S. (2004). Business intelligence. *Communications of the Association for Information Systems*, *13*(1), 15. doi:10.17705/1CAIS.01315

Newsroom. (2021). *Wells Fargo Announces New Digital Infrastructure Strategy and Strategic Partnerships With Microsoft, Google Cloud.* NewsRoom. https://newsroom.wf.com/English/news-releases/news-release-details/2021/Wells-Fargo-Announces-New-Digital-Infrastructure-Strategy-and-Strategic-Partnerships-With-Microsoft-Google-Cloud/default.aspx

Ohno, T. (1988). *Toyota Production Systems: Beyond Large Scale Production.* QAD. https://www.qad.com/blog/2018/03/taiichi-ohno-toyota-production-system

Ong, I. L., Siew, P. H., & Wong, S. F. (2011). A five-layered business intelligence architecture. *Communications of the IBIMA*, *2011*, 1–11. doi:10.5171/2011.695619

Oracle. (2018). What is ERP? *Oracle.* https://www.oracle.com/erp/what-is-erp/#:~:text=Enterprise%20resource%20planning%20(ERP)%20refers,compliance%2C%20and%20supply%20chain%20operations

Parry, G. C., & Turner, C. E. (2006). Application of lean visual process management tools. *Production Planning and Control*, *17*(1), 77–86. doi:10.1080/09537280500414991

Russom, P. (2011). Big data analytics. *TDWI best practices report, fourth quarter, 19*(4), 1-34.

Sarker, I. H. (2022). AI-Based Modeling: Techniques, Applications and Research Issues Towards Automation, Intelligent and Smart Systems. *SN Computer Science*, *3*(2), 158. doi:10.1007/s42979-022-01043-x PMID:35194580

Shah, R., & Ward, P. T. (2007). Defining and developing measures of lean production. *Journal of Operations Management*, *25*(4), 785–805. doi:10.1016/j.jom.2007.01.019

Tornjanski, V., Petrovic, D., & Nesic, S. (2020). Effectiveness of knowledge transfer between project team members in digitally disrupted organizations. *Management: Journal of Sustainable Business and Management Solutions in Emerging Economies*, *25*(2), 1–14.

Zahedi, M., Shahin, M., & Ali Babar, M. (2016). A systematic review of knowledge sharing challenges and practices in global software development. *International Journal of Information Management*, *36*(6, 6, Part A), 995–1019. doi:10.1016/j.ijinfomgt.2016.06.007

KEY TERMS AND DEFINITIONS

Application Programming Interface (API): Mechanisms enable two or more computer software or programs to communicate with each other.

Artificial Intelligence Model: A set of programs to analyze data to find patterns and make forecasting.

Artificial Intelligence: An advanced technique enables developing smart machines to perform tasks and think and function as human beings.

Business Intelligence: Business Intelligence is a software process for data analysis and management of business information through integrating strategies and technologies used by companies.

Data Lake: A centralized data repository to store, management, process, and secure all structured and unstructured data at any scale.

Data mart: A subset of data warehouse specializing in a particular business line, department, or subject.

Lean theory: A philosophy of manufacturing and operation integrating a set of principles, techniques, and tools into various operational processes to improve effectiveness, human resources, assets, and overall productivity and quality.

Online Analytical Processing (OLAP): A technology good at processing a large amount of data from different dimensions.

Online Transaction Processing (OLTP): A type of data processing enables the online real-time execution of a large number of transactions by a large number of people.

Chapter 8
Examining the Effectiveness of Machine Learning Models for Interest Rate Prediction

Vandana Sharma
https://orcid.org/0000-0002-9612-7721
J.C. Bose University of Science and Technology YMCA, India

ABSTRACT

The banking sector plays a vital role in economic growth, offering financial services and determining interest rates, influencing borrowing and investment decisions. Traditional uniform rates based on risk assessments and market conditions may not suit today's diverse economic landscape. Leveraging big data and machine learning, the idea of personalized interest rates is explored. The proposed work examines the effectiveness of two machine learning based classification algorithms logistic regression and K-Nearest Neighbours (KNN) for predicting personalized interest rates in the banking sector. The study collects and explores a dataset from Lending Club by conducting thorough exploratory data analysis (EDA). Despite getting low accuracies, this research is pioneering in the field of interest rate prediction and provides a foundation for further research in this area. The EDA conducted during the study contributes valuable insights into the dataset's structure, enabling better understanding and identification of potential challenges and improvements for future models.

1. INTRODUCTION

Interest rates are the lifeblood of financial markets, driving investment decisions, shaping economic policies, and influencing the choices of individuals and businesses. Traditional methods of forecasting interest rates have relied heavily on economic indicators, historical trends, and expert judgment. While these approaches have served us well, the ever-increasing complexity of global financial markets demands a more agile and data-centric methodology as the global

DOI: 10.4018/979-8-3693-1331-2.ch008

economy is projected to grow 6.0% in 2021 and 4.9% in 2022 (Abedin et al., 2021). The ability to accurately predict changes in interest rates has profound implications for financial institutions, investors, and policymakers alike. Machine learning, with its capacity to analyze vast amounts of data and identify subtle patterns, presents a promising avenue for enhancing our understanding of interest rate dynamics. As we stand on the cusp of a data-driven revolution, machine learning algorithms have emerged as powerful tools capable of extracting patterns and insights from vast datasets. This research paper embarks on a journey to harness the capabilities of machine learning in the realm of finance, specifically in the context of "Predicting Interest Rates." This approach, in turn, provides a competitive advantage to banks, attracting and retaining more customers in a fiercely competitive market. Moreover, the precise evaluation of individual creditworthiness and risk empowers banks to improve their profitability through optimized lending portfolios and reduced provisioning. Personalized interest rates also play a key role in promoting financial inclusion, making credit more accessible to those with limited credit histories or belonging to underserved communities, thereby fostering a more inclusive banking environment. Also, interest rates based on individual profile contribute to economic stability by enabling prudent lending practices and reducing the likelihood of systemic risks. In light of these compelling reasons, interest rate predictions have the potential to revolutionize the banking sector, benefiting both financial institutions and their customers.

The motivation behind this research paper is twofold. First, it recognizes the growing demand for accurate and timely interest rate predictions, given the pivotal role of interest rates in economic decision-making. Second, it acknowledges the vast troves of data available today, encompassing financial market indicators, macroeconomic variables, social sentiment, and more. The convergence of these factors underscores the opportunity to employ machine learning to predict interest rates more effectively than ever before. This study aims to provide a comprehensive exploration of the application of machine learning techniques to interest rate prediction. It will delve into the various machine learning models and algorithms to assess their suitability and performance in predicting interest rate movements. Additionally, the research will consider the significance of different data sources and features in improving prediction accuracy.

Financial crises such as the Global Financial Crisis of 2007–2008, and crisis induced by the COVID-19 pandemic have effects on both commodity and financial markets (Abedin et al., 2021). By analyzing historical interest rate data, macroeconomic factors, and financial market indicators, this research paper will seek to uncover hidden patterns and relationships that traditional forecasting methods may overlook. It will also evaluate the potential challenges and limitations associated with machine learning-based predictions, such as model interpretability and data quality. Through the evaluation of machine learning algorithms like Logistic Regression and K-Nearest Neighbors, this research aims to provide valuable insights to empower banking institutions in adopting customer-centric and data-driven approaches to interest rate setting, ultimately fostering a sustainable and customer-friendly financial ecosystem. The outcomes of this research endeavor have the potential to reshape how we approach interest rate predictions, providing stakeholders with more robust and timely insights. It is our hope that this exploration into the fusion of finance and machine learning will contribute to a deeper understanding of interest rate dynamics and open new avenues for informed decision-making in the ever-evolving landscape of global finance.

2. BACKGROUND

Interest represents a charge imposed on the borrower for the use of an asset. The borrowed assets may encompass currency, goods, vehicles, and property. As a consequence, interest rates are at times denoted as the "price of borrowing" due to their augmentation of the cost for obtaining the same sum of money. Therefore, most transactions involving loans and borrowing are subject to interest rates. Individuals secure loans to purchase homes, fund ventures, establish or expand businesses, or address educational expenses. Enterprises utilize loans to finance capital outlays and expand by acquiring long-term, fixed assets such as property, equipment, and structures. The reimbursement of borrowed capital can be effectuated through monthly installments or a lump sum settled by a predetermined due date. The present interest rate and the state of the local economy are the main reasons for defaults. These variables' relative importance varies from nation to nation, but they are always the most important factors in terms of explanatory power across the board (Barbaglia et al., 2023).

2.1 Understanding Interest Rates

In the context of loans, the initial sum, which is the complete loan amount, is influenced by the interest rate. This rate signifies both the profit rate for the lender and the debt cost for the borrower. Because lenders seek compensation for the use of funds they lacked during the loan period, the outstanding sum generally exceeds the borrowed amount. Throughout this period, the lender might have instead invested the money, enabling the asset to generate income, rather than offering it as a loan. The interest levied is the contrast between the overall repayment and the original loan value. The borrower frequently pays lesser interest rates if the lender deems them to be less-risky borrowers. A higher interest rate will be applied to a borrower deemed to pose a greater risk, hence increasing the cost of the loan.

2.2 How Are Interest Rates Determined?

Bank interest rates are influenced by several variables, including the overall health of the economy. The interest rate that a nation's central bank sets determines the range of annual percentage rates that individual banks offer. The cost of debt increases when interest rates are set high by the central bank. A high cost of debt deters people from taking out loans and reduces demand from consumers. Inflation also has a tendency to raise interest rates. To combat inflation, banks can opt to elevate reserve mandates, constrict the money supply, or boost the demand for credit. In economies characterized by elevated interest rates, individuals tend to save more because the interest on savings accounts yields a greater profit. As a consequence of investors favoring the allure of higher savings rates over stock market investments, which offer lower returns, the stock market experiences a downturn. Furthermore, the limitations on businesses' access to debt-based capital funding lead to an economic downturn. Because borrowers may obtain loans at cheap rates during these times, economies are frequently boosted. Entrepreneur and consumers have great tendency or inclination to pay out money and buy precarious expenditures like stocks since savings interest rates are low. Spending like this stimulates the economy and injects cash into the markets, which leads to economic growth. Lower interest rates are preferred by governments, but they eventually cause market disequilibrium, which increases inflation when demand exceeds supply. Interest rates rise in the presence of inflation. The primary institutional bank factors that affect interest rates are shown in Figure 1.

Figure 1. Factors determining interest rates

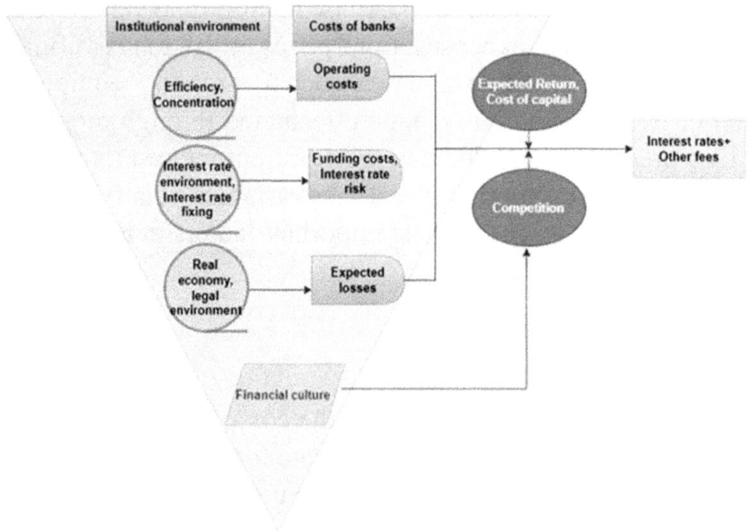

In brief, the interest rate is the percentage a lender imposes on a borrower, calculated based on the initial loan amount lent. The annual percentage rate (APR) is the standard method used to indicate the interest rate on a loan. It determines the annual percentage of the principal pay by factoring in monthly payments and other charges. The annual percentage rate (APR) is also the interest rate paid on assets each year, excluding the interest that compounds over the course of the year. The periodic interest rate is multiplied by the number of times in a year that it was applied to determine the annual percentage rate, or APR. The funds earned from holding savings in a bank or credit union, such as in a savings account or certificate of deposit (CD), can also be affected by an interest rate. The interest gained from these deposit accounts is commonly known as the annual percentage yield (APY).

2.3 Machine Learning: An Overview

Through the use of preprogrammed algorithms that gather and process input variables, machine learning generates results as output data that fall between suitable classes. These algorithms build "intelligence" over time by improving their operations to boost performance and learning from new data as it is supplied to them. The four types of machine learning algorithms are reinforcement learning, unsupervised learning, semi-supervised learning, and supervised learning.

2.3.1 Supervised Learning

Supervised learning involves training the machine through modeling. The machine learning system must figure out how to obtain the required inputs and outputs from a provided dataset, with the operator having knowledge of the correct solutions. The algorithm learns from observations, identifies data patterns, and generates predictions. This iterative process continues until the algorithm performs with a high level of accuracy. The operator refines the algorithm as it produces predictions. Supervised learning encompasses tasks like classification, regression, and prediction.

1. **Classification**: When performing a classification job, a machine learning algorithm must infer a conclusion from observed values and decide which category fresh observations fall into. For instance, the software must examine current observational data and classify emails as "spam" or "not spam" in accordance.
2. **Regression**: In tasks involving regression, a machine learning software must estimate and comprehend the connections between variables. Regression analysis is very helpful for prediction and forecasting since it concentrates on one dependent variable and a number of other changing factors.
3. **Prediction**: Often used to analyze trends, predicting is the act of forecasting about the future based on the past and current data.

2.3.2 Semi-Supervised Learning

Semi-supervised learning, which utilizes a combination of labeled and unlabeled data, bears a resemblance to supervised learning. In order for the algorithm to interpret the data, the information must have relevant tags, which is what labeled data primarily consists of. Unlabelled data is devoid of these tags. Machine learning algorithms may acquire the ability to label unlabelled data by utilizing this combination.

2.3.3 Unsupervised Learning

In this scenario, the machine learning system examines data independently to uncover patterns. There is no predefined response key or human operator for guidance. Instead, the system scrutinizes the available data to uncover relationships and associations. An unsupervised learning process entails providing a substantial volume of data to a machine learning algorithm, allowing it to analyze and respond as necessary. The algorithm endeavors to organize the data in a manner that reveals its underlying structure, which could involve grouping or structuring the data more coherently. As it evaluates additional data, the algorithm progressively improves its ability to make decisions based on that information. Below techniques fall under the category of unsupervised learning:

1. **Clustering:** To organize linked data collections (using preset criteria). Data may be categorized and analyzed for patterns by breaking the data up into smaller groups.

2. **Dimension reduction:** To discover the precise information needed, dimension reduction decreases the number of factors taken into account.

2.3.4 Reinforcement Learning

Reinforcement learning is focused on systematic learning procedures, involving the provision of actions, parameters, and target objectives to a machine learning algorithm. Once the criteria are set, the algorithm supervises and assesses each output to ascertain the optimal choice. It seeks to explore various alternatives and possibilities. Reinforcement learning is essentially a process of training the machine through experimentation. It gains insights from past mistakes and adapts its strategies based on the current context to achieve the most favorable outcome.

The suitability of a machine learning algorithm for use is determined by a combination of factors, including the volume, quality, and diversity of the data, as well as the specific insights organizations aim to derive from it. Numerous additional elements, including as parameters, data points, training length, accuracy, and many more, are also crucial. Thus, choosing the right algorithm necessitates taking into account the specification, experimentation, business necessity, and available time. Without initially evaluating alternatives, even the most experienced data scientists are unable to determine which algorithm will perform best. The following are the most popular and widely used machine learning formulas:

1. Naïve Bayes Classifier Algorithm (Supervised Learning - Classification)
   The Naive Bayes classifier employs the Bayes theorem to classify each value as though it's unrelated to all other values. It enables us to make predictions about a particular category or class using probability, relying on a given dataset. Despite its simplicity, this classifier is commonly utilized because it often surpasses more complex classification methods in performance.
2. K Means Clustering Algorithm (Unsupervised Learning - Clustering)
   Unsupervised learning methods like as the K Means Clustering approach are employed for the classification of unlabeled data, or data that lacks well-defined groups or categories. The variable K indicates the number of groups detected by the procedure, which locates groups in the data. It then proceeds to repeatedly assign every point of data to one of K groups depending on the specified attributes.
3. Support Vector Machine Algorithm (Supervised Learning - Classification)
   In regression analysis and classification, data is examined through the application of support vector machine methods. This model efficiently categorizes features by using training examples that are labeled as belongs to particular category. Subsequently, the technique proceeds to construct a model that assigns new data points to one or both of these classes.
4. Linear Regression (Supervised Learning/Regression)
   Linear regression stands as the fundamental form of regression analysis. Employing simple linear regression, we gain insights into the associations among two continuous features.
5. Logistic Regression (Supervised learning – Classification)
   This methods is mainly used to categorize categorical dataset that contain some independent variable with a dependent variable. Logistic regression converts independent variables into

expression of probability between 0 and 1 with related to the dependent variable which contains binary values.

6. Artificial Neural Networks (Reinforcement Learning)
   It is composed of 'units' that are linked to layers on both sides. This method is inspired from the working of human brain. It is a large network of linked processing units that work together to solve certain problems. They pick up knowledge from experience and action as well.
7. Decision Trees (Supervised Learning – Classification/Regression)
   A decision tree, resembling a flowchart, represents potential outcomes for each action by branching out. At each node, which represents a test for a specific variable, the tree displays the results of the tests performed.
8. Random Forests (Supervised Learning – Classification/Regression)
   An ensemble learning technique called random forests uses many algorithms to improve task-related outcomes like regression and classification. All of the classifiers are weak on their own, even if they perform best when combined. The method creates a "decision tree," or hierarchal representation of inferences, with an input positioned above. As the data descends the tree, it is then split up into even smaller groups based on predetermined standards.
9. K Nearest Neighbors (Supervised Learning)
   This method is used to assess the probability of an observation belonging with specific class. This approach analyzes nearby data item in order to ascertain the group affiliation of a given data point. For instance, when this algorithm is determining whether a data point, placed on a grid, is from Group A or Group B, it analyzes other data items in the vicinity to identify the predominant group among them.

Role of Machine Learning in Banking Innovation

In recent years, machine learning has emerged as a transformative paradigm in the field of computer science and data analysis. This efficient approach involves constructing models and algorithms that allow computers to acquire knowledge from data and render forecasts or decisions without the necessity of explicit coding. Machine learning has found applications in a wide range of domains, including natural language processing, image recognition, healthcare, finance, and more. Its ability to extract meaningful patterns and insights from complex datasets has made it a pivotal tool for researchers and practitioners alike. This background section provides an overview of the fundamental concepts and significance of machine learning, highlighting its growing importance in addressing diverse research challenges and fostering innovation across various disciplines. Machine learning can play a valuable role in helping banks decide interest rates in several ways:

1. **Risk Assessment:** Machine learning models can analyze vast amounts of data, including credit scores, income levels, employment history, and transaction history, to assess the creditworthiness of borrowers. By predicting the likelihood of default or late payments, banks can determine the appropriate interest rate to charge to mitigate their risk.

2. **Market Analysis:** Machine learning algorithms can process real-time economic and market data, including inflation rates, interest rates set by central banks, and trends in financial markets. This analysis can help banks adjust their interest rates in response to changing market conditions to remain competitive and profitable.
3. **Customer Segmentation:** Banks can use machine learning to segment their customer base into different groups based on various factors such as age, income, spending habits, and financial goals. Different interest rates can then be offered to each segment to better meet their specific needs and maximize profitability.
4. **Fraud Detection:** Machine learning models can detect fraudulent activities and transactions in real-time. By identifying and preventing fraud, banks can reduce their losses and, consequently, may be able to offer more competitive interest rates to their customers.
5. **Predictive Analytics:** Predictive modeling can help banks anticipate changes in interest rates and economic conditions. By incorporating these predictions into their decision-making processes, banks can make proactive adjustments to interest rates to optimize their profitability.
6. **Customer Feedback Analysis:** Machine learning offers the means to assess customer feedback, sentiment on social media, and online reviews, enabling a deeper understanding of customer contentment and inclinations. Banks can leverage this data to make well-informed choices regarding interest rates and other financial offerings.
7. **Optimizing Loan Pricing:** Machine learning can help banks optimize loan pricing by considering a range of factors, such as the cost of funds, operational expenses, and desired profit margins. This can lead to more competitive interest rates for borrowers while still ensuring the bank's profitability.
8. **Dynamic Pricing:** Machine learning empowers banks to adopt flexible pricing tactics, allowing for the real-time adaptation of interest rates in response to demand, risk variables, and market dynamics. This methodology allows banks to optimize their profits while providing borrowers with competitive interest rates.
9. **Compliance and Regulation:** Machine learning can assist banks in ensuring compliance with regulatory requirements related to interest rate determination. By automating compliance checks, banks can avoid penalties and legal issues.
10. **Portfolio Management:** Machine learning can help banks optimize their loan portfolios by predicting which loans are more likely to default or become delinquent. This allows banks to make informed decisions about interest rates for specific loans or classes of loans.

In summary, machine learning can enhance the decision-making process for banks when it comes to setting interest rates by improving risk assessment, market analysis, customer segmentation, fraud detection, predictive analytics, and more. However, it's essential to use these technologies responsibly and ethically, considering factors such as fairness, transparency, and data privacy when implementing machine learning in financial decision-making processes.

3. LITERATURE REVIEW

For an extensive literature survey it is of vital importance to explore and analyze most relevant articles to know about the research state, pertinent gaps and various state of the art models. Choosing relevant keywords for exploring related articles is a foremost step in a review process. Various keywords and substrings are applied for getting appropriate research articles. A word cloud is depicted in Figure 2 by using all the titles of various research papers used in the study such as Interest rates, Banking, Machine Learning, Personalized rates etc.

Figure 2. Word cloud

The basic outline of a methodical approach applied for the review process is depicted in Figure 3.

Figure 3. Methodology

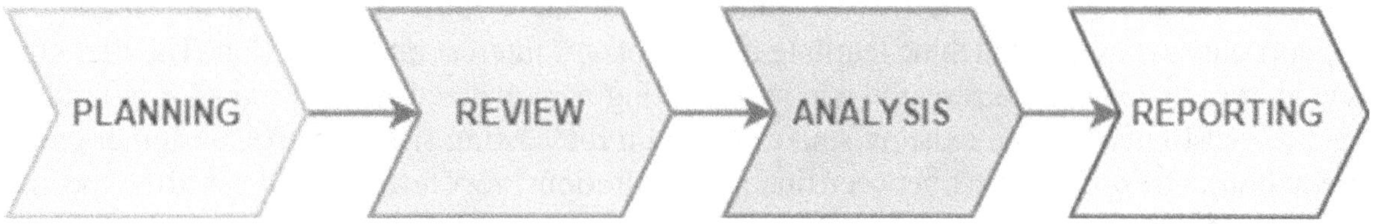

1. **Plan:** In the planning stage of literature review, we establish a clear roadmap for how we will gather and analyze relevant literature for our research on interest rate prediction using machine learning algorithms. We begin by clearly defining the objectives and goals of our literature review. Thus we state that the primary aim is to evaluate the existing literature on machine learning algorithms in the context of interest rate prediction. Then we define the scope of our literature review by specifying the types of sources (academic journals, conference papers, books, etc.) and any criteria for inclusion (e.g., publication date, relevance to your research). By detailing the strategies we will employ to search for relevant literature. This might include using academic databases, keywords, and Boolean operators to identify articles and papers related to the topic.
2. **Review:** The review phase involves systematically collecting and assessing the identified literature. It describes how we collect the relevant literature based on our search strategy. It mentions the sources used and any databases or academic search engines explored. It may explain the process of extracting key information from each source, such as the title, authors, publication date, research methodology, and findings. It can helps in categorizing the literature into relevant themes or topics related to machine learning algorithms and interest rate prediction.
3. **Analyze:** This step involves critically evaluating and synthesizing the information gathered from the literature. It mention how critically one assess the quality of each source, considering factors like the credibility of the authors, the rigor of the research methodology, and the relevance to the research. It describes how to compare and synthesize the findings and insights from different sources. This involves identifying common trends, contradictions, gaps in the literature, and any emerging patterns. Key concepts are highlighted using theories, and approaches in the literature that are pertinent to the proposed model.
4. **Report:** In this final step, the results of the literature review are compiled into a coherent report. Explain it as follows. It helps in summarizing the main findings and defining a conclusion from the literature review. It may provide recommendations for future research based on the gaps and insights that are identified during the analysis. It emphasizes that one must properly cite all the sources used in accordance with a specific citation style and create a bibliography or reference list.

By following these four steps—plan, review, analyze, and report—we systematically conducted our literature review, ensuring that we gather, assess, and synthesize relevant information to support our research on machine learning algorithms for interest rate prediction. The literature review revealed a notable research gap in predicting personalized interest rates for individual banking customers. While existing studies focus on forecasting risk in banks, customer churn prediction, and exchange rates between financial institutions, very few have addressed the specific challenge of predicting interest rates for individual customers. This research aims to fill this gap by developing an innovative machine learning model that accurately predicts personalized interest rates. Some of the research outcome of the notable researchers in the domain is highlighted.

Abedin et al. (2021) presented Bi-LSTM BR, an ensemble deep learning method designed to predict exchange rates for 21 different currencies compared to the USD in both pre-COVID-19 and COVID-19 timeframes. This novel model surpasses conventional and deep learning-driven algorithms in its ability to forecast exchange rates, exhibiting reduced prediction errors. Nonetheless, it's worth noting that the model's performance fluctuates considerably in volatile market conditions, underscoring its significance during such periods. The study provides valuable advantages to foreign exchange traders by enhancing predictive accuracy and identifying the currencies most impacted, thereby aiding in potential trading gains and risk mitigation in the context of the pandemic.

Barbaglia et al. (2023) conducted an analysis of 12 million residential mortgages in various European countries to gain insights into the patterns of loan defaults. By employing machine learning algorithms, the research identifies borrower characteristics, loan-specific factors, and local economic conditions as significant predictors of default. Compared to logistic regression, machine learning models offer more accurate predictions, emphasizing the importance of region-specific risk-assessment policies in Europe, particularly considering interest rates and local economic characteristics.

Bellotti et al. (2021) conducted a comparison of diverse regression methods and data mining techniques in relation to predicting failed loan repayment rates. Rule-based algorithms, such as Cubist, boosted trees, and random forests, exhibit superior performance when contrasted with alternative approaches. Furthermore, the inclusion of variables linked to the bank's recovery process, such as the history of interactions with defaulted clients and client reimbursements, enhances the precision of all algorithms in discerning debtors with differing repayment capabilities and prospects for recovery.

Goncu (2019) utilizes a variety of machine learning regression techniques, including Ridge, decision tree, support vector, and linear regression, to forecast exchange rates for the following month. This prediction takes into account various factors such as domestic money supply, real interest rates, the Federal Funds rate, and the previous month's exchange rate. The Ridge regression approach provides precise forecasts, with errors measuring less than 60 basis points, which proves valuable for investors and policymakers in assessing the impact of interest rates on exchange rates.

Wei et al. (2021) tackle the deficiencies present in existing performance evaluation research for commercial banks, which predominantly concentrate on individual characteristics and lack comprehensive analysis. Their study introduces a groundbreaking method that utilizes an adaptively reduced step-size gradient boosting regression tree algorithm for evaluating bank performance.By considering multidimensional features and unobservable data, this method provides better classification results for rural banks' performance in China.

Muneer et al. (2022) aims to predict churning customers, particularly in the banking sector, using three intelligent models: random forest, AdaBoost, and support vector machine. By applying the synthetic minority oversampling technique (SMOTE) to address imbalanced data, the proposed approach achieved remarkable results, with an F1 score of 91.90% and 88.7% overall accuracy using the random forest model. Notably, the random forest model also performed well on fully feature-selected datasets.

Naeem et al. (2021) introduced a machine learning methodology for predicting currency exchange rates through sentiment analysis of Twitter posts. They prepared and annotated data from a forex website and finance-related tweets to determine whether exchange rates would rise or fall. Employing multiple classifiers, including logistic, random forest, bagging, naïve Bayes, and support vector machines, the research attained an 82.14% accuracy in forecasting USD to PKR exchange rates.

Suimon et al. (2020) focuses on the impact of overseas financial crises and changes in US and European monetary policies on the Japanese interest rates market. By incorporating machine learning methods and data from overseas rates markets, the study developed a forecasting model for Japanese interest rates. The inclusion of US interest rates data notably improved the prediction accuracy of Japanese long-term interest rates, especially after 2006, indicating the usefulness of overseas interest rates information in forecasting the Japanese rates market.

Sun et al. (2020) introduces LSTM-B, a novel ensemble deep learning method integrating LSTM neural network and bagging strategy. It focuses not only on accurate exchange rate forecasting but also on improving trading profitability. LSTM-B outperforms other benchmarks in both forecasting accuracy and potential trading profitability, demonstrating its effectiveness in advising professional trading decisions for major currency exchange rates.

A Scientometric analysis is performed to assess and analyze previous research based on Machine Learning for Banking and Finance. Figure 4 depicts the Documents published between 2009 and 2023. As we can see there is a significant increase of research in the year 2022.

Figure 4. Documents by year

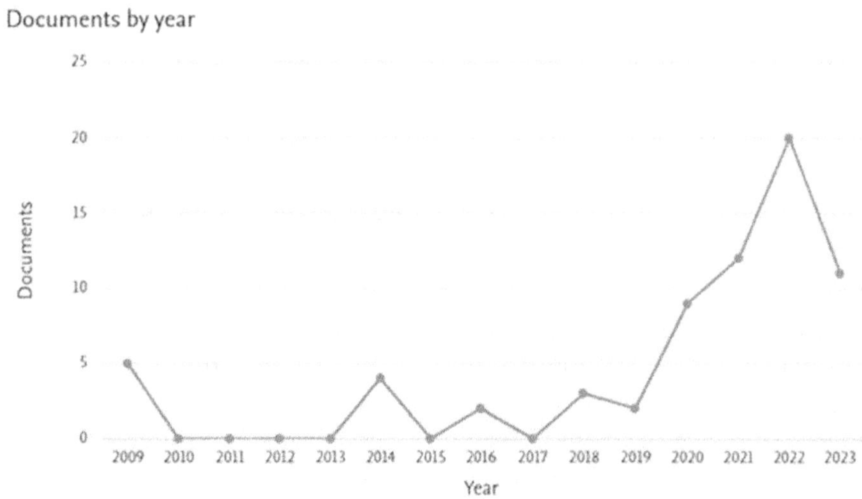

Below figure 5 represents the published research papers in the field of finance using machine learning. India is the country that leads the table with highest number of research papers.

Figure 6 describes many different subject areas in which researchers have published their work. Computer Science is the area with leading research articles followed by Engineering and Business management domain.

The type of research publications are represented in figure 7 that depicts the highest ratio of Conference research papers and Research articles.

Figure 5. Documents by country

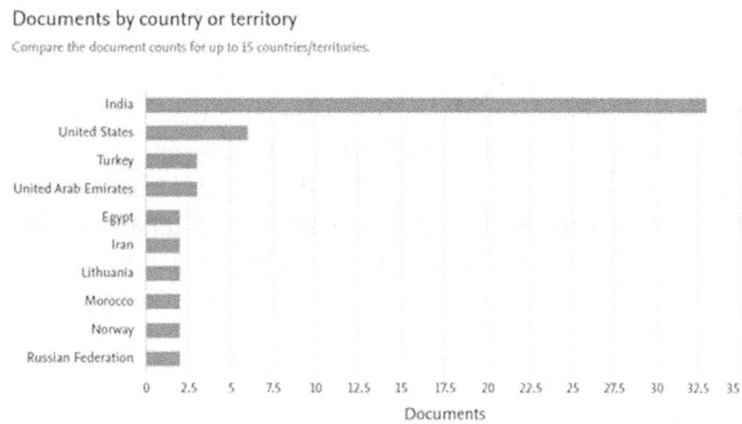

Figure 6. Documents by subject area

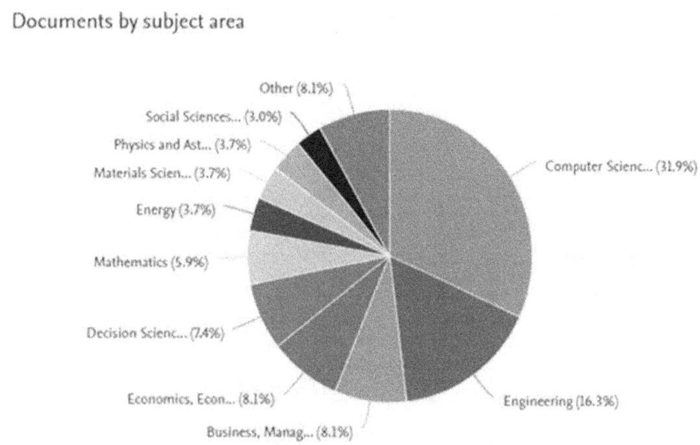

Figure 7. Documents by type

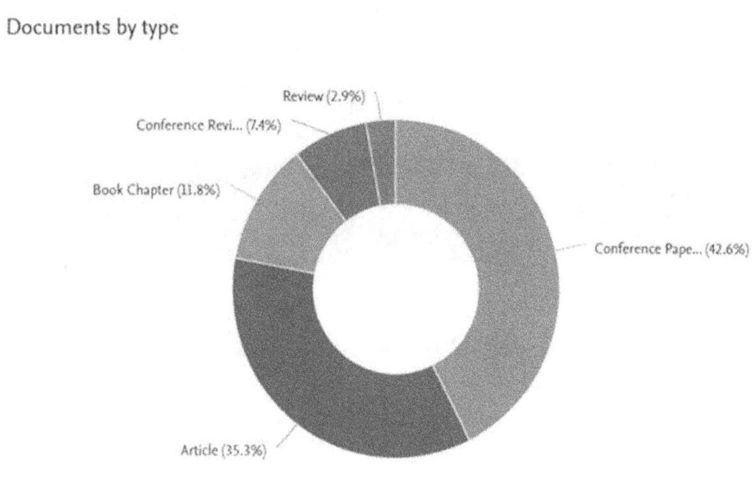

The existing research in the field lacks a machine learning model capable of predicting personalized interest rates for individual bank customers based on their past history or performance. This critical gap in the literature hinders the ability to offer tailored interest rates, potentially limiting customer satisfaction and overall growth in the banking sector. Moreover analysing and forecasting exchange rates is a challenging task for the scientific community due to its nonlinear, complex and irregular structural feature (Sun, 2020). In response to this research gap, our study proposes a novel machine learning approach specifically designed to predict personalized interest rates for individual banking customers. By leveraging historical data and customer performance metrics, our model aims to bridge this gap and provide valuable insights for the banking industry, enabling more personalized and customer-centric interest rate offerings.

4. METHODOLOGY

The architecture presents a clear and systematic representation of the research approach used in this study. Figure 8 illustrates the step-by-step process of how data was collected, processed, and analyzed to achieve the research objectives.

Figure 8. Proposed model architecture

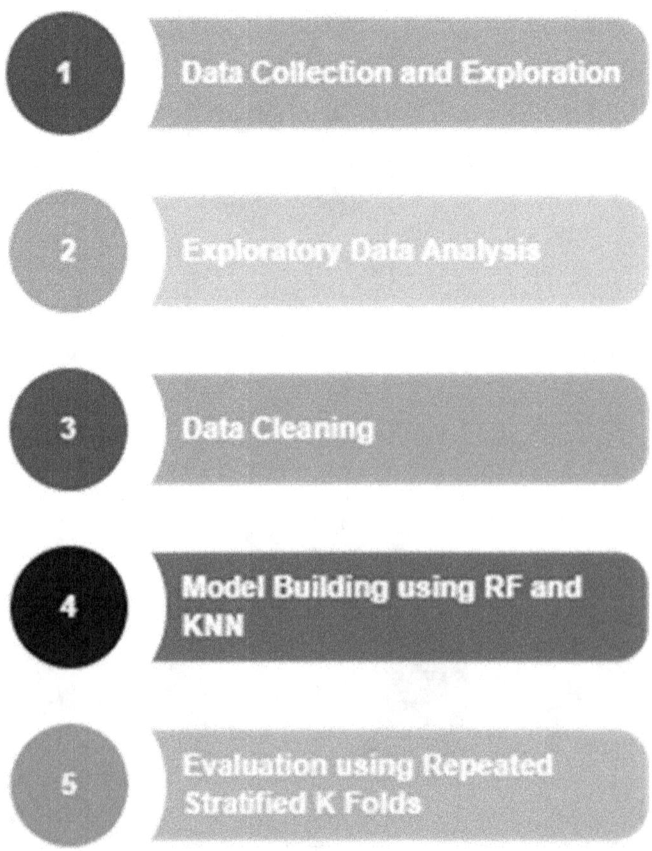

The first stage involves data collection from Lending Club, a US based P2P financial organization. Through EDA, we gain valuable insights into the dataset's characteristics, identify patterns, and detect potential anomalies or trends. Histograms scatter plots, and box plots are utilized as visual aids to comprehend the distribution and associations among variables. The next step focuses on data cleaning, which includes data preprocessing, transformation, and feature engineering to ensure the data is suitable for analysis. After data cleaning, two machine learning algorithms, Random Forest and KNN are applied to the dataset for prediction of interest rates. The model is then trained and tested using Repeated Stratified K folds and various other evaluation metric to assess its performance.

4.1 Data Collection and Exploration

A dataset named Lending Club banking data is collected from Kaggle. The dataset contains 164,309 rows and 14 columns, including various independent features and a target variable as depicted in Figure 9.

Figure 9. Feature list

```
train.dtypes
```

```
Loan_ID                      int64
Loan_Amount_Requested        int64
Length_Employed             object
Home_Owner                  object
Annual_Income              float64
Income_Verified             object
Purpose_Of_Loan             object
Debt_To_Income             float64
Inquiries_Last_6Mo           int64
Months_Since_Deliquency    float64
Number_Open_Accounts         int64
Total_Accounts               int64
Gender                      object
Interest_Rate                int64
dtype: object
```

Data dictionary of all the columns employed in the dataset are represented in Table 1 below:

Table 1. Data dictionary

COLUMNS	DESCRIPTION
Annual_Income	The annual income that the customer declared on their own when they registered.
Home_Owner	The state of the borrower's house ownership as disclosed at registration. Rent, Own, Mortgage and others are our values.
Loan_id	A distinct LC-assigned identifier for the loan listing.
Inquiries_Last_6Mo	The quantity of questions over the last six months (not include queries about cars and mortgages)
Interest_Rate	It denotes the interest rate applied on loan.
Loan_Amount_ Requested	The stated loan amount that the applicant has applied for. This figure is updated if the credit division decides to lower the loan amount at any stage.
Purpose_Of_Loan	A category provided by the borrower for the loan request.
Month_Since_ Deliquency	The count of months since the borrower's most recent delinquency.
Total_Accounts	The overall amount of credit agreements that have been acquired by the applicant
Income_Verified	Specifies whether or not the income was validated by LC, whether the income source was verified, or neither.
Debt_To_Income	The proportion determined by dividing the applicant's self-reported monthly income by the total amount of payments made each month towards all debt commitments, except the requested LC loan and the mortgage.
Length_Employed	Period of employment in years. There are ten possible values, 0 denoting less than a year and 10 denoting ten or more years.
Gender	Gender of a person such as male and female

The python code imports necessary libraries such as pandas, numpy, matplotlib, seaborn, and sets some configurations. Then reads the training and testing datasets from CSV files. The code then explores the dataset by checking the data types of each column, identifying categorical and continuous variables, and visualizing some variables' distributions and relationships.

4.2 Exploratory Data Analysis

Exploratory Data Analysis (EDA) is an essential phase in the data analysis process that focuses on gaining a deep understanding of the dataset before applying more advanced statistical or machine learning techniques. EDA involves examining and visualizing the data to uncover patterns, relationships, anomalies, and insights that can inform subsequent analyses. EDA serves as the foundation for hypothesis generation, feature selection, and data preprocessing, making it a critical step in the data science workflow. EDA encompasses a variety of techniques and methods to extract meaningful information from data. Some key types of EDA that are employed in the research work are explained below:

1. **Univariate Analysis**: This type of EDA focuses on examining individual variables in isolation. Common Univariate techniques include histograms, bar charts, box plots, and summary statistics (mean, median, mode, variance, etc.). Univariate analysis helps identify the distribution, central tendency, and spread of each variable and also helps in deciding the target variable. In our case target variable is loan_status. All key variables are analyzed one by one such as Interest_Rate, Gender, Home_owner, Income_verified etc.
2. **Bivariate Analysis**: Bivariate analysis explores the relationships between pairs of variables. Scatter plots, correlation matrices, and two-way tables are commonly used tools in this type of analysis. Bivariate EDA helps uncover associations, dependencies, and potential cause-and-effect relationships between variables. It helps in analyzing all other variables with respect to the target variable to measure correlation between them.
3. **Multivariate Analysis**: Multivariate analysis extends the exploration to three or more variables simultaneously. Techniques such as 3D scatter plots, heat maps, and dimensionality reduction methods (e.g., PCA or t-SNE) are employed. Multivariate EDA is essential for understanding complex interactions among multiple variables. It helps in finding multicollinearity by comparing many variables altogether.

The choice of EDA techniques depends on the nature of the data, research questions, and goals of the analysis. EDA not only helps identify data issues but also provides valuable insights that guide subsequent data preprocessing, modeling, and hypothesis testing. A well-executed EDA phase is essential for making informed decisions and drawing meaningful conclusions from data.EDA helps researchers understand their data better, make informed decisions, and prepare for further analysis or modeling. Here are some of the visualization outputs provided below: From figure 10 to figure 16 individual variables such as Interest_Rate, Gender, Home_owner, Income_verified, Purpose_of_Loan, Length_Employed, Loan_Amount_Requested etc are analyzed to get more insights into feature values.

Figure 10. Interest rate plot

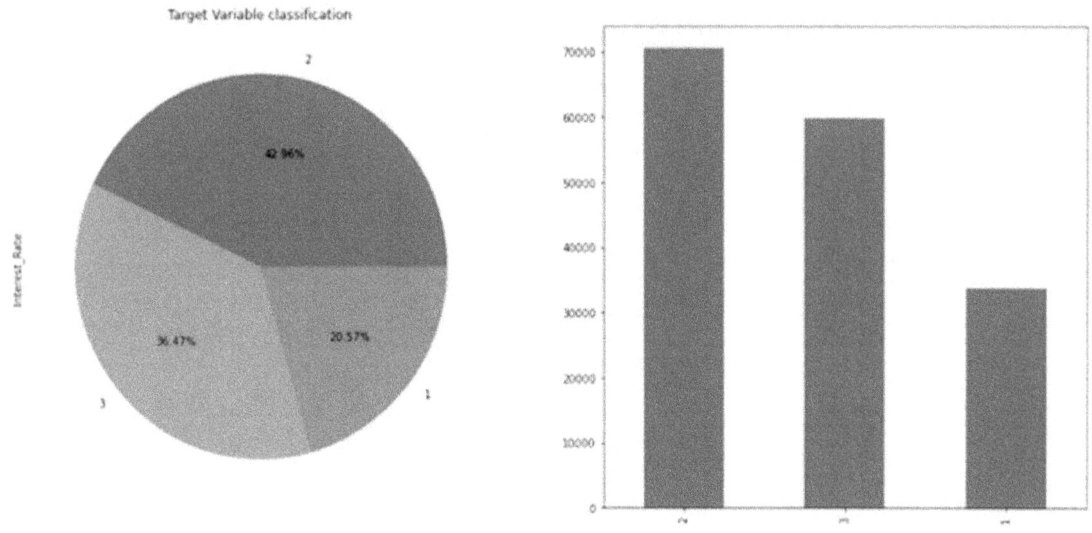

Figure 11. Gender and Homeowner plot

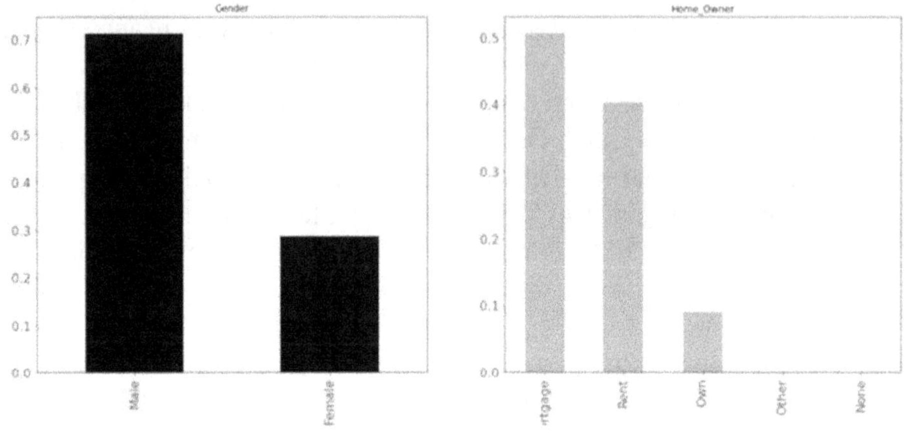

Figure 12. Income-verified and Purpose_of_loan plot

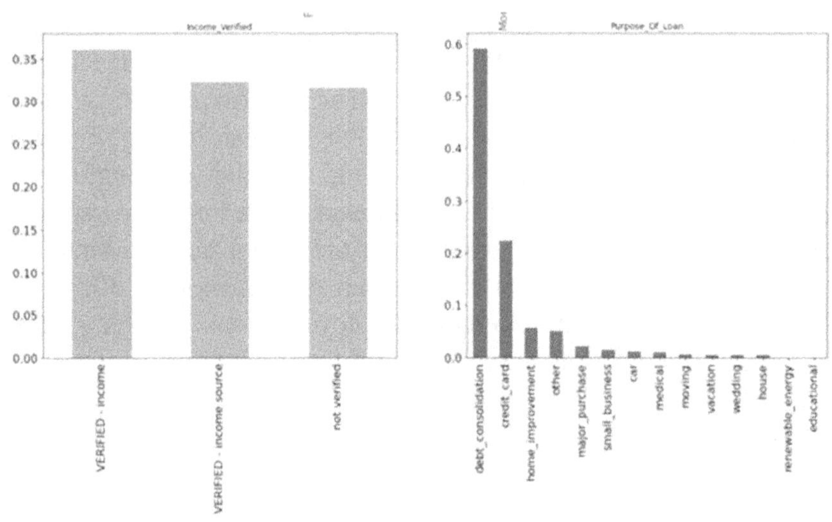

Figure 13. Income-verified and Purpose_of_loan plot

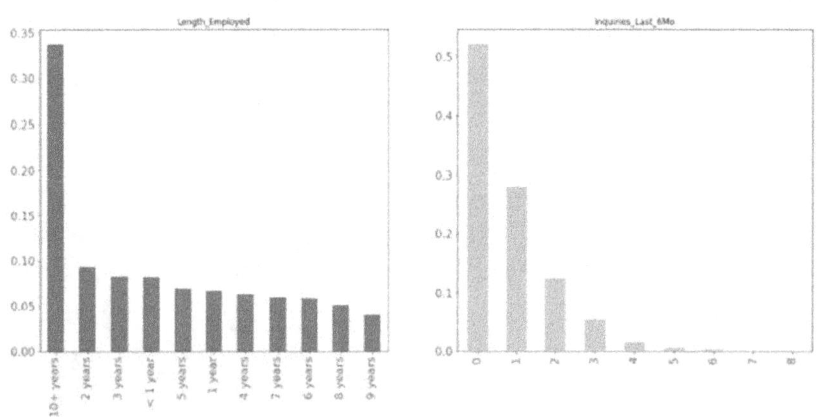

Up to this point, the categorical and ordinal variables are examined, now some of the numerical variables will be examined such as Loan_Amount_Requested, Annual_Income, Debt_to_Income, Month_since_deliquency etc.

Figure 14. Loan_Amount_Requested plot

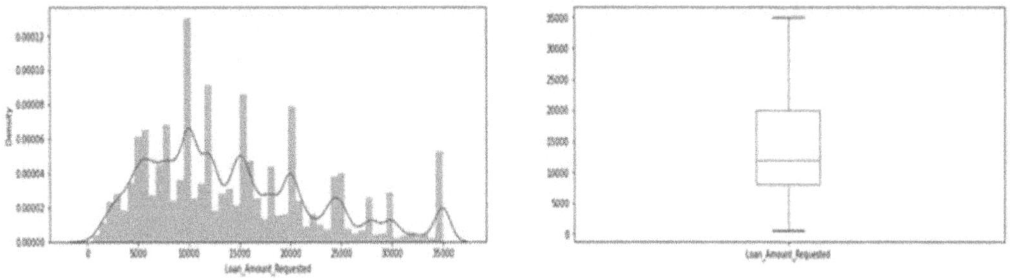

Figure 15. Loan_Amount_Requested plot

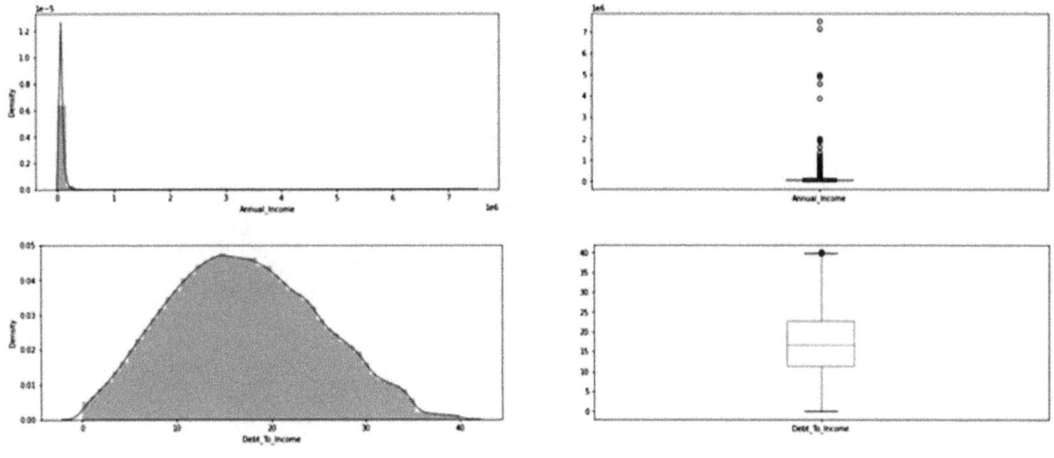

Next a bivariate analysis is performed as depicted from figure 17 to figure 20. Since the target variable is Interest_rate all other features are compared with the target variable to check correlation between them.

Moreover, a comprehensive analysis is conducted to examine the correlation between the target variable and the other two feature variables, employing multivariate techniques as shown .

Below, a heatmap analysis in figure 23 illustrates the correlations between each of the features in the banking dataset.

Figure 16. Month_since_Deliquency and Number_of_Open_Account plot

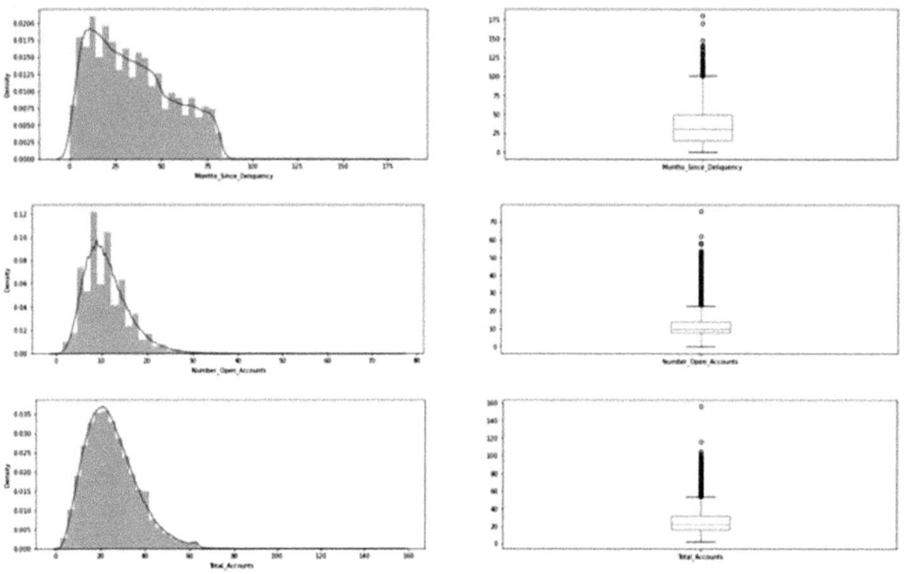

Figure 17. Home_owner vs. Interest_rate visualization

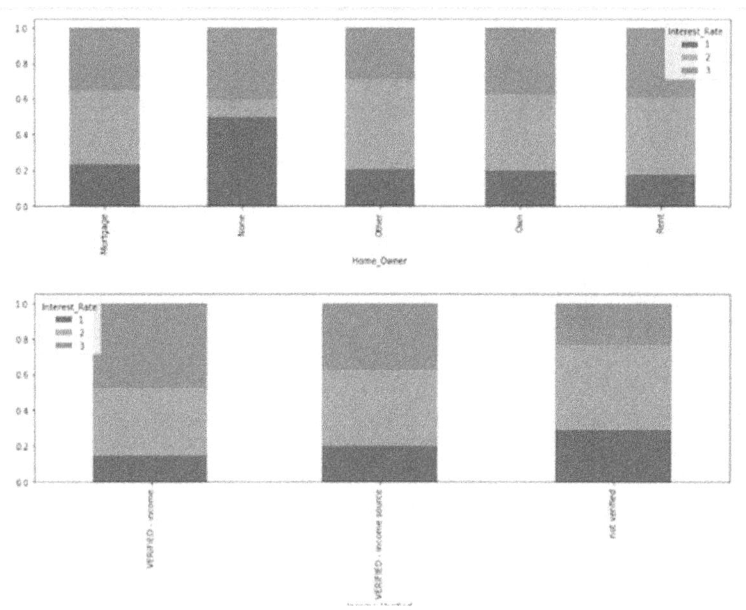

Figure 18. Purpose_Of_Loan vs. Interest_Rate visualization

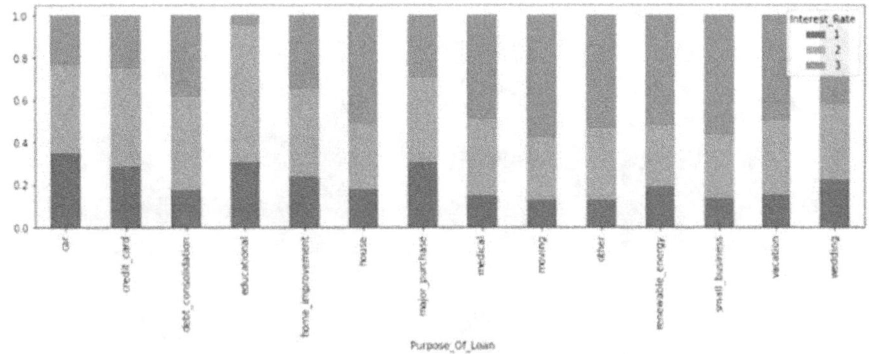

Figure 19. Gender vs. Interest_rate visualization

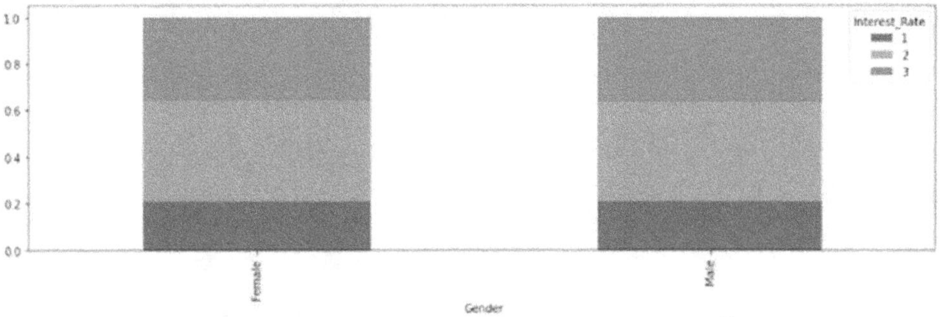

Figure 20. Length_Employed, Inquiries_Last_6mo vs Interest_rate visualization

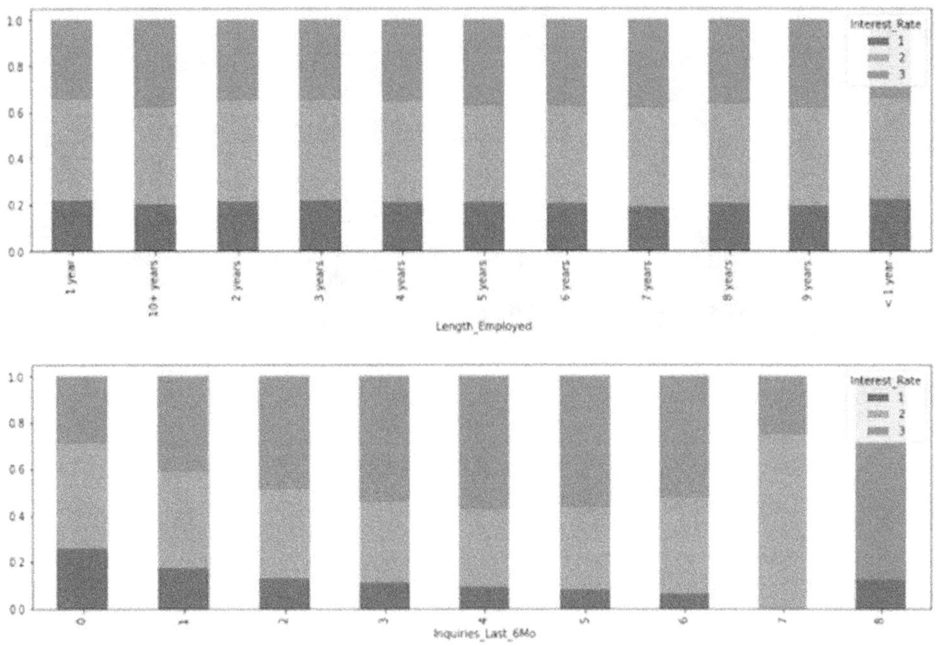

Figure 21. Annual_Income vs Interest_rate visualization

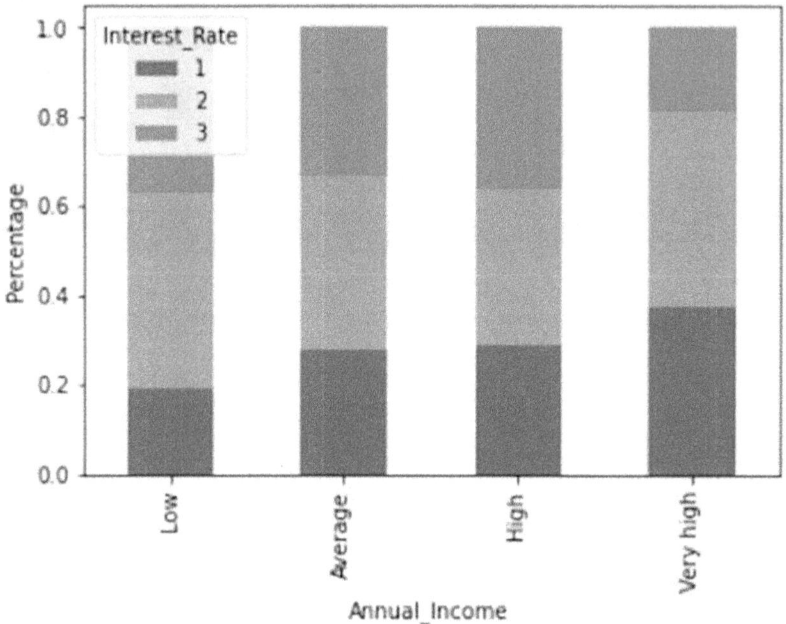

Figure 22. Loan_Amount vs Interest_rate visualization

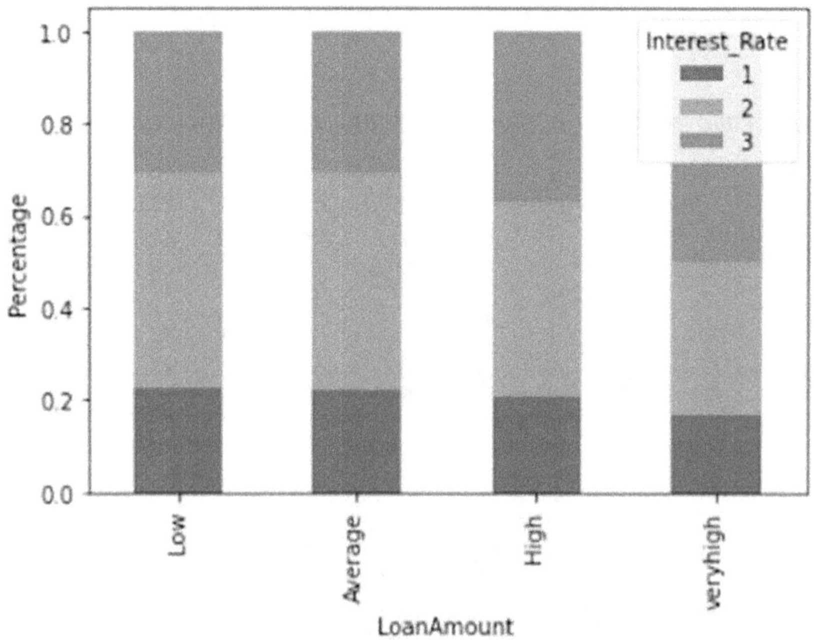

Figure 23. Heatmap visualization

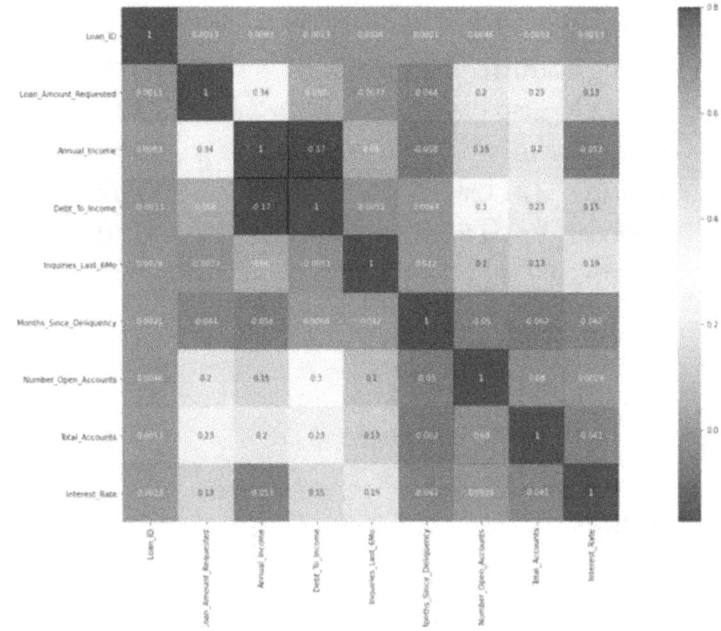

4.3 Data Cleaning

An essential step within the data preparation process involves data cleansing, often known as data wrangling and data purging as well. It entails finding and fixing mistakes, discrepancies, errors, and missing values in the data in order to make sure the information is valid, dependable, and acceptable for analysis. Data cleaning is essential because real-world data is often messy and imperfect, and the quality of our analysis depends on the quality of our data. It is an iterative process, and it may require multiple rounds of inspection and correction. The goal is to transform raw data into a clean, well-structured dataset that is ready for analysis, modeling, or visualization. The research work systematically handles missing values in the columns 'Length_Employed', 'Home_Owner', and 'Annual_Income' by filling them with the mode and median values. Figure 24 depicts the number of missing values presented in dataset.

The column 'Months_Since_Deliquency' is removed because of a substantial quantity of absent data points. The scatter plot in the Figure 25 clearly depicts the occurrence of outliers in the data.

The python code detects and handles outliers in the 'Annual_Income', 'Number_Open_Accounts', and 'Total_Accounts' columns using z-scores. It replaces the outliers with the respective maximum or minimum values to prevent model bias.Sub sequentially extracts numerical information from the 'Length_Employed' column and converts it to an integer. It also applies a square root transformation to 'Number_Open_Accounts' and 'Total_Accounts' to deal with zero values and improve their distributions.

Figure 24. Missing values

```
Loan_ID                       0
Loan_Amount_Requested         0
Length_Employed            7371
Home_Owner                25349
Annual_Income             25102
Income_Verified               0
Purpose_Of_Loan               0
Debt_To_Income                0
Inquiries_Last_6Mo            0
Months_Since_Deliquency   88379
Number_Open_Accounts          0
Total_Accounts                0
Gender                        0
Interest_Rate                 0
Annual_Income_bin         25102
LoanAmount_bin                0
dtype: int64
```

Figure 25. Missing value representation

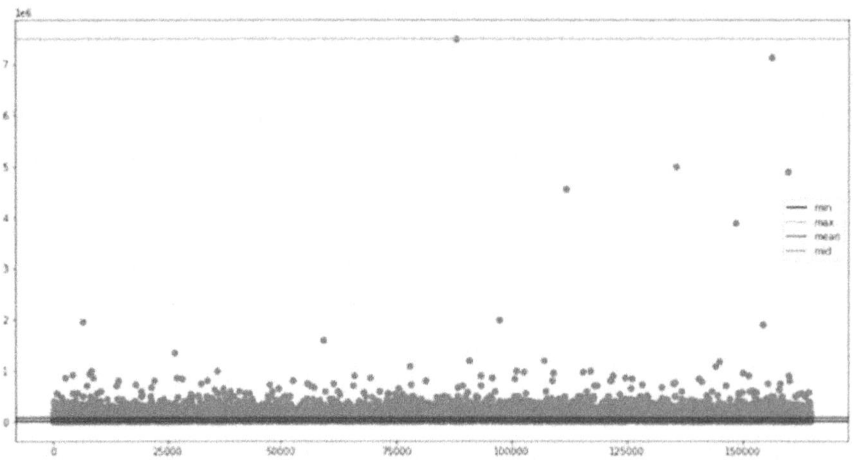

4.4 MODEL BUILDING

As our proposed model is a classification problem this work applies various classification based ML algorithms. After dividing the dataset as training and testing data into the ratio of 7:3, two classification algorithms logistic regression and k nearest neighbor are used for building a model. The code prepares the data for model training by dropping the 'Loan_ID' column and divides the dataset into features (X) and the target variable (y).

4.4.1 Logistic Regression

Predicting a qualitative class or a quantitative result is a common task in machine learning. The earlier type is called a regression issue in general. A continuous parameter is the input and a numerical number is the prediction in a linear regression case. If the input parameter is categorical in nature or we can say if it the input and predicted outcomes are qualitative, it is known to be a classification problem. The However, not all algorithms can be neatly classified into these two categories; one such example is logistic regression. Being a member of the regression family, logistic regression makes predictions about outcomes based on quantitative connections between variables. Its result is qualitative, unlike linear regression, and it takes both continuous and discrete data as input. Furthermore, it anticipates a definite class, like "True/False" or "Yes/No."

Figure 26. Sigmoid function

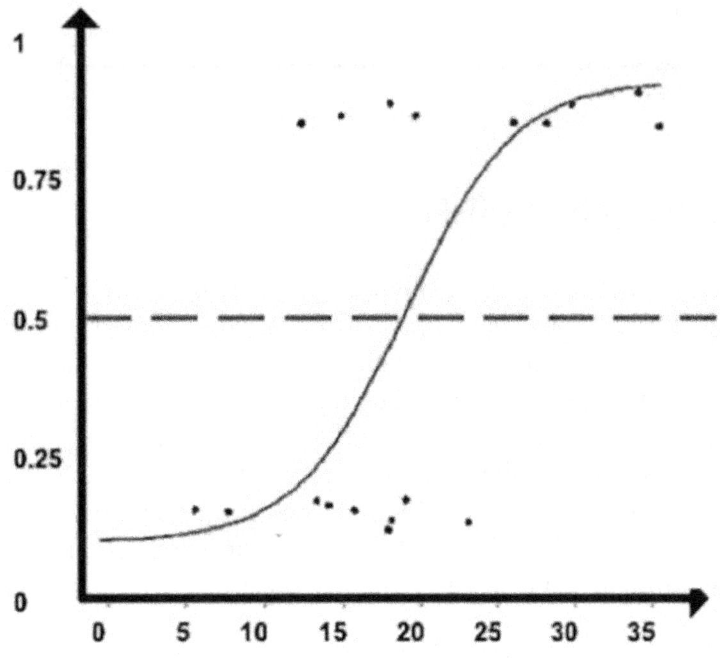

Correlation amongst variables is analyzed by the logistic regression technique. A Sigmoid function in logistic regression as show in figure 26 is basically used to convert various independent variables into expression of probability that lies between 0 and 1 in terms of dependent variable. A binary prediction is performed using mainly 0.5 cut-off value to divide the population or dataset into two groups. One group denotes everything that is assessed to be above 0.5 and group B includes everything that is assessed to be below. A decision line also known as hyperplane is used to divide two sets of data once data points are classified using the Sigmoid function. This hyperplane may then be used to forecast the category of future data points.

Figure 27. Decision boundary

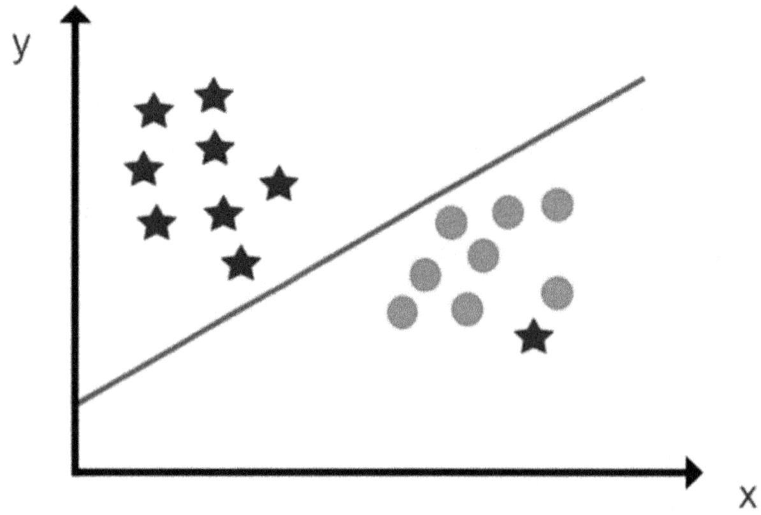

4.4.2 K-Nearest Neighbors (KNN)

K-Nearest Neighbors is one of the most often used methods in classification and regression prediction problems. Predicted on the median of the K nearest observations in the parameter space, or the majority group, it forecasts the class or value of a new data point. The distance among the data points is frequently calculated using the Euclidean distance formula. KNN does not presume any baseline variation in the data and is non-parametric. It is simple to implement but may have challenges with high-dimensional or large datasets. Selecting the appropriate value for K is crucial for optimal performance. In KNN, the most commonly used distance metric is the Euclidean distance. The Euclidean distance between two data points $X(x_1, x_2, \ldots, x_i)$ and $Y(y_1, y_2, \ldots, y_i)$ in an i-dimensional space is calculated as:

$$d(X,Y) = \sqrt{(x1 - y1)^2 + (x2 - y2)^2 \ldots + (xi - yi)^2}$$

Here, $d(X,Y)$ is the Euclidean distance across points of data X and Y; $x1, x2, \dots, xi$ and $y1, y2, \dots, yi$ are the feature values of the data points X and Y in each dimension.

For classification problems, a majority vote determines the class label; that is, the label that is most frequently used in relation to a specific data point is selected.

4.3 Model Evaluation

After applying both the classification algorithms the proposed model successfully predicted the interest rate value out of "1" "2" or "3" for individual customer. The interest rate values assigned with these particular numbers are provided in Figure 28.

Figure 28. Interest rate values for prediction

```
2    70580
3    59923
1    33806
Name: Interest_Rate, dtype: int64
```

Some of the predicted values are denoted in Figure 29. To enhance the model accuracy and mitigate any bias, the Repeated Stratified K-Fold cross-validation technique is employed in this research.

Figure 29. Predicted loan values

	Loan_ID	Interest_Rate
0	10164310	3
1	10164311	2
2	10164312	2
3	10164313	2
4	10164314	2

By simply executing the cross-validation process several times (based on the n_repeats number), Repeated Stratified K Fold enables increasing the predicted performance of a model trained using machine learning, and presenting the mean result for every fold obtained by all runs. Using Repeated Stratified K Fold indicates that the dataset would be divided into various stratified k-folds each time the technique was performed, and as a result, the performance results would vary. The choice of K for the K-Fold cross-validation was set to 5. This approach ensured that the dataset was effectively partitioned into five subsets, with each fold maintaining the same class distribution as the original data. By repeatedly reshuffling the dataset and performing the K-Fold cross-validation multiple times, it is able to obtain more reliable and robust estimates of the model's performance. The use of Repeated Stratified K-Fold cross-validation with K=5 enabled us to validate our predictive models rigorously and ascertain their application on diverse subsets of the data, ultimately leading to more reliable and accurate results. Figure 30 depicts accuracies achieved by different folds.

Figure 30. Accuracies at various folds

```
1 of kfold 5
accuracy_score 0.5099202726553466

2 of kfold 5
accuracy_score 0.5171018197309963

3 of kfold 5
accuracy_score 0.513389325056296

4 of kfold 5
accuracy_score 0.5168279471730266

5 of kfold 5
accuracy_score 0.510696570402605
```

Accuracies achieved for two algorithms based on default parameters is provided below in Table 2.

Table 2. Accuracies achieved

Model	*best_score*	*best_params*
Logistic Regression	*0.51*	*{}*
KNN	*0.45*	*{}*

5. CONCLUSION

In conclusion, this research work has explored the application of logistic regression and K-Nearest Neighbors (KNN) for predicting personalized interest rates of bank customers. The study also involved an extensive exploratory data analysis (EDA) of the banking dataset, which provided valuable insights into the data's distribution, patterns, and relationships among variables. However, despite the thorough EDA, the obtained accuracies for both models were relatively low, with logistic regression achieving an accuracy of 0.51 and KNN achieving 0.45.Despite these low accuracies, this study holds immense value in the domain of interest rate prediction for individual bank customers. It pioneers the exploration of machine learning methods in this area and lays the groundwork for future research endeavors. By identifying the limitations of the current models, such as the need for more sophisticated algorithms and feature engineering, this study opens up avenues for further advancements in the field. Additionally, the EDA conducted during the research process provided essential information about the dataset's characteristics and enabled better understanding of the data's underlying structure. This comprehensive analysis also helped in identifying potential challenges and opportunities for model improvement.

5.1 Competing Interest

The authors of this publication declare there are no competing interests.

5.2 Funding

This research received no specific grant from any funding agency in the public, commercial, or not-for-profit sectors.

REFERENCES

Abedin, M. Z., Moon, M. H., Hassan, M. K., & Hajek, P. (2021). Deep learning-based exchange rate prediction during the COVID-19 pandemic. *Annals of Operations Research*. Advance online publication. doi:10.1007/s10479-021-04420-6 PMID:34848909

Barbaglia, L., Manzan, S., & Tosetti, E. (2023). Forecasting Loan Default in Europe with Machine Learning. *Journal of Financial Econometrics*, *21*(2), 569–596. doi:10.1093/jjfinec/nbab010

Bellotti, A., Brigo, D., Gambetti, P., & Vrins, F. (2021). Forecasting recovery rates on non-performing loans with machine learning. *International Journal of Forecasting*, *37*(1), 428–444. doi:10.1016/j.ijforecast.2020.06.009

Beutel, J., List, S., & Von Schweinitz, G. (2019). Does machine learning help us predict banking crises? *Journal of Financial Stability*, *45*, 100693. doi:10.1016/j.jfs.2019.100693

Goncu, A. (2019). Prediction of exchange rates with machine learning. *Proceedings of the International Conference on Artificial Intelligence, Information Processing and Cloud Computing*, (pp. 1–5). ACM. 10.1145/3371425.3371448

Li, J.-P., Mirza, N., Rahat, B., & Xiong, D. (2020). Machine learning and credit ratings prediction in the age of fourth industrial revolution. *Technological Forecasting and Social Change, 161*, 120309. doi:10.1016/j.techfore.2020.120309

Muneer, A., Faizan Ali, R., Alghamdi, A., Mohd Taib, S., Almaghthawi, A., & Ghaleb, E. A. A. (2022). Predicting customers churning in banking industry: A machine learning approach. *Indonesian Journal of Electrical Engineering and Computer Science, 26*(1), 539. doi:10.11591/ijeecs.v26.i1.pp539-549

Naeem, S., Khan Mashwani, W., Ali, A., Irfan Uddin, M., Mahmoud, M., Jamal, F., & Chesneau, C. (2021). Machine Learning-based USD/PKR Exchange Rate Forecasting Using Sentiment Analysis of Twitter Data. *Computers, Materials & Continua, 67*(3), 3451–3461. doi:10.32604/cmc.2021.015872

Suimon, Y., Sakaji, H., Izumi, K., Shimada, T., & Matsushima, H. (2020). Japanese Interest Rate Forecast Considering the Linkage of Global Markets Using Machine Learning Methods. *International Journal of Smart Computing and Artificial Intelligence, 4*(1), 1–17. doi:10.52731/ijscai.v4.i1.500

Sun, S., Wang, S., & Wei, Y. (2020). A new ensemble deep learning approach for exchange rates forecasting and trading. *Advanced Engineering Informatics, 46*, 101160. doi:10.1016/j.aei.2020.101160

Wei, J., Ye, T., & Zhang, Z. (2021). A Machine Learning Approach to Evaluate the Performance of Rural Bank. *Complexity, 2021*, 1–10. doi:10.1155/2021/4281006

KEY TERMS AND DEFINITIONS

Heat Map: A heat map is a visual representation of data where values are depicted as colors, typically used to show the distribution or intensity of a phenomenon over a two-dimensional space.

Interest rates: Interest rates are the cost of borrowing money or the return on investment, expressed as a percentage of the principal amount.

K Nearest Neighbor (KNN): K Nearest Neighbors (KNN) is a supervised machine learning algorithm that classifies a data point based on the majority class of its k nearest neighbors in a feature space.

Random Forest (RF): A random forest is an ensemble machine learning model that builds a multitude of decision trees and merges them together to improve accuracy and reduce over fitting.

Scientometric Analysis: Scientometric analysis is the quantitative study and measurement of scientific research output, productivity, and impact, often involving the analysis of publications and citations.

Chapter 9
The Evolution of CSR Information Disclosure From Web 1.0 to Web 2.0

Jiaxu Du
https://orcid.org/0009-0007-2443-3547
University of Leicester, UK

Kangding Wang
https://orcid.org/0009-0002-0256-5120
University of Bath, UK

ABSTRACT

This chapter explores the effects of technological advancements on corporate social responsibility (CSR) disclosure. It examines how the evolving use of new technology is reshaping the demand for CSR disclosure from diverse stakeholders and the interconnected dynamics between them. As technology continues to evolve, understanding its far-reaching impact on CSR disclosure is critical for businesses and society as a whole. The evolution of Internet technologies at all stages, from the pre-Internet era to Web 2.0, dramatically affects the way firms interact with stakeholders. This chapter will critically examine the transformative impact of technology in CSR disclosure, as well as how these technologies in turn shape stakeholder engagement. This chapter also provides suggestions for addressing corresponding challenges in the social media era.

1. INTRODUCTION

Information technology is ever-changing and crucial to the development of businesses, economies, and societies. The introduction of computers and the proliferation of the networks have far-reaching effects on the way businesses are run. Over the past 40 years, the use of technology has facilitated and accelerated the CSR debate and changed the nature of the CSR discussion. Leung et al. (2013) review the past literature on media platform and observe a scarcity of papers

DOI: 10.4018/979-8-3693-1331-2.ch009

specifically addressing CSR practices within social media. This highlights a research gap in examining how firms communicate CSR through social media platforms. Hence, it's crucial to grasp the influence of the technological revolution on CSR disclosure. This chapter intends to investigate the influence of technological advancements on CSR disclosure channels. It will examine the interconnected relationships between evolving technology and the evolving requirements of stakeholders at various stages of technological transformation.

Before the advent of Web 1.0, firms mainly use annual reports and traditional media to disclose CSR (Figure 1). The dissemination of CSR statements is limited due to the limited communication capacity and audience. Annual reports, being subject to audit, serve as the official means through which companies release their CSR information, as opposed to press releases and advertisements. However, firms' CSR information and themes vary greatly depending on how they identify their stakeholders. For example, between 1973 and 1974, the CSR information disclosed by FTSE 500 firms in their annual reports vary from year to year (Abbott & Monsen, 1979). In addition, firms are unable to obtain timely comments and feedback from stakeholders after releasing CSR-related information. With the rise of Web 1.0 in the 1990s, firms start to complement their annual reports by introducing stand-alone reports and online CSR disclosures. These stand-alone reports effectively address the absence of CSR disclosure in conventional annual reports, addressing the fragmentation of CSR information in terms of its comprehensiveness and depth. Meanwhile, the emergence of Internet accountability arising from Web 1.0 helps to rise CSR information transparency. The widespread adoption of Web 1.0 technologies not only raise awareness of CSR, but also prompted firms to assess the accessibility of CSR information to a wider group of stakeholders. Although Web 1.0 is only the initial stage of Internet development, compared with today's highly interactive Web 2.0 stage, the Internet during this period was only a static web page that did not involve user activities.

Figure 1. Internet technology impacts on CSR disclosure channels over the years

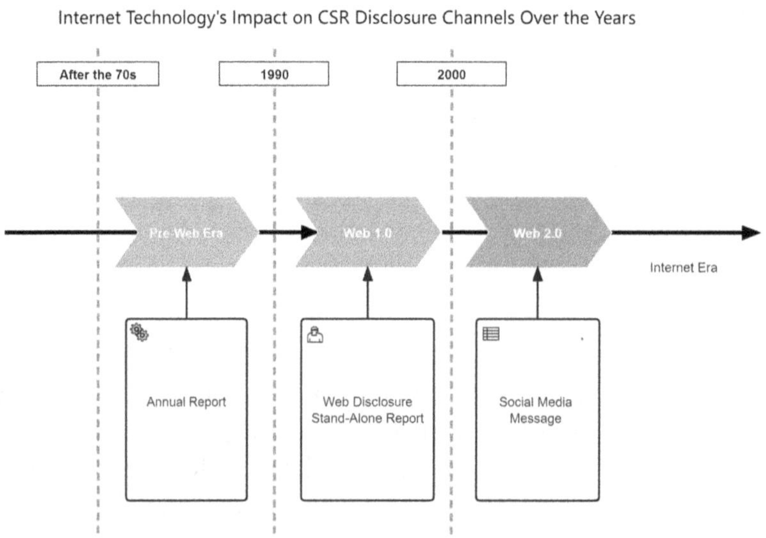

Web 2.0, a dynamic and interactive online environment, has fundamentally changed how information is created and shared (Chen et al., 2011). This transformative phase has significantly influenced business practices, especially concerning CSR disclosure. Web 2.0 technologies enable individuals and organizations to participate in two-way communication, promoting transparency and authenticity. The emergence of social networks and CEOs' presence on these platforms has further shaped businesses' interactions with stakeholders. This shift in engagement from Web 1.0 to Web 2.0 signifies a move from static, one-way communication to real-time, two-way dialogue, enhancing CSR transparency and effectiveness.

Overall, in the era of rapidly advancing Internet technology, CSR disclosure has undergone significant transformation. It is important for stakeholders, firms and policymakers to understand the far-reaching impact of technology on CSR disclosure. While Web 2.0, represented by online social media, enable firms to disseminate information more efficiently, it also brings new challenges that require serious consideration, such as authenticity of CSR Information, selective CSR practices and disclosure behaviours and different preferences in CSR communication channels. This chapter also make corresponding suggestions on these issues. The following sections shed light on the implications of technological transformations on CSR disclosure.

2. BACKGROUND

2.1 CSR Talk and Walk

CSR is inevitably understood in terms of 'talk' and 'walk', which are often seen as the two main domains of understanding CSR (Colucci et al., 2020). CSR talk refers to the image that a firm constructs of itself through the delivery of information, whereas CSR walk is the specific CSR policies, structures and processes that a firm implements (Wickert et al, 2016). The rationale for the academic split of CSR into talk and walk is that, in previous studies, it is often the case that firms tend to prefer talk, between talk and walk, and that companies are willing to discuss a large volume of CSR information to fulfil their purposes (Brunton et al., 2017; Kallio, 2007; Lomborg, 2003).

The application of Internet technology has facilitated and accelerated CSR talk and transformed the nature of CSR talk over the past 40 years. The following sections will delve into the evolution of CSR talk over the past 40 years, highlighting the transformative impact of Web 1.0 technology both before and after its introduction. It also discusses the potential impact of this technology on the CSR walk.

2.2 Dawn: CSR Talk Before the Advent of Web 1.0

Before the advent of Web 1.0, companies predominantly utilized annual reports and traditional media, like press releases and print advertisements for CSR disclosure (Gray et al., 1995). The restrictive dissemination capacity of traditional media and communication channels resulted in CSR talk only being spread to a limited extent. This means that the extent of dissemination of CSR information are both limited, and the group of people who can receive and understand CSR information is also limited. In this context, CSR disclosure and communication were targeted primarily at a specific demographic, believed to have the power to influence corporate behaviour (Freeman, 1984). "The process of communicating the social and environmental effects of organisations' economic actions to particular interest groups within society and to society at large" (Gray et al., 1988, p. 9).

At this stage, CSR talk mainly involves publishing relevant information in the annual reports, and, for a few companies, it is supplemented by press releases, print advertisements, and public lectures and seminars (Abbott & Monsen, 1979; Gray et al., 1995). Corporate annual reports have always been regarded as the official channel for firms to release CSR information, especially for listed companies whose annual reports have to be reviewed by the relevant authorities, mainly the stock exchange (Wilmshurst & Frost, 2000). In addition, annual reports also brings corporate annual reports under higher regulatory pressure from social accountability as compared to the supplementary channels mentioned above. This accountability pressure confers a high degree of credibility on corporate annual reports that are not shared by other disclosure methods and channels(Haniffa & Cooke, 2005; Tilt, 1994).

The disclosure of CSR information in companies' annual reports is varied. As mentioned earlier, the CSR published by companies is limited by the identification of their stakeholders, and the CSR information and themes published vary considerably between companies depending on the differences in their identification of stakeholders. These themes cover a wide range of topics such as environmental issues, community involvement, and product quality. Moreover, society's perception of CSR is constantly evolving and being constructed at this stage. The CSR information disclosed by companies in their annual reports also varied from year to year. Abbott & Monsen (1979) found through a content analysis that the CSR information disclosed by FTSE 500 companies in their annual reports varied from year to year between 1973 and 1974. There was a 13.4% increase in environmental information published by the sample companies between 1973 and 1974, however, there was a limited increase in disclosure on other topics.

In addition, press releases and print advertisements are also the tools used by companies to demonstrate their CSR performance and results (Manheim & Pratt, 1986; Zeghal & Ahmed, 1990). especially for environmentally sensitive industries such as energy, extractive industries and textile industries. However, press releases and advertisements are not the primary platforms for CSR talk.

3. WEB 1.0: NAVIGATING THE DIGITAL LANDSCAPE OF CORPORATE RESPONSIBILITY

3.1 Twilight: Challenges in CSR Communication Preceding Web 1.0

Initially, the accessibility of information was quite restricted. While annual reports provided a means for stakeholders to access a firm's financial and operational data, these reports were typically disseminated through public channels aimed at specific audiences such as investors and analysts. This approach made it challenging for non-specialists to access such information prior to the advent of Web 1.0 technologies. As Louwers (1996) observed, annual reports were primarily distributed in the form of computer-printed textual documents. This traditional method, often involving costly paper-based reports, discouraged companies from widespread distribution due to the associated expenses (Khadaroo, 2005). Consequently, the limited accessibility impeded the oversight and engagement of broader stakeholder groups in the discourse and implementation of CSR—referred to as CSR "talk" and "walk." This resulted in a scenario where both CSR communication and action were predominantly influenced by the companies themselves and a select group of stakeholders.

In addition, corporate annual report disclosure practices restrict the effectiveness of CSR information dissemination, resulting in information that may not be timely or out of touch with current corporate business practices (Courtis, 1986). The limitation of CSR information dissemination through corporate annual reports is bidirectional. From the perspective of stakeholders, traditional annual report information reflects a firm's social and environmental performance over a specific past period, potentially preventing stakeholders from gaining real-time insights into the firm's most recent performance. Conversely, companies may not promptly obtain stakeholders' views and feedback after releasing CSR information, causing the information disclosed in a subsequent period not to accurately address stakeholders' concerns. Particularly in cases of unforeseen environmental or social problems, real-time communication and interaction between companies and stakeholders may not be feasible.

Press releases, brochures and print advertisements traditionally served as supplementary channels to address the delay in disseminating CSR communication through annual reports (Zeghal & Ahmed, 1990). However, the simplification of messages in press releases and advertisements, which is often necessary to capture audience attention, can inadvertently dilute the depth of a firm's CSR communication. Moreover, Companies posting information in non-annual reporting channels are likely not motivated by a social welfare purpose. Lill et al. (1986) conducted a content analysis of CSR messages in 1967, 1972, 1975,1977 and 1984 published in magazine advertisements. They found that these messages tended to fulfill marketing strategies more than public services objectives.

3.2 Beacon: Illuminating CSR Communication in the Web 1.0 Era

Web 1.0 was introduced in the 1990s and this not only shifted firm CSR talk from mainly relying on annual reports, but also enhanced it so that an annual report releases remained primary, supplemented by stand-alone report releases and web disclosures. Moreover, the use of Web 1.0 technology has also profoundly affected the dissemination and promotion of CSR. In the following section, the impact of Web 1.0 on CSR disclosure will be discussed from two perspectives: stand-alone CSR reports and web disclosures.

As mentioned above, before the introduction of Web 1.0, companies could only disseminate their CSR activities and performance to specific stakeholder groups through annual reports. However, the popularity of the Internet has promoted stakeholder communication (Gowthorpe & Amat, 1999; Thornburg, 1995), and accelerated public awareness of CSR and environmental responsibility, stimulating the participation of a wider audience including consumers, governments, and social organizations in the CSR talk and walk (Esrock & Leichty, 1998).

The widespread adoption of Web 1.0 technology has not only heightened awareness about CSR but also prompted companies to evaluate the accessibility of CSR information to a broader array of stakeholder groups. Consequently, companies have recognized that traditional disclosures, often succinct in annual reports, are no longer adequate to meet the diversified needs of their audience. Under Web 1.0, firms were compelled to unveil a wider variety and depth of CSR information to cater to the demands of various groups.

Furthermore, Corporate disclosure within annual reports is under the monopoly of the company's control (Parker, 1982), the advent of Internet technology dismantles the corporate monopoly on CSR information. Stakeholders can access data regarding the social and environmental performance of not only the companies themselves but also their suppliers, competitors, and partners through the Internet. This information flow circumvents barriers established by companies, enabling stakeholders to verify the accuracy and authenticity of the data. Therefore, Web 1.0 technology facilitates enhanced transparency, thereby bolstering stakeholder trust in the information that firms disclose on non-annual reporting platforms.

3.2.1 Emergence: The Rise of Stand-Alone CSR Reporting

Based on the above background, the world's first stand-alone report on CSR information was published in 1989 (Kolk, 2004). This was called the "Sustainability Report". In terms of content, standalone reports provide depth and comprehensiveness of CSR information compared to traditional annual reports. The topics cover a wide range of employee engagement, resource utilization, air and water emissions, health management, sustainability and local community issues.

Moreover, stand-alone reports have not only increased the extent of information disclosed but also the quantity of firms involved in the disclosure of these topics has increased since the advent of Web 1.0 technology (KPMG, 1997).The emergence of stand-alone reports effectively compensates for the lack of CSR information disclosure in traditional annual reports, and, in terms of both extent and depth, compensates for the fragmentation of CSR information in annual reports.

3.2.2 Transformation: New Forms of Online CSR Communication

The emergence of Web 1.0 technology not only indirectly promotes the comprehensive disclosure of CSR, but more importantly, it directly affects the communication of CSR information. Although Web 1.0 was only the initial stage of Internet development, compared to the highly interactive Web 2.0 stage today, the Internet in this period was only a static webpage without involving user activities. However, these static web pages provided companies with a new channel to demonstrate their business results and promoted the development of companies beyond their business results to Internet users, such as environmental, social and sustainable development.

Companies now have the option to share CSR information on their self-created web pages, thereby transitioning from conventional print and distribution channels for CSR reports to online disclosure. This notable transition does more than just expand the audience, which, in the traditional reporting format, was geographically confined and predominantly composed of specific stakeholder groups. It eradicates the time and geographical constraints inherent in the previous reporting format. Now, companies can publish and refresh their CSR updates at any moment and from any location, ensuring that their disclosures remain adaptable and timely in the information age

3.2.3 Duality: Challenges and Opportunities in Web 1.0 CSR Disclosure

1. Enhanced Transparency

Transparency is a major feature displayed in the Web 1.0 era, especially in CSR disclosure. The introduction of Web 1.0 subversively changes the difficulty and complexity of information access. In the context of CSR disclosure dominated by annual report disclosure and traditional media disclosure, the flow of CSR information is controlled and restricted by firms and information publishers (Parker, 1982). However, the popularization of Internet technology broke this "information black box", and the control of firms over the flow of information has decreased significantly (Sun & Bhattacherjee, 2014).

Social and environmental information has become part of the public domain, and the cost to companies of blocking and concealing information has risen significantly (Gajewski & Li, 2015). Stakeholders are now able to utilize Internet channels to directly affect corporate disclosure policy (García-Sánchez & Noguera-Gámez, 2017). For example, if firms claim to have outstanding environmental practices, consumers, investors and supervisors can use Internet to more easily access the corresponding data published by the firm in other sources and verify the veracity of the claim.

Thus, it is clear that Web 1.0 played a crucial role in enhancing corporate transparency. In an era of increasing democratization of information, firms have to adapt to this change and consider transparency not only as a responsibility but also as a means of strengthening the bonds with stakeholders and to continuously pursue truthfulness, accuracy and timeliness on the path of information disclosure.

2. The emergence of Internet accountability

Internet users have emerged along with the Web 1.0, and unlike traditional stakeholder groups, this user group is no longer limited by time and space. The emergence of this group breaks the original stakeholder identification approach constructed by firms, such as power priority, legitimacy priority, urgency priority, and so on (Ryan & Schneider, 2003). This means that companies need to give more comprehensive cater of the needs of non-traditional stakeholder groups in the process of releasing CSR information (Sriramesh et al., 2013). Meanwhile, the rapid spread of Web 1.0 technology has led to a geometric increase in the quantity of this group. This increase in quantity has led to the amplification and aggregation of the opinions of this group, creating a force for accountability that cannot be ignored (Neu et al., 2019). This power makes firms not only have to meet the disclosure needs of this group when disclosing CSR information but also understand and consider responding to the voice of this group.

3. The Construction of an International CSR Branding Strategy

As repeatedly emphasized in the previous section, the advent of the Internet era has broken the time and space restrictions, which enables the impact of an firm's social and environmental performance to be not limited to the firm's internal and specific stakeholder groups (Palazzo et al., 2020). Through the Internet, firms can disseminate these CSR walks across regions and countries, thus building a multinational social and environmental brand influence. With the growth in the number of Internet users, the CSR brand can spread rapidly within the online user community, which can break through the traditional word-of-mouth influence to achieve wider image dissemination.

4. Concerns about the authenticity of information

The emergence of Web 1.0 technology has realized a communication effect that cannot be achieved by traditional media, however, the Internet also has the inherent problem of the authenticity of information in traditional media (Zhang et al., 2015). Internet platforms and Internet users are unable to judge and identify the authenticity of CSR information, and the emergence of Internet technology has improved the barriers to accessing and verifying information in traditional media (Flanagin & Metzger, 2000), but it cannot completely avoid the problem of misreporting and underreporting of information.

3.3 WEB 2.0: REVOLUTIONIZING CSR INFORMATION DISCLOSURE

3.3.1 The CSR Social Media Revolution

During the early days of the Internet, Web 1.0 primarily acted as an information repository, providing static web pages with minimal user interaction. It was a time when the Internet was more of a one-way street, where organizations would publish content for passive consumption. However, with the advent of the Web 2.0 era, this landscape underwent a remarkable transformation. Hence, the arrival of Web 2.0 mark a notable shift in how information is shared, distributed, and accessed on the Internet. Web 2.0 embodies a dynamic and interactive online environment, where users are active participants in creating and sharing information (Chen et al., 2011). This transformative phase in the development of the Internet has had profound implications for various aspects of society, including business practices and CSR disclosure.

The advent of the Web 2.0 era, with social media as its prime example, has expanded the avenues available to companies for sharing CSR information. Web 2.0 technologies include various interactive platforms and tools like social media, wikis, blogs, and user-generated content websites. These technologies have democratized the online landscape, allowing individuals and organizations to engage in two-way communication, collaborate, and share information with unprecedented ease (Lee et al., 2013). The count of CEOs with social media accounts has risen substantially since 2020, and an online presence is now more crucial than ever. This trend is further amplified by the increased use of mobile apps during the pandemic. As of August 2022, around 70% of Fortune 500 CEOs had profiles on at least one of the major social communication platforms like LinkedIn, Twitter, Instagram, or Facebook (Mcivor, 2022).

As a result, the Web 2.0 era has become a pivotal driver in shaping how companies engage with their stakeholders, particularly in the context of CSR disclosure (Figure 2). Past study highlights the growing utilization of CSR on corporate websites (Basil & Erlandson, 2008). As an illustration, the fast fashion brand H&M produced an online music video ad featuring musicians, motivating customers to recycle unwanted clothing in its stores and join H&M's World Recycle Week sustainability campaign (Sutton, 2016). Another instance is Disney's initiative to inspire its fans to share photos of themselves wearing Mickey Mouse ears, pledging to donate $5 to the Make-A-Wish Foundation for each photo (Disney, 2018). In addition to for-profit organizations, public interest organizations such as the Red Cross employ a range of tools, including websites, blogs, Twitter, and Facebook, to foster connections. They emphasize volunteer recruitment and retention, provide community updates on disaster preparedness and response, and engage with the media, as evidenced by studies by Briones et al. (2011). These instances showcase the influence of social media. Currently organizations mainly deliver CSR-related information through their official social media accounts and the personal accounts of their CEOs (Zhou et al., 2023). Therefore, the CEO is sometimes seen as the public face of the organization, e.g. Mark Zuckerberg (Facebook CEO), Elon Musk (Tesla and SpaceX CEO) and Tim Cook (Apple CEO). For example, Mark Zuckerberg frequently posts about Facebook's internal CSR and external CSR efforts. In addition, he posted about launching the Chan Zuckerberg Initiative to help cure childhood diseases. Although this is his personal appeal, it certainly demonstrates Facebook's inclination towards CSR (Wang & Huang, 2018).

Figure 2. Social media disclosure with stakeholder(s)

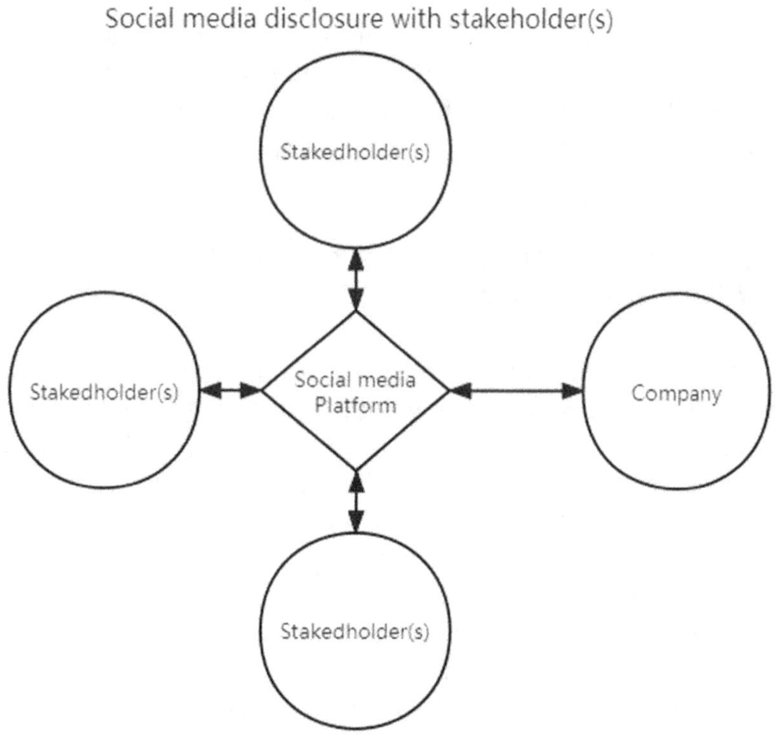

Social media and CSR development should work in parallel, as they have multiple interrelated and complementary relationships. Social media provides an open platform for companies to share their CSR efforts more transparently (Dutot et al., 2016; Yang et al., 2020). Social media can help companies identify and respond to CSR-related risks in a more timely manner to reduce the likelihood of reputational damage. This helps build trust as information about a company's social and environmental commitments is more readily available, thus increasing accountability. On top of that, social media allows stakeholders to provide feedback, comments, and suggestions, which helps companies improve their CSR initiatives (Briones et al, 2011; Cortado & Chalmeta, 2016; Manetti & Bellucci, 2016; Saxton et al., 2019). Firms can use these suggestions to optimize their sustainability strategies to better meet social and environmental expectations (Briones et al, 2011). In addition to this, positive CSR shared on social media can boost brand awareness and foster customer loyalty (Yan et al., 2010; Kang & Hustvedt, 2014; Jin & Phua, 2014; Dwivedi et al., 2021). Social media platforms allow companies to build stronger connections with consumers, share CSR stories, and engage consumers to resonate with the company's core values (Chu et al., 2020). Therefore, the synergy of social media and CSR can lead to better engagement and more meaningful relationships with a variety of stakeholders.

Currently, the integrated discussion on social media and CSR disclosure is still in the exploratory stage, and there is fewer related literature. For example, Briones et al. (2011) provide useful insights for nonprofits on strategically applying social media to build dialogic relationships with stakeholders, following principles like providing valuable info, encouraging interaction, and monitoring conversations. However, this is also limited to non-profit organizations. This chapter would delve into how these technologies have altered the dynamics of corporate communication, influenced stakeholder expectations, and reshaped the strategies employed by organizations to communicate their CSR initiatives and commitments. To fully comprehend the implications of the Web 2.0 era on CSR disclosure, it is essential to assess the progression of online communication, the emergence of social media platforms, and their role in shaping corporate transparency and responsibility.

3.4 Embracing Web 2.0: Advantages of social media in CSR Communication

Lately, sharing CSR information via media platform has recently been a hot topic in the corporate realm. When it comes to communicating with the company's stakeholders, the CEO and the company's social media accounts are often one in the same (Zhou et al., 2023). Compared to traditional CSR reporting methods, social media is a cost-effective way to disseminate CSR information (Etter, 2013). It eliminates the need for costly print materials and allows for immediate updates without the expense of reprinting. Furthermore, in terms of credibility, media platform is a good venue for CSR initiatives, such as green advertising, through electronic word of mouth, which is often seen as more trustworthy than commercial advertising (Minton et al., 2012). There are several compelling reasons why this trend is widely recognized by businesses, and it has fundamentally changed the way social media interacts with businesses.

1. Interactive Engagement Redefined

As the Web evolves from version 1.0 to version 2.0, one of the most notable transformations has been the redefinition of interactive engagement. Web 1.0 was primarily characterized by static websites and one-way communication, where companies would publish CSR reports and information without meaningful interaction with their stakeholders (Brennan & Merkl-Davies,

2018). This unidirectional approach often resulted in a lack of engagement and dialogue between businesses and their audiences.

With the advent of Web 2.0, the landscape of interactive engagement has undergone a profound shift. Social media platforms, blogs, and other Web 2.0 technologies have empowered stakeholders to actively participate in discussions surrounding CSR initiatives. Social media's ability for two-way communication can enhance stakeholder engagement (Du & Vieira, 2012, Lee et al., 2013; Zhang & Lin, 2015; Dutot et al., 2016). Users can now comment on, share, and even co-create content related to firm's CSR activities. This newfound interactivity has fostered a sense of transparency and authenticity, allowing for real-time conversations and feedback loops (Briones et al, 2011; Cortado & Chalmeta, 2016; Manetti & Bellucci, 2016; Saxton et al., 2019). Du & Vieira (2012) suggest that utilizing media platform for CSR communication is valuable as it could help alleviate public skepticism towards CSR. These studies indicate that social communication platform is useful for communicating with CSR as it promotes two-way dialogue with stakeholders by giving customers a voice in the firms' CSR efforts.

Furthermore, companies have recognized the value of this redefined engagement. They have embraced the opportunity to not only broadcast their CSR efforts but also to listen to the concerns and expectations of their stakeholders. Briones et al (2011) examines how the American Red Cross leverages social media to communicate and relationship-building with key stakeholders, finding that social media allows the Red Cross to have two-way dialogues and conversations with stakeholders. This helps the organization get feedback, spread awareness about its mission and services, and foster engagement. This bidirectional communication has enabled businesses to tailor their CSR strategies more effectively, addressing specific issues and showcasing a sincere dedication to social and environmental responsibility (Chu et al., 2020). Men & Tsai (2016) find that public engagement with the CEO also directly affects the quality of public relations reporting. Furthermore, the study by Sisson (2017) shows that donors' impression of interactivity and the likelihood that they will provide social media material for an organization both increase when they interact with the nonprofit's social media pages. However, in the case of the hotel industry, Zizka (2017) find that it primarily utilizes social media for one-way CSR messaging. This raises questions about the industry's commitment to genuine stakeholder engagement and whether they are missing out on the potential benefits of a more interactive and responsive approach. Hence, even though there is an increasing acknowledgment of the significance of two-way CSR communication, it's crucial to rigorously assess the genuineness and efficiency of these initiatives and their effect on addressing social and environmental concerns. Companies should not merely use such communication as a facade but should genuinely commit to responsible practices and responsiveness to stakeholders' concerns.

2. Real-time Insights for Real-time Impact

Web 2.0 ushered in a new era of real-time engagement and information dissemination, bidding farewell to the static nature of Web 1.0. This shift towards real-time updates has not only ensured the accuracy and timeliness of CSR information but has also fortified the reliability of disclosures, enabling organizations to have a more immediate and impactful interaction with their stakeholders.

In the Web 2.0 era, firms could give real-time updates on their CSR activities and initiatives. This ability to share information as it unfolds allows stakeholders to stay informed about the latest developments and progress. Whether it's announcing a new sustainability project, sharing live updates from CSR events, or responding promptly to stakeholder inquiries, real-time updates offer a dynamic and responsive approach to CSR disclosure. For example, through interviews, Briones et al (2011) find that public relations practices through social media are effective and necessary. In the USA, Twitter and Facebook are the main platforms used, allowing real-time interaction and monitoring of conversations. This provides faster services to communities in need, generating more media coverage, and receiving input to improve the organization. This new approach contrasts with the traditional Web 1.0 approach, where information was typically static and updated only in annual reports.

In the past, annual and stand-alone CSR reports were usually issued once a year, leading to a lag in conveying current activities and achievements. This time gap between actions and reporting often left stakeholders uninformed about firms' most recent CSR efforts. However, Web 2.0 technologies have bridged this gap by allowing companies to share information in real time. As a result, stakeholders can access up-to-the-minute data, enabling them to make more informed decisions, hold companies accountable, and engage in timely discussions about CSR initiatives.

This emphasis on real-time insights not only enhances transparency but also empowers stakeholders to actively participate in shaping corporate responsibility strategies. It fosters a sense of trust and credibility as stakeholders witness organizations being responsive to their concerns and committed to their CSR promises in real time.

3. User-generated Content and Transparency

The era of Web 2.0 has introduced a powerful concept in the realm of CSR disclosure: user-generated content on social media platforms. This phenomenon is highly significant in promoting corporate transparency and enhancing stakeholder trust in CSR information, ushering in an era of more dynamic and interactive communication (Calvano, 2008; Lee et al., 2013). The proliferation of social networking platforms has transformed stakeholders from passive information recipients into active contributors and assessors of content (Dellarocas, 2003). These aspects offer substantial opportunities and challenges for companies. Crafting strategic plans on how to effectively showcase their CSR commitment to stakeholders has become a critical concern (Dawkins, 2005).

The interactive nature of Web 2.0 allows viewers to challenge the content they encounter, promoting greater transparency and accuracy in the process (Insch, 2008). The interactive nature of Web 2.0 allows viewers to challenge the content they encounter, thus increasing the transparency and accuracy of the process (Insch, 2008). This questioning interaction undoubtedly enhances the implementation of accountability. Lyon & Montgomery (2013) suggest that the advent of social media has changed the way businesses report their environmental performance, improving CSR communication while decreasing "greenwash" practices. Lee et al. (2013) indicate that social media aids in increasing CSR communication awareness, allowing internet users to freely voice their opinions on matters without requiring the firm's approval. Therefore, when discrepancies or inaccuracies are identified, stakeholders can swiftly address them, prompting companies to rectify and clarify their CSR disclosures. This iterative feedback loop not only improves the quality of information but also ensures that CSR reports align with actual practices. User-generated content acts as a built-in system of checks and balances, helping to keep companies accountable for their CSR commitments. However, there are hurdles in fully utilizing social network for CSR communication. The primary audience on social network platforms tends to be younger individuals, and older board members and volunteers, who may be less familiar with these tools, constitute a significant portion of a company's stakeholders. When companies choose to disseminate CSR information primarily through online channels, there is a risk that a portion of their stakeholders, particularly those who are not well-versed in social media, may not have access to this type of information. This digital divide can result in certain segments of the population not receiving the information, limiting the reach of CSR communication efforts. For example, one obstacle to social media usage is its potential to isolate the older generation, which constitutes a significant portion of volunteers and donors. One interviewee argues that older generations are not familiar with the concept of social media, which poses a challenge to utilise social media to build relationships (Briones et al., 2011).

It is acknowledged that neither channel can ensure that all demographic groups have access to CSR information. But on the basis of a larger range of possible demographic groups, it is essential for organizations to consider how to bridge the gap to ensure that more demographic groups have access to CSR information. It's crucial to acknowledge that social media platforms provide a distinct environment for more comprehensive and diverse discussions. These platforms enable the sharing of diverse perspectives and experiences, facilitating a deeper and more comprehensive understanding of a company's CSR efforts among stakeholders. This richness in perspective contributes to a more informed and dynamic dialogue, which can, in turn, facilitate the collaborative development of CSR strategies that better align with the diverse expectations and needs of stakeholders. Thus, by addressing the digital divide and leveraging the inclusive nature of social media, organizations can not only enhance accountability but also promote more effective and inclusive CSR communication.

3.5 The Momentum: Exploring the Popularity of Web 2.0 CSR Communication

Social media is a way of spreading information close to life. Compared to Web 1.0 firm websites and stand-alone CSR reports, social media offers a richer level of interaction and engagement. Social media can benefit organizations in several ways: gaining customer insights, enhancing brand awareness and loyalty, providing real-time results through targeted advertising, and attracting potential customers with improved conversion rates (Yan et al., 2010; Kang & Hustvedt, 2014; Jin & Phua, 2014; Dwivedi et al., 2021). In addition, this heightened interactivity allows companies to achieve multiple objectives in different ways, not just marketing (Haigh et al. 2013; Haigh & Wigley, 2015). Through social media, companies can communicate messages that are relevant to CSR but not to marketing, thus demonstrating their ethical and corporate citizenship side. Meanwhile, social media also acts as a channel for corporate public relations, helping companies to respond to negative events and repair their reputation through timely interactions (Men & Tsai, 2016). This interactivity also helps to reach out to a wider range of stakeholders, especially consumers, fulfilling their demand for more information and transparency from companies. Hence, social media not only helps to fulfil the needs of the companies themselves but also satisfies the needs of social media users for additional information and interaction, creating a mutually beneficial scenario.

While the previous discussion highlighted the potential exclusion of older individuals or those less familiar with social media concepts when disclosing CSR information through these platforms, it is worth noting that social networking usage among older adults has significantly increased. In 2009, the percentage of older adults engaging in social networking doubled from 22 percent to 42 percent (Madden, 2010). This trend indicates a growing openness among this demographic to utilize social media, suggesting that their engagement with these platforms is on the rise. Therefore, the Internet has evolved into one of the most vital platforms for word-of-mouth communication (Berthon et al., 2012; Minton et al., 2012). Engaging in CSR activities can bring various advantages to organizations, including the enhancement of corporate reputation, trust, brand image, and word-of-mouth (Sen & Bhattacharya, 2001; Hur et al. 2014; Du et al., 2011; Plewa et al., 2015 and Vo et al., 2019). People would refer to reviews on the Internet before making purchases (Chu & Kim, 2011). Bickart & Schindler (2001) empirically show that people are more likely to trust evaluations made by people on Internet platforms than offline word-of-mouth. In today's fast-paced digital age, the immediacy of social media aligns perfectly with the demand for instant access to CSR information and updates.

In additional, stakeholders, from consumers to investors, now expect a higher level of transparency from businesses. Social media allows companies to showcase their CSR efforts transparently, building trust and goodwill among their audience. One study examines the impact of companies' CSR efforts on consumer purchases (Kang & Hustvedt, 2014), suggesting that advertisements with a clear CSR message increase consumers' willingness to purchase a particular brand.

Finally, social media has the significant advantage of reaching billions of users around the world, allowing companies to reach a broad and diverse audience and thus multiply the impact of their CSR initiatives. This reach is not limited by geography or demographics, making social media an attractive channel for global CSR communications. Nonetheless, it's crucial to highlight that CSR information shared via social media doesn't automatically guarantee its authenticity and comparability. There is a diversity of CSR information on social media and a lack of uniformity. This information can be qualitative or quantitative and varies, making it difficult to compare the CSR initiatives of different companies. Whilst social media provides increased access to CSR information for a wide audience, companies and stakeholders still need to interpret and evaluate this information carefully to ensure accuracy and credibility.

4. SOLUTIONS AND RECOMMENDATIONS

In the evolving landscape of corporate communication, Internet technology plays a pivotal role. It has driven significant changes in businesses approach and handle CSR disclosure. However, this transformation is not without its challenges. While technology has brought about many positive shifts, there are still some hurdles in the process that deserve attention:

1. Authenticity

As discussed earlier, the authenticity of information is one of the primary concerns of the public. This chapter suggests that companies can adopt a third-party independent organization to review its social and environmental behaviors and reports, which not only improves the authenticity of the information but also further enhances the public's trust in the firm. Moreover, different stakeholders can be encouraged to participate in the release of information to encourage the public to monitor the CSR behavior of the firm. Finally, companies can open a feedback mechanism on their social accounts.

2. Cyber Accountability

Cyber Accountability may affect the routine CSR practices of companies. The rise of social media platforms enables the public to readily assemble and engage in discussions on specific subjects, and these conversations are progressively emerging as a force for social accountability (Colleoni, 2013). This accountability is also potentially affecting corporate CSR disclosure, and companies may adopt selective CSR practices and disclosure behaviors to cater to the accountability expectations and pressures from specific groups. However, this selective strategy may result in some stakeholders being neglected.

This chapter suggests that companies can provide other channels to interact with stakeholders beyond social media. For instance, seminars, online meetings, emails, and other ways to connect with stakeholders. Furthermore, organizations can also consider conducting regular reviews of their CSR practices and sharing and discussing the results with stakeholders. This will enable the organization to identify and adjust any deficiencies in CSR practices.

3. Preferences of CSR communication

Firms are expanding the channels for CSR disclosure through the advancement of internet technology. In focusing and emphasizing on disclosure in social media, firms may reduce disclosure in annual reports. However, as mentioned earlier, an entity's annual report is an official document of the firm, which is a formal, instrumental document. It has an essential reference for investors and other primary stakeholders. The selective transfer and release of CSR information to informal channels may be seen as an attempt to minimize the supervision of the government and exchanges.

This chapter raises the following concerns about CSR disclosure in light of the Internet changes. First, companies need to actively engage in CSR practices and communications. This chapter finds that information transparency and openness is an inevitable trend with the development of Internet technology, which implies that businesses will encounter further challenges and hardships in controlling and manipulating social and environmental information. Secondly, companies need to consider the interests of a broader group of stakeholders. The transition from Web 1.0 to Web 2.0 is a process of expanding the number of information participants, which creates a constant necessity for companies to expand their identification of stakeholders and to satisfy the interests of increasingly identified stakeholder groups. Finally, companies need to be truthful in executing socially and environmentally responsible behavior. Internet transformation has been effective in enhancing corporate disclosure and communication, but it is not capable of directly engaging corporate social and environmental behaviors.

5. CONCLUSION

This chapter assesses the effects and transformation of CSR disclosure and communication in the context of Internet technology, and explores in depth the potential reasons for this transformation, as well as the opportunities and challenges it presents from the perspective of both companies and stakeholders. Internet technology emerged in the late 20th century and has since gone through numerous iterations and advancements (Hafner, 1998); The advent of Web 1.0 has accelerated the dissemination of information, breaking down the information barriers traditionally constructed by time and space distances (Castells, 2003). Further, this transformation broke the "Information Control" constructed by traditional media and business, and Internet users began to have the initiative to filter and identify CSR information (Abelson, Ledeen and Lewis, 2008). The iteration of Internet technology from Web 1.0 to Web 2.0 is of milestone significance in terms of information interaction. Social media users engage in the communication and discussion of corporate social and environmental information, which completely shapes the corporate CSR walk rather than just talk.

In terms of business practices, Before Web 1.0, companies started to look at communicating and presenting CSR information, and fragmented information by publishing it in corporate annual reports. In addition, newspapers, press releases, and print advertisements were utilized to tailor responses to the social and environmental issues or scandal encountered by companies. However, as the section headings "Dawn" and "Twilight" imply, although companies and society have begun to pay attention to corporate`s social and environmental issues, the recognition of CSR practices and information dissemination remains limited. Substantial gaps persist in both the CSR disclosure and their implementation.

A catalyst is needed to drive the transformation of CSR talk and walk, and Web 1.0 serves as a "beacon" to expedite the spread and popularization of CSR awareness among the public and businesses. Companies began to issue stand-alone reports to systematically and comprehensively discuss their social and environmental performance. Web 1.0 static web pages provide a straightforward platform for public and businesses access, understand, and showcase CSR information, as opposed to the traditional, complicated, and cumbersome methods of obtaining corporate annual reports. Web 1.0 laid the groundwork for raising public and corporate awareness about social and environmental responsibility. With the arrival of Web 2.0, companies and the public engage in discussions and interact regarding CSR information through social media. It's evident that the advancement of internet technology has significantly impacted corporate CSR practices and communication.

6. FUTURE RESEARCH DIRECTIONS

This chapter critically discuss the evolution of CSR disclosure under the development of Internet technology. Future research could consider focusing on whether and how Internet technologies also drive corporate social and environmental practices, and attempt to discuss and examine whether corporate CSR talk and walk are consistent under the development of Internet technologies.

REFERENCES

Abbott, W. F., & Monsen, R. J. (1979). On the Measurement of Corporate Social Responsibility: Self-Reported Disclosures as a Method of Measuring Corporate Social Involvement. *Academy of Management Journal*, *22*(3), 501–515. doi:10.2307/255740

Abelson, H., Ledeen, K., & Lewis, H. (2012). *Blown to bits: your life, liberty, and happiness after the digital explosion*. Addison-Wesley Professional.

Basil, D. Z., & Erlandson, J. (2008). Corporate social responsibility website representations: A longitudinal study of internal and external self-presentations. *Journal of Marketing Communications*, *14*(2), 125–137. doi:10.1080/13527260701858497

Berthon, P. R., Pitt, L. F., Plangger, K., & Shapiro, D. (2012). Marketing meets Web 2.0, social media, and creative consumers: Implications for international marketing strategy. *Business Horizons*, *55*(3), 261–271. doi:10.1016/j.bushor.2012.01.007

Brammer, S., Millington, A., & Rayton, B. (2007). The contribution of corporate social responsibility to organizational commitment. *International Journal of Human Resource Management*, *18*(10), 1701–1719. doi:10.1080/09585190701570866

Brennan, N. M., & Merkl-Davies, D. M. (2018). Do firms effectively communicate with financial stakeholders? A conceptual model of corporate communication in a capital market context. *Accounting and Business Research*, *48*(5), 553–577. doi:10.1080/00014788.2018.1470143

Briones, R. L., Kuch, B., Liu, B. F., & Jin, Y. (2011). Keeping up with the digital age: How the American Red Cross uses social media to build relationships. *Public Relations Review*, *37*(1), 37–43. doi:10.1016/j.pubrev.2010.12.006

Brunton, M., Eweje, G., & Taskin, N. (2017). Communicating corporate social responsibility to internal stakeholders: Walking the walk or just talking the talk? *Business Strategy and the Environment*, *26*(1), 31–48. doi:10.1002/bse.1889

Calvano, L. (2008). Multinational corporations and local communities: A critical analysis of conflict. *Journal of Business Ethics*, *82*(4), 793–805. doi:10.1007/s10551-007-9593-z

Castells, M. (2002). *The Internet galaxy: Reflections on the Internet, business, and society*. Oxford University Press. doi:10.1093/acprof:oso/9780199255771.001.0001

Chen, Y., Fay, S., & Wang, Q. (2011). The role of marketing in social media: How online consumer reviews evolve. *Journal of Interactive Marketing*, *25*(2), 85–94. doi:10.1016/j.intmar.2011.01.003

Chu, S. C., Chen, H. T., & Gan, C. (2020). Consumers' engagement with corporate social responsibility (CSR) communication in social media: Evidence from China and the United States. *Journal of Business Research*, *110*, 260–271. doi:10.1016/j.jbusres.2020.01.036

Chu, S. C., & Kim, Y. (2011). Determinants of consumer engagement in electronic word-of-mouth (eWOM) in social networking sites. *International Journal of Advertising*, *30*(1), 47–75. doi:10.2501/IJA-30-1-047-075

Colleoni, E. (2013). CSR communication strategies for organizational legitimacy in social media. *Corporate Communications*, *18*(2), 228–248. doi:10.1108/13563281311319508

Colucci, M., Tuan, A., & Visentin, M. (2020). An empirical investigation of the drivers of CSR talk and walk in the fashion industry. *Journal of Cleaner Production*, *248*, 119200. doi:10.1016/j.jclepro.2019.119200

Cortado, F. J., & Chalmeta, R. (2016). Use of social networks as a CSR communication tool. *Cogent business & management, 3*(1), 1187783.

Courtis, J. K. (1986). An investigation into annual report readability and corporate risk-return relationships. *Accounting and Business Research*, *16*(64), 285–294. doi:10.1080/00014788.1986.9729329

David, D. T. (1995). Welcome to the communication age. *Internet Research*, *5*(1), 64–70. doi:10.1108/10662249510084471

Dawkins, J. (2005). Corporate responsibility: The communication challenge. *Journal of Communication Management (London)*, *9*(2), 108–119. doi:10.1108/13632540510621362

Dellarocas, C. (2003). The digitization of word of mouth: Promise and challenges of online feedback mechanisms. *Management Science*, *49*(10), 1407–1424. doi:10.1287/mnsc.49.10.1407.17308

Disney. (2018). The Walt Disney Company and Make-A-Wish® Invite Fans to "Share Your Ears" to Help Grant Wishes in Celebration of 90 Years of Mickey Mouse. *Business Wire*. https://www.businesswire.com/news/home/20181104005033/en/The-Walt-Disney-Company-and-Make-A-Wish%C2%AE-Invite-Fans-to-%E2%80%9CShare-Your-Ears%E2%80%9D-to-Help-Grant-Wishes-in-Celebration-of-90-Years-of-Mickey-Mouse

Du, S., Bhattacharya, C. B., & Sen, S. (2011). Corporate social responsibility and competitive advantage: Overcoming the trust barrier. *Management Science*, *57*(9), 1528–1545. doi:10.1287/mnsc.1110.1403

Du, S., & Vieira, E. T. Jr. (2012). Striving for legitimacy through corporate social responsibility: Insights from oil companies. *Journal of Business Ethics*, *110*(4), 413–427. doi:10.1007/s10551-012-1490-4

Dutot, V., Lacalle Galvez, E., & Versailles, D. W. (2016). CSR communications strategies through social media and influence on e-reputation: An exploratory study. *Management Decision, 54*(2), 363–389. doi:10.1108/MD-01-2015-0015

Dwivedi, Y. K., Ismagilova, E., Hughes, D. L., Carlson, J., Filieri, R., Jacobson, J., Jain, V., Karjaluoto, H., Kefi, H., Krishen, A. S., Kumar, V., Rahman, M. M., Raman, R., Rauschnabel, P. A., Rowley, J., Salo, J., Tran, G. A., & Wang, Y. (2021). Setting the future of digital and social media marketing research: Perspectives and research propositions. *International Journal of Information Management, 59*, 102168. doi:10.1016/j.ijinfomgt.2020.102168

Esrock, S. L., & Leichty, G. B. (1998). Social responsibility and corporate web pages: Self-presentation or agenda-setting? *Public Relations Review, 24*(3), 305–319. doi:10.1016/S0363-8111(99)80142-8

Etter, M. (2013). Reasons for low levels of interactivity:(Non-) interactive CSR communication in Twitter. *Public Relations Review, 39*(5), 606–608. doi:10.1016/j.pubrev.2013.06.003

Flanagin, A. J., & Metzger, M. J. (2000). Perceptions of Internet information credibility. *Journalism & Mass Communication Quarterly, 77*(3), 515–540. doi:10.1177/107769900007700304

Freeman, R. E. (1984). *Strategic management: A stokcholder approach.* Pitman.

Gajewski, J. F., & Li, L. (2015). Can Internet-based disclosure reduce information asymmetry? *Advances in Accounting, 31*(1), 115–124. doi:10.1016/j.adiac.2015.03.013

García-Sánchez, I. M., & Noguera-Gámez, L. (2017). Integrated reporting and stakeholder engagement: The effect on information asymmetry. *Corporate Social Responsibility and Environmental Management, 24*(5), 395–413. doi:10.1002/csr.1415

Gowthorpe, C., & Amat, O. (1999). External reporting of accounting and financial information via the Internet in Spain. *European Accounting Review, 8*(2), 365–371. doi:10.1080/096381899336096

Gray, R., Kouhy, R., & Lavers, S. (1995). Corporate social and environmental reporting: A review of the literature and a longitudinal study of UK disclosure. *Accounting, Auditing & Accountability Journal, 8*(2), 47–77. doi:10.1108/09513579510146996

Gray, R., Owen, D., & Maunders, K. (1988). Corporate social reporting: Emerging trends in accountability and the social contract. *Accounting, Auditing & Accountability Journal, 1*(1), 6–20. doi:10.1108/EUM0000000004617

Hafner, K., & Lyon, M. (1998). *Where wizards stay up late: The origins of the Internet.* Simon and Schuster.

Haigh, M. M., Brubaker, P., & Whiteside, E. (2013). Facebook: Examining the information presented and its impact on stakeholders. *Corporate Communications, 18*(1), 52–69. doi:10.1108/13563281311294128

Haigh, M. M., & Wigley, S. (2015). Examining the impact of negative, user-generated content on stakeholders. *Corporate Communications, 20*(1), 63–75. doi:10.1108/CCIJ-02-2013-0010

Haniffa, R. M., & Cooke, T. E. (2005). The impact of culture and governance on corporate social reporting. *Journal of Accounting and Public Policy*, *24*(5), 391–430. doi:10.1016/j.jaccpubpol.2005.06.001

Hur, W. M., Kim, H., & Woo, J. (2014). How CSR leads to corporate brand equity: Mediating mechanisms of corporate brand credibility and reputation. *Journal of Business Ethics*, *125*(1), 75–86. doi:10.1007/s10551-013-1910-0

Insch, A. (2008). Online communication of Corporate Environmental Citizenship: A study of New Zealand's electricity and gas retailers. *Journal of Marketing Communications*, *14*(2), 139–153. doi:10.1080/13527260701858505

Iqbal Khadaroo, M. (2005). Business reporting on the internet in Malaysia and Singapore: A comparative study. *Corporate Communications*, *10*(1), 58–68. doi:10.1108/13563280510578204

Jin, S. A. A., & Phua, J. (2014). Following celebrities' tweets about brands: The impact of twitter-based electronic word-of-mouth on consumers' source credibility perception, buying intention, and social identification with celebrities. *Journal of Advertising*, *43*(2), 181–195. doi:10.1080/00913367.2013.827606

Kallio, T. J. (2007). Taboos in corporate social responsibility discourse. *Journal of Business Ethics*, *74*(2), 165–175. doi:10.1007/s10551-006-9227-x

Kang, J., & Hustvedt, G. (2014). Building trust between consumers and corporations: The role of consumer perceptions of transparency and social responsibility. *Journal of Business Ethics*, *125*(2), 253–265. doi:10.1007/s10551-013-1916-7

Kolk, A. (2004). A decade of sustainability reporting: Developments and significance. *International Journal of Environment and Sustainable Development*, *3*(1), 51–64. doi:10.1504/IJESD.2004.004688

KPMG. (1997). *KPMG International survey of environmental reporting 1999*. KPMG. https://www.researchgate.net/publication/254796996_KPMG_International_survey_of_environmental_reporting_1999

Lee, H. H. M., Van Dolen, W., & Kolk, A. (2013). On the role of social media in the 'responsible' food business: Blogger buzz on health and obesity issues. *Journal of Business Ethics*, *118*(4), 695–707. doi:10.1007/s10551-013-1955-0

Leung, D., Law, R., Van Hoof, H., & Buhalis, D. (2013). Social media in tourism and hospitality: A literature review. *Journal of Travel & Tourism Marketing*, *30*(1-2), 3–22. doi:10.1080/10548408.2013.750919

Lill, D., Gross, C., & Peterson, R. (1986). The inclusion of social-responsibility themes by magazine advertisers: A longitudinal study. *Journal of Advertising*, *15*(2), 35–41. doi:10.1080/00913367.1986.10673003

Lomborg, B. (2003). *The skeptical environmentalist: measuring the real state of the world* (Vol. 1). Cambridge University Press.

Louwers, T., Pasewark, W. R., & Typpo, E. W. (1996). The Internet: Changing the way corporations tell their story. *The CPA Journal*, *66*(11), 24.

Lyon, T. P., & Montgomery, A. W. (2013). Tweetjacked: The impact of social media on corporate greenwash. *Journal of Business Ethics*, *118*(4), 747–757. doi:10.1007/s10551-013-1958-x

Madden, M. (2010). *Older adults and social media*. PewInternet and American Life Project.

Manetti, G., & Bellucci, M. (2016). The use of social media for engaging stakeholders in sustainability reporting. *Accounting, Auditing & Accountability Journal*, *29*(6), 985–1011. doi:10.1108/AAAJ-08-2014-1797

Manheim, J. B., & Pratt, C. B. (1986). Communicating corporate social responsibility. *Public Relations Review*, *12*(2), 9–18. doi:10.1016/S0363-8111(86)80022-4

Mcivor, M. (2022). How Many Fortune 500 CEOs are on Social Media in 2022? *Influential Executive*. https://influentialexecutive.com/how-many-fortune-500-ceos-social-media-2022/

Men, L. R., & Tsai, W. H. S. (2016). Public engagement with CEOs on social media: Motivations and relational outcomes. *Public Relations Review*, *42*(5), 932–942. doi:10.1016/j.pubrev.2016.08.001

Minton, E., Lee, C., Orth, U., Kim, C. H., & Kahle, L. (2012). Sustainable marketing and social media: A cross-country analysis of motives for sustainable behaviors. *Journal of Advertising*, *41*(4), 69–84. doi:10.1080/00913367.2012.10672458

Neu, D., Saxton, G., Rahaman, A., & Everett, J. (2019). Twitter and social accountability: Reactions to the Panama Papers. *Critical Perspectives on Accounting*, *61*, 38–53. doi:10.1016/j.cpa.2019.04.003

Palazzo, M., Vollero, A., & Siano, A. (2020). From strategic corporate social responsibility to value creation: An analysis of corporate website communication in the banking sector. *International Journal of Bank Marketing*, *38*(7), 1529–1552. doi:10.1108/IJBM-04-2020-0168

Parker, L. D. (1982). Corporate annual reporting: A mass communication perspective. *Accounting and Business Research*, *12*(48), 279–286. doi:10.1080/00014788.1982.9728820

Plewa, C., Conduit, J., Quester, P. G., & Johnson, C. (2015). The impact of corporate volunteering on CSR image: A consumer perspective. *Journal of Business Ethics*, *127*(3), 643–659. doi:10.1007/s10551-014-2066-2

Saxton, G. D., Gómez, L., Ngoh, Z., Lin, Y. P., & Dietrich, S. (2019). Do CSR messages resonate? Examining public reactions to firms' CSR efforts on social media. *Journal of Business Ethics*, *155*(2), 359–377. doi:10.1007/s10551-017-3464-z

Sen, S., & Bhattacharya, C. B. (2001). Does doing good always lead to doing better? Consumer reactions to corporate social responsibility. *JMR, Journal of Marketing Research*, *38*(2), 225–243. doi:10.1509/jmkr.38.2.225.18838

Sisson, D. C. (2017). Control mutuality, social media, and organization-public relationships: A study of local animal welfare organizations' donors. *Public Relations Review*, *43*(1), 179–189. doi:10.1016/j.pubrev.2016.10.007

Sriramesh, K., Rivera-Sánchez, M., & Soriano, C. (2013). Websites for stakeholder relations by corporations and non-profits: A time-lag study in Singapore. *Journal of Communication Management (London)*, *17*(2), 122–139. doi:10.1108/13632541311318738

Sun, Y., & Bhattacherjee, A. (2014). Looking inside the "IT black box": Technological effects on IT usage. *Journal of Computer Information Systems*, *54*(2), 1–15. doi:10.1080/08874417.2014.11645681

Sutton, J. (2016). *Why Social Media and Sustainability Should Go Hand in Hand*. Triple Pundit. https://www.triplepundit.com/2016/06/social-mediasustainability-go-hand-hand/

Tilt, C. A. (1994). The Influence of External Pressure Groups on Corporate Social Disclosure: Some Empirical Evidence. *Accounting, Auditing & Accountability Journal*, *7*(4), 47–72. doi:10.1108/09513579410069849

Trevor, D. W., & Geoffrey, R. F. (2000). Corporate environmental reporting. A test of legitimacy theory. *Accounting, Auditing & Accountability Journal*, *13*(1), 10–26. doi:10.1108/09513570010316126

Vo, T. T., Xiao, X., & Ho, S. Y. (2019). How does corporate social responsibility engagement influence word of mouth on Twitter? Evidence from the airline industry. *Journal of Business Ethics*, *157*(2), 525–542. doi:10.1007/s10551-017-3679-z

Wang, R., & Huang, Y. (2018). Communicating corporate social responsibility (CSR) on social media: How do message source and types of CSR messages influence stakeholders' perceptions? *Corporate Communications*, *23*(3), 326–341. doi:10.1108/CCIJ-07-2017-0067

Wickert, C., Scherer, A. G., & Spence, L. J. (2016). Walking and Talking Corporate Social Responsibility: Implications of Firm Size and Organizational Cost. *Journal of Management Studies*, *53*(7), 1169–1196. doi:10.1111/joms.12209

Wilmshurst, T. D., & Frost, G. R. (2000). Corporate environmental reporting: A test of legitimacy theory. *Accounting, Auditing & Accountability Journal*, *13*(1), 10–26. doi:10.1108/09513570010316126

Yan, R. N., Ogle, J. P., & Hyllegard, K. H. (2010). The impact of message appeal and message source on Gen Y consumers' attitudes and purchase intentions toward American Apparel. *Journal of Marketing Communications*, *16*(4), 203–224. doi:10.1080/13527260902863221

Yang, J., Basile, K., & Letourneau, O. (2020). The impact of social media platform selection on effectively communicating about corporate social responsibility. *Journal of Marketing Communications*, *26*(1), 65–87. doi:10.1080/13527266.2018.1500932

Zeghal, D., & Ahmed, S. A. (1990). Comparison of social responsibility information disclosure media used by Canadian firms. *Accounting, Auditing & Accountability Journal*, *3*(1), 0-0.

Zhang, C. B., & Lin, Y. H. (2015). Exploring interactive communication using social media. *Service Industries Journal*, *35*(11-12), 670–693. doi:10.1080/02642069.2015.1064396

Zhang, Z., Zhang, Z., & Li, H. (2015). Predictors of the authenticity of Internet health rumours. *Health Information and Libraries Journal*, *32*(3), 195–205. doi:10.1111/hir.12115 PMID:26268517

Zizka, L. (2017). The (mis) use of social media to communicate CSR in hospitality: Increasing stakeholders'(dis) engagement through social media. *Journal of Hospitality and Tourism Technology*, *8*(1), 73–86. doi:10.1108/JHTT-07-2016-0037

ADDITIONAL READING

Fieseler, C., & Fleck, M. (2013). The Pursuit of Empowerment through Social Media: Structural Social Capital Dynamics in CSR-Blogging. *Journal of Business Ethics*, *118*(4), 759–775. doi:10.1007/s10551-013-1959-9

Saxton, G. D., Gomez, L., Ngoh, Z., Lin, Y.-P., & Dietrich, S. (2019). Do CSR Messages Resonate? Examining Public Reactions to Firms' CSR Efforts on Social Media. *Journal of Business Ethics*, *155*(2), 359–377. doi:10.1007/s10551-017-3464-z

Saxton, G. D., Ren, C., & Guo, C. (2021). Responding to Diffused Stakeholders on Social Media: Connective Power and Firm Reactions to CSR-Related Twitter Messages. *Journal of Business Ethics*, *172*(2), 229–252. doi:10.1007/s10551-020-04472-x

Zhou, J., Ye, S., & Liu, X. (2023). More Social, More Socially Responsible? The Impact of CEO Social Media Use on Corporate Social Performance. *British Journal of Management*, 1467-8551.12774. doi:10.1111/1467-8551.12774

KEY TERMS AND DEFINITIONS

CSR Talk and Walk: The discrepancy between what a firm claims (talk) and actually does (walk) regarding its CSR initiatives.

CSR: Business practices that involve initiatives beneficial to society and promote sustainable development.

Green Washing: Misleading practices where a firm falsely presents itself as environmentally friendly.

Social Media: A digital communication platform that enables users to create, share, and interact with content in real-time, fostering a dynamic and interactive online environment.

Stakeholder: An individual or group affected by or can affect a firm's actions and decisions.

Stand-Alone Report: A report that is published separately, not part of another document or annual report, often focusing on a single topic or area, such as sustainability, CSR, or financials.

Sustainability Report: A report published by a firm to showcase its economic, environmental, social, and governance performance and impacts.

Web 1.0: The first, static phase of the Internet with primarily read-only content.

Web 2.0: The evolution of the Internet into a platform for user-generated, collaborative, and interactive content.

Chapter 10
AI-Driven Hospital Accounting: A Path to Financial Health

Jaspreet Kaur
Chandigarh University, India

ABSTRACT

When it comes to maintaining their financial stability, healthcare organisations confront particular difficulties. Hospitals are constantly under pressure to maximise their financial operations due to the growing expense of healthcare, shifting reimbursement structures, and the requirement to deliver high-quality patient care. In this quickly changing environment, traditional hospital accounting techniques might not be sufficient anymore. This chapter examines how artificial intelligence (AI) can revolutionise hospital accounting and provide a way to improve financial stability. AI-driven hospital accounting uses automation, data analytics, and sophisticated machine learning algorithms to increase accuracy, expedite financial procedures, and facilitate well-informed decision-making.

1. INTRODUCTION

In the field of computer science and technology, artificial intelligence, or AI for short, has become one of the most exciting and revolutionary disciplines. It includes a broad range of approaches, strategies, and technological advancements that let machines mimic human intellect and carry out operations that were previously thought to be the sole purview of humans. This essay explores the foundations of artificial intelligence (AI), illuminating its various subfields and applications while also addressing its central ideas. Fundamentally, artificial intelligence (AI) seeks to give robots the capacity to learn, understand, and adapt similarly to how humans do. This includes the ability to think, solve problems, come to judgements, and comprehend spoken language. Artificial intelligence (AI) systems are built to process enormous volumes of data, identify patterns, and utilise that knowledge to make deft decisions (Vesty et al.,2023).

DOI: 10.4018/979-8-3693-1331-2.ch010

1.1 Computer Learning: The AI Workhorse

The backbone of AI is machine learning (ML), a subset of it. Systems that aren't explicitly coded can learn from data thanks to machine learning techniques. Machines may identify patterns and make predictions based on previously unknown data by being exposed to training data. Multimedia learning (ML) includes a number of methods, including as supervised learning (training the algorithm on labelled data), unsupervised learning (finding patterns in data), and reinforcement learning (learning from interacting with the environment).

Deep learning, a kind of machine learning, is so good at tackling complicated problems, it has attracted a lot of interest. Artificial neural networks, which draw inspiration from the human brain, are at the centre of it all. These networks are made up of data-processing neurons arranged in interconnected layers. Natural language processing, driverless cars, image and audio recognition, and other fields have benefited greatly from the application of deep learning (Kilanko, 2023).

Another important area of artificial intelligence is natural language processing (NLP). NLP is concerned with making computers capable of comprehending, interpreting, and producing human language. It is used in sentiment analysis, text production, language translation, and chatbots. Significant progress has been achieved in bridging the communication gap between humans and machines with NLP technology.

1.2 AI Applications

The impact of AI is seen in many industries, such as robotics, healthcare, finance, and automotive. AI helps with medication research, patient care, and diagnostics in the healthcare industry. AI is used by financial institutions for risk assessment, investment strategies, and fraud detection. Artificial intelligence (AI) powers autonomous decision-making in industrial robots and self-driving automobiles, as well as speech recognition and natural language comprehension in personal assistants like Siri and Alexa (Kaur, 2023).

1.3 The Social and Ethical Aspects

Although artificial intelligence (AI) has many benefits, it also brings up social and ethical issues. The deployment of AI has brought up a number of issues, including algorithmic bias, data privacy, employment displacement, and the necessity of openness in AI decision-making processes. To properly utilise AI's potential, these issues must be resolved (Mohammad et al., 2023).

With its foundations in deep learning, machine learning, and natural language processing, artificial intelligence is a shining example of technological progress. It is currently the impetus behind several inventions and breakthroughs in a wide range of industries, having evolved from being just a notion. Gaining an appreciation of AI's potential and the ongoing revolutionary effects it has on our world requires an understanding of its foundations. As AI develops, it will be our obligation to negotiate the ethical and sociological ramifications of this technology while also embracing its potential to improve both our communities and the global community. After all, tremendous power comes with great responsibility (Meslamani, 2023).

1.4 AI's Changing Place in Healthcare

The way artificial intelligence (AI) is being used in healthcare is a testament to how technology can revolutionise patient care, operational efficiency, and medical research. AI is changing healthcare in a number of ways, and its influence is only increasing. This essay examines how artificial intelligence (AI) is evolving in the healthcare industry and the several domains where it is having a substantial impact as depicted in figure 1 below.

Figure 1. Ways in which AI is changing healthcare

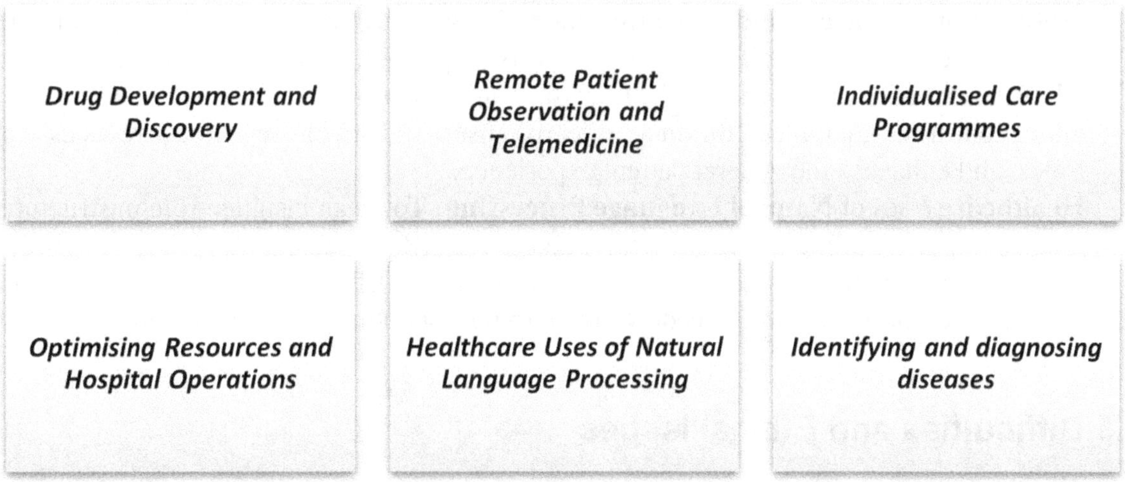

- **Identifying and diagnosing diseases:** The field of diagnostics and disease detection is one of the most important areas where artificial intelligence is being used in healthcare. Large volumes of medical data, including lab results, patient records, and medical imaging, can be analysed using machine learning algorithms to find trends and abnormalities. As a result, AI-powered diagnostic solutions for diseases like diabetes, cancer, and cardiovascular disorders have been developed. AI is now used by radiologists to help interpret MRIs, CT scans, and X-rays, resulting in faster and more accurate diagnosis (Huraysi et al., 2023).
- **Individualised Care Programmes:** Personalised treatment regimens for patients are made possible by AI's capacity to analyse massive databases and extract insights. AI is able to make personalised medicine and therapy recommendations by examining genetic information, medical history, and treatment results. By ensuring that patients receive the best possible care with the fewest possible side effects, this enhances their whole healthcare experience.
- **Drug Development and Discovery:** AI is essential for expediting the development of new drugs. AI is used by pharmaceutical companies to simulate molecular interactions, find possible medication candidates, and forecast drug behaviour. This lowers related ex-

penses while simultaneously accelerating the medication development process. AI has played a significant role in the search for cures and vaccinations against newly developing illnesses like COVID-19 (Monlezun, 2023).

- **Remote Patient Observation and Telemedicine:** AI technology has been essential in driving the adoption of telehealth and remote patient monitoring during the COVID-19 epidemic. AI systems can analyse real-time patient data collected by wearable devices and Internet of Things sensors. While the patient is comfortable in their own home, healthcare experts can remotely monitor the vital signs of their patients, identify any abnormalities, and take required action. AI-powered telehealth services make it possible for people in remote or underdeveloped locations to receive healthcare by facilitating virtual consultations.
- **Optimising Resources and Hospital Operations:** AI is being utilised to optimise resource allocation and hospital operations. By using predictive analytics to forecast patient admission rates, hospitals may make necessary adjustments to staffing levels and resource allocation. This guarantees the most effective use of available resources, reduces wait times, and enhances the general patient experience.
- **Healthcare Uses of Natural Language Processing:** To glean insights from unstructured medical data, including electronic health records (EHRs), medical literature, and clinical notes, natural language processing (NLP) is utilised. NLP contributes to the efficiency and accuracy of healthcare procedures by automating coding, billing, and administrative tasks.

1.5 Difficulties and Ethical Issues

Even with its major contributions, artificial intelligence's growing position in healthcare is not without difficulties. Data security, privacy, algorithmic bias, and the requirement for legal frameworks are still major factors to take into account. Healthcare talks revolve around ethical challenges related to artificial intelligence, including the responsible use of patient data and openness in AI decision-making (Patil & Shankar, 2023).

AI's developing position in healthcare is characterised by advancement, creativity, and a dedication to enhancing patient outcomes and the effectiveness of the healthcare system. As AI technologies develop, they have the potential to improve healthcare accessibility and personalization while also improving our capacity to identify, cure, and prevent diseases. To guarantee the ethical and advantageous integration of AI in healthcare, it is essential that technologists, legislators, and healthcare practitioners collaborate to fully use AI's potential while tackling its related ethical and legal issues (Wysocki et al., 2023).

1.6 AI Innovations Associated With Hospital Accounting

In hospital accounting, artificial intelligence (AI) technologies are crucial because they enable healthcare organisations improve overall financial health, expedite financial procedures, cut down on errors, and improve revenue cycle management (Stafford, 2023). The following AI innovations are pertinent to hospital accounting as depicted in figure 2 below:

Figure 2. AI innovation in hospital accounting

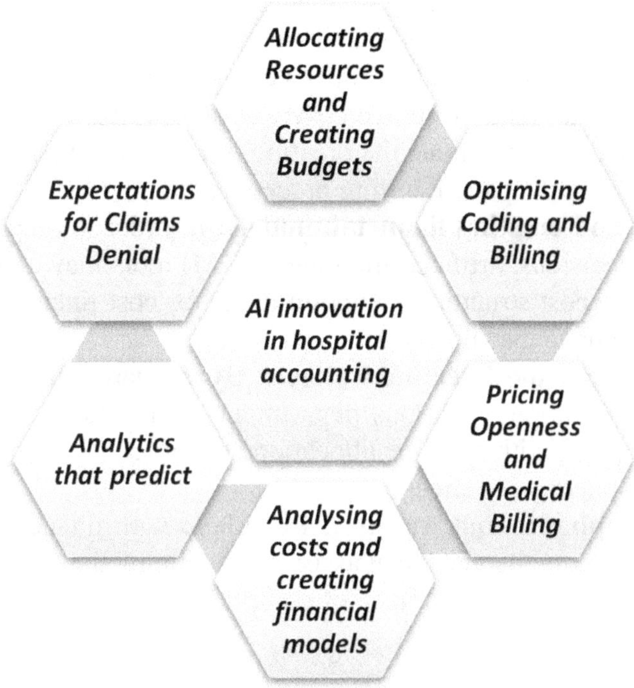

Automation of robotic processes (RPA): RPA automates repetitive, rule-based work in accounting and finance processes by utilising software robots, often known as bots. RPA is used in hospital accounting for managing accounts payable and receivable, handling payroll, and processing invoices. RPA can boost productivity, decrease human mistake rates, and free up employees to work on more strategically important financial activities (Kaur,2023).

Analytics that predict: AI algorithms are used in predictive analytics to examine past financial data and forecast future trends. Predictive analytics can be used in hospital accounting to optimise financial planning, identify possible problems, and forecast revenue. Predicting cash flow, patient volumes, and revenue cycle performance can be made easier with its help.

- **Expectations for Claims Denial:** AI can be used to forecast which insurance claims for medical care are most likely to be rejected. AI technologies can assist hospitals in reducing claim denials by examining past claims data and spotting recurring denial patterns. This can lower administrative expenses and enhance cash flow (Federspiel et al.,2023).
- **Fraud Encounters:** Financial data can be analysed by AI-based fraud detection systems to find anomalies and possibly fraudulent activity. This is essential to avoiding monetary losses brought on by dishonest accounting and billing practises.
- **NLP, or natural language processing**: NLP is a useful tool for analysing unstructured data in accounting and financial documents, including financial reports and contracts. It can assist in obtaining important data, spotting irregularities, and guaranteeing adherence to accounting guidelines (Jabri & Tim, 2023).

- **Optimising Coding and Billing:** AI-powered tools that recommend suitable codes based on clinical documentation can help with medical billing and coding. This streamlines the reimbursement process, lowers errors, and guarantees proper billing.
- **Pricing Openness and Medical Billing:** AI can help by giving payers and patients precise cost estimates that take insurance coverage and available treatments into consideration. Additionally, it can facilitate the creation of customised payment plans and billing statements, enhancing the patient billing procedure.
- **Analysing costs and creating financial models:** In order to help hospitals make data-driven financial decisions, artificial intelligence (AI) tools may analyse financial data to reveal insights into cost structures, pinpoint areas for cost reduction, and give financial modelling (Chintamaneni et al., 2023).
- **Allocating Resources and Creating Budgets:** By evaluating past financial data and optimising budget allocation to various departments and initiatives, artificial intelligence (AI) can help hospitals with resource allocation and budget planning. This guarantees the effective use of monetary resources.
- **Support for Compliance and Audits:** AI can help with financial record auditing and regulatory standard compliance. It can assist in automating the tracking of financial transactions, which facilitates the assurance of compliance with financial regulations (Zahlan et al., 2023).

Hospitals may optimise revenue, cut expenses, improve financial management, and improve their overall financial health by utilising these AI technologies. But in order to protect patient and financial data security and privacy as well as compliance with healthcare legislation, it is imperative that these technologies be implemented cautiously.

1.7 Healthcare's Complicated Financial Environment

Healthcare finance is a very complex and dynamic field that is influenced by many different stakeholders, laws, and variables. It includes the monetary facets of insurance, administration, reimbursement, and healthcare delivery. Policymakers, healthcare organisations, and industry participants must all comprehend this complexity. We'll look at a few of the major factors that make up the intricate financial picture in healthcare here.

Healthcare payment schemes come in a variety of intricate forms. Value-based care, capitation, fee-for-service, and bundled payments are a few of them. These models have an effect on the payment of healthcare providers for their services, and they frequently call for sophisticated financial and administrative administration (Kumar et al., 2023).

- **Health Insurance:** The intricacy is increased by the abundance of both public and commercial health insurance carriers. Healthcare facilities like hospitals have to deal with different payer criteria, coding schemes, and billing processes. The financial operations of healthcare organisations are closely linked to health insurance claims, denials, and reimbursements.
- **Rules and Compliance:** With a plethora of federal and state rules, the healthcare sector is one of the most strictly regulated. Dedicated financial resources and specialised knowl-

edge are needed to ensure compliance with rules such as the Affordable Care Act (ACA), the Health Insurance Portability and Accountability Act (HIPAA), and other Medicare and Medicaid regulations.

- **Revenue Cycle Management:** In the healthcare industry, patient registration, insurance verification, coding, billing, and collections are all part of the intricate revenue cycle process. Any disruption in this cycle may result in monetary losses. To effectively manage this cycle, healthcare organisations require cutting-edge technologies and specialised knowledge.
- **Accounting and Reporting:** Financial reporting for the healthcare industry must follow certain healthcare accounting standards and generally accepted accounting principles (GAAP). Healthcare accounting is a specialised field. Financial transparency and regulatory compliance depend on accurate accounting and financial reporting (Bold et al., 2023).
- **Costs and Pricing:** The expenses associated with providing healthcare are complex, encompassing not just the direct costs of patient care but also the costs of capital projects, administrative overhead, and regulatory compliance. Accurately estimating costs for services and procedures is a difficult process that is frequently impacted by agreements with payers and government initiatives.
- **Value-based Care:** The goal of the move to value-based care models is to reduce costs and enhance patient outcomes. For this shift to be financially sustainable and demonstrate value, large investments in data analytics, infrastructure, and care coordination are needed.
- **Investments in Technology:** To handle revenue cycle management, electronic health records (EHRs), and data analytics, hospitals and other healthcare organisations need to make investments in cutting-edge healthcare information systems. These expenditures can add up, and they need constant upkeep.
- **Financial Aid and Charity treatment:** Underinsured and uninsured patients frequently receive financial aid and charity treatment from healthcare facilities. This makes financial management much more difficult and necessitates tracking, reporting, and adherence to federal regulations (Dogheim & Hussain, 2023).
- **Economic Factors:** Reimbursement rates, patient financial responsibility, and healthcare utilisation can all be impacted by the overall state of the economy, which includes elements like economic recessions, unemployment rates, and government fiscal policies.
- **Acquisitions and Mergers**: In the healthcare sector, integration and consolidation can bring about financial challenges in the form of combining operations, systems, and financial reporting.
- **Global Health Challenges:** The COVID-19 pandemic and other events have exposed the flaws in healthcare financing and highlighted the significance of emergency planning for healthcare institutions. Healthcare administration, finance, compliance, and technological experience are all need to successfully navigate this complicated financial environment. To maintain patient satisfaction, high-quality care, and financial viability, healthcare organisations must make strategic decisions and adjust to the changing financial landscape. Through prospective reforms and modifications to healthcare finance systems, policymakers and regulators also have a significant impact on the financial landscape.

1.8 Traditional Hospital Accounting's Drawbacks

Numerous drawbacks of traditional hospital accounting techniques can impede healthcare organisations' ability to manage finances and make wise decisions. Several of these restrictions consist of:

- **Lack of detail:** Financial reporting from traditional accounting systems frequently lacks sufficient detail. They might not separate expenses and income into particular categories, which makes it challenging to pinpoint precise instances of financial inefficiencies or potential cost-cutting measures.
- **Inaccurate Cost Allocation:** Expenses may not be appropriately allocated to particular departments, services, or operations using traditional accounting methods. This might lead to distorted cost statistics, which makes it difficult to assess the actual profitability of various services or the price of treating a specific patient (Gaddum & Chapiro, 2023).
- **Complexity of Revenue Recognition:** There are many different payment structures and sources of revenue in the healthcare industry, such as insurance reimbursements, government programmes, and patient payments, which make the revenue recognition process complex. It's possible that conventional accounting techniques lack the adaptability needed to appropriately address this complexity.
- **Lack of Transparency:** Healthcare organisations may find it challenging to monitor and comprehend their financial performance due to traditional accounting systems' possible lack of transparency in financial reporting. This may hinder their capacity to pinpoint places in need of development.
- **Limited Real-time Data:** Because traditional accounting systems frequently rely on periodic financial statements, there is a lack of real-time financial data. Decision-making may become delayed as a result, and one may find it more difficult to respond swiftly to financial possibilities or obstacles.
- **Ineffective predicting and Budgeting:** In the fast-paced world of healthcare, traditional accounting techniques can be burdensome for predicting and budgeting. It is difficult to use standard methods to simulate different scenarios and evaluate the effects of changes in patient volumes, payment rates, and other aspects for healthcare organisations.
- **Insufficient for Value-Based Care:** As the healthcare sector moves towards value-based care, existing accounting systems can find it difficult to accurately reflect the cost and calibre of patient care. Value-based care places a stronger emphasis on patient happiness and outcomes, necessitating more precise financial evaluation.
- **Challenges with Regulatory Compliance:** Complex healthcare laws like HIPAA, the Affordable Care Act, and Medicare/Medicaid standards may be too difficult for healthcare organisations to comply with when using traditional accounting procedures. Financial fines may arise from noncompliance (Unver, 2023).
- **Difficulty in Determining Cost Drivers:** Conventional accounting may lack the instruments and processes necessary to precisely determine the causes of expenses. Making educated choices on the distribution of resources and the lowering of prices requires an understanding of the elements that influence costs.

- **Difficulties with Data Integration:** Healthcare companies frequently employ a variety of software programmes, such as accounting, revenue cycle management, and electronic health records (EHRs). Using typical accounting techniques to integrate data from various different systems into a coherent financial picture might be difficult.

In order to get around these restrictions, a lot of healthcare companies are switching to more sophisticated financial management systems that can handle the intricate revenue and expense structures that are exclusive to the healthcare sector, give real-time data, and provide strong financial analytics. To better handle the particular opportunities and difficulties given by the healthcare financial landscape, these systems frequently include components of financial management and reporting that are exclusive to the healthcare industry (Vesty et al.,2023).

1.9 Revenue Cycle Management With AI

Predictive analytics powered by AI can examine past claims data to find trends and patterns connected to claim denials. AI is able to forecast the possibility that a claim would be rejected by looking at a number of data elements, including as patient data, billing details, and coding accuracy. This makes it possible for healthcare organisations to improve paperwork, code accurately, and follow billing standards in order to prevent denials. Revenue is maximised and RCM becomes more effective by addressing denials before they happen.

Increasing Coding Precision: By providing medical coders with coding support tools, AI can greatly improve coding accuracy. These technologies evaluate clinical documentation and provide appropriate procedure and diagnosis codes using Natural Language Processing (NLP) and machine learning techniques. This lowers the likelihood that coding errors will occur and increases the likelihood that the codes chosen will be approved by payers, resulting in more precise compensation and more income (Kilanko, 2023).

Optimising the Patient Billing Process: The patient billing process can be improved in a number of ways using AI technologies. They can offer simple payment choices, clearly explain prices, and customise billing statements. AI can also forecast a patient's financial situation and adjust payment schedules appropriately. In addition to making patient billing more enjoyable, this also raises the possibility of effective revenue collection. Through the automation and simplification of numerous process steps, it also lessens the administrative load associated with patient billing.

Finding Inefficiencies and Revenue Leakage: AI is capable of analysing operational and financial data to find possible sources of inefficiency and income leakage. This entails finding underutilised services, identifying invoicing problems, and optimising administrative procedures. AI can also be used to find possibilities to increase revenue and optimise the use of resources. Healthcare organisations may greatly improve their financial health by resolving these problems, which will guarantee that they collect all available funds and reduce inefficiencies that could result in losses. All things considered, applying AI to revenue cycle management can make healthcare companies run more smoothly, save money, increase coding accuracy, and streamline patient billing procedures. In addition, it makes proactive claim denial management possible and can spot possible income leakage and inefficiencies, all of which can lead to better financial results and happier patients. But it's crucial to apply AI solutions cautiously, making sure that legal criteria are met and that patient data is kept secure and private (Mohammad et al., 2023).

1.10 Using AI to Drive Expense Management: Changing Accuracy and Efficiency

For companies of all sizes, expense management is an essential component of financial control and optimisation. For an organisation to maintain sustainability and financial health, costs must be properly tracked, evaluated, and managed. Artificial Intelligence (AI) has become a potent tool to transform spending management in today's data-driven society. This section examines the advantages and ramifications of artificial intelligence (AI)-driven expense management, illuminating the ways in which this technology improves accuracy and efficiency in financial operations.

1.11 AI's Place in Expense Management

The use of artificial intelligence technology to optimise, automate, and streamline the entire process of controlling corporate expenses is known as AI-driven expense management. This strategy covers a number of topics, such as data analysis, policy enforcement, receipt processing, and expenditure reporting. Let's examine the primary ways that artificial intelligence is changing this field.

- **Automated Data Extraction and Receipt Scanning:** AI-driven systems for managing expenses have the ability to automatically extract pertinent data from invoices and receipts. Employees will save significant time and errors by not having to enter data by hand.
- **Policy Enforcement and Compliance:** By looking for policy infractions in expense reports and receipts, AI can police expense policies. AI can flag an expenditure claim for additional examination or rejection if it deviates from the company's policies (Meslamani, 2023).
- **Expense Categorization and Tagging:** Artificial Intelligence can automatically classify and tag expenses, guaranteeing precise and uniform accounting. In addition to making expense monitoring easier, this improves data accuracy for financial analysis.
- **Predictive analytics:** AI-powered solutions for managing spending can forecast future costs by analysing past data. As a result, businesses are better able to manage resources, prepare budgets, and proactively find areas where they may save money.
- Artificial Intelligence (AI) has the capability to detect anomalies in expenditure reports and trends of fraudulent cost submissions. It can assist organisations avoid financial losses by highlighting possible fraud situations for inquiry.
- **Effective Approval Workflows:** By automatically assigning costs to the right employees, artificial intelligence (AI) can improve approval workflow efficiency. For quicker processing, it might give priority to high-value or urgent charges (Huraysi et al., 2023).

1.12 AI-Powered Expense Management's Advantages

The following are some advantages that organisations can gain by integrating AI into expense management:

- **Enhanced Efficiency:** Manual cost management procedures take a lot of time and are prone to mistakes. Many of these duties are automated by AI, freeing up staff members to concentrate on more strategic work.
- **Cost savings**: Artificial intelligence (AI) can find areas where money can be saved by examining expenditure data and looking for inefficiencies or non-compliant spending.
- **Enhanced Precision:** Automation and the ability to extract data result in more precise data, which lowers the possibility of accounting errors (Patil & Shankar, 2023).
- **Enhanced Policy Compliance:** AI lowers the likelihood of non-compliance by ensuring that cost claims follow corporate policies.
- **Simplified Auditing**: AI can identify possible problems, which makes auditing more accurate and efficient.
- **Real-time Reporting and Insights:** AI gives businesses instant access to spending information and insights, enabling them to act quickly on data-driven decisions.

Expense management powered by AI is revolutionary for businesses trying to streamline their financial processes. It provides efficiency, precision, and automation, which lessens the administrative load and frees up staff members to work on other worthwhile projects. AI may also improve policy compliance, yield insightful discoveries, and present cost-saving options that have a big influence on an organization's bottom line. Businesses who implement AI will have a competitive advantage in financial control and decision-making as the technology's use in spending management grows.

1.13 AI-Powered Expense Management: Revolutionising Accuracy and Efficiency

For companies of all sizes, expense management is an essential component of financial control and optimisation. For an organisation to maintain sustainability and financial health, costs must be properly tracked, evaluated, and managed. Artificial Intelligence (AI) has become a potent tool to transform spending management in today's data-driven society. This section examines the advantages and ramifications of artificial intelligence (AI)-driven expense management, illuminating the ways in which this technology improves accuracy and efficiency in financial operations (Wysocki et al., 2023).

1.14 AI's Place in Expense Management

The use of artificial intelligence technology to optimise, automate, and streamline the entire process of controlling corporate expenses is known as AI-driven expense management. This strategy covers a number of topics, such as data analysis, policy enforcement, receipt processing, and expenditure reporting. Let's examine the primary ways that artificial intelligence is changing this field:

Automated Data Extraction and Receipt Scanning: AI-driven systems for managing expenses have the ability to automatically extract pertinent data from invoices and receipts. Employees will save significant time and errors by not having to enter data by hand.

Policy Enforcement and Compliance: By looking for policy infractions in expense reports and receipts, AI can police expense policies. AI can flag an expenditure claim for additional examination or rejection if it deviates from the company's policies.

Expense Categorization and Tagging: Artificial Intelligence can automatically classify and tag expenses, guaranteeing precise and uniform accounting. In addition to making expense monitoring easier, this improves data accuracy for financial analysis.

Predictive analytics: AI-powered solutions for managing spending can forecast future costs by analysing past data. As a result, businesses are better able to manage resources, prepare budgets, and proactively find areas where they may save money (Stafford, 2023).

Artificial Intelligence (AI) has the capability to detect anomalies in expenditure reports and trends of fraudulent cost submissions. It can assist organisations avoid financial losses by highlighting possible fraud situations for inquiry.

Effective Approval Workflows: By automatically assigning costs to the right employees, artificial intelligence (AI) can improve approval workflow efficiency. For quicker processing, it might give priority to high-value or urgent charges.

1.15 AI-Powered Expense Management's Advantages

The following are some advantages that organisations can gain by integrating AI into expense management:

- **Enhanced Efficiency:** Manual cost management procedures take a lot of time and are prone to mistakes. Many of these duties are automated by AI, freeing up staff members to concentrate on more strategic work.
- **Cost savings:** Artificial intelligence (AI) can find areas where money can be saved by examining expenditure data and looking for inefficiencies or non-compliant spending.
- **Enhanced Precision**: Automation and the ability to extract data result in more precise data, which lowers the possibility of accounting errors.
- **Enhanced Policy Compliance:** AI lowers the likelihood of non-compliance by ensuring that cost claims follow corporate policies.
- **Simplified Auditing:** AI can identify possible problems, which makes auditing more accurate and efficient.
- **Real-time Reporting and Insights:** AI gives businesses instant access to spending information and insights, enabling them to act quickly on data-driven decisions (Jabri & Tim, 2023).

Expense management powered by AI is revolutionary for businesses trying to streamline their financial processes. It provides efficiency, precision, and automation, which lessens the administrative load and frees up staff members to work on other worthwhile projects. AI may also improve policy compliance, yield insightful discoveries, and present cost-saving options that have a big influence on an organization's bottom line. Businesses who implement AI will have a competitive advantage in financial control and decision-making as the technology's use in spending management grows.

1.16 AI-Powered Financial Forecasting

For companies and organisations to prepare and make wise financial decisions about their future, financial forecasting is an essential activity. It entails forecasting future financial results, such as earnings, costs, and revenues. Artificial Intelligence (AI) has been a potent tool to improve financial forecasting's efficacy and accuracy in recent years. The relevance of precise financial forecasts, the function of AI models in financial forecasting, and the significance of data-driven decision-making in this context are all examined in this section. Precise financial projections are crucial for multiple reasons:

- Financial projections serve as the cornerstone of strategic planning. They support businesses in establishing their financial objectives and creating plans to meet them.
- Resource Allocation: Budgets are in line with anticipated financial needs thanks to the guidance provided by forecasts. This stops money from being spent too much or too little in important areas.
- Risk management: Organisations can create backup plans and risk-reduction techniques by identifying possible financial risks and uncertainties.
- Accurate forecasts contribute to increased investor trust. Financial predictions are a crucial tool for stakeholders, lenders, and investors to make well-informed judgements when deciding whether to support or invest in a firm.
- Performance Assessment: Real financial performance is assessed using forecasts as a reference point. Companies can evaluate the efficacy of their financial management by comparing projected and actual results (Kilanko, 2023).

1.17 AI-Based Financial Forecasting Models

Financial forecasting has undergone a revolution thanks to AI models, which provide sophisticated skills over old techniques. The following are a few AI-driven methods for financial forecasting:

Machine Learning (ML): To find patterns and relationships in historical financial data, ML algorithms can examine the data. Based on these patterns, one can utilise regression analysis, time series analysis, and deep learning approaches to forecast future financial results.

Natural language processing, or NLP, is used to evaluate text data extracted from social media, news articles, and financial reports in order to determine sentiment and derive information that may have an impact on financial forecasts (Meslamani, 2023).

Predictive analytics is a subfield of artificial intelligence that forecasts future financial performance based on past data. For the analysis of customer behaviour, demand forecasting, and revenue forecasting, this is especially helpful.

AI-Enhanced Financial Models: By offering more precise inputs and real-time data updates, artificial intelligence can improve conventional financial models. This lowers human data entry errors and increases the accuracy of financial forecasts.

1.18 Data-Informed Judgmentation

The foundation of effective financial forecasting with AI is data-driven decision-making. Data is the foundation of AI models, and the relevance, volume, and quality of the data used determine how accurate the projections are. Additionally, organisations that use data-driven decision-making are encouraged to:

Utilise Real-Time Data: AI's ability to handle massive amounts of data in real time enables businesses to respond swiftly to shifting market dynamics or financial difficulties.

Adapt to Market Dynamics: In order to account for changes in the market, financial predictions need to be adaptable. Based on real-time data, AI models can offer continuing insights and modifications, guaranteeing that projections stay accurate and pertinent.

Determine chances and dangers: Data-driven financial forecasting helps to identify potential dangers as well as chances for growth in addition to predicting financial outcomes.

Boost Resource Allocation: Organisations may cut waste and distribute resources more effectively by using data-driven projections (Gaddum & Chapiro, 2023).

Ensure that Financial Decisions Support the Overarching Mission: Data-driven financial projections assist organisations in ensuring that financial objectives are in line with more general strategic goals.

All things considered; AI-powered financial forecasting is revolutionising how businesses make financial plans. It is impossible to overestimate the importance of accurate financial predictions because they form the basis for risk management, resource allocation, strategic planning, and investor trust. Organisations can use cutting-edge methods and real-time data to develop more accurate and flexible financial projections by utilising AI models that are powered by data-driven decision-making. This enhances financial decision-making and performance (Unver, 2023)

1.19 AI in Healthcare Fraud Detection and Prevention: The Increasing Problem of Healthcare Fraud

Healthcare fraud is a widespread issue that jeopardises the integrity of global healthcare systems. Every year, fraudulent acts cost billions of dollars and compromise the standard of care that patients receive. Since conventional techniques for preventing and detecting fraud are frequently insufficient, integrating AI algorithms is an essential first step in guaranteeing adherence to legal requirements. This essay examines the application of AI to the fight against healthcare fraud, emphasising the use of AI algorithms to identify abnormalities and guarantee regulatory compliance.

The Increasing Problem of Medical Fraud: A wide range of illegal behaviours, such as identity theft, prescription fraud, kickbacks, and billing fraud, are included in healthcare fraud. The complexity of healthcare billing systems, the growth of telehealth services, and the growing dependence on electronic health records (EHRs) are some of the causes contributing to the rising incidence of healthcare fraud. Because of these difficulties, it is now more challenging to identify fraudulent activity using conventional techniques (Patil & Shankar, 2023).

AI Techniques for Finding Disparities: Healthcare fraud is a critical issue that AI algorithms help to resolve. In order to find anomalies in large datasets—which is crucial for identifying fraudulent activity—these algorithms make use of machine learning and data analytics. The following are some essential AI methods for spotting fraud:

Machine Learning: Healthcare data is analysed using machine learning methods, which include supervised and unsupervised learning. While unsupervised learning approaches can spot odd patterns or anomalies in the data, supervised learning models can be trained to identify patterns linked to fraudulent claims.

Natural language processing, or NLP, is used to examine textual information included in insurance claims and medical records. NLP can identify inconsistencies, contradictions, and suspicious language that can point to fraud by analysing and comprehending the text.

Predictive analytics: By examining past data patterns, AI-powered predictive models are able to identify future instances of fraud. This aids in proactively stopping deception and reducing monetary losses.

Neural networks and other deep learning algorithms are capable of recognising intricate patterns and relationships within huge datasets. This is especially helpful in identifying fraud schemes that are sophisticated and dynamic.

Behavioural Analytics: For patients, payers, and healthcare providers, AI can create a baseline of typical behaviour. The early detection of fraud is made possible by the flagging of deviations from these baselines as possible anomalies. Making Certain Regulatory Standards Are Followed:

In addition to aiding in the detection of fraud, AI algorithms are essential for guaranteeing adherence to legal requirements. Strict restrictions are enforced by regulatory agencies, such the Health Insurance Portability and Accountability Act (HIPAA) in the United States, to protect patient data and stop fraud. AI can help with the following:

Real-time Monitoring: AI can keep an eye on healthcare transactions and data in order to spot any suspicious or non-compliant behaviour and make sure that organisations follow the law (Wysocki et al., 2023).

AI can assist with the implementation of strong data encryption and access control systems, protecting patient information and thwarting illegal access.

Audit Trails: AI-driven audit trails ensure accountability and transparency, two things that are critical for compliance by maintaining a thorough record of all data accesses and transactions.

Reporting and Documentation: AI systems have the ability to generate compliance reports automatically, which makes it simpler for healthcare organisations to prove to auditors that they are adhering to regulations.

Adopting cutting-edge technologies, such artificial intelligence (AI), is vital to efficiently detect and prevent fraudulent actions in light of the growing problem of healthcare fraud. The use of AI algorithms to identify abnormalities and procedures to guarantee adherence to legal requirements are essential parts of this endeavour. Healthcare companies may save a significant amount of money, protect patient data, and uphold the confidence of both patients and regulatory agencies by utilising AI. AI will become much more important in preventing fraud and improving compliance as the healthcare industry develops.

1.20 Healthcare Automation of Reporting and Compliance: Managing the Regulatory Environment

Numerous laws and regulations are in place to protect patient data, guarantee high-quality care, and preserve financial transparency, which makes the regulatory environment in which the healthcare industry functions complex. Financial reporting and compliance management are essential components of hospital administration, and they may be made much more efficient with the use of automation technologies. This paper examines the regulatory environment in the healthcare industry, the function of automation in managing compliance, and the advantages of financial reporting simplification (Federspiel et al.,2023).

- **The Healthcare Regulatory Environment:** Numerous local, national, and international regulations apply to the healthcare sector. In the healthcare industry, important regulatory frameworks include:
- The Health Insurance Portability and Accountability Act (HIPAA) controls the exchange of medical information and guarantees the security and privacy of patient data. The goal of the Affordable Care Act (ACA) is to increase access, affordability, and quality of healthcare in the US. An international standard for medical diagnosis coding is the International Classification of Diseases (ICD).
- **Regulations from the Food and Drug Administration (FDA):** Oversee the creation and authorization of medications and medical devices.
- The Clinical Laboratory Improvement Amendments (CLIA) set forth requirements for clinical laboratories' level of quality.
- **Various accrediting bodies:** The Joint Commission and other organisations set criteria for the safety and quality of healthcare.
- **Regulations pertaining to Medicare and Medicaid:** Control financing and reimbursement for medical services. Automation in the Management of Compliance: Automation is essential for overseeing and guaranteeing adherence to these rules. The following are some ways that automation can improve healthcare compliance management:

Continuous Monitoring: In order to spot any deviations from regulatory requirements, automated tools are able to continuously monitor data, processes, and transactions. This proactive strategy aids in problem solving immediately (Jabri & Tim, 2023).

Automation can be used to enforce access rules and data encryption to guarantee that patient data is kept private and safe, as mandated by laws such as HIPAA. Automated systems generate comprehensive audit trails that facilitate the tracking and verification of regulatory compliance. This is particularly advantageous during audits.

- **Documents and Reporting:** Automation is capable of producing and keeping track of the records, documents, and reports needed to prove compliance with different regulatory standards.
- **Risk assessment:** Organisations can quickly resolve non-compliance or vulnerabilities in healthcare operations by using automated risk assessment solutions.

- **Simplifying Accounting Reports**: Automation has the potential to greatly enhance financial reporting in the healthcare industry in addition to compliance management. Healthcare financial reporting is complicated because it involves many parties, big datasets, and strict regulations. This procedure can be made more efficient by automation in a few ways:
- **Data Integration:** By integrating financial data from several sources, automated solutions can lower the risk of human mistake and manual data entry.
- **Real-time reports:** Healthcare companies may swiftly make well-informed decisions thanks to automation's ability to provide real-time financial reports.
- **Standardised Reporting Templates:** Information may be shared with appropriate stakeholders more easily when automation techniques are used to create standardised financial reports that meet regulatory criteria (Jabri & Tim, 2023).
- **Predictive analytics:** Healthcare companies can better understand their financial performance and are ready for future issues by utilising advanced analytics and forecasting models that are made possible by automation. It can be difficult to navigate the regulatory environment in the healthcare industry, but financial reporting and compliance management are essential to making sure healthcare organisations follow the law. Automation technology provides a number of benefits, including process simplification, less non-compliance risk, increased productivity, and improved overall healthcare service quality. Healthcare organisations can better fulfil their regulatory requirements while concentrating more on patient care, research, and innovation by embracing automation. Automation will be more and more crucial to healthcare reporting and compliance as the regulatory landscape changes.

1.21 Personalised Services and Better Patient Experiences: Healthcare is Transforming Through the Use of AI for Patient Analytics

In the medical field, patient-centric healthcare has become a crucial paradigm shift. Healthcare providers are realising that it's crucial to customise their services to each patient's unique needs rather than taking a one-size-fits-all strategy. Leading the charge in allowing this shift is artificial intelligence (AI), which makes it easier to provide individualised services that improve patient experiences and provide insightful data on patient demographics. The function of artificial intelligence (AI) in patient analytics, its effect on patient-centric healthcare, and how it enhances patient experiences are all covered in this section.

Patient-First Medical Care: The patient is the focal point of medical decision-making and treatment delivery in patient-centric healthcare. It puts the patient's requirements, preferences, and results first, with an emphasis on enhancing their general health and well-being. The empowering of individuals to make educated decisions about their own health is one of the main tenets of patient-centric healthcare, along with cooperation, transparency, and communication (Chintamaneni et al., 2023).

AI-Powered Patient Demographic Information: Data Gathering and Integration: AI systems are capable of collecting, analysing, and integrating enormous volumes of patient data, including demographic, lifestyle, and social determinants of health information as well as medical records. Healthcare professionals are able to get a more comprehensive picture of each patient thanks to this extensive data collecting.

Predictive analytics: By examining patient data, AI algorithms are able to forecast health risks and results. This enhances patient outcomes and preventative treatment by enabling medical professionals to recognise at-risk individuals and take proactive measures to address them.

Segmentation and Personalization: AI is capable of grouping patients according to their preferences, health status, or demographics. More effective care is produced when physicians can better tailor interventions, therapies, and communication to each group's specific requirements thanks to this segmentation.

Enhanced Patient Experiences with Tailored Services: AI assists in the creation of individualised treatment programmes that take a patient's genetic predispositions, medical history, and lifestyle choices into account. Better health outcomes follow from more efficient and patient-specific therapies (Zahlan et al., 2023).

Engagement and Communication: AI-powered patient analytics allow medical professionals to get in touch with patients more quickly and individually. AI-driven chatbots, for instance, can respond to patient inquiries right away, increasing engagement and satisfaction.

Medication Management: By tracking adherence and sending out reminders, artificial intelligence (AI) can help patients better manage their prescriptions. Better health management and medication compliance are facilitated by this customisation.

Telehealth and Remote Monitoring: Patients can have continuous care from the comfort of their homes with the help of AI-powered remote monitoring systems. Real-time monitoring of vital signs and health data by healthcare professionals enables timely intervention when necessary.

Data-Driven Insights: AI uses patient data to produce insights that are then used to influence decisions on how best to allocate resources, build healthcare facilities, and make general improvements to the way that care is delivered, all of which have the potential to improve the patient experience.

Patient-centric care is becoming the norm in healthcare because to AI-driven patient data. It equips medical professionals with the knowledge and resources needed to provide individualised treatment that enhances patient satisfaction, outcomes, and experiences. AI's contribution to healthcare will only grow as technology develops, eventually changing the industry to the advantage of both patients and healthcare professionals. One of the most important steps in realising the goal of genuinely patient-centric healthcare is the incorporation of AI (Kumar et al., 2023).

1.22 AI-Driven Hospital Accounting Implementation: Ensuring Performance, Data Security, and Ethical Obligation

Financial management in healthcare organisations could undergo a transformation with the use of AI-driven hospital accounting. Artificial Intelligence has the potential to optimise operations, boost precision, cut expenses, and automate accounting procedures. However, careful planning, an emphasis on data security and privacy, and a dedication to resolving the ethical implications of AI use are necessary for the successful deployment of AI in this context. These three crucial facets of implementing AI in hospital accounting are covered in this section.

- **Needs Analysis:** It is crucial to carry out an exhaustive needs analysis prior to integrating AI into hospital accounting. This entails determining which particular accounting jobs may be automated, comprehending the infrastructure that is currently in place, and matching AI solutions with the hospital's budgetary objectives.
- **Buy-in from Stakeholders:** Ascertain that the implementation strategy has the support of all relevant parties, such as top management, IT departments, and finance teams. Gaining support requires training and effective communication.
- **Choosing the Best AI Solutions:** Pick AI solutions that are compatible with the accounting specifications of the hospital. These solutions ought to be scalable to accommodate changing requirements and effortlessly interface with current systems.
- **Data Quality:** The effectiveness of AI-driven accounting depends on having high-quality data. To guarantee the precision and dependability of financial data, hospitals ought to allocate resources towards data cleansing, normalisation, and validation procedures.
- **Privacy and Data Security Considerations:** Regulation Compliance: Healthcare organisations are required to follow data security laws such as the General Data Protection Regulation (GDPR) and the Health Insurance Portability and Accountability Act (HIPAA). AI solutions ought to be created with adherence to these rules in mind. Use robust data encryption techniques to shield private patient and financial information from hacking or illegal access (Bold et al., 2023).
- **Access Control:** Limit authorised personnel's access to financial data. To protect user privacy, role-based access controls ought to be implemented in AI systems.
- **Frequent Audits and Monitoring:** To identify any irregularities, security lapses, or improper use of data, keep a close eye on AI systems and do routine audits.

1.23 Responsible AI Use and Its Ethical Consequences

Transparency: AI systems utilised in hospital accounting must to be transparent and able to justify the decisions they make. Trust among stakeholders is bolstered by this transparency.

Bias Mitigation: Hospitals should actively work to eliminate any biases that might be present in AI systems, particularly in areas where financial judgement is involved. It is necessary to regularly audit AI systems for bias and impartiality.

Obtaining informed consent is essential when using AI systems to handle patient financial transactions. Patients need to know about the possible financial repercussions of how their data is being utilised.

Accountability: For choices made with AI, hospitals need to set up distinct channels of accountability. This entails determining accountability for the results of AI-driven financial decisions and guaranteeing error-recovery procedures (Bold et al., 2023).

Although implementing AI-driven hospital accounting has the potential to significantly improve financial management, there are planning, data security, and ethical considerations that must be taken into consideration. Healthcare organisations can take use of AI while maintaining patient confidentiality and public trust by doing a comprehensive requirements assessment, protecting data, and implementing responsible AI practises. Implementing AI-driven hospital accounting successfully eventually requires a comprehensive strategy that strikes a balance between accountability and innovation.

1.24 Examples of AI-Powered Hospital Accounting in the Real World

- **AI-Enhanced Revenue Cycle Management at Cleveland Clinic:** The Cleveland Clinic, a leading healthcare organisation, has integrated AI into its revenue cycle management. Predictive analytics powered by AI can be used to pinpoint areas where financial performance can be enhanced, such increasing revenue capture and decreasing claim denials. Their financial operations have significantly improved as a result of their use of AI.
- **AI-Enabled Financial Forecasting at Mayo Clinic**: The Mayo Clinic, which is well-known for its patient-centered treatment, employs AI in its financial forecasting. They use machine learning to optimise staffing levels, forecast patient flows, and deploy resources effectively. This maintains a balance between stable finances and high-quality medical treatment (Dogheim & Hussain, 2023).
- **AI in Cost Control at Intermountain Healthcare**: AI is used in cost control at Intermountain Healthcare, a non-profit health system. Artificial intelligence (AI)-driven algorithms examine the cost structure and assist in locating areas where costs might be cut without sacrificing the standard of patient care. Significant cost reductions have resulted from this strategy.

1.25 Best Practices and Lessons Learned

- **Data Quality Is Everything:** Successful AI-driven hospital accounting is built on top-notch data. Hospitals should spend money on data normalisation, validation, and cleansing to make sure AI systems operate with correct and trustworthy data.
- **Clear Objectives and KPIs**: Establish clear objectives and key performance indicators (KPIs) prior to deployment. Setting clear goals makes it easier to assess AI's impact.
- **Interoperability and Integration:** Make sure AI solutions can easily interact with the financial and accounting systems that are currently in place. Improved data and insight flow and decreased friction are two benefits of interoperability.
- **Involve Stakeholders**: It is essential to include top management, IT staff, and financial teams in the planning and execution phases. Success depends on their cooperation, support, and input.
- **Regulation Compliance:** Hospitals need to make sure AI-powered accounting systems abide by laws pertaining to data security and healthcare. Failing to do so may have financial and legal repercussions (Federspiel et al.,2023).
- **Frequent Updates and Training:** Employees must receive ongoing education and training on AI systems in order to fully utilise the technology. Employees should be informed when AI changes. Hospitals should actively address biases in AI systems and make sure their financial decision-making procedures are transparent in order to uphold ethical standards. The influence on patients and the larger community must be taken into account while using AI ethically.
- **Accountability and Recourse:** Clearly state who is responsible for AI-driven choices and set up procedures for taking corrective action in the event that mistakes or unexpected effects occur.

- **Continuous Improvement:** The process of implementing AI in hospital accounting is never-ending. Evaluate and improve AI systems on a regular basis to adjust to shifting legal and financial environments.
- **Patient Data Privacy:** Informed consent and strong data privacy safeguards are necessary when AI systems use patient data in financial transactions. Patients ought to be in charge of their information and be informed about how it is used. The possible advantages and difficulties of AI-driven hospital accounting are highlighted by these real-world instances and best practises. If AI is successfully incorporated into hospital financial management, it can optimise financial operations, increase efficiency, and improve patient care—as long as it is done so with careful planning, ethical responsibility, and compliance.

1.26 Hospitals' Best Bets for AI-Powered Hospital Accounting in the Future

Invest in Knowledge and Skill in AI: Hospitals that want to employ and train AI specialists, data scientists, and financial analysts who can handle the intricacies of AI-driven accounting should make this investment. Establishing an internal team with the requisite knowledge is essential for sustained success.

Adopt a thorough approach to AI: Create a comprehensive AI plan that covers all financial operations, including forecasting, cost control, and revenue cycle management. Make sure AI is in line with the hospital's overarching operational and financial objectives.

Data Management and Governance: To preserve high-quality data, give data governance and management a priority. To guarantee that the information used to generate AI-driven insights is accurate, put in place data governance guidelines, data cleansing procedures, and frequent audits (Jabri & Tim, 2023).

Integration & Interoperability: Make sure AI solutions are made to work with the accounting and finance systems that are already in place. Financial operations may be streamlined and data silos can be avoided with seamless data flow and integration between AI and older systems.

Keep an Eye on and Improve AI Systems Constantly: Keep an eye on AI systems and improve algorithms often to adjust to shifting legal and financial landscapes. Artificial Intelligence needs constant upkeep and development; it cannot be implemented once.

Transparent and Ethical AI Use: Hospitals need to actively address algorithmic biases and be open about using AI to make financial decisions. Adoption of AI should be heavily influenced by ethical considerations.

Privacy of Patient Data and Informed Consent: Obtain informed consent and guarantee that strong data protection controls are in place when patient data is used in financial transactions. Patients ought to have control over their information and be informed about how it is used.

Working Together and Communicating: Encourage cooperation and honest dialogue across the clinical, IT, and finance divisions. Better patient care and more efficient financial operations can result from effective cross-departmental collaboration.

Invest in Education and Training: Staff should receive ongoing training and education on AI technologies and how they might be used in hospital accounting. A workforce with knowledge and awareness is better positioned to take full use of AI technologies.

1.27 Review and Update Compliance Measures on a Regular Basis

Stay up to date on the latest changes in data privacy and healthcare standards. To make sure AI-driven accounting stays compliant with the law, regularly examine and update compliance controls.

Provide Accountability and Recourse Mechanisms: Set up procedures for recourse in the event of mistakes or unforeseen repercussions, and clearly clarify the lines of accountability for choices made using AI (Zahlan et al., 2023).

Strategic Alliances: Think about forming strategic alliances with AI providers or consulting companies that specialise in healthcare accounting. The hospital's AI projects may benefit from these collaborations' insightful contributions and plentiful resources.

Assess and Disseminate Success Stories: Share success stories inside the company and track the effects of AI-driven hospital accounting on a regular basis. Maintaining stakeholder support and buy-in can be facilitated by showcasing concrete advantages. AI-driven hospital accounting has a lot of potential to improve financial operations, improve patient care, and guarantee regulatory compliance in the future. Hospitals will be well-positioned to prosper in this changing environment if they proactively adopt AI while resolving ethical and privacy concerns and upholding a commitment to data integrity.

2. CONCLUSION

An important step towards the financial stability and operational excellence of healthcare organisations has been taken with the incorporation of AI-driven technologies into hospital accounting. Hospital financial management is changing as a result of AI's revolutionary potential, which also increases accuracy, efficiency, and the capacity to provide patient-centered care. By improving revenue cycle management, reducing expenses, and improving forecasting accuracy, artificial intelligence (AI) has the potential to completely transform financial management in the healthcare industry. The best practises and real-world examples provided show that artificial intelligence (AI) is not just a theoretical idea but also a workable and tested solution for hospitals. Hospitals must, however, make significant investments and thoughtful decisions if they are to fully realise the transformative potential of AI. This entails promoting data quality, guaranteeing data security and privacy, addressing moral considerations, and instituting an accountable and transparent culture. AI-driven hospital accounting presents a viable route to both financial stability and operational excellence as healthcare organisations continue to negotiate the complicated regulatory environment and pursue patient-centric care. Hospitals will be better prepared to prosper in this dynamic and changing healthcare environment if they strategically embrace AI, involve their stakeholders, and invest in knowledge and technology. By doing this, they will be able to provide better treatment for patients as well as the larger community, all while achieving financial stability.

REFERENCES

Al Meslamani, A. Z. (2023). Applications of AI in pharmacy practice: A look at hospital and community settings. *Journal of Medical Economics*, *26*(1), 1081–1084. doi:10.1080/13696998.2023.2249758 PMID:37594444

Bold, B., Lkhagvajav, Z., & Dorjsuren, B. (2023). Role of artificial intelligence in achieving universal health coverage: A Mongolian perspective. *Korean Journal of Radiology*, *24*(9), 821. doi:10.3348/kjr.2023.0668 PMID:37634636

Chintamaneni, S., Yatham, P., & Stumbar, S. (2023). From East to West: A Narrative Review of Healthcare Models in India and the United States. *Cureus*, *15*(8). doi:10.7759/cureus.43456 PMID:37711922

Dogheim, G. M., & Hussain, A. (2023). Patient Care through AI-driven Remote Monitoring: Analyzing the Role of Predictive Models and Intelligent Alerts in Preventive Medicine. *Journal of Contemporary Healthcare Analytics*, *7*(1), 94–110.

Federspiel, F., Mitchell, R., Asokan, A., Umana, C., & McCoy, D. (2023). Threats by artificial intelligence to human health and human existence. *BMJ Global Health*, *8*(5), e010435. doi:10.1136/bmjgh-2022-010435 PMID:37160371

Gaddum, O., & Chapiro, J. (2023). An Interventional Radiologist's Guide to Critical Appraisal of Artificial Intelligence Research. *Journal of Vascular and Interventional Radiology*. PMID:37769940

Huraysi, N. A., Kattan, W. M., Alqurashi, M. A., Fadel, B. A., & Al-Hanawi, M. K. (2023). Preferences on Policy Options for Ensuring the Financial Sustainability of Healthcare Services in the Kingdom of Saudi Arabia. *Risk Management and Healthcare Policy*, *16*, 1033–1047. doi:10.2147/RMHP.S414823 PMID:37333981

Jabri, F., & Tim, I. S. (2023). *RESEARCH ESSAY DATA SCIENCE AND ANALYTICS IN HEALTHCARE.*

Kaur, J. (2023). Robotic Process Automation in Healthcare Sector. In *E3S Web of Conferences* (Vol. 391, p. 01008). EDP Sciences.

Kaur, J. (2023, May). How is Robotic Process Automation Revolutionising the Way Healthcare Sector Works? In *International Conference on Information, Communication and Computing Technology* (pp. 1037-1055). Singapore: Springer Nature Singapore. 10.1007/978-981-99-5166-6_70

Kumar, S., Lim, W. M., Sivarajah, U., & Kaur, J. (2023). Artificial intelligence and blockchain integration in business: Trends from a bibliometric-content analysis. *Information Systems Frontiers*, *25*(2), 871–896. PMID:35431617

Mohammad Amini, M., Jesus, M., Fanaei Sheikholeslami, D., Alves, P., Hassanzadeh Benam, A., & Hariri, F. (2023). Artificial Intelligence Ethics and Challenges in Healthcare Applications: A Comprehensive Review in the Context of the European GDPR Mandate. *Machine Learning and Knowledge Extraction*, *5*(3), 1023–1035. doi:10.3390/make5030053

Monlezun, D. J. (2023). *The Thinking Healthcare System: Artificial Intelligence and Human Equity*. Elsevier.

Patil, S., & Shankar, H. (2023). Transforming Healthcare: Harnessing the Power of AI in the Modern Era. *International Journal of Multidisciplinary Sciences and Arts*, *2*(1), 60–70.

Stafford, A. (2023). New development: Using counter accounting as a methodology in public accountability and management research. *Public Money & Management*, *43*(7), 709–712. doi:10.1080/09540962.2023.2251765

Unver, M. B. (2023). Governing fiduciary relationships or building up a governance model for trust in AI? Review of healthcare as a socio-technical system. *International Review of Law Computers & Technology*, *37*(2), 1–29. doi:10.1080/13600869.2023.2192569

Vesty, G., Kokshagina, O., Jansson, M., Cheong, F., & Butler-Henderson, K. (2023). Accounting, valuing and investing in health care: Dealing with outdated accounting models. *Meditari Accountancy Research*, *31*(1), 52–77. doi:10.1108/MEDAR-06-2021-1334

Wysocki, O., Davies, J. K., Vigo, M., Armstrong, A. C., Landers, D., Lee, R., & Freitas, A. (2023). Assessing the communication gap between AI models and healthcare professionals: Explainability, utility and trust in AI-driven clinical decision-making. *Artificial Intelligence*, *316*, 103839. doi:10.1016/j.artint.2022.103839

Zahlan, A., Ranjan, R. P., & Hayes, D. (2023). Artificial intelligence innovation in healthcare: Literature review, exploratory analysis, and future research. *Technology in Society*, *74*, 102321. doi:10.1016/j.techsoc.2023.102321

Compilation of References

Aaker, D. A., & Jacobson, R. (1994). The Financial Information Content of Perceived Quality. *Journal of Marketing Research (JMR), 31*(2), pp. 191–201. https://eds-s-ebscohost-com.ez.xjtlu.edu.cn/eds/detail/detail?vid=0&sid=b8d20eb7-83c8-4c90-83f8-70f2a37f3053%40redis&bdata=JnNpdGU9ZWRzLWxpdmUmc2NvcGU9c2l0ZQ%3d%3d#AN=9411112939&db=bsu.

Abbott, W. F., & Monsen, R. J. (1979). On the Measurement of Corporate Social Responsibility: Self-Reported Disclosures as a Method of Measuring Corporate Social Involvement. *Academy of Management Journal, 22*(3), 501–515. doi:10.2307/255740

Abd Rahman, M. S. B., Mohamad, E., & Abdul Rahman, A. A. B. (2021). Development of IoT—Enabled data analytics enhance decision support system for lean manufacturing process improvement. *Concurrent Engineering, Research and Applications, 29*(3), 208–220. doi:10.1177/1063293X20987911

Abedin, M. Z., Moon, M. H., Hassan, M. K., & Hajek, P. (2021). Deep learning-based exchange rate prediction during the COVID-19 pandemic. *Annals of Operations Research*. Advance online publication. doi:10.1007/s10479-021-04420-6 PMID:34848909

Abelson, H., Ledeen, K., & Lewis, H. (2012). *Blown to bits: your life, liberty, and happiness after the digital explosion*. Addison-Wesley Professional.

ACCA. (2019). *Audit and Technology*. The Association of Chartered Certified Accountants.

Accenture. (2019). *More than half of consumers would pay more for sustainable products designed to be reused or recycled, Accenture survey finds*. Accenture. https://newsroom.accenture.com/news/2019/more-than-half-of-consumers-would-pay-more-for-sustainable-products-designed-to-be-reused-or-recycled-accenture-survey-finds

Afolabi, H., Ram, R., & Rimmel, G. (2022). Harmonization of sustainability reporting regulation: Analysis of a contested arena. *Sustainability (Basel), 14*(9), 5517. doi:10.3390/su14095517

Agnew, H. (2016). Technology transforms Big 4 hiring practices. *Financial Times*. https://www.ft.com/content/d5670764-15d2-11e6- b197-a4af20d5575e.

Ahmeti, Y., & Iseni, E. (2022). Factors Affecting Profitability of Insurance Companies. *Academicus,* (25), pp. 122–142. [Online]. https://eds-s-ebscohost-com.ez.xjtlu.edu.cn/eds/detail/detail?vid=0&sid=00dd95f5-c2a7-417f-bbb4-2760d329b36a%40redis&bdata=JnNpdGU9ZWRzLWxpdmUmc2NvcGU9c2l0ZQ%3d%3d#db=hlh&AN=154767036

Akram Afzal, M. (2017). Risks in new product development (NPD) projects. ebsCohost. https://search-ebscohost-com.ez.xjtlu.edu.cn/login.aspx?direct=true&db=edsble&AN=edsble.738624&site=eds-live&scope=site

Al Meslamani, A. Z. (2023). Applications of AI in pharmacy practice: A look at hospital and community settings. *Journal of Medical Economics, 26*(1), 1081–1084. doi:10.1080/13696998.2023.2249758 PMID:37594444

Al-Huneidi, A. M., & Schreurs, J. (2011). Constructivism Based Blended Learning in Higher Education. [iJET]. *International Journal of Emerging Technologies in Learning.*

Ali, A. (2000). The Impact of Innovativeness and Development Time on New Product Performance for Small Firms. *Marketing Letters, 11*(2), 151–163. https://search-ebscohost-com.ez.xjtlu.edu.cn/login.aspx?direct=true&db=edsjsr&AN=edsjsr.40216567&site=eds-live&scope=site

Alles, M. G. (2015). Drivers of the use and facilitators and obstacles of the evolution of big data by the audit profession. *Accounting Horizons, 29*(2), 439–449. doi:10.2308/acch-51067

Alves, P., Miranda, L., & Morais, C. (2017). The Influence of Virtual Learning Environments in Students' Performance, *Universal. The Journal of Educational Research, 5*(3), 517–527.

Andaleeb, S. S., & Hasan, K. (2016) *Strategic Marketing Management in Asia : Case Studies and Lessons Across Industries.* [Place of publication not identified]: Emerald Group Publishing Limited. [Online]. https://search-ebscohost-com.ez.xjtlu.edu.cn/login.aspx?direct=true&db=edsebk&AN=1423724&site=eds-live&scope=site

Andrade, C. (2021). Z Scores, Standard Scores, and Composite Test Scores Explained. *Indian Journal of Psychological Medicine, 43*(6), 555–557. https://eds-s-ebscohost-com.ez.xjtlu.edu.cn/eds/detail/detail?vid=0&sid=58922e84-ed8e-4cb8-9d9d-c2e19877d938%40redis&bdata=JnNpdGU9ZWRzLWxpdmUmc2NvcGU9c2l0ZQ%3d%3d#AN=153685949&db=asn

Appelbaum, D. A., Kogan, A., & Vasarhelyi, M. A. (2017). Big data and analytics in the modern audit engagement: Research needs. *Auditing, 36*(4), 1–27. doi:10.2308/ajpt-51684

Auer, R., Haslhofer, B., Kitzler, S., Saggese, P., & Victor, F. (2023). *The Technology of Decentralized Finance (DeFi).* Bank for International Settlements, Monetary and Economic Department. doi:10.1007/s42521-023-00088-8

AWS. (2023a). *What is a data lake?* AWS. https://aws.amazon.com/big-data/datalakes-and-analytics/what-is-a-data-lake/

AWS. (2023b). *What is an API (Application Programming Interface)?* AWS. https://aws.amazon.com/what-is/api/#:~:text=API%20stands%20for%20Application%20Programming,other%20using%20requests%20and%20responses

Baiman, S., & Verrecchia, R. E. (1996). The relation among capital markets, financial disclosure, production efficiency, and insider trading. *Journal of Accounting Research, 34*(1), 1–22. doi:10.2307/2491329

Barbaglia, L., Manzan, S., & Tosetti, E. (2023). Forecasting Loan Default in Europe with Machine Learning. *Journal of Financial Econometrics, 21*(2), 569–596. doi:10.1093/jjfinec/nbab010

Bar-Gera, H. (2017). The Target Parameter of Adjusted R-Squared in Fixed-Design Experiments. *American Statistician, 71*(2), 112–119. https://eds-p-ebscohost-com.ez.xjtlu.edu.cn/eds/detail/detail?vid=0&sid=d23f04d3-7f78-46a0-b9d0-bfe8b0f789a5%40redis&bdata=JnNpdGU9ZWRzLWxpdmUmc2NvcGU9c2l0ZQ%3d%3d#db=asn&AN=123952667

Basil, D. Z., & Erlandson, J. (2008). Corporate social responsibility website representations: A longitudinal study of internal and external self-presentations. *Journal of Marketing Communications, 14*(2), 125–137. doi:10.1080/13527260701858497

Beasley, M. S., Carcello, J. V., Hermanson, D. R., & Lapides, P. D. (2000). Fraudulent financial reporting: Consideration of industry traits and corporate governance mechanisms. *Accounting Horizons, 14*(4), 441–454. doi:10.2308/acch.2000.14.4.441

Bebchuk, L. A., Brav, A., Jiang, W., & Keusch, T. (2020). Dancing with activists. *Journal of Financial Economics, 137*(1), 1–41. doi:10.1016/j.jfineco.2020.01.001

Bebchuk, L. A., & Weisbach, M. S. (2010). The state of corporate governance research. *Review of Financial Studies*, *23*(3), 939–961. doi:10.1093/rfs/hhp121

Belissent, J. (2021). Chief data officers: invest in your data sharing programs now. *Forrester.* https://www.forrester.com/report/chiefdata-officers-invest-in-your-data-sharing-programsnow/RES164496

Bellotti, A., Brigo, D., Gambetti, P., & Vrins, F. (2021). Forecasting recovery rates on non-performing loans with machine learning. *International Journal of Forecasting*, *37*(1), 428–444. doi:10.1016/j.ijforecast.2020.06.009

Benito, B., Montesinos, V., & Bastida, F. (2008). An example of creative accounting in public sector: The private financing of infrastructures in Spain. *Critical Perspectives on Accounting*, *19*(7), 963–986. doi:10.1016/j.cpa.2007.08.002

Berthon, P. R., Pitt, L. F., Plangger, K., & Shapiro, D. (2012). Marketing meets Web 2.0, social media, and creative consumers: Implications for international marketing strategy. *Business Horizons*, *55*(3), 261–271. doi:10.1016/j.bushor.2012.01.007

Beutel, J., List, S., & Von Schweinitz, G. (2019). Does machine learning help us predict banking crises? *Journal of Financial Stability*, *45*, 100693. doi:10.1016/j.jfs.2019.100693

Beverland, M. B., Gemser, G., & Karpen, I. O. (2017). Design, consumption and marketing: outcomes, process, philosophy and future directions. *Journal of Marketing Management*, 33(3/4), pp. 159–172. https://eds-s-ebscohost-com.ez.xjtlu.edu.cn/eds/detail/detail?vid=0&sid=3f3dedd8-5c7d-4dd9-9885-c5bd60ab08e9%40redis&bdata=JnNpdGU9ZWRzLWxpdmUmc2NvcGU9c2l0ZQ%3d%3d#AN=121630773&db=bsu (Accessed: 21 November 2022).

Bhatti, G., Mohan, H., & Raja Singh, R. (2021). Towards the future of smart electric vehicles: Digital twin technology. *Renewable and Sustainable Energy Reviews, 141.* https://eds-s-ebscohost-com.ez.xjtlu.edu.cn/eds/detail/detail?vid=0&sid=fd935fcc-49df-4462-b790-1e03b402e74a%40redis&bdata=JnNpdGU9ZWRzLWxpdmUmc2NvcGU9c2l0ZQ%3d%3d#AN=S1364032121000964&db=edselp

Bhutada, G. (2022). *Visualizing 10 Years of Global EV Sales by Country* [Online]. Visual Capitolist. https://www.visualcapitalist.com/visualizing-10-years-of-global-ev-sales-by-country/

Biais, B., Capponi, A., Cong, L. W., Gaur, V., & Giesecke, K. (2023). Advances in blockchain and crypto economics. *Management Science*, *69*(11), 6417–6426. doi:10.1287/mnsc.2023.intro.v69.n11

Bog, A., Kruger, J., & Schaffner, J. (2008). A Composite Benchmark for Online Transaction Processing and Operational Reporting. Paper presented at the *2008 IEEE Symposium on Advanced Management of Information for Globalized Enterprises (AMIGE).* IEEE. 10.1109/AMIGE.2008.ECP.30

Bold, B., Lkhagvajav, Z., & Dorjsuren, B. (2023). Role of artificial intelligence in achieving universal health coverage: A Mongolian perspective. *Korean Journal of Radiology*, *24*(9), 821. doi:10.3348/kjr.2023.0668 PMID:37634636

Bond, C. E., Shipton, Z. K., Jones, R., Butler, R. W. H., & Gibbs, A. D. (2007). Knowledge transfer in a digital world: Field data acquisition, uncertainty, visualization, and data management. *Geosphere*, *3*(6), 568–576. doi:10.1130/GES00094.1

Bouras, M. A., Lu, Q., Zhang, F., Wan, Y., Zhang, T., & Ning, H. (2020). Distributed ledger technology for eHealth identity privacy: State of the art and future perspective. *Sensors (Basel)*, *20*(2), 483. doi:10.3390/s20020483 PMID:31952172

Bowen, S. A. (2014). The relationship between corporate social responsibility and greenwashing: An exploratory study. *Business & Society*, *53*(1), 38–72.

Brammer, S., Millington, A., & Rayton, B. (2007). The contribution of corporate social responsibility to organizational commitment. *International Journal of Human Resource Management*, *18*(10), 1701–1719. doi:10.1080/09585190701570866

Brennan, N. M., & Merkl-Davies, D. M. (2018). Do firms effectively communicate with financial stakeholders? A conceptual model of corporate communication in a capital market context. *Accounting and Business Research, 48*(5), 553–577. doi:10.1080/00014788.2018.1470143

Briones, R. L., Kuch, B., Liu, B. F., & Jin, Y. (2011). Keeping up with the digital age: How the American Red Cross uses social media to build relationships. *Public Relations Review, 37*(1), 37–43. doi:10.1016/j.pubrev.2010.12.006

Broadbent, J., & Laughlin, R. (2009). Performance Management Systems: A conceptual model. *Management Accounting Research, 20*(4), 283–295. doi:10.1016/j.mar.2009.07.004

Broccardo, E., Hart, O., & Zingales, L. (2022). Exit versus voice. *Journal of Political Economy, 130*(12), 3101–3145. doi:10.1086/720516

Brogaard, J., Li, D., & Xia, Y. (2017). Stock liquidity and default risk. *Journal of Financial Economics, 124*(3), 486–502. doi:10.1016/j.jfineco.2017.03.003

Brown-Liburd, H., Issa, H., & Lombardi, D. (2015). Behavioral implications of big data's impact on audit judgment and decision making and future research directions. *Accounting Horizons, 29*(2), 451–468. doi:10.2308/acch-51023

Brunton, M., Eweje, G., & Taskin, N. (2017). Communicating corporate social responsibility to internal stakeholders: Walking the walk or just talking the talk? *Business Strategy and the Environment, 26*(1), 31–48. doi:10.1002/bse.1889

Brydon, D. (2019). *Assess, assure and inform: improving audit quality and effectiveness*. Assets. https://assets.publishing.service.gov.uk/government/uploads/system/uploads/attac hment_data/file/852960/brydon-review-final-report.pdf

Buchholz, R. A., & Rosenthal, S. B. (2005). Toward a contemporary conceptual framework for stakeholder theory. *Journal of Business Ethics, 58*(1-3), 137–148. doi:10.1007/s10551-005-1393-8

Bukhbinder, G., Krumenaker, M., & Phillips, A. (2005). *Insurance Industry Decision Support: Data Marts*. OLAP and Predictive Analytics.

Butera, F., Sommet, N., & Darnon, C. (2019). Sociocognitive Conflict Regulation: How to Make Sense of Diverging Ideas. *Current Directions in Psychological Science, 28*(2), 145–151. doi:10.1177/0963721418813986

Buterin, V. (2016). *On Public and Private Blockchain*. Ethereum. https://blog.ethereum.org/2015/08/07/on-public-and-private-blockchains

Calvano, L. (2008). Multinational corporations and local communities: A critical analysis of conflict. *Journal of Business Ethics, 82*(4), 793–805. doi:10.1007/s10551-007-9593-z

Cao, S., Cong, L. W., & Yang, B. (2019). *Financial reporting and blockchains: Audit pricing, misstatements, and regulation. Misstatements, and Regulation*. (Working Paper).

Cao, M., Chychyla, R., & Stewart, T. (2015). Big data analytics in financial statement audits. *Accounting Horizons, 29*(2), 423–429. doi:10.2308/acch-51068

Cao, S., Cong, L. W., Han, M., Hou, Q., & Yang, B. (2020). Blockchain architecture for auditing automation and trust building in public markets. *Computer, 53*(7), 20–28. doi:10.1109/MC.2020.2989789

Casoni, G. (2010). Design and creativity in open innovation processes: The case of Italian industrial districts. *Strategic Design Research Journal, 3*(2), 33–40. https://eds-s-ebscohost-com.ez.xjtlu.edu.cn/eds/detail/detail?vid=0&sid=62795653-a518-46da-a314-4fd50176908a%40redis&bdata=JnNpdGU9ZWRzLWxpdmUmc2NvcGU9c2l0ZQ%3d%3d#AN=60870568&db=asn

Castells, M. (2002). *The Internet galaxy: Reflections on the Internet, business, and society*. Oxford University Press. doi:10.1093/acprof:oso/9780199255771.001.0001

Catalini, C., & Gans, J. S. (2020). Some simple economics of the blockchain. *Communications of the ACM*, *63*(7), 80–90. doi:10.1145/3359552

CGMA. (2016). *Business Analytics and Decision Making? The human dimension*. CGMA. www.cgma.org/resources/reports/business-analytics-and-decision-making.html

Chandler, R. A. (2017). Questions of ethics and etiquette in the Society of Accountants in Edinburgh, 1853–1951. *Accounting History*, *22*(2), 179–192. doi:10.1177/1032373216675912

Cheng, S. C. (2014). *Effects of Socio-Cognitive Conflicts on Group Cognition and Group Performance*. [Unpublished doctoral dissertation, Harvard Graduate School of Education].

Chen, Y., Fay, S., & Wang, Q. (2011). The role of marketing in social media: How online consumer reviews evolve. *Journal of Interactive Marketing*, *25*(2), 85–94. doi:10.1016/j.intmar.2011.01.003

Cheung, W. M., Chung, R., & Fung, S. (2015). The effects of stock liquidity on firm value and corporate governance: Endogeneity and the REIT experiment. *Journal of Corporate Finance*, *35*, 211–231. doi:10.1016/j.jcorpfin.2015.09.001

Chiarini, A., & Kumar, M. (2021). Lean Six Sigma and Industry 4.0 integration for Operational Excellence: Evidence from Italian manufacturing companies. *Production Planning and Control*, *32*(13), 1084–1101. doi:10.1080/09537287.2020.1784485

Chintamaneni, S., Yatham, P., & Stumbar, S. (2023). From East to West: A Narrative Review of Healthcare Models in India and the United States. *Cureus*, *15*(8). doi:10.7759/cureus.43456 PMID:37711922

Chiu, J., & Koeppl, T. V. (2019). Blockchain-based settlement for asset trading. *Review of Financial Studies*, *32*(5), 1716–1753. doi:10.1093/rfs/hhy122

Chod, J., & Lyandres, E. (2023). Product market competition with crypto tokens and smart contracts. *Journal of Financial Economics*, *149*(1), 73–91. doi:10.1016/j.jfineco.2023.04.011

Chukleang, T., & Jandaeng, C. (2022, September). Security Enhancement in Smart Logistics with Blockchain Technology: A Home Delivery Use Case. In Informatics (Vol. 9, No. 3, p. 70). MDPI. doi:10.3390/informatics9030070

Chu, S. C., Chen, H. T., & Gan, C. (2020). Consumers' engagement with corporate social responsibility (CSR) communication in social media: Evidence from China and the United States. *Journal of Business Research*, *110*, 260–271. doi:10.1016/j.jbusres.2020.01.036

Chu, S. C., & Kim, Y. (2011). Determinants of consumer engagement in electronic word-of-mouth (eWOM) in social networking sites. *International Journal of Advertising*, *30*(1), 47–75. doi:10.2501/IJA-30-1-047-075

Čiarnienė, R., & Vienažindienė, M. (2012). Lean manufacturing: theory and practice. *Economics and management*, *17*(2), 726-732. doi:10.5755/j01.em.17.2.2205

Coase, R. H. (1937). The Nature of the Firm. *Economica*, *4*(16), 386–405. doi:10.1111/j.1468-0335.1937.tb00002.x

Cojoianu, T., Hoepner, A. G. F., Ifrim, G., & Lin, Y. (2020). *Greenwatch-shing: Using AI to Detect Greenwashing*. https://papers.ssrn.com/sol3/papers.cfm?abstract_id= 3627157

Colleoni, E. (2013). CSR communication strategies for organizational legitimacy in social media. *Corporate Communications*, *18*(2), 228–248. doi:10.1108/13563281311319508

Colucci, M., Tuan, A., & Visentin, M. (2020). An empirical investigation of the drivers of CSR talk and walk in the fashion industry. *Journal of Cleaner Production, 248*, 119200. doi:10.1016/j.jclepro.2019.119200

Cong, L. W., & He, Z. (2019). Blockchain disruption and smart contracts. *Review of Financial Studies, 32*(5), 1754–1797. doi:10.1093/rfs/hhz007

Conn, S. S. (2005). OLTP and OLAP data integration: a review of feasible implementation methods and architectures for real time data analysis. Paper presented at *IEEE SoutheastCon, 2005*. IEEE.

Cooper, R. G., Edgett, S. J., & Kleinschmidt, E. J. (2004). Benchmarking Best Npd Practices-Ii', *Research Technology Management, 47*(3), pp. 50–59. https://search-ebscohost-com.ez.xjtlu.edu.cn/login.aspx?direct=true&db=edsjsr&AN=edsjsr.43238109&site=eds-live&scope=site

Cornett, M. M., Marcus, A. J., & Tehranian, H. (2008). Corporate governance and pay-for-performance: The impact of earnings management. *Journal of Financial Economics, 87*(2), 357–373. doi:10.1016/j.jfineco.2007.03.003

Cortado, F. J., & Chalmeta, R. (2016). Use of social networks as a CSR communication tool. *Cogent business & management, 3*(1), 1187783.

Courtis, J. K. (1986). An investigation into annual report readability and corporate risk-return relationships. *Accounting and Business Research, 16*(64), 285–294. doi:10.1080/00014788.1986.9729329

Curtis, A., McVay, S., & Toynbee, S. (2020). The changing implications of research and development expenditures for future profitability [Preprint]. *Review of Accounting Studies, 25*(2), 405–437. doi:10.1007/s11142-019-09528-6

Dabbagh, N., Marra, R. M., & Howland, J. L. (2018). *Meaningful Online Learning: Integrating Strategies, Activities, and Learning Technologies for Effective Designs* (1st ed.). Routledge. doi:10.4324/9781315528458

Dai, J., & Vasarhelyi, M. A. (2017). Toward blockchain-based accounting and assurance. *Journal of Information Systems, 31*(3), 5–21. doi:10.2308/isys-51804

David, D. T. (1995). Welcome to the communication age. *Internet Research, 5*(1), 64–70. doi:10.1108/10662249510084471

Dawkins, J. (2005). Corporate responsibility: The communication challenge. *Journal of Communication Management (London), 9*(2), 108–119. doi:10.1108/13632540510621362

De Santis, F., & D'Onza, G. (2021). Big data and data analytics in auditing: In search of legitimacy. *Meditari Accountancy Research, 29*(5), 1088–1112. doi:10.1108/MEDAR-03-2020-0838

Deepa, N., Pham, Q. V., Nguyen, D. C., Bhattacharya, S., Prabadevi, B., Gadekallu, T. R., & Pathirana, P. N. (2022). A survey on blockchain for big data: Approaches, opportunities, and future directions. *Future Generation Computer Systems, 131*, 209–226. doi:10.1016/j.future.2022.01.017

Dellarocas, C. (2003). The digitization of word of mouth: Promise and challenges of online feedback mechanisms. *Management Science, 49*(10), 1407–1424. doi:10.1287/mnsc.49.10.1407.17308

Deloitte. (2022). *Deloitte us survey findings on esg disclosure and preparedness*. Deloitte. https://www2.deloitte.com/content/dam/Deloitte/us/Documents/audit/us-survey-findings-on-esg-disclosure-and-preparedness.pdf

Deloitte. (2022a). *Simplifying risk technology for deeper insights and lower cost risk and regulatory data and technology insights*. Deloitte. https://www2.deloitte.com/content/dam/Deloitte/au/Documents/risk/deloitte-au-simplifying-risktechnology-25052022.pdf

Deloitte. (2022b). *TechTrends*. Deloitte. https://www2.deloitte.com/au/en/pages/technology/ articles/tech-trends.html

Deming, W. E. (1986). *Out of the Crisis*. MIT Press.

Demirdöğen, G., Işık, Z., & Arayici, Y. (2020). Lean management framework for healthcare facilities integrating BIM, BEPS and big data analytics. *Sustainability (Basel)*, *12*(17), 7061. doi:10.3390/su12177061

Di Vaio, A., Hassan, R., & Palladino, R. (2023). Block chain technology and gender equality: A systematic literature review. *International Journal of Information Management*, *68*, 102517. doi:10.1016/j.ijinfomgt.2022.102517

Ding, H. (2022). *Vehicle Driving Risk Prediction Model by Reverse Artificial Intelligence Neural Network*. Computational Intelligence & Neuroscience. https://eds-p-ebscohost-com.ez.xjtlu.edu.cn/eds/detail/detail?vid=0&sid=cf20a4ef-0ea7-4827-b638-900d1c5f2f19%40redis&bdata=JnNpdGU9ZWRzLWxpdmUmc2NvcGU9c2l0ZQ%3d%3d#AN=159695525&db=asn doi:10.1155/2022/3100509

Disney. (2018). The Walt Disney Company and Make-A-Wish® Invite Fans to "Share Your Ears" to Help Grant Wishes in Celebration of 90 Years of Mickey Mouse. *Business Wire*. https://www.businesswire.com/news/home/20181104005033/en/The-Walt-Disney-Company-and-Make-A-Wish%C2%AE-Invite-Fans-to-%E2%80%9CShare-Your-Ears%E2%80%9D-to-Help-Grant-Wishes-in-Celebration-of-90-Years-of-Mickey-Mouse

Dixon, L. (2020). Autonowashing: The greenwashing of vehicle automation. *Transportation Research Interdisciplinary Perspectives*, *5*, 100113. doi:10.1016/j.trip.2020.100113

Dogheim, G. M., & Hussain, A. (2023). Patient Care through AI-driven Remote Monitoring: Analyzing the Role of Predictive Models and Intelligent Alerts in Preventive Medicine. *Journal of Contemporary Healthcare Analytics*, *7*(1), 94–110.

Dong Soo, K. (2022). Recent ESG disclosure trends and greenwashing. *Future Growth Research*, *8*(1), 101–107.

DongHai Securities. (2022). *Automotive Industry Weekly Report*. DongHai Securities. http://www.iwencai.com/unified-wap/infodetail?uid=1b11ba4603306623&w=小鹏销量&querytype=report

Du, S., Bhattacharya, C. B., & Sen, S. (2011). Corporate social responsibility and competitive advantage: Overcoming the trust barrier. *Management Science*, *57*(9), 1528–1545. doi:10.1287/mnsc.1110.1403

Du, S., & Vieira, E. T. Jr. (2012). Striving for legitimacy through corporate social responsibility: Insights from oil companies. *Journal of Business Ethics*, *110*(4), 413–427. doi:10.1007/s10551-012-1490-4

Dutot, V., Lacalle Galvez, E., & Versailles, D. W. (2016). CSR communications strategies through social media and influence on e-reputation: An exploratory study. *Management Decision*, *54*(2), 363–389. doi:10.1108/MD-01-2015-0015

Dwivedi, Y. K., Ismagilova, E., Hughes, D. L., Carlson, J., Filieri, R., Jacobson, J., Jain, V., Karjaluoto, H., Kefi, H., Krishen, A. S., Kumar, V., Rahman, M. M., Raman, R., Rauschnabel, P. A., Rowley, J., Salo, J., Tran, G. A., & Wang, Y. (2021). Setting the future of digital and social media marketing research: Perspectives and research propositions. *International Journal of Information Management*, *59*, 102168. doi:10.1016/j.ijinfomgt.2020.102168

Earley, C. E. (2015). Data analytics in auditing: Opportunities and challenges. *Business Horizons*, *58*(5), 493–500. doi:10.1016/j.bushor.2015.05.002

Elgendy, N., & Elragal, A. (2014). Big Data Analytics: A Literature Review Paper. Paper presented at the *Advances in Data Mining*. Applications and Theoretical Aspects, Cham.

Ernst, H., Hoyer, W. D., & Rübsaamen, C. (2010). Sales, Marketing, and Research-and-Development Cooperation Across New Product Development Stages: Implications for Success', *Journal of Marketing*, *74*(5), 80–92. https://search-ebscohost-com.ez.xjtlu.edu.cn/login.aspx?direct=true&db=edsjsr&AN=edsjsr.41228575&site=eds-live&scope=site

Ertel, W. (2018). *Introduction to artificial intelligence*. Springer.

Esrock, S. L., & Leichty, G. B. (1998). Social responsibility and corporate web pages: Self-presentation or agenda-setting? *Public Relations Review*, *24*(3), 305–319. doi:10.1016/S0363-8111(99)80142-8

Etter, M. (2013). Reasons for low levels of interactivity:(Non-) interactive CSR communication in Twitter. *Public Relations Review*, *39*(5), 606–608. doi:10.1016/j.pubrev.2013.06.003

EY. (2022). *C-suite insights sustainability and esg trends index*. EY. https://assets.ey.com/content/dam/ey-sites/ey-com/en_us/topics/sustainability/ey-c-suite-insights-sustainability-and-esg-trends-index.pdf

Fama, E. F., & Jensen, M. C. (1983a). Separation of ownership and control. *The Journal of Law & Economics*, *26*(2), 301–325. doi:10.1086/467037

Fama, E. F., & Jensen, M. C. (1983b). Agency problems and residuals claims. *The Journal of Law & Economics*, *26*(2), 327–349. doi:10.1086/467038

Fang, H. S. A. (2021). Commercially successful blockchain healthcare projects: A scoping review. *Blockchain in Healthcare Today*, 4. doi:10.30953/bhty.v4.166 PMID:36777489

Far, S. B., Rad, A. I., & Assar, M. R. (2023). *Block chain and its derived technologies shape the future generation of digital businesses: A focus on decentralized finance and the Metaverse*. Data Science and Management.

Fayard, D., Lee, L. S., Leitch, R. A., & Kettinger, W. J. (2012). Effect of internal cost management, information systems integration, and absorptive capacity on inter-organizational cost management in supply chains. *Accounting, Organizations and Society*, *37*(3), 168–187. doi:10.1016/j.aos.2012.02.001

Federspiel, F., Mitchell, R., Asokan, A., Umana, C., & McCoy, D. (2023). Threats by artificial intelligence to human health and human existence. *BMJ Global Health*, *8*(5), e010435. doi:10.1136/bmjgh-2022-010435 PMID:37160371

Ferreira, D., Li, J., & Nikolowa, R. (2023). Corporate capture of blockchain governance. *Review of Financial Studies*, *36*(4), 1364–1407. doi:10.1093/rfs/hhac051

Ferri, L., Spanò, R., Ginesti, G., & Theodosopoulos, G. (2020). Ascertaining auditors' intentions to use blockchain technology: Evidence from the big 4 accountancy firms in Italy. *Meditari Accountancy Research*, *29*(5), 1063–1087. doi:10.1108/MEDAR-03-2020-0829

Fifka, M. (2012). The development and state of research on social and environmental reporting in global comparison. *Journal Für Betriebswirtschaft*, *62*(1), 45–84. doi:10.1007/s11301-012-0083-8

Financial Conduct Authority. (2022). *FCA Proposes New Rules to Tackle Greenwashing*. FCA. https://www.fca.org.uk/news/press-releases/fca-proposes-new-rules-tackle-greenwashing

Flanagin, A. J., & Metzger, M. J. (2000). Perceptions of Internet information credibility. *Journalism & Mass Communication Quarterly*, *77*(3), 515–540. doi:10.1177/107769900007700304

Flannery, R. (2022). China EV Maker XPeng Loss More Than Doubles Amid Covid Woes. *Forbes*. https://search-ebscohost-com.ez.xjtlu.edu.cn/login.aspx?direct=true&db=bsu&AN=157033656&site=eds-live&scope=site

Florén, H. (2018). Critical success factors in early new product development: a review and a conceptual model. *International Entrepreneurship and Management Journal*, *14*(2), 411–427. https://eds-s-ebscohost-com.ez.xjtlu.edu.cn/eds/detail/detail?vid=0&sid=29e5f1f5-2243-4556-b322-7dfeb350965d%40redis&bdata=JnNpdGU9ZWRzLWxpdmUmc2NvcGU9c2l0ZQ%3d%3d#AN=edssjs.F01DC038&db=edssjs

Fox, J., Lorsch, J. W., & What, G. A. S. (2012). What are good shareholders? *Harvard Business Review*. https://hbr.org/2012/07/what-good-are-shareholders

Fox, R. (2022). XPeng Stock Shows Strong Q2 Delivery Numbers; Is It A Buy Now? Here's What Charts, Analysis Show. *Investors Business Daily.* https://search-ebscohost-com.ez.xjtlu.edu.cn/login.aspx?direct=true&db=bwh&AN=159350087&site=eds-live&scope=site

Fox, J., & Lorsch, J. W. (2012). What good are shareholders. *Harvard Business Review, 90*(7/8), 48–57.

Freeman, R. E. (1984). *Strategic management: A stokcholder approach.* Pitman.

Gaddum, O., & Chapiro, J. (2023). An Interventional Radiologist's Guide to Critical Appraisal of Artificial Intelligence Research. *Journal of Vascular and Interventional Radiology.* PMID:37769940

Gadekallu, T. R., Huynh-The, T., Wang, W., Yenduri, G., Ranaweera, P., Pham, Q. V., & Liyanage, M. (2022). *Blockchain for the metaverse: A review.* arXiv preprint arXiv:2203.09738.

Gajewski, J. F., & Li, L. (2015). Can Internet-based disclosure reduce information asymmetry? *Advances in Accounting, 31*(1), 115–124. doi:10.1016/j.adiac.2015.03.013

García-Sánchez, I. M., & Noguera-Gámez, L. (2017). Integrated reporting and stakeholder engagement: The effect on information asymmetry. *Corporate Social Responsibility and Environmental Management, 24*(5), 395–413. doi:10.1002/csr.1415

George, M. (2005) *Fast Innovation: Achieving Superior Differentiation, Speed to Market, and Increased Profitability.* McGraw-Hill Education. https://eds-s-ebscohost-com.ez.xjtlu.edu.cn/eds/detail/detail?vid=0&sid=59cb4dbc-5523-480d-bdc5-5fb0e798b719%40redis&bdata=JnNpdGU9ZWRzLWxpdmUmc2NvcGU9c2l0ZQ%3d%3d#AN=edsely.0071457895&db=edsely (Accessed: 4 October 2022).

Ghiasi, M., Dehghani, M., Niknam, T., Kavousi-Fard, A., Siano, P., & Alhelou, H. H. (2021). Cyber-attack detection and cyber-security enhancement in smart DC-microgrid based on blockchain technology and Hilbert Huang transform. *IEEE Access : Practical Innovations, Open Solutions, 9*, 29429–29440. doi:10.1109/ACCESS.2021.3059042

Goncu, A. (2019). Prediction of exchange rates with machine learning. *Proceedings of the International Conference on Artificial Intelligence, Information Processing and Cloud Computing*, (pp. 1–5). ACM. 10.1145/3371425.3371448

Gowthorpe, C., & Amat, O. (1999). External reporting of accounting and financial information via the Internet in Spain. *European Accounting Review, 8*(2), 365–371. doi:10.1080/096381899336096

Gramlich, V., Guggenberger, T., Principato, M., Schellinger, B., & Urbach, N. (2023). A multivocal literature review of decentralized finance: Current knowledge and future research avenues. *Electronic Markets, 33*(1), 11. doi:10.1007/s12525-023-00637-4

Gray, R., Kouhy, R., & Lavers, S. (1995). Corporate social and environmental reporting: A review of the literature and a longitudinal study of UK disclosure. *Accounting, Auditing & Accountability Journal, 8*(2), 47–77. doi:10.1108/09513579510146996

Gray, R., Owen, D., & Maunders, K. (1988). Corporate social reporting: Emerging trends in accountability and the social contract. *Accounting, Auditing & Accountability Journal, 1*(1), 6–20. doi:10.1108/EUM0000000004617

Gupta, S., Modgil, S., & Gunasekaran, A. (2020). Big data in lean six sigma: A review and further research directions. *International Journal of Production Research, 58*(3), 947–969. doi:10.1080/00207543.2019.1598599

Hafner, K., & Lyon, M. (1998). *Where wizards stay up late: The origins of the Internet.* Simon and Schuster.

Haigh, M. M., Brubaker, P., & Whiteside, E. (2013). Facebook: Examining the information presented and its impact on stakeholders. *Corporate Communications, 18*(1), 52–69. doi:10.1108/13563281311294128

Haigh, M. M., & Wigley, S. (2015). Examining the impact of negative, user-generated content on stakeholders. *Corporate Communications*, *20*(1), 63–75. doi:10.1108/CCIJ-02-2013-0010

Han, H., Shiwakoti, R. K., Jarvis, R., Mordi, C., & Botchie, D. (2023). Accounting and auditing with block chain technology and artificial Intelligence: A literature review. *International Journal of Accounting Information Systems*, *48*, 100598. doi:10.1016/j.accinf.2022.100598

Haniffa, R. M., & Cooke, T. E. (2005). The impact of culture and governance on corporate social reporting. *Journal of Accounting and Public Policy*, *24*(5), 391–430. doi:10.1016/j.jaccpubpol.2005.06.001

Hemonnet, G. A., Manceau, D., & Abecassis, M. C. (2019). Drivers and Pathways of NPD Success in the Marketing–External Design Relationship. *Journal of Product Innovation Management*, *36*(2), 196–223. https://eds-p-ebscohost-com.ez.xjtlu.edu.cn/eds/pdfviewer/pdfviewer?vid=1&sid=ea2bb025-ba8d-4eba-812c-534f7d1dba62%40redis

Hermalin, B., & Weisbach, M. S. (2007). *Transparency and corporate governance*.

Herzig, C., & Schaltegger, S. (2006). Corporate sustainability reporting: An overview. In S. Schaltegger, M. Bennett & R. L. Burritt (Eds.), *Sustainability Accounting and Reporting* (pp. 301-324). Springer. https://www.sec.gov/news/statement/lee-statement-esg-052522

Hirschman, A. O. (1972). *Exit, voice, and loyalty: Responses to decline in firms, organizations, and states*. Harvard university press.

Holweg, M. (2007). The genealogy of lean production. *Journal of Operations Management*, *25*(2), 420–437. doi:10.1016/j.jom.2006.04.001

Hossain, M., & Lassen, A. H. (2017). How do digital platforms for ideas, technologies, and knowledge transfer act as enablers for digital transformation? *Technology Innovation Management Review*, *7*(9), 55–60. doi:10.22215/timreview/1106

Hunt, E. B. (2014). *Artificial intelligence*. Academic Press.

Huraysi, N. A., Kattan, W. M., Alqurashi, M. A., Fadel, B. A., & Al-Hanawi, M. K. (2023). Preferences on Policy Options for Ensuring the Financial Sustainability of Healthcare Services in the Kingdom of Saudi Arabia. *Risk Management and Healthcare Policy*, *16*, 1033–1047. doi:10.2147/RMHP.S414823 PMID:37333981

Hur, W. M., Kim, H., & Woo, J. (2014). How CSR leads to corporate brand equity: Mediating mechanisms of corporate brand credibility and reputation. *Journal of Business Ethics*, *125*(1), 75–86. doi:10.1007/s10551-013-1910-0

IAASB. (2020). *Technology Frequently Asked Questions, November 2020*. IFAC. https://www.ifac.org/ system/files/publications/files/IAASB-TechnologyFAQ-Automated-Tools-Techniques.pdf

IBM. (2019). *What is business intelligence?* IBM. https://www.ibm.com/topics/business-intelligence

IBM. (2021). *What is OLTP?* IBM. https://www.ibm.com/topics/oltp#:~:text=OLTP%2C%20or%20online%20transactional%20processing,of%20data%20in%20a%20database

IBM. (2023). *What is a data mart?* IBM. https://www.ibm.com/topics/data-mart

IESBA. (2021). *Handbook of the international code of ethics for professional accountants*. IESBA. https://www.ethicsboard.org/publications/2021- handbook-international-code-ethics-professional accountants.

Im, H., Kim, K. H., & Kim, J. H. (2020, January). Privacy and ledger size analysis for healthcare blockchain. In *2020 International Conference on Information Networking (ICOIN)* (pp. 825-829). IEEE. 10.1109/ICOIN48656.2020.9016624

Insch, A. (2008). Online communication of Corporate Environmental Citizenship: A study of New Zealand's electricity and gas retailers. *Journal of Marketing Communications*, *14*(2), 139–153. doi:10.1080/13527260701858505

Insideevs. (2022). 'XPeng Electric Car Sales Decreased By Almost 63% In November 2022. Inside EVS. https://insideevs.com/news/624618/xpeng-electric-car-sales-november2022/

IPE & PECC. (2021a). *Tesla & More Electric Vehicle Investigative Report I.* IPE. https://wwwoa.ipe.org.cn/Upload/202109140452005929.pdf

IPE & PECC. (2021b). *Tesla & More Electric Vehicle Investigative Report II.* IPE. https://wwwen.ipe.org.cn/reports/report_21270.html

Iqbal Khadaroo, M. (2005). Business reporting on the internet in Malaysia and Singapore: A comparative study. *Corporate Communications*, *10*(1), 58–68. doi:10.1108/13563280510578204

Jabarulla, M. Y., & Lee, H. N. (2021, August). A blockchain and artificial intelligence-based, patient-centric healthcare system for combating the COVID-19 pandemic: Opportunities and applications. In Healthcare (Vol. 9, No. 8, p. 1019). MDPI.

Jabarulla, M. Y., & Lee, H. N. (2020). Blockchain-based distributed patient-centric image management system. *Applied Sciences (Basel, Switzerland)*, *11*(1), 196. doi:10.3390/app11010196

Jabbar, R., Fetais, N., Krichen, M., & Barkaoui, K. (2020, February). Blockchain technology for healthcare: Enhancing shared electronic health record interoperability and integrity. In *2020 IEEE International Conference on Informatics, IoT, and Enabling Technologies (ICIoT)* (pp. 310-317). IEEE.

Jabri, F., & Tim, I. S. (2023). *RESEARCH ESSAY DATA SCIENCE AND ANALYTICS IN HEALTHCARE.*

Jakobsen, M., Mitchell, F., Nørreklit, H., & Trenca, M. (2019). Educating Management Accountants as Business Partners. *Qualitative Research in Accounting & Management*, *16*(4), 517–541. doi:10.1108/QRAM-10-2017-0099

Jayaram, J., & Narasimhan, R. (2007). The Influence of New Product Development Competitive Capabilities on Project Performance. *IEEE Transactions on Engineering Management, Engineering Management, IEEE Transactions on, IEEE Trans. Eng. Manage, 54*(2), 241–256. https://eds-p-ebscohost-com.ez.xjtlu.edu.cn/eds/detail/detail?vid=0&sid=cfdf6fb5-162f-4cae-a39f-c31c10920c1f%40redis&bdata=JnNpdGU9ZWRzLWxpdmUmc2NvcGU9c2l0ZQ%3d%3d#AN=edseee.4160162&db=edseee

Jayasinghe, K. (2021). Constructing constructivism in management accounting education: Reflections from a teaching cycle with innovative learning elements. *Qualitative Research in Accounting & Management*, *18*(2), 282–309. doi:10.1108/QRAM-05-2020-0067

Jensen, J. R., von Wachter, V., & Ross, O. (2021). An introduction to decentralized finance (defi). *Complex Systems Informatics and Modeling Quarterly*, (26), 46–54. doi:10.7250/csimq.2021-26.03

Jensen, M. C., & Meckling, W. H. (1976). Theory of the firm: Managerial behavior, agency costs and ownership structure. *Journal of Financial Economics*, *3*(4), 305–360. doi:10.1016/0304-405X(76)90026-X

Jin, S. A. A., & Phua, J. (2014). Following celebrities' tweets about brands: The impact of twitter-based electronic word-of-mouth on consumers' source credibility perception, buying intention, and social identification with celebrities. *Journal of Advertising*, *43*(2), 181–195. doi:10.1080/00913367.2013.827606

KaiYuan Securities. (2022). *XPeng total deliveries until September 2022.* IWENCAI. http://www.iwencai.com/unifiedwap/inforesult?w=%E5%B0%8F%E9%B9%8F&querytype=report&tab=2

Kallio, T. J. (2007). Taboos in corporate social responsibility discourse. *Journal of Business Ethics*, *74*(2), 165–175. doi:10.1007/s10551-006-9227-x

Kamran, R., Khan, N., & Sundarakani, B. (2021). Blockchain technology development and implementation for global logistics operations: A reference model perspective. *Journal of Global Operations and Strategic Sourcing*, *14*(2), 360–382. doi:10.1108/JGOSS-08-2020-0047

Kang, J., & Hustvedt, G. (2014). Building trust between consumers and corporations: The role of consumer perceptions of transparency and social responsibility. *Journal of Business Ethics*, *125*(2), 253–265. doi:10.1007/s10551-013-1916-7

Kashyap, S., Bhushan, B., Kumar, A., & Nand, P. (2022). Quantum blockchain approach for security enhancement in cyberworld. In *Multimedia Technologies in the Internet of Things Environment* (Vol. 3, pp. 1–22). Springer Singapore.

Kassen, M. (2023). Blockchain and digital governance: Decentralization of decision making policy. *The Review of Policy Research*, ropr.12585. Advance online publication. doi:10.1111/ropr.12585

Kaur, J. (2023, May). How is Robotic Process Automation Revolutionising the Way Healthcare Sector Works? In International Conference on Information, Communication and Computing Technology (pp. 1037-1055). Singapore: Springer Nature Singapore. 10.1007/978-981-99-5166-6_70

Kaur, J. (2024). Green Finance 2.0: Pioneering Pathways for Sustainable Development and Health Through Future Trends and Innovations. In Sustainable Investments in Green Finance (pp. 294-319). IGI Global.

Kaur, J. (2023). Robotic Process Automation in Healthcare Sector. In *E3S Web of Conferences* (Vol. 391, p. 01008). EDP Sciences.

Kaur, S., Singh, S., Gupta, S., & Wats, S. (2023). Risk analysis in decentralized finance (DeFi): A fuzzy-AHP approach. *Risk Management*, *25*(2), 13. doi:10.1057/s41283-023-00118-0

Kemp, A. (2018). *Taiichi Ohno: Hero of the Toyota Production System*. QAD. https://www.qad.com/blog/2018/03/taiichi-ohno-toyota-production-system

Kend, M., & Nguyen, L. A. (2020). Big data analytics and other emerging technologies: The impact on the Australian audit and assurance profession. *Australian Accounting Review*, *30*(4), 269–282. doi:10.1111/auar.12305

Kend, M., & Nguyen, L. A. (2022). The emergence of audit data analytics in existing audit spaces: Findings from three technologically advanced audit and assurance service markets. *Qualitative Research in Accounting & Management*, *19*(5), 540–563. doi:10.1108/QRAM-01-2021-0005

Kessler, E. H., & Bierly, P. E., III. (2002). Is faster better? An empirical test of the implications of innovation speed. *IEEE Transactions on Engineering Management, Engineering Management, IEEE Transactions on, IEEE Trans. Eng. Manage*, *49*(1), 2–12. https://eds-p-ebscohost-com.ez.xjtlu.edu.cn/eds/detail/detail?vid=0&sid=a42b9fe2-a446-45e7-8cda-fa16525054c1%40redis&bdata=JnNpdGU9ZWRzLWxpdmUmc2NvcGU9c2l0ZQ%3d%3d#AN=edseee.985742&db=edseee

Kim, J. S., Sim, J. B., Kim, Y. J., Park, M. K., Oh, S. J., & Doo, I. C. (2023). Establishment of NLP-Based Greenwashing Pattern Detection Service. In J. S. Park, L. T. Yang, Y. Pan, & J. H. Park (Eds.), *Advances in Computer Science and Ubiquitous Computing* (pp. 1–9). Springer. doi:10.1007/978-981-99-1252-0_32

King, S., & Nadal, S. (2012). Ppcoin: Peer-to-peer crypto-currency with proof-of-stake. *Self-Published Paper*.

Kirkpatrick, G. (2009). The corporate governance lessons from the financial crisis. *OECD Journal: Financial Market Trends*, *2009*(1), 61–87. doi:10.1787/fmt-v2009-art3-en

Kiss, A. N., & Barr, P. S. (2017). New Product Development Strategy Implementation Duration and New Venture Performance. *Journal of Management, 43*(4), 1185–1210. https://eds-p-ebscohost-com.ez.xjtlu.edu.cn/eds/detail/detail?vid=0&sid=750872be-f362-44c6-a5c4-02a88cdccbdb%40redis&bdata=JnNpdGU9ZWRzLWxpdmUmc2NvcGU9c2l0ZQ%3d%3d#AN=121615690&db=bsu

Kitzler, S., Victor, F., Saggese, P., & Haslhofer, B. (2023). Disentangling decentralized finance (DeFi) compositions. *ACM Transactions on the Web*, *17*(2), 1–26. doi:10.1145/3532857

Kokina, J., & Davenport, T. H. (2017). The emergence of artificial intelligence: How automation is changing auditing. *Journal of Emerging Technologies in Accounting*, *14*(1), 115–122. doi:10.2308/jeta-51730

Kolk, A. (2004). A decade of sustainability reporting: Developments and significance. *International Journal of Environment and Sustainable Development*, *3*(1), 51–64. doi:10.1504/IJESD.2004.004688

Kolk, A. (2010). Trajectories of sustainability reporting by MNCs. *Journal of World Business*, *45*(4), 367–374. doi:10.1016/j.jwb.2009.08.001

Kordestani, H., Barkaoui, K., & Zahran, W. (2020, August). HapiChain: a blockchain-based framework for patient-centric telemedicine. In *2020 IEEE 8th International Conference on Serious Games and Applications for Health (SeGAH)* (pp. 1-6). IEEE. 10.1109/SeGAH49190.2020.9201726

KPMG. (1997). *KPMG International survey of environmental reporting 1999*. KPMG. https://www.researchgate.net/publication/254796996_KPMG_International_survey_of_environmental_reporting_1999

KPMG. (2011). *KPMG International Survey of Corporate Responsibility Reporting*. KPMG. https://www.in.kpmg.com/securedata/aci/files/corporateresponsibility2011.pdf

KPMG. (2022). *Big shifts, small steps, Survey of Sustainability Reporting 2022*. KPMG. https://kpmg.com/xx/en/home/insights/2022/09/survey-of-sustainability-reporting-2022.html

Kumar, M., Townsend, J. D., & Vorhies, D. W. (2015). Enhancing Consumers' Affection for a Brand Using Product Design. *Journal of Product Innovation Management*, *32*(5), 716–730. https://eds-p-ebscohost-com.ez.xjtlu.edu.cn/eds/detail/detail?vid=0&sid=6d3ea559-8df6-4500-9968-a7e770a918c1%40redis&bdata=JnNpdGU9ZWRzLWxpdmUmc2NvcGU9c2l0ZQ%3d%3d#AN=108541949&db=bsu

Kumar, S., Lim, W. M., Sivarajah, U., & Kaur, J. (2023). Artificial intelligence and blockchain integration in business: Trends from a bibliometric-content analysis. *Information Systems Frontiers*, *25*(2), 871–896. PMID:35431617

Kutzin, J., & World Health Organization. (1995). *Experience with organizational and financing reform of the health sector*. WHO.

Kuwashima, K., & Fujimoto, T. (2013). Performance Measurement in Product Development Research: A Literature Review. *Annals of Business Administrative Science*, *12*(4), 213–223. https://eds-s-ebscohost-com.ez.xjtlu.edu.cn/eds/detail/detail?vid=0&sid=35581885-aa72-4407-ae9a-77b232e4df7a%40redis&bdata=JnNpdGU9ZWRzLWxpdmUmc2NvcGU9c2l0ZQ%3d%3d#AN=119369235&db=bsu (Accessed: 21 November 2022).

La Porta, R., Lopez-de-Silanes, F., Shleifer, A., & Vishny, R. (2000). Investor protection and corporate governance. *Journal of Financial Economics*, *58*(1-2), 3–27. doi:10.1016/S0304-405X(00)00065-9

Langerak, F., & Hultink, E. J. (2005). The impact of new product development acceleration approaches on speed and profitability: lessons for pioneers and fast followers. *IEEE Transactions on Engineering Management, Engineering Management, IEEE Transactions on, IEEE Trans. Eng. Manage.* IEEE. https://eds-p-ebscohost-com.ez.xjtlu.edu.cn/eds/detail/detail?vid=0&sid=fe052f67-ee0d-4fac-81f7-c5d5d1bfc36a%40redis&bdata=JnNpdGU9ZWRzLWxpdmUmc2NvcGU9c2l0ZQ%3d%3d#AN=edseee.1388696&db=edseee

Langerak, F., & Hultink, E. J. (2006). The Impact of Product Innovativeness on the Link between Development Speed and New Product Profitability. *Journal of Product Innovation Management, 23*(3), 203–214. https://eds-s-ebscohost-com.ez.xjtlu.edu.cn/eds/detail/detail?vid=0&sid=e4a18c29-bdcb-4c00-bf29-eb3c8878a64a%40redis&bdata=JnNpdGU9ZWRzLWxpdmUmc2NvcGU9c2l0ZQ%3d%3d#AN=20535319&db=bsu

Laplume, A. O., Sonpar, K., & Litz, R. A. (2008). Stakeholder theory: Reviewing a theory that moves us. *Journal of Management, 34*(6), 1152–1189. doi:10.1177/0149206308324322

Lee, A. R., Kim, M. G., & Kim, I. K. (2019, November). SHAREChain: Healthcare data sharing framework using Blockchain-registry and FHIR. In *2019 IEEE International Conference on Bioinformatics and Biomedicine (BIBM)* (pp. 1087-1090). IEEE. 10.1109/BIBM47256.2019.8983415

Lee, H. H. M., Van Dolen, W., & Kolk, A. (2013). On the role of social media in the 'responsible' food business: Blogger buzz on health and obesity issues. *Journal of Business Ethics, 118*(4), 695–707. doi:10.1007/s10551-013-1955-0

Lehner, M., Ittonen, K., Silvola, H., & Strom, E. (2022). Artificial intelligence based intelligence-based decision-making in accounting and auditing, ethical challenges and normative thinking. *Accounting, Auditing & Accountability Journal, 35*(9), 109–135. doi:10.1108/AAAJ-09-2020-4934

Leung, D., Law, R., Van Hoof, H., & Buhalis, D. (2013). Social media in tourism and hospitality: A literature review. *Journal of Travel & Tourism Marketing, 30*(1-2), 3–22. doi:10.1080/10548408.2013.750919

Li, J.-P., Mirza, N., Rahat, B., & Xiong, D. (2020). Machine learning and credit ratings prediction in the age of fourth industrial revolution. *Technological Forecasting and Social Change, 161*, 120309. doi:10.1016/j.techfore.2020.120309

Lill, D., Gross, C., & Peterson, R. (1986). The inclusion of social-responsibility themes by magazine advertisers: A longitudinal study. *Journal of Advertising, 15*(2), 35–41. doi:10.1080/00913367.1986.10673003

Li, M., Chen, L., Zhao, J., & Li, Q. (2021). Sentiment analysis of Chinese stock reviews based on BERT model. *Applied Intelligence, 51*(7), 5016–5024. doi:10.1007/s10489-020-02101-8

Limited, J. S. E. (2022). *Leading the Way for a Better Tomorrow: JSE Sustainability Disclosure Guidance.* JSE. https://www.jse.co.za/sites/default/files/media/documents/JSE%20Sustainability%20Disclosure%20Guidance%20June%202022.pdf

Li, Q., Li, A., Wang, T., & Cai, Y. (2021). Interconnected hybrid AC-DC microgrids security enhancement using blockchain technology considering uncertainty. *International Journal of Electrical Power & Energy Systems, 133*, 107324. doi:10.1016/j.ijepes.2021.107324

Littley, J. (2012). *Leveraging data analytics and continuous auditing processes for improved audit planning, effectiveness, and efficiency.* (KPMG White Paper).

Lomborg, B. (2003). *The skeptical environmentalist: measuring the real state of the world* (Vol. 1). Cambridge University Press.

Louwers, T., Pasewark, W. R., & Typpo, E. W. (1996). The Internet: Changing the way corporations tell their story. *The CPA Journal, 66*(11), 24.

Lozano, R., & Huisingh, D. (2011). Inter-linking issues and dimensions in sustainability reporting. *Journal of Cleaner Production*, *19*(2-3), 99–107. doi:10.1016/j.jclepro.2010.01.004

Lyon, T. P., & Montgomery, A. W. (2013). Tweetjacked: The impact of social media on corporate greenwash. *Journal of Business Ethics*, *118*(4), 747–757. doi:10.1007/s10551-013-1958-x

Macpherson, M., Gasperini, A., & Bosco, M. (2021). Implications for Artificial Intelligence and ESG Data. SSRN Electronic Journal. doi:10.2139/ssrn.3863599

Madden, M. (2010). *Older adults and social media*. PewInternet and American Life Project.

Manetti, G., & Bellucci, M. (2016). The use of social media for engaging stakeholders in sustainability reporting. *Accounting, Auditing & Accountability Journal*, *29*(6), 985–1011. doi:10.1108/AAAJ-08-2014-1797

Manheim, J. B., & Pratt, C. B. (1986). Communicating corporate social responsibility. *Public Relations Review*, *12*(2), 9–18. doi:10.1016/S0363-8111(86)80022-4

Manita, R., Elommal, N., Baudier, P., & Hikkerova, L. (2020). The digital transformation of external audit and its impact on corporate governance. *Technological Forecasting and Social Change*, *150*, 119751. doi:10.1016/j.techfore.2019.119751

Manne, H. G. (1966). Insider Trading and the Administrative Process. *The George Washington Law Review*, *35*, 473.

MathWorks. (2022) *BootCI*. Mathworks. https://de.mathworks.com/help/stats/bootci.html

Mcivor, M. (2022). How Many Fortune 500 CEOs are on Social Media in 2022? *Influential Executive*. https://influentialexecutive.com/how-many-fortune-500-ceos-social-media-2022/

McNally, R. C., Akdeniz, M. B., & Calantone, R. J. (2011). New Product Development Processes and New Product Profitability: Exploring the Mediating Role of Speed to Market and Product Quality. *Journal of Product Innovation Management*, (s1), 63–77. https://eds-s-ebscohost-com.ez.xjtlu.edu.cn/eds/detail/detail?vid=0&sid=0349b761-5727-41bb-9841-cea04d0046cd%40redis&bdata=JnNpdGU9ZWRzLWxpdmUmc2NvcGU9c2l0ZQ%3d%3d#AN=66592359&db=bsu

Meadows, M., Merendino, A., Dibb, S., Garcia-Perez, A., Hinton, M., Papagiannidis, S., Pappas, I., & Wang, H. (2022). Tension in the data environment: How organisations can meet the challenge. *Technological Forecasting and Social Change*, *175*, 121315. doi:10.1016/j.techfore.2021.121315

Meisami, S., Meisami, S., Yousefi, M., & Aref, M. R. (2023). Combining Block chain and IOT for Decentralized Healthcare Data Management. arXiv preprint arXiv:2304.00127.

Mena Report. (2022). EB CoHost. https://search-ebscohost-com.ez.xjtlu.edu.cn/login.aspx?direct=true&db=edsgea&AN=edsgcl.693449837&site=eds-live&scope=site (Accessed: 17 October 2022).

Men, L. R., & Tsai, W. H. S. (2016). Public engagement with CEOs on social media: Motivations and relational outcomes. *Public Relations Review*, *42*(5), 932–942. doi:10.1016/j.pubrev.2016.08.001

Microsoft. (2020). *Online analytical processing (OLAP)*. Microsoft. https://learn.microsoft.com/en-us/azure/architecture/data-guide/relational-data/online-analytical-processing

Millson, M. R., & Wilemon, D. (2019). The Npd Speed-Market Success Relationship: A Meta-Analysis', *International Journal of Innovation Management*, *23*(6), N.PAG. https://eds-s-ebscohost-com.ez.xjtlu.edu.cn/eds/detail/detail?vid=0&sid=c5118752-88cf-467b-9168-d98359264dc6%40redis&bdata=JnNpdGU9ZWRzLWxpdmUmc2NvcGU9c2l0ZQ%3d%3d#AN=137684240&db=edb

Min, Y. L., Zheng, Q., & Zhu, Y. (2022) *MGTF 490 capstone project: identify "Greenwashing" funds using NLP in firms' prospectuses, as you sow*. Semantic Scholar. https://www.semanticscholar.org/paper/MGTF-490-Capstone-Project%3A-Identify-%E2%80%9CGreenwashing%E2%80%9D-Li-Hsu/aa59e82a5ed86ab76272925bb73ce6d298527a71

Minton, E., Lee, C., Orth, U., Kim, C. H., & Kahle, L. (2012). Sustainable marketing and social media: A cross-country analysis of motives for sustainable behaviors. *Journal of Advertising*, *41*(4), 69–84. doi:10.1080/00913367.2012.10672458

Mitchell, T. M. (1997). *Machine Learning*. McGraw-Hill.

Mohammad Amini, M., Jesus, M., Fanaei Sheikholeslami, D., Alves, P., Hassanzadeh Benam, A., & Hariri, F. (2023). Artificial Intelligence Ethics and Challenges in Healthcare Applications: A Comprehensive Review in the Context of the European GDPR Mandate. *Machine Learning and Knowledge Extraction*, *5*(3), 1023–1035. doi:10.3390/make5030053

Moloughney, T. (2021). XPeng G3 Earns Top Quality Ranking By J.D. Power In Latest Study. Inside EVS. https://insideevs.com/news/524097/xpeng-g3-jd-power-quality/

Monlezun, D. J. (2023). *The Thinking Healthcare System: Artificial Intelligence and Human Equity*. Elsevier.

MSCI. (2023). *Tesla ESG rating report*. MSCI. https://www.alliancebernstein.com/sites/ campaign/theme/resources/pdfs/msci_tsla_esg_ratings_report.pdf

Muneer, A., Faizan Ali, R., Alghamdi, A., Mohd Taib, S., Almaghthawi, A., & Ghaleb, E. A. A. (2022). Predicting customers churning in banking industry: A machine learning approach. *Indonesian Journal of Electrical Engineering and Computer Science*, *26*(1), 539. doi:10.11591/ijeecs.v26.i1.pp539-549

Musamih, A., Salah, K., Jayaraman, R., Yaqoob, I., Puthal, D., & Ellahham, S. (2022). NFTs in healthcare: Vision, opportunities, and challenges. *IEEE Consumer Electronics Magazine*. doi:10.1109/MCE.2022.3217660

Musk, E. (2022a). *ESG is an outrageous scam! Shame on SPGlobal* [Twitter]. https://twitter.com/elonmusk/status/1526957672200908801

Musk, E. (2022b). *Exxon is rated top ten best in world for environment, social & governance (ESG) by S&P 500, while Tesla didn't make the list! ESG is a scam. It has been weaponized by phony social justice warriors* [Twitter]. https://twitter.com/elonmusk/status/1526958110023245829

Naeem, S., Khan Mashwani, W., Ali, A., Irfan Uddin, M., Mahmoud, M., Jamal, F., & Chesneau, C. (2021). Machine Learning-based USD/PKR Exchange Rate Forecasting Using Sentiment Analysis of Twitter Data. *Computers, Materials & Continua*, *67*(3), 3451–3461. doi:10.32604/cmc.2021.015872

Nair, K., & Gupta, R. (2021). Application of AI technology in modern digital marketing environment. *World Journal of Entrepreneurship, Management and Sustainable Development*, *7*(3), 318–328. doi:10.1108/WJEMSD-08-2020-0099

Nakamoto, S. (2008). *Bitcoin: A Peer-to-Peer Electronic Cash System.*

Negash, S. (2004). Business intelligence. *Communications of the Association for Information Systems*, *13*(1), 15. doi:10.17705/1CAIS.01315

Nemes, N., Scanlan, S. J., Smith, P., Smith, T., Aronczyk, M., Hill, S., Lewis, S. L., Montgomery, A. W., Tubiello, F. N., & Stabinsky, D. (2022). An integrated framework to assess greenwashing. *Sustainability (Basel)*, *14*(8), 4431. doi:10.3390/su14084431

Neu, D., Saxton, G., Rahaman, A., & Everett, J. (2019). Twitter and social accountability: Reactions to the Panama Papers. *Critical Perspectives on Accounting*, *61*, 38–53. doi:10.1016/j.cpa.2019.04.003

Newsroom. (2021). *Wells Fargo Announces New Digital Infrastructure Strategy and Strategic Partnerships With Microsoft, Google Cloud.* NewsRoom. https://newsroom.wf.com/English/news-releases/news-release-details/2021/Wells-Fargo-Announces-New-Digital-Infrastructure-Strategy-and-Strategic-Partnerships-With-Microsoft-Google-Cloud/default.aspx

Ning, X., Yim, D., & Khuntia, J. (2021). Online Sustainability Reporting and Firm Performance: Lessons Learned from Text Mining. *Sustainability (Basel), 13*(3), 1069. doi:10.3390/su13031069

Ohno, T. (1988). *Toyota Production Systems: Beyond Large Scale Production.* QAD. https://www.qad.com/blog/2018/03/taiichi-ohno-toyota-production-system

Ong, I. L., Siew, P. H., & Wong, S. F. (2011). A five-layered business intelligence architecture. *Communications of the IBIMA, 2011*, 1–11. doi:10.5171/2011.695619

Oracle. (2018). What is ERP? *Oracle.* https://www.oracle.com/erp/what-is-erp/#:~:text=Enterprise%20resource%20planning%20(ERP)%20refers,compliance%2C%20and%20supply%20chain%20operations

Ozili, P. K. (2023). Assessing global interest in decentralized finance, embedded finance, open finance, ocean finance and sustainable finance. *Asian Journal of Economics and Banking, 7*(2), 197–216. doi:10.1108/AJEB-03-2022-0029

Palazzo, M., Vollero, A., & Siano, A. (2020). From strategic corporate social responsibility to value creation: An analysis of corporate website communication in the banking sector. *International Journal of Bank Marketing, 38*(7), 1529–1552. doi:10.1108/IJBM-04-2020-0168

Parker, L. D. (1982). Corporate annual reporting: A mass communication perspective. *Accounting and Business Research, 12*(48), 279–286. doi:10.1080/00014788.1982.9728820

Parry, G. C., & Turner, C. E. (2006). Application of lean visual process management tools. *Production Planning and Control, 17*(1), 77–86. doi:10.1080/09537280500414991

Patel, N. S. (2021). Establishing Social Presence for an Engaging Online Teaching and Learning Experience. *International Journal of TESOL Studies, 3*(1), 162–178.

Patil, S., & Shankar, H. (2023). Transforming Healthcare: Harnessing the Power of AI in the Modern Era. *International Journal of Multidisciplinary Sciences and Arts, 2*(1), 60–70.

Pearl, J. (1988). *Probabilistic reasoning in intelligent systems: networks of plausible inference.* Morgan Kaufmann Publishers.

Pearl, J. (2019). *The Book of Why.* Penguin.

Pearson, J. (2010). Turning Point. Are We Doing the Right Thing? Leadership and Prioritisation for Public Benefit. *Journal of Corporate Citizenship, 2010*(37), 37–40. doi:10.9774/GLEAF.4700.2010.sp.00006

Perrons, R. K., & Cosby, T. (2020). Applying blockchain in the geoenergy domain: The road to interoperability and standards. *Applied Energy, 262*, 114545. doi:10.1016/j.apenergy.2020.114545

Petani, F. J., Ramirez, C., & Gendron, Y. (2021). Special issue on Digitalization, work, and professions. *Critical Perspectives on Accounting, 79*(C), 102354. doi:10.1016/j.cpa.2021.102354

Piñeiro-Chousa, J., Šević, A., & González-López, I. (2023). Impact of social metrics in decentralized finance. *Journal of Business Research, 158*, 113673. doi:10.1016/j.jbusres.2023.113673

Plewa, C., Conduit, J., Quester, P. G., & Johnson, C. (2015). The impact of corporate volunteering on CSR image: A consumer perspective. *Journal of Business Ethics, 127*(3), 643–659. doi:10.1007/s10551-014-2066-2

PwC. (2023). *Comparison of the big three sustainability frameworks.* PwC. https://viewpoint.pwc.com/dt/gx/en/pwc/in_depths/in_depths_INT/in_depths_INT/Navigating-the-ESG-landscape.html?ep=eml_15_08_2023_gx_en_ext

Quattrone, P. (2016). Management accounting goes digital: Will the move make it wiser? *Management Accounting Research, 31*, 118–122. doi:10.1016/j.mar.2016.01.003

Raisch, S., & Krakowski, S. (2021). Artificial intelligence and management: The automation–augmentation paradox. *Academy of Management Review, 46*(1), 192–210. doi:10.5465/amr.2018.0072

Rappaport, A. (1986). *Creating Shareholder Value: The New Standard for Business Performance*. Free Press.

Richins, G., Stapleton, A., Stratopoulos, T., & Wong, C. (2017). Big data analytics: Opportunity or threat for the accounting profession? *Journal of Information Systems, 31*(3), 63–79. doi:10.2308/isys-51805

Rivera, D. A., Frenay, M., & Swaen, V. (2023). The Learning Design of MOOC Discussion Forums: An Analysis of Forum Instructions and Their Role in Supporting the Social Construction of Knowledge. *Technology, Knowledge, and Learning.*

Roulstone, D. T. (2003). The relation between insider-trading restrictions and executive compensation. *Journal of Accounting Research, 41*(3), 525–551. doi:10.1111/1475-679X.00115

Russom, P. (2011). Big data analytics. *TDWI best practices report, fourth quarter, 19*(4), 1-34.

Saleh, F. (2021). Blockchain without waste: Proof-of-stake. *Review of Financial Studies, 34*(3), 1156–1190. doi:10.1093/rfs/hhaa075

Sarker, I. H. (2022). AI-Based Modeling: Techniques, Applications and Research Issues Towards Automation, Intelligent and Smart Systems. *SN Computer Science, 3*(2), 158. doi:10.1007/s42979-022-01043-x PMID:35194580

Saxton, G. D., Gómez, L., Ngoh, Z., Lin, Y. P., & Dietrich, S. (2019). Do CSR messages resonate? Examining public reactions to firms' CSR efforts on social media. *Journal of Business Ethics, 155*(2), 359–377. doi:10.1007/s10551-017-3464-z

Sen, S., & Bhattacharya, C. B. (2001). Does doing good always lead to doing better? Consumer reactions to corporate social responsibility. *JMR, Journal of Marketing Research, 38*(2), 225–243. doi:10.1509/jmkr.38.2.225.18838

Sensharma, S., Sinha, M., & Sharma, D. (2022). Do Indian firms engage in greenwashing? Evidence from Indian firms. *Australasian Accounting. Business and Finance Journal, 16*(5), 67–88. doi:10.14453/aabfj.v16i5.06

Seo, J. Y. (2016). What Factors Influence Profitability in the Korean Credit Card Business?. *International Journal of Business & Society, 17*(1), 19–27. https://search-ebscohost-com.ez.xjtlu.edu.cn/login.aspx?direct=true&db=bsu&AN=116157302&site=eds-live&scope=site (Accessed: 8 October 2022).

Sethi, R. (2000). New Product Quality and Product Development Teams. *Journal of Marketing, 64*(2), 1–14. https://eds-s-ebscohost-com.ez.xjtlu.edu.cn/eds/detail/detail?vid=0&sid=46478820-e48d-43e9-b952-0f1ed41b8dba%40redis&bdata=JnNpdGU9ZWRzLWxpdmUmc2NvcGU9c2l0ZQ%3d%3d#AN=3043546&db=bsu

Shah, R., & Ward, P. T. (2007). Defining and developing measures of lean production. *Journal of Operations Management, 25*(4), 785–805. doi:10.1016/j.jom.2007.01.019

Sharma, A., Hung, Y. H., Agarwal, P., & Kalra, M. (2019). A study on blockchain applications in healthcare. In Frontier Computing: Theory, Technologies and Applications (FC 2018) 7 (pp. 623-628). Springer Singapore. doi:10.1007/978-981-13-3648-5_75

Sheehy, B. (2014). Greenwashing in corporate environmental discourse: A discursive approach. *Journal of Business Ethics, 123*(3), 635–649.

Shrestha, R., Nam, S. Y., Bajracharya, R., & Kim, S. (2020). Evolution of V2X communication and integration of blockchain for security enhancements. *Electronics (Basel)*, *9*(9), 1338. doi:10.3390/electronics9091338

Shuaib, M., Alam, S., Alam, M. S., & Nasir, M. S. (2021). Self-sovereign identity for healthcare using blockchain. *Materials Today: Proceedings*.

Silva, R., Rodrigues, R., & Leal, C. (2021). Games-based learning in accounting education – which dimensions are the most relevant? *Accounting Education*, *30*(2), 159–187. doi:10.1080/09639284.2021.1891107

Sina Finance. (2020). 中国第二大酒店华住集团上市前夜遭做空 华住紧急回应. Sina Finance. https://finance.sina.com.cn/stock/hkstock/ggscyd/2020-09-22/doc-iivhuipp5842766.shtml

Singh, A. P., Pradhan, N. R., Luhach, A. K., Agnihotri, S., Jhanjhi, N. Z., Verma, S., Kavita, Ghosh, U., & Roy, D. S. (2020). A novel patient-centric architectural framework for blockchain-enabled healthcare applications. *IEEE Transactions on Industrial Informatics*, *17*(8), 5779–5789. doi:10.1109/TII.2020.3037889

Singh, V., & Thurman, A. (2019). How Many Ways Can We Define Online Learning? A Systematic Literature Review of Definitions of Online Learning (1988–2018). *American Journal of Distance Education*, *33*(4), 289–306. doi:10.1080/08923647.2019.1663082

Sisson, D. C. (2017). Control mutuality, social media, and organization-public relationships: A study of local animal welfare organizations' donors. *Public Relations Review*, *43*(1), 179–189. doi:10.1016/j.pubrev.2016.10.007

Sivasubramaniam, N., Liebowitz, S. J., & Lackman, C. L. (2012). Determinants of New Product Development Team Performance: A Meta-analytic Review. *Journal of Product Innovation Management*, *29*(5), 803–820. https://eds-p-ebscohost-com.ez.xjtlu.edu.cn/eds/detail/detail?vid=0&sid=0973782c-e37f-47fc-a0b6-c0d1609cf14e%40redis&bdata=JnNpdGU9ZWRzLWxpdmUmc2NvcGU9c2l0ZQ%3d%3d#AN=78301272&db=bsu

Smith, N. C., & Rönnegard, D. (2016). Shareholder primacy, corporate social responsibility, and the role of business schools. *Journal of Business Ethics*, *134*(3), 463–478. doi:10.1007/s10551-014-2427-x

Sriramesh, K., Rivera-Sánchez, M., & Soriano, C. (2013). Websites for stakeholder relations by corporations and non-profits: A time-lag study in Singapore. *Journal of Communication Management (London)*, *17*(2), 122–139. doi:10.1108/13632541311318738

Stafford, A. (2023). New development: Using counter accounting as a methodology in public accountability and management research. *Public Money & Management*, *43*(7), 709–712. doi:10.1080/09540962.2023.2251765

Suimon, Y., Sakaji, H., Izumi, K., Shimada, T., & Matsushima, H. (2020). Japanese Interest Rate Forecast Considering the Linkage of Global Markets Using Machine Learning Methods. *International Journal of Smart Computing and Artificial Intelligence*, *4*(1), 1–17. doi:10.52731/ijscai.v4.i1.500

Sun, D. (2000). Selection of the Linear Regression Model According to the Parameter Estimation. *JOURNAL OF NATURAL SCIENCES*, *5*(4), 400–405. https://search-ebscohost-com.ez.xjtlu.edu.cn/login.aspx?direct=true&db=edscoj&AN=edscoj.whdxxb.e200004005&site=eds-live&scope=site.

Sun, S., Wang, S., & Wei, Y. (2020). A new ensemble deep learning approach for exchange rates forecasting and trading. *Advanced Engineering Informatics*, *46*, 101160. doi:10.1016/j.aei.2020.101160

Sun, Y., & Bhattacherjee, A. (2014). Looking inside the "IT black box": Technological effects on IT usage. *Journal of Computer Information Systems*, *54*(2), 1–15. doi:10.1080/08874417.2014.11645681

Sutton, J. (2016). *Why Social Media and Sustainability Should Go Hand in Hand*. Triple Pundit. https://www.triplepundit.com/2016/06/social-mediasustainability-go-hand-hand/

Swann, C., Jackman, P. C., Lawrence, A., Hawkins, R. M., Goddard, S. G., Williamson, O., Schweickle, M. J., Vella, S. A., Rosenbaum, S., & Ekkekakis, P. (2023). The (over) use of SMART goals for physical activity promotion: A narrative review and critique. *Health Psychology Review*, *17*(2), 211–226. doi:10.1080/17437199.2021.2023608 PMID:35094640

Swink, M., Talluri, S., & Pandejpong, T. (2006). Faster, better, cheaper: A study of NPD project efficiency and performance tradeoffs. *Journal of Operations Management*, *24*(5), 542–562. https://eds-p-ebscohost-com.ez.xjtlu.edu.cn/eds/detail/detail?vid=0&sid=7409c5bb-9ebd-4d23-845b-e103f0cec522%40redis&bdata=JnNpdGU9ZWRzLWxpdmUmc2NvcGU9c2l0ZQ%3d%3d#AN=S0272696305001488&db=edselp

Szabo, N. (1997). *The Idea of Smart Contracts.*

Tahir, R., Athar, M. R., & Afzal, A. (2020). The impact of greenwashing practices on green employee behaviour: Mediating role of employee value orientation and green psychological climate. *Cogent Business & Management*, *7*(1), 1781996. doi:10.1080/23311975.2020.1781996

Tan, Y., & Floros, C. (2014). Risk, Profitability, and Competition: Evidence from the Chinese Banking Industry. *Journal of Developing Areas*, *48*(3), 303–319. https://eds-s-ebscohost-com.ez.xjtlu.edu.cn/eds/detail/detail?vid=0&sid=b5a78bbc-27f3-4183-b7ae-c92a21a751ca%40redis&bdata=JnNpdGU9ZWRzLWxpdmUmc2NvcGU9c2l0ZQ%3d%3d#AN=97125404&db=bsu (Accessed: 6 October 2022).

Tapscott, D., & Tapscott, A. (2016). *Blockchain Revolution: How the Technology Behind Bitcoin is Changing Money, Business, and The World.* Penguin.

TerraChoice. (2009). *The seven sins of greenwashing: Summary Report.* TerraChoice. https://www.e-education.psu.edu/emsc302/sites/www.e-education.psu.edu.emsc302/files/TerraChoice_2010.pdf

Tesla Inc. (2020). *Impact Report 2020.* Tesla. https://www.tesla.com/ns_videos/2020-tesla-impact-report.pdf

Tesla Inc. (2021). *Impact Report 2021.* Tesla. https://www.tesla.com/ns_videos/2021-tesla-impact-report.pdf

Tesla Inc. (2022). *Impact Report 2022.* Tesla. https://www.tesla.com/ns_videos/2022-tesla-impact-report.pdf

Tettamanzi, P., Venturini, G., & Murgolo, M. (2022). Sustainability and financial accounting: A critical review on the ESG dynamics. *Environmental Science and Pollution Research International*, *29*(11), 16758–16761. doi:10.1007/s11356-022-18596-2 PMID:35025042

Thakur, A. (2022). A comprehensive study of the trends and analysis of distributed ledger technology and blockchain technology in the healthcare industry. *Frontiers in Blockchain*, *5*, 844834. doi:10.3389/fbloc.2022.844834

Thomas, D. R., Chappell, S. F., & Bright, D. S. (2020). *Classroom as Organization.* Edward Elgar Publishing. doi:10.4337/9781788979856

Tiberius, V., & Hirth, S. (2019). Impacts of digitization on auditing: A Delphi study for Germany. *Journal of International Accounting, Auditing & Taxation*, *37*, 100288. doi:10.1016/j.intaccaudtax.2019.100288

Tilt, C. A. (1994). The Influence of External Pressure Groups on Corporate Social Disclosure: Some Empirical Evidence. *Accounting, Auditing & Accountability Journal*, *7*(4), 47–72. doi:10.1108/09513579410069849

Tornjanski, V., Petrovic, D., & Nesic, S. (2020). Effectiveness of knowledge transfer between project team members in digitally disrupted organizations. *Management: Journal of Sustainable Business and Management Solutions in Emerging Economies*, *25*(2), 1–14.

Tóth, Z., Bessenyei, I. (2008). *Moodle and social constructivism.* NETIS textbook

Townley, B., Cooper, D. J., & Oakes, L. (2003). Performance Measures and the Rationalization of Organizations. *Organization Studies*, *24*(7), 1045–1071. doi:10.1177/0170840603024700З

Trevor, D. W., & Geoffrey, R. F. (2000). Corporate environmental reporting. A test of legitimacy theory. *Accounting, Auditing & Accountability Journal*, *13*(1), 10–26. doi:10.1108/09513570010316126

Truhlar, A. M., Williams, K. M., & Walter, M. T. (2018). Case study: Student engagement with course content and peers in synchronous online discussions. *Online Learning : the Official Journal of the Online Learning Consortium*, *22*(4), 289–312.

Tycho, T., De Back, A., Tinga, M., & Louwerse, M. (2021). Learning in immersed collaborative virtual environments: Design and implementation. *Interactive Learning Environments*, *31*(1), 1–19.

U.S. Securities and Exchange Commission (2022). It's Not Easy Being Green: Bringing Transparency and Accountability to Sustainable

U.S. Securities and Exchange Commission. (2022). *It's Not Easy Being Green: Bringing Transparency and Accountability to Sustainable Investing*. U.S. Securities and Exchange Commission. https://www.sec.gov/news/statement/lee-statement-esg-052522

Unver, M. B. (2023). Governing fiduciary relationships or building up a governance model for trust in AI? Review of healthcare as a socio-technical system. *International Review of Law Computers & Technology*, *37*(2), 1–29. doi:10.1080/13600869.2023.2192569

Uyar, A., Karaman, A. S., & Kilic, M. (2020). Is corporate social responsibility reporting a tool of signaling or greenwashing? Evidence from the worldwide logistics sector. *Journal of Cleaner Production*, *253*, 119997. doi:10.1016/j.jclepro.2020.119997

van der Elst, C., & Lafarre, A. (2024). The Viability of Blockchain in Corporate Governance. In *Board-Shareholder Dialogue: Best Practices, Legal Constraints and Policy Options*. Cambridge University Press.

Van der Stede, W. A. (2016). Management accounting in context: Industry, regulation and informatics. *Management Accounting Research*, *31*, 100–102. doi:10.1016/j.mar.2016.02.005

Verhoef, P. C., & Leeflang, P. S. (2009). Understanding the Marketing Department's Influence Within the Firm', *Journal of Marketing*, *73*(2), 14–37. https://eds-s-ebscohost-com.ez.xjtlu.edu.cn/eds/detail/detail?vid=0&sid=e93cac68-4161-4f9c-a461-06f8f5a61d2f%40redis&bdata=JnNpdGU9ZWRzLWxpdmUmc2NvcGU9c2l0ZQ%3d%3d#AN=36441948&db=bsu

Vesty, G., Kokshagina, O., Jansson, M., Cheong, F., & Butler-Henderson, K. (2023). Accounting, valuing and investing in health care: Dealing with outdated accounting models. *Meditari Accountancy Research*, *31*(1), 52–77. doi:10.1108/MEDAR-06-2021-1334

Vinuesa, R., Azizpour, H., Leite, I., Balaam, M., Dignum, V., Domisch, S., Felländer, A., Langhans, S. D., Tegmark, M., & Fuso Nerini, F. (2020). The role of artificial intelligence in achieving the Sustainable Development Goals. *Nature Communications*, *11*(1), 233. doi:10.1038/s41467-019-14108-y PMID:31932590

Vo, T. T., Xiao, X., & Ho, S. Y. (2019). How does corporate social responsibility engagement influence word of mouth on Twitter? Evidence from the airline industry. *Journal of Business Ethics*, *157*(2), 525–542. doi:10.1007/s10551-017-3679-z

Wachira, M. (2018). Constructionism in Accounting Research: An Investigative Tool for Corporate Social Disclosure Practices'. *European Journal of Business and Management*, *10*, 10.

Wang, R., & Huang, Y. (2018). Communicating corporate social responsibility (CSR) on social media: How do message source and types of CSR messages influence stakeholders' perceptions? *Corporate Communications*, *23*(3), 326–341. doi:10.1108/CCIJ-07-2017-0067

Wang, Y., He, J., Zhu, N., Yi, Y., Zhang, Q., Song, H., & Xue, R. (2021). Security enhancement technologies for smart contracts in the blockchain: A survey. *Transactions on Emerging Telecommunications Technologies*, *32*(12), e4341. doi:10.1002/ett.4341

Wei, J., Ye, T., & Zhang, Z. (2021). A Machine Learning Approach to Evaluate the Performance of Rural Bank. *Complexity*, *2021*, 1–10. doi:10.1155/2021/4281006

Weinberger, A., Ertl, B., Fischer, F., & Mandl, H. (2005). Epistemic and social scripts in computer–supported collaborative learning. *Instructional Science*, *33*(1), 1–30. doi:10.1007/s11251-004-2322-4

Wenhua, Z., Qamar, F., Abdali, T. A. N., Hassan, R., Jafri, S. T. A., & Nguyen, Q. N. (2023). Block chain technology: Security issues, healthcare applications, challenges and future trends. *Electronics (Basel)*, *12*(3), 546. doi:10.3390/electronics12030546

Werner, S., Perez, D., Gudgeon, L., Klages-Mundt, A., Harz, D., & Knottenbelt, W. (2022, September). Sok: Decentralized finance (defi). In *Proceedings of the 4th ACM Conference on Advances in Financial Technologies* (pp. 30-46). ACM. 10.1145/3558535.3559780

Wichers, C. R. (1975). The Detection of Multicollinearity: A Comment. *The Review of Economics and Statistics*, *57*(3), 366–368. https://search-ebscohost-com.ez.xjtlu.edu.cn/login.aspx?direct=true&db=edsjsr&AN=edsjsr.10.2307.1923926&site=eds-live&scope=site

Wickert, C., Scherer, A. G., & Spence, L. J. (2016). Walking and Talking Corporate Social Responsibility: Implications of Firm Size and Organizational Cost. *Journal of Management Studies*, *53*(7), 1169–1196. doi:10.1111/joms.12209

Widuri, R., & Gautama, Y. (2020). Computer-Assisted Audit Techniques (CAATs) for financial fraud detection: a qualitative approach. *2020 International Conference on Information Management and Technology (ICIMTech)*. KPMG. www.kpmg.com/US/en/IssuesAndInsights/ArticlesPublications/Documents/data-analytics-continuous-auditing.pdf

Wieandt, A., & Heppding, L. (2023). Centralized and decentralized finance: Coexistence or convergence? In *The Fintech Disruption: How Financial Innovation Is Transforming the Banking Industry* (pp. 11–51). Springer International Publishing. doi:10.1007/978-3-031-23069-1_2

Wronka, C. (2023). Financial crime in the decentralized finance ecosystem: New challenges for compliance. *Journal of Financial Crime*, *30*(1), 97–113. doi:10.1108/JFC-09-2021-0218

Wu, X. Y., Fan, Z. P., & Cao, B. B. (2023). An analysis of strategies for adopting block chain technology in the fresh product supply chain. *International Journal of Production Research*, *61*(11), 3717–3734. doi:10.1080/00207543.2021.1894497

Wysocki, O., Davies, J. K., Vigo, M., Armstrong, A. C., Landers, D., Lee, R., & Freitas, A. (2023). Assessing the communication gap between AI models and healthcare professionals: Explainability, utility and trust in AI-driven clinical decision-making. *Artificial Intelligence*, *316*, 103839. doi:10.1016/j.artint.2022.103839

XPeng. (2020) *2020 Annual Report* [Online]. XPeng. https://ir.xiaopeng.com/static-files/c75210a2-1b8d-4a52-8a41-8190e000822c

XPeng. (2021a) *2021 Environmental, Social and Governance Report* [Online]. XPeng. https://ir.xiaopeng.com/system/files-encrypted/nasdaq_kms/assets/2022/05/25/21-12-58/2021-ESG-220524-vS-EN.pdf (Accessed: 1 October 2022).

XPeng. (2021b) *2021 Annual Report* [Online]. XPeng. https://ir.xiaopeng.com/static-files/8707a7a3-2645-45a7-9cb4-02364ce5cf57 (Accessed: 4 October 2022).

XPeng. (2022a) *XPENG CORPORATE STORY* [Online]. XPeng. https://heyxpeng.com/brand?prentId=5 (Accessed: 1 October 2022).

XPeng. (2022b) *XPeng Reports Second Quarter 2022 Unaudited Financial Results* [Online]. XPang. https://ir.xiaopeng.com/static-files/fd52d251-717e-49b6-b39e-f5bb5c66b44c

XPeng. (2022c) *XPeng Reports Third Quarter 2022 Unaudited Financial Results* [Online]. XPeng. https://ir.xiaopeng.com/static-files/d18ce2b8-2d45-4b7d-961b-b74e0b7766f7

XPeng. (2023) *2022 Environmental, Social and Governance Report* [Online]. XPeng. https://ir.xiaopeng.com/system/files-encrypted/nasdaq_kms/assets/2023/04/12/5-18-25/小鹏汽车2022年ESG报告-英文版.pdf

XPeng. (n.d.) *About XPeng*. XPeng. https://ir.xiaopeng.com/?mobile=1

Yang, C. (2022). China's Popular EV Companies Enter Crucial Earnings Season. *Bloomberg*. https://search-ebscohost-com.ez.xjtlu.edu.cn/login.aspx?direct=true&db=bsu&AN=158489758&site=eds-live&scope=site

Yang, Y., & Xu, D. (2017). A methodology for assessing the effect of portfolio management on NPD performance based on Bayesian network scenarios. *Expert Systems*, *34*(2). https://eds-p-ebscohost-com.ez.xjtlu.edu.cn/eds/detail/detail?vid=0&sid=535cc033-c759-4831-a8e1-81a49f94d36e%40redis&bdata=JnNpdGU9ZWRzLWxpdmUmc2NvcGU9c2l0ZQ%3d%3d#AN=122404448&db=bsu

Yang, J., Basile, K., & Letourneau, O. (2020). The impact of social media platform selection on effectively communicating about corporate social responsibility. *Journal of Marketing Communications*, *26*(1), 65–87. doi:10.1080/13527266.2018.1500932

Yan, R. N., Ogle, J. P., & Hyllegard, K. H. (2010). The impact of message appeal and message source on Gen Y consumers' attitudes and purchase intentions toward American Apparel. *Journal of Marketing Communications*, *16*(4), 203–224. doi:10.1080/13527260902863221

Yim, W. W., Yetisgen, M., Harris, W. P., & Kwan, S. W. (2016). Natural language processing in oncology: A review. *JAMA Oncology*, *2*(6), 797–804. doi:10.1001/jamaoncol.2016.0213 PMID:27124593

Yoon, K., Lucas, H., & Zhang, L. (2015). Big data as complementary audit evidence. *Accounting Horizons*, *29*(2), 431–438. doi:10.2308/acch-51076

Zahedi, M., Shahin, M., & Ali Babar, M. (2016). A systematic review of knowledge sharing challenges and practices in global software development. *International Journal of Information Management*, *36*(6, 6, Part A), 995–1019. doi:10.1016/j.ijinfomgt.2016.06.007

Zahlan, A., Ranjan, R. P., & Hayes, D. (2023). Artificial intelligence innovation in healthcare: Literature review, exploratory analysis, and future research. *Technology in Society*, *74*, 102321. doi:10.1016/j.techsoc.2023.102321

Zeghal, D., & Ahmed, S. A. (1990). Comparison of social responsibility information disclosure media used by Canadian firms. *Accounting, Auditing & Accountability Journal*, *3*(1), 0-0.

Zetzsche, D. A., Arner, D. W., & Buckley, R. P. (2020). Decentralized finance (defi). *Journal of Financial Regulation*, *6*(2), 172–203. doi:10.1093/jfr/fjaa010

Zhang, C. B., & Lin, Y. H. (2015). Exploring interactive communication using social media. *Service Industries Journal*, *35*(11-12), 670–693. doi:10.1080/02642069.2015.1064396

Zhang, J. Z., He, W., Shetty, S., Tian, X., He, Y., Behl, A., & Veetil, A. K. V. (2023). Understanding governance and control challenges of block chain technology in healthcare and energy sectors: A historical perspective. *Journal of Management History*. doi:10.1108/JMH-12-2022-0086

Zhang, P., White, J., Schmidt, D. C., Lenz, G., & Rosenbloom, S. T. (2018). FHIRChain: Applying blockchain to securely and scalably share clinical data. *Computational and Structural Biotechnology Journal*, *16*, 267–278. doi:10.1016/j.csbj.2018.07.004 PMID:30108685

Zhang, Z., Zhang, Z., & Li, H. (2015). Predictors of the authenticity of Internet health rumours. *Health Information and Libraries Journal*, *32*(3), 195–205. doi:10.1111/hir.12115 PMID:26268517

Zhao, H. X. (2019) *R&D investment and enterprise profitability*. R&D. https://www.fx361.com/page/2019/0910/10034472.shtml

Zheng, R. (2010). Effects of situated learning on students' knowledge acquisition: An individual differences perspective. *Journal of Educational Computing Research*, *43*(4), 467–487. doi:10.2190/EC.43.4.c

ZheShang Securities. (2022). *Weekly report for the automotive industry*. ZheSheng. http://www.iwencai.com/unifiedwap/inforesult?w=%E5%B0%8F%E9%B9%8F%20%E7%90%86%E6%83%B3%20%E8%94%9A%E6%9D%A5%20%E6%AF%9B%E5%88%A9&querytype=report&tab=2

Zhou, L., Xiong, X., Ernstberger, J., Chaliasos, S., Wang, Z., Wang, Y., & Gervais, A. (2023, May). Sok: Decentralized finance (defi) attacks. In *2023 IEEE Symposium on Security and Privacy (SP)* (pp. 2444-2461). IEEE. 10.1109/SP46215.2023.10179435

Zhuang, Y., Sheets, L. R., Chen, Y. W., Shae, Z. Y., Tsai, J. J., & Shyu, C. R. (2020). A patient-centric health information exchange framework using blockchain technology. *IEEE Journal of Biomedical and Health Informatics*, *24*(8), 2169–2176. doi:10.1109/JBHI.2020.2993072 PMID:32396110

Zizka, L. (2017). The (mis) use of social media to communicate CSR in hospitality: Increasing stakeholders' (dis) engagement through social media. *Journal of Hospitality and Tourism Technology*, *8*(1), 73–86. doi:10.1108/JHTT-07-2016-0037

About the Contributors

Samuel Kwok is a story scientist and an expert in cross-border bullion finance. He holds a Doctorate in Professional Studies from Middlesex University London. He is a practice-led researcher who has developed a unique approach to role-based narrative policy framework and Policy-actors group research for branding management. Dr Kwok is an FHEA with extensive experience in conducting educational research and authoring business cases published and reprinted internationally. His monograph 'Strategy of China Bullion Market Integration and its Financial Impact' published by People's Daily Press, China, highlights his exceptional expertise in the field. Dr Kwok is a member of Chartered Accountants Worldwide (CAW) and is listed as an FCA on the FCA's Register in the UK. He has several professional qualifications, including FCCA, HKICPA, FAIA(Acad), FCEC, and ICEC-USA. Dr Kwok is a distinguished columnist. He has also been recognized as an Industry Expert by the Bureau of Science & Technology of Suzhou Municipal People's Government since 2020. With his extensive knowledge and expertise, Dr Kwok has worked with the Executive Education of IBSS as Academic Director on corporate training programs for CRRC, Sodexo, and Santoni. His views have been featured by major media outlets such as Xinhua News Agency, AB Magazine (ACCA), 21st Century Business Herald, NHK, Jakarta Post, ABC-Australia, The Campus (TIMES Higher Education), The CONVERSATION, and Channel News Asia. Before starting his consultancy firm in 2012, Dr Kwok worked for KPMG and Deloitte and served as a board executive member of two publicly listed firms in Hong Kong. Dr Kwok is a constructive and forward-thinking expert in his field, and his contributions to the industry are invaluable.

Mohamed Omran is currently working as a Senior Associate Professor in Accounting at International Business School Suzhou (IBSS), Xi'an Jiaotong-Liverpool University (XJTLU). He gained his PhD in Accounting in 2008 from La Trobe University, Australia. Dr Omran is a member of both CPA and CMA Australia. He possesses long international experience (over 30 years) in teaching accounting subjects in different universities around the globe (i.e., China, Australia, Kuwait, and Egypt). Before joining XJTLU, Dr Omran worked as a Senior Lecturer of Accounting at Central Queensland University (Australia) and Associate Professor of Accounting at Gulf University for Sciences and Technology (Kuwait). Dr Omran taught various accounting subjects, including financial accounting, management accounting, and auditing. His research interests include corporate financial reports and disclosure, corporate social responsibility, and corporate governance issues. Dr Omran has published widely in accounting and finance journals. He is currently AE for the Journal of Applied Accounting Research. He is also a member of CPA & CMA Australia.

Poshan (Sam) Yu a Chinese Australian, is a versatile individual who excels in a range of roles and industries. With a dynamic skill set, he serves as a consultant, adjunct professor, keynote speaker, research award winner, SSCI journal editor, author, ad-hoc reviewer, entrepreneur, venture capitalist, and OzAsia festival ambassador. Additionally, he brings his financial expertise to over 30 media platforms in China as a guest financial news commentator. Sam's academic contributions extend to various prestigious institutions. He teaches at the University of Victoria Program at Soochow University in China and holds the position of an external professor of financial technology and finance at SKEMA Business School, China. Furthermore, he is a visiting professor at Krirk University in Thailand, EU-Asia research coordinator at the European Business Institute of Luxembourg, and a visiting researcher at the Australian Studies Centre of Shanghai University. Notably, he is also a guest professor at Emlyon Business School China and an adjunct faculty member at George Washington University's master program at Renmin University of China. Previously, he taught as a casual academic at the University of South Australia Business School and was a visiting scholar at the Chinese University of Hong Kong. Furthermore, Sam is actively engaged with several organizations and holds significant positions. As a regional partner in China for FasterCapital, based in Dubai, United Arab Emirates, he plays a vital role in fostering entrepreneurship. He also serves as a vice president at Tinbowah Investment in Beijing and holds an honorary vice president position at the Belt and Road Blockchain Association. Additionally, he contributes as a business mentor for AIC RAISE in Coimbatore, India, the Griffith Industry Mentoring Program in Australia, and University College London. Beyond his professional endeavors, Sam acts as the marketing manager at CAMathories™, an organization founded by a group of Cambridge University alumni and faculty members dedicated to early childhood education, mathematics, science, and advanced technologies. Sam's research interests are extensive and encompass a wide range of topics. They include public-private partnerships, financial technology, regulatory technology, educational technology, mergers and acquisitions, private equity, venture capital, start-ups, intellectual property, art finance, wine, and China's "One Belt One Road" policy.

* * *

Wang Jiaqi holds a MSc in Professional Accounting from the University of Liverpool under the supervision of Professor Samuel Kim Kwong Kwok. Mr. Wang has been engaged deeply in the Data Analytics projects in APPLE INC. China. He is now a PhD candidate in the University of Liverpool.

Jaspreet Kaur is currently working as an Assistant Professor in University Business School, Chandigarh University, Mohali, Punjab. She is a post graduate (MBA-H.R) from Panjab University,Chandigarh. She has also qualified UGC NET JRF in Human Resource Management/Labour and Social Welfare and has completed PhD in Business Management from Chandigarh University, Mohali. She has over 8 years of experience in academic and administrative assignments. She also received & Best Teacher of the Department Award & in the year 2019 and 2021 in the field of imparting quality education. Her research interests include Employee Engagement, Management of Organizational Change and Organization Development. She has published several research papers and articles in reputed international and national journals and has presented papers in various national and international conferences. She also contributed one edited book and 10 book chapters on various topics.

Jean-Yves Le Corre is an Educational Developer and Associate Professor of Practice at the Academy of Future Education, Xi'an Jiaotong- Liverpool University (XJTLU). His role at the Educational Development Unit of XJLTU is to support the implementation of XJTLU's vision in Learning and Teaching philosophy. His research aims to investigate innovative instructional models for Managerial Control and Accounting education in Virtual Learning Environments, focusing on constructivist learning pedagogy and learner's behaviours towards the resolution of socio-cognitive conflicts.

Jiaman Xu is an Assistant Professor of Finance at UCD School of Business. She obtained her doctorate from the University of Edinburgh in 2022. She has published in leading finance and accounting journals, such as Journal of Business Finance and Accounting, Journal of Financial Stability, and European Journal of Finance.

Shaozhe Xu, currently a Computer Science undergraduate student at the University of Liverpool. Since joining the university in 2019, he has demonstrated interest in the field of computer science, including AI, Robotics, front-end and back-end development, as well as computer vision, achieving excellent academic results. He collaborated with Dr Jean-Yves LE CORRE to write the chapter titled "Immersive Learning in Management Accounting Education: A Prototype of Classroom-as-Organization Supported by Learning Management System and Virtual Reality,". This chapter focuses on the prototype of immersive learning, incorporating a computer science and VR technology perspective, emphasizing the unique contributions and value of this prototype. Shaozhe Xu has a keen interest in future research endeavors. He plans to delve deeper into the technology and looks forward to making further contributions.

Index

K

L

M

N

O

P

R

S

T

V

W

X

www.ingramcontent.com/pod-product-compliance
Lightning Source LLC
LaVergne TN
LVHW080646011026
849160LV00014B/1339
* 9 7 9 8 3 6 9 3 4 6 5 9 4 *